AF252064

FINE LINES

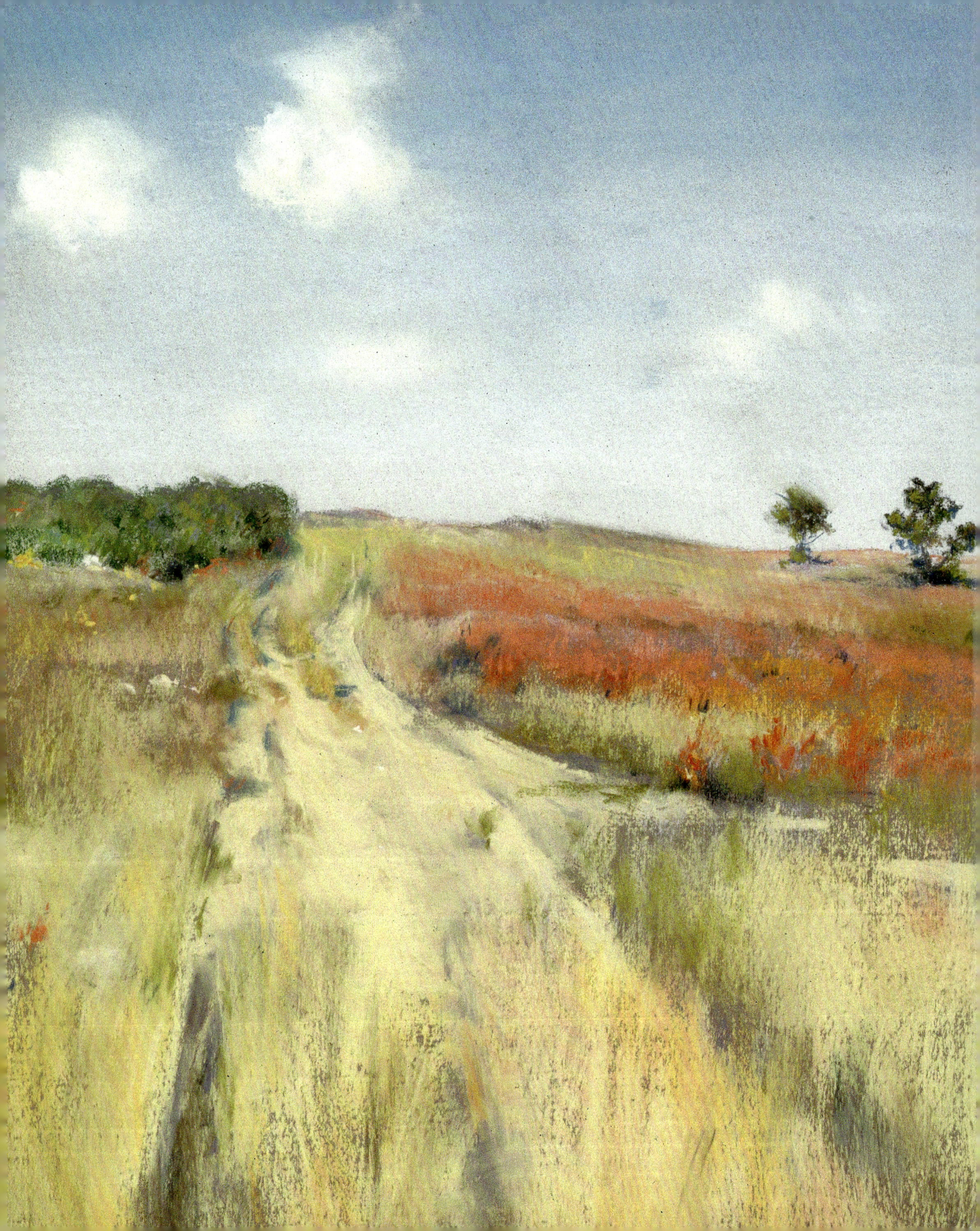

FINE LINES

AMERICAN DRAWINGS FROM THE
BROOKLYN MUSEUM

KAREN A. SHERRY

with contributions by

CAROLINE GILLASPIE and CAITLIN JENKINS

BROOKLYN MUSEUM
in association with D GILES LIMITED, LONDON

 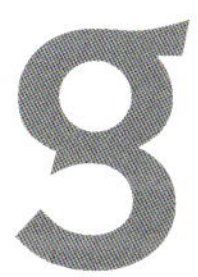

Published on the occasion of the exhibition *Fine Lines: American Drawings from the Brooklyn Museum*, organized by the Brooklyn Museum and held March 1 through May 26, 2013.

Generous support for this exhibition and the accompanying catalogue was provided by Leonard and Ellen Milberg. Additional funding for the exhibition was provided by the Robert E. Blum Fund. The catalogue was also supported by Linda E. Scher; Furthermore: a program of the J. M. Kaplan Fund; and a Brooklyn Museum publications endowment established by the Iris and B. Gerald Cantor Foundation and the Andrew W. Mellon Foundation.

For the Brooklyn Museum:
James Leggio, Head of Publications and Editorial Services
Editor: Joanna Ekman
Copyeditor: Fronia W. Simpson
Proofreaders: Marian Appellof and Laura L. Morris

Photography of Brooklyn Museum objects by Digital Collections and Services, Brooklyn Museum: new photography by Sarah DeSantis and Christine Gant, and by Anita Cruz-Eberhard with support of a generous grant from the Institute of Museum and Library Services (IMLS); digitization of historical images by Sarah Gentile. Unless otherwise indicated, photographs for figure illustrations were provided by the institutions or owners.

Brooklyn Museum
200 Eastern Parkway
Brooklyn, NY 11238-6052
www.brooklynmuseum.org

First published in 2013 by GILES
an imprint of D Giles Limited
4 Crescent Stables
139 Upper Richmond Road, London, SW15 2TN, UK

For D Giles Limited:
Proofread by Sarah Kane and David Rose
Designed by Helen Swansbourne
Printed and bound in China

Library of Congress Cataloging-in-Publication Data

Fine lines: American drawings from the Brooklyn Museum / Karen A. Sherry ; with contributions by Caroline Gillaspie and Caitlin Jenkins.
     p. cm.
  "Published on the occasion of the exhibition Fine Lines: American Drawings from the Brooklyn Museum, held at the Brooklyn Museum from March 1 to May 26, 2013."
  Includes bibliographical references and index.
  ISBN 978-1-907804-14-4 (hardcover) -- ISBN 978-0-87273-171-4 (pbk.)
  1. Brooklyn Museum--Exhibitions. 2. Drawing, American--Exhibitions. 3. Drawing--New York (State)--New York--Exhibitions. I. Sherry, Karen A. II. Gillaspie, Caroline. III. Jenkins, Caitlin. IV. Brooklyn Museum.

  NC105.F56 2013
  741.973'07474723--dc23

              2012023149

Front cover: J. Carroll Beckwith. *Portrait of Minnie Clark* (detail), circa 1890s. Brooklyn Museum, Gift of J. Carroll Beckwith, 17.127 (number 52)

Back cover: Gaston Lachaise. *Back of a Nude Woman*, 1929. Brooklyn Museum, Gift of Carl Zigrosser, 38.183. © Estate of Gaston Lachaise (number 14)

Frontispiece: William Merritt Chase. *Shinnecock Hills* (detail), circa 1895. Brooklyn Museum, Gift of William A. Putnam, 19.96 (number 92)

Opposite: Benjamin Osro Eggleston. *Little Girl Holding an Apple*, 1927. Brooklyn Museum, Dick S. Ramsay Fund, 75.187 (number 40)

CONTENTS

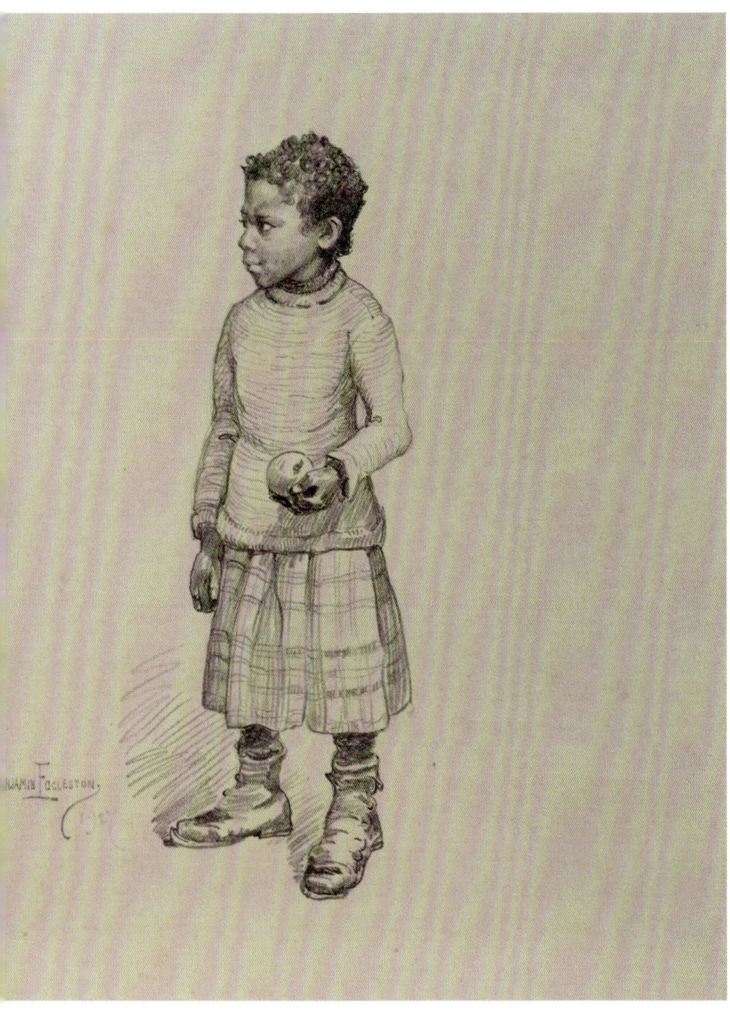

FOREWORD

From the colonial period to the present day, drawing has held an important place in American art. Embracing it as a fundamental creative practice, artists have used drawing to train the hand, record impressions, and experiment with ideas and styles. Although the Brooklyn Museum has been collecting American drawings for more than a century, this volume and the exhibition it accompanies constitute the first major presentation of the institution's rich holdings of these works. To introduce the breadth and scope of the collection, *Fine Lines: American Drawings from the Brooklyn Museum* offers a selection of more than a hundred of our most significant drawings and sketchbook pages produced before 1945 in a variety of graphic media.

Fine Lines continues the Museum's long-standing leadership in supporting exhibitions and scholarship in the field of American art and advances this institution's commitment to documenting our renowned permanent collections and making them accessible to diverse audiences. Following in the tradition of such publications as the award-winning collection catalogue *American Paintings in the Brooklyn Museum: Artists Born by 1876*, by Teresa A. Carbone (2006), and the exhibition catalogue *Masters of Color and Light: Homer, Sargent, and the American Watercolor Movement*, by Linda S. Ferber and Barbara Dayer Gallati (1998), *Fine Lines* examines the distinctive character of our drawings collection while also situating these important and engaging works within the broader history of art of the United States.

We are deeply grateful to Leonard and Ellen Milberg for their generous support of the exhibition and catalogue. We also extend our sincere thanks to Linda E. Scher and Furthermore for their support of this publication.

I want to thank the Brooklyn Museum's extraordinary staff for its dedicated efforts in realizing this publication and exhibition. I am particularly grateful to Karen A. Sherry, now Curator of American Art at the Portland Museum of Art, Maine, and former Associate Curator of American Art at the Brooklyn Museum, who organized the exhibition and is the primary author of the catalogue, which offers an insightful discussion of these remarkable works of art. Caroline Gillaspie, Research Assistant, also contributed commentaries. Caitlin Jenkins, former Andrew W. Mellon Fellow in Paper Conservation, provided an essay and glossary that expand our understanding of these drawings through an examination of their material properties and techniques.

For the ongoing support of the Museum's Trustees, we extend special gratitude to John S. Tamagni, Chair, and every member of our Board. Without the confidence and active engagement of our Trustees, it would not be possible to initiate and maintain the high level of exhibition and publication programming exemplified by *Fine Lines: American Drawings from the Brooklyn Museum.*

ARNOLD L. LEHMAN
Director
Brooklyn Museum

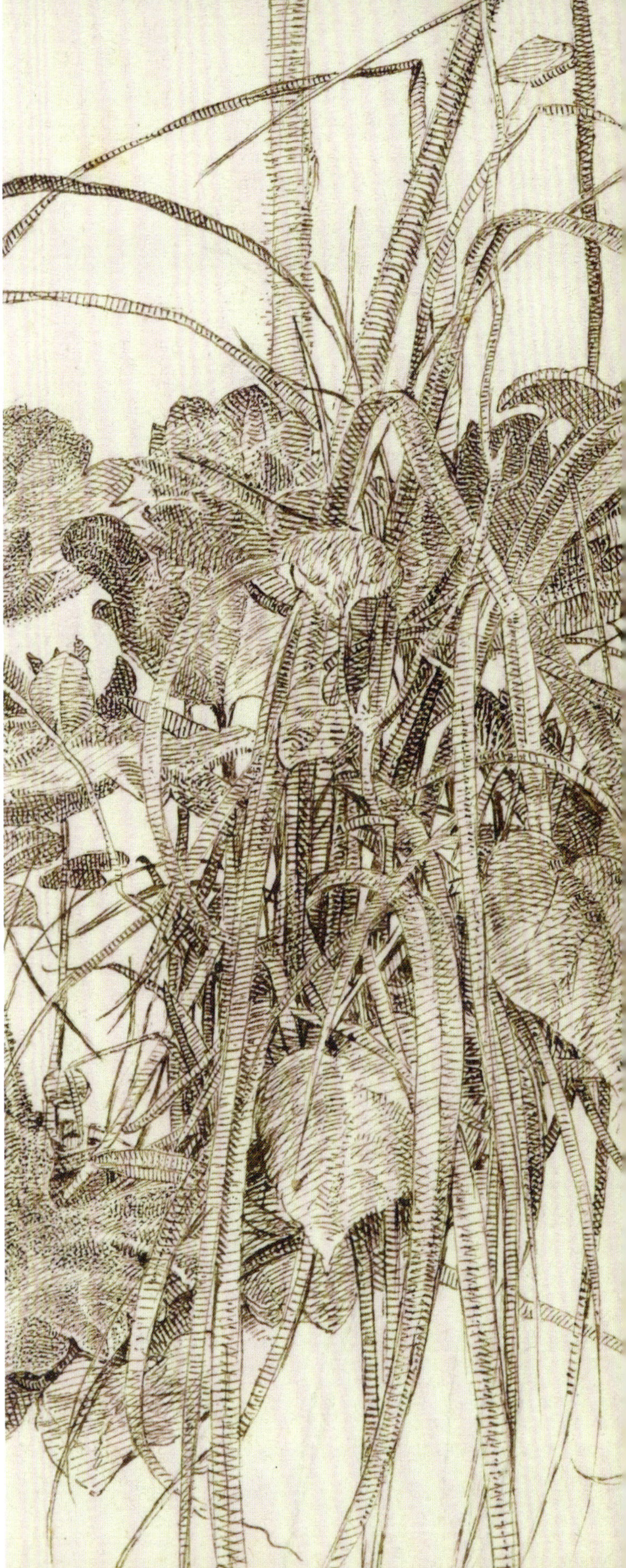

Esther Frances (Francesca) Alexander.
S. Zita, 1874–82.
Detail of number 85

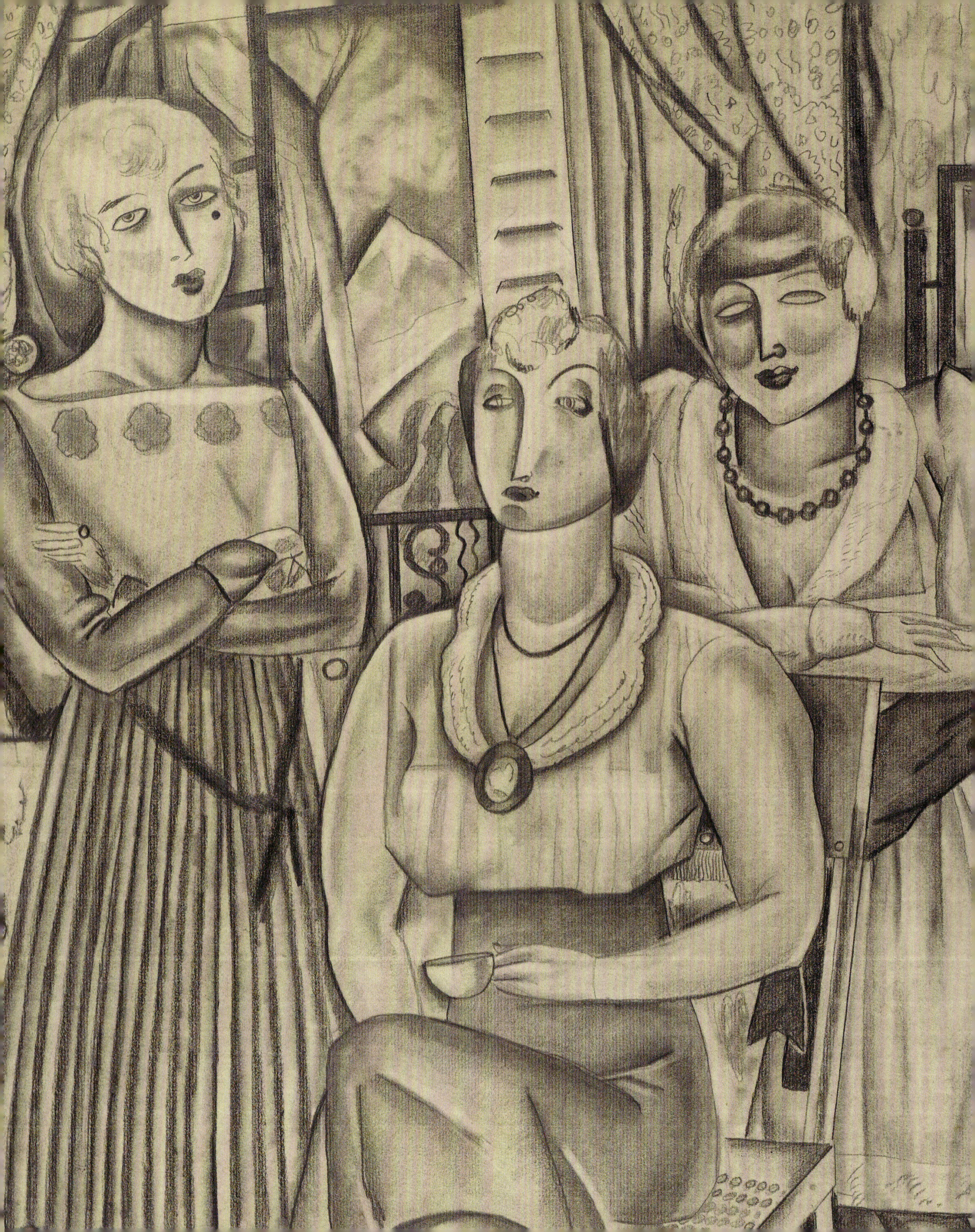

PREFACE AND ACKNOWLEDGMENTS

The Brooklyn Museum's world-renowned collection of American art originated in the mid-nineteenth century with the commission of two paintings from leading artists of the day. The collection expanded exponentially over the course of the twentieth century, and it continues to grow, resulting in holdings of remarkable breadth and depth. In its long-standing commitment to American art, the Museum has also supported notable exhibitions and publications in the field, which have helped to familiarize audiences with many of the treasures in the collection, especially the paintings and watercolors. Brooklyn's American drawings, however, have had significantly less exposure. Although the Museum began acquiring in this area early in the twentieth century—Robert Blum's stunning pastel *Woman in a Japanese Costume* was among the first drawings to enter the collection, in 1911 (see number 35)—and American drawings have been included in gallery installations, special exhibitions, and publications, no major, comprehensive publication or exhibition has before now been devoted to these works. As a result, the Museum's drawings collection remains largely unfamiliar both to specialists in American art and to general audiences.

This lacuna is not unique to the Brooklyn Museum, and, indeed, there is a relative dearth of scholarship on drawings in the field of American art history. Theodore Stebbins's *American Master Drawings and Watercolors*, published more than thirty years ago, remains the single most comprehensive historical survey on the practice of drawing in America. The reasons why drawings have received less attention from scholars are manifold and complex, but a few warrant mention here. First, works on paper are fragile and light-sensitive—properties that strictly limit opportunities for their display on museum walls. Moreover, art historians have often deemed drawings to be ancillary to other media, particularly paintings and sculpture, and thus have focused their energies on works that are considered more finished and historically significant. Finally, whereas many museums have large caches of works on paper in their collections, they lack the staff and other resources to devote to studying such collections in depth and utilizing them in gallery installations.

This situation is changing, as the field of American art history becomes more inclusive and sophisticated in an effort to consider all facets of creative production for a better understanding of American culture. Over the past decade, many museums have begun to produce collection catalogues to document more systematically their holdings of American drawings. These

OPPOSITE:
Louis Bouché. *The Three Sisters*, 1918.
Detail of number 44

institutions include the Metropolitan Museum of Art (2002), the Princeton University Art Museum (2004), the Columbus Museum in Georgia (2006), and the New-York Historical Society (2008), among others. Their endeavors have brought to light a diverse range of objects and have fostered appreciation for the vitality of graphic practices in America. An addition to this growing body of literature, *Fine Lines: American Drawings from the Brooklyn Museum* provides the first introduction to the Museum's holdings of drawings. It presents 114 of the collection's most aesthetically remarkable and historically significant works, produced by seventy-four artists active between the late eighteenth and the mid-twentieth century. The accompanying exhibition will give museum visitors the opportunity to enjoy firsthand these rarely displayed masterpieces, many of which have not left storage for decades.

The Brooklyn Museum owns more than three thousand American drawings in various media dating from the colonial era through the present day. Selecting only a fraction of the vast collection for this exhibition and catalogue necessarily required the application of certain delimiting parameters. Works whose primary medium is watercolor were excluded because the Museum's famous and superb holdings of American water-colors have already been the subject of numerous publications and exhibitions. This volume provides an exciting opportunity to shine the spotlight on less familiar, though equally note-worthy, works on paper in graphite, ink, pastel, crayon, and other graphic media. In addition, *Fine Lines* features drawings produced before the mid-1940s by artists trained in and prac-ticing Western graphic traditions. (Native American ledger drawings, for example, are not included.) Limiting the breadth of this study increases its depth by allowing for a more focused

examination of certain trends and themes in the practice of drawing within the chosen historical time frame. Yet even within these parameters, more than 1,800 drawings were considered during the preparation of *Fine Lines*. The final selection of highlights provides a representative sampling of the great treasures contained in the Brooklyn Museum's collection of American drawings.

From the documentary sketches of indigenous people, flora, and fauna made by early European and American explorers to the expressive and experimental images by contemporary artists, drawing has always played an important role in American art. Artists have used drawing in myriad ways—as a mode of recording the world around them, as an expression of a creative impulse, as preparation for work in other formats, and as an autonomous form of art. Furthermore, drawing has been regarded, since the Renaissance, as the basis of creative design and, therefore, the foundation for other forms of art—painting, sculpture, and architecture. For this reason, drawing became a pillar of artistic training, and its status was codified in artists' manuals for professionals and amateurs, as well as in the art academies established throughout Europe during the seventeenth and eighteenth centuries and in the United States during the nineteenth century. The preeminence of draftsman-ship in the traditional academic curriculum is signaled by the fact that the École des Beaux-Arts in Paris did not provide aspiring painters with advanced technical instruction in painting until 1863. The drawings presented in this volume reflect the variety and vitality of the graphic arts in America across nearly two centuries of this longer history—a time period bracketed by Benjamin West's historical composition *Know Thy Self* of 1768 (see number 61) and Max Weber's modernist figure study *The Dancer* of 1946 (see number 24). Within this great diversity of media, techniques, and styles, certain enduring themes emerge that encompass many of the broader preoccupations that were shaping American art. This volume is arranged in six sections devoted to these themes: the human body, costume studies, portraiture, narrative subjects, the landscape, and urban imagery.

To enhance our understanding of the practice of drawing in the United States and of the distinctive nature of the master-pieces in the Brooklyn Museum's collection, the volume concludes with an essay and glossary by the paper conservator Caitlin Jenkins that present the different drawing materials and processes and a review of their use in this country. The com-bination of art-historical and conservation analysis yields a rich and engaging story not only about individual works on paper in the Brooklyn Museum's collection but also about the importance of drawing within the history of American art. It is hoped that *Fine Lines: American Drawings from the Brooklyn Museum* will foster a new appreciation for these heretofore little-known treasures and inspire additional work with the drawings collection in the form of exhibitions and scholarship.

This project began several years ago with a survey of the Brooklyn Museum's American drawings collection. From the moment I opened the first box of drawings in storage, I have been assisted by many individuals at every stage of organizing the exhibition and its accompanying publication. It gives me great pleasure to acknowledge their efforts here. First and foremost, I thank Caroline Gillaspie, my indispensable and indefatigable research assistant. She compiled a wealth of information on the collection, wrote insightful catalogue entries,

and made myriad other contributions with her characteristic intelligence and good cheer. I am also deeply indebted to Teresa A. Carbone, Andrew W. Mellon Curator of American Art, who provided unwavering encouragement and astute advice at every juncture.

For their strong support of *Fine Lines*, I extend my thanks to Arnold L. Lehman, Director; Kevin Stayton, Chief Curator; Ken Moser, Carol Lee Shen Chief Conservator and Vice Director for Collections; Sallie Stutz, Director of Merchandising; and Sally Williams, Public Information Officer. Numerous other members of the Museum's extraordinary staff helped with the production of this publication and exhibition. Curatorial Assistants Rima Ibrahim and Emily Sessions applied their usual high degree of organizational efficiency, intelligence, and good humor to the project. I am also indebted to a talented group of volunteers and interns for their contributions: Charnia Adelman, John Gribowich, Kelsey Gustin, Sonia Pace, Nina Accorsini Sangimino, and Nicholas Wise. Past and present curatorial colleagues generously shared advice and camaraderie: Patrick Amsellem, Rich Aste, Judith Dolkart, Linda S. Ferber, Barry Harwood, Marilyn Kushner, Nancy Rosoff, and Susan Kennedy Zeller.

I had the great privilege of working closely with the Museum's gifted paper conservators and preparators— including Antoinette Owen, Beatriz Centeno, Rachel Danzing, Keith Duquette, Pavlos Kapetanakis, Elaine Komorowski, and Lisa Nelson—who ensured the preservation and beautiful presentation of these works, and taught me a great deal about the drawings in the process. An integral part of this team, Caitlin Jenkins, former Andrew W. Mellon Fellow in Paper Conservation, also contributed an informative essay and glossary that add an important technical dimension to this publication. Maria Fredericks, Drue Heinz Book Conservator at the Thaw Conservation Center, The Morgan Library and Museum, expertly treated several of the sketchbooks.

In the Brooklyn Museum's Library and Archives, Deirdre Lawrence, Sandy Wallace, and Angie Park helped to procure crucial resources for my research. Marguerite Vigliante, Coordinator, Works on Paper, helped with the access to the drawings and their curatorial files. I am also grateful to the Registrars and Collections Management staff: Terri O'Hara and Chrisy Tselentakis cheerfully fielded numerous inquiries about collection records, Liz Reynolds and other registrars managed the logistical arrangements for the exhibition, and Walter Andersons and the art handlers ensured the safe movement of objects. Matthew Yokobosky and his design team created an inspired installation. The support of Sharon Matt Atkins, Lisa Small, Dolores Pukki, and Amanda Dietz in the Exhibitions Division was instrumental in the organization of this exhibition.

Many colleagues from outside the Museum have generously shared their expertise and enthusiasm for this project, especially Alan Braddock, Sarah Cash, Sarah Kelly, John F. McGuigan, Jr., Mary K. McGuigan, Roberta J. M. Olson, and Paul W. Worman. I would like to give special thanks to Mary Lublin for her intellectual and practical support and to Leonard and Ellen Milberg, Linda E. Scher, and Furthermore for providing crucial funding.

The production of this book was expertly guided by James Leggio, Head of Publications and Editorial Services. Deborah Wythe coordinated the images for the volume; the stunning new photography of the Museum's drawings was done by Sarah DeSantis, Christine Gant, and Anita Cruz-Eberhard, and Alice Cork handled photo research for the ancillary illustrations. I thank Dan Giles, Sarah McLaughlin, Allison Giles, and Pat Barylski at D Giles Limited, London, for their dedication and support of this project, and Helen Swansbourne for the book's beautiful design. Finally, my profound gratitude goes to Fronia W. Simpson, copyeditor, and, especially, Joanna Ekman, Senior Editor at the Brooklyn Museum, for their astute comments, meticulous attention to detail, and infinite patience.

KAREN A. SHERRY

OPPOSITE:
Robert Frederick Blum.
Woman in a Japanese Costume, circa 1890–92.
Detail of number 35

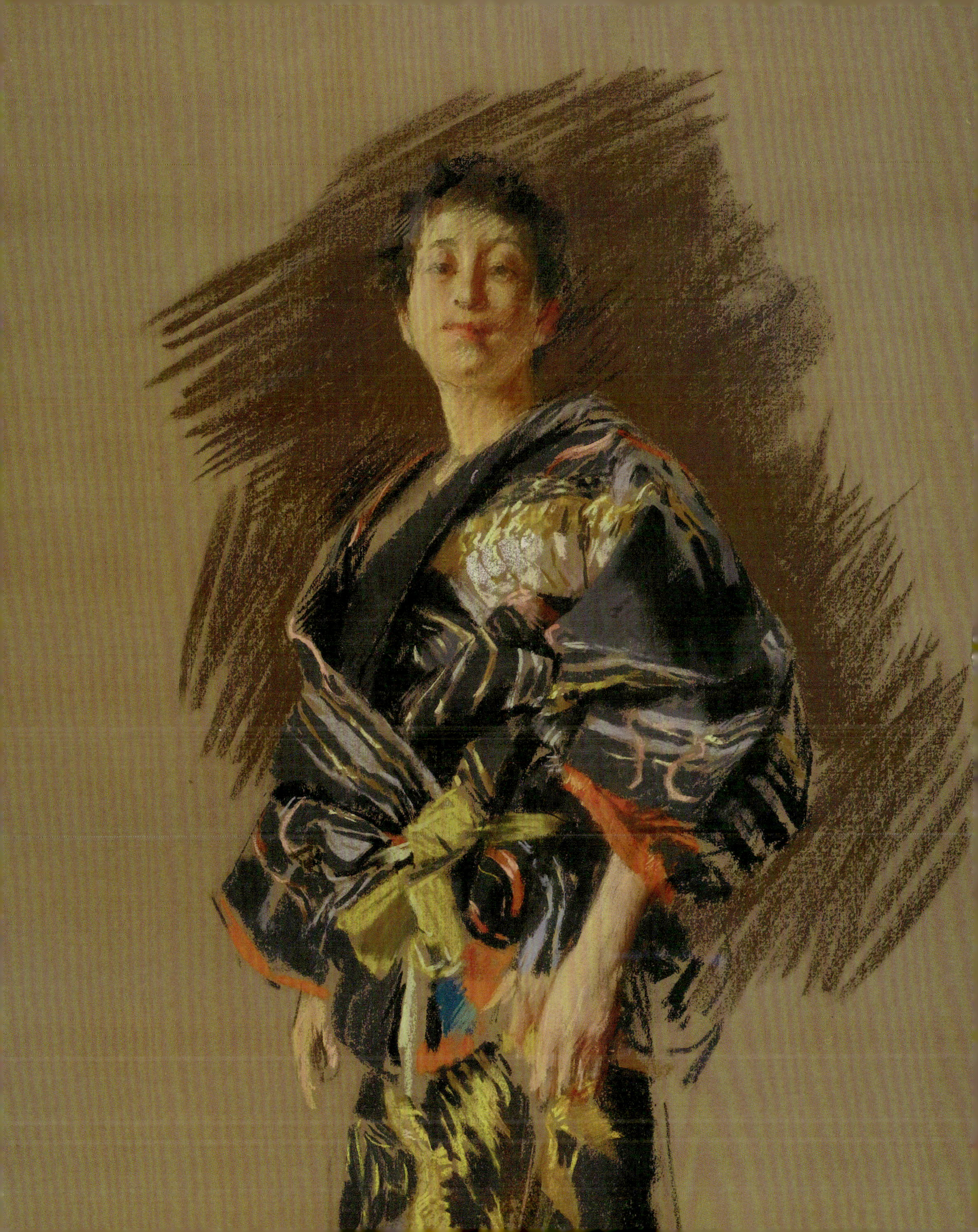

CATALOGUE

All catalogue works are in the collection of the
Brooklyn Museum. Measurements are in inches and
centimeters, given with height first, followed by
width and (for sketchbooks) by depth. Within each
entry, the first reference to another artist in the
catalogue appears in boldface.

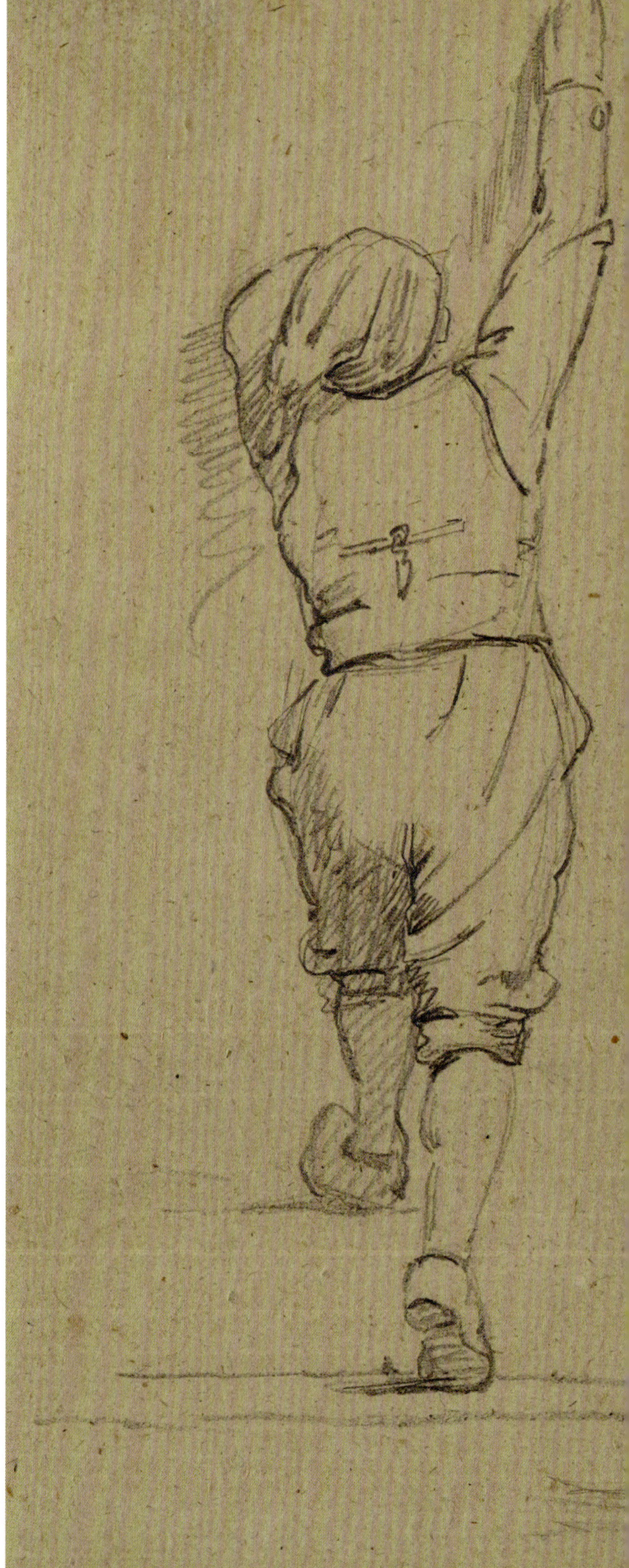

Eastman Johnson.
Three Dutch Figures, circa 1852.
Detail of number 27

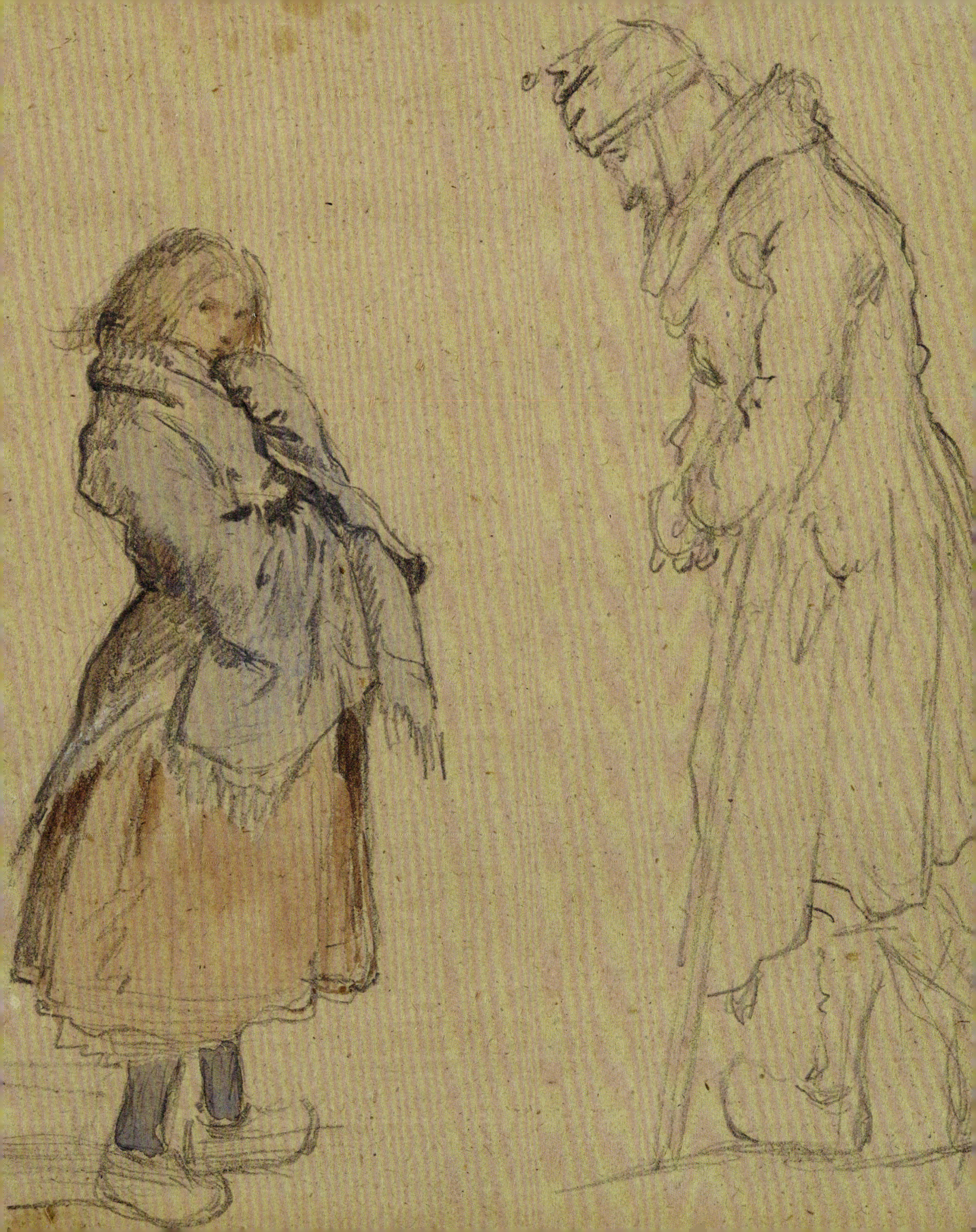

RECORDING ANATOMY

The great richness and diversity of images of the human body featured in this section underscore the centrality of figure drawing to artistic practice. Considered an essential component of an artist's professional training, figure drawing was incorporated into the curricula of the first art academies (modeled on European art schools) established in the United States in the early nineteenth century, the most prominent of which were the Pennsylvania Academy of the Fine Arts (1805) in Philadelphia and the National Academy of Design (1825) in New York. Indeed, figure study was so fundamental to academic training that the drawings of the nude that were required of art students were called "academies." With its complex anatomical structure, its combination of concave and convex contours, and its seemingly endless variety of poses, the human body was considered the most challenging subject in art. Artists learned to depict the body by drawing from casts of canonical examples of classical sculpture—regarded as embodying Western ideals of physical perfection—and from live models. Even as progressive artists began to reject the conventional practices and idealized naturalism of academic art in the late nineteenth century, the nude figure maintained a vital presence in American art. Artists used the body to explore new styles, such as Cubism and abstraction, and shifting conceptions about the nature of human physicality and sexuality.

The drawings in this section range from conventional academies, anatomical studies, and other figural exercises that reflect the enduring legacy of the academic tradition to works that take a more frank and realistic approach to the nude. Modernist artists experimented with new modes of figuration, such as reducing the body to its essential structure, and exploited the expressive potential of the human form in representations of dancers and other figures in motion.

Eastman Johnson

American, 1824–1906

1 Anatomy Sketchbook, 1849

Graphite on beige, medium-weight, slightly textured laid paper, 17⅛ × 11¹¹⁄₁₆ × ⅜ in. (43.5 × 28.1 × 1 cm)
Gift of Albert Duveen, 40.61

This sketchbook contains twenty-one pages of carefully delineated anatomical studies that Eastman Johnson made in 1849 while enrolled in the open anatomy class at the Düsseldorf Royal Academy.[1] The school's emphasis on graphic technique is evident in the meticulous precision of Johnson's drawings and the almost scientific rigor of his exercises. The images depict parts of the human skeleton—a skull, foot, rib cage, and arm and leg bones—often shown from multiple angles, and the male and female body in outline form. On many of the pages, Johnson also included faint guidelines (such as grids and other geometric shapes) and notations about proportions of and relationships between body parts. These inscriptions cite anatomical rules or calculations of canonical formulas, as in the text accompanying a schematic drawing of the female figure on page 18, which includes notations such as "The height of head 8 in.," "from the chin to the *halsgrube* [jugular notch] 3 in.," and "Width of head thro the brows 6 in.—width of neck thro the chin 3½."

The two drawings of the bones of the right foot on page 1 typify Johnson's skeletal studies and demonstrate his masterful draftsmanship. Using crisp pencil lines, the artist rendered the distinctive contours of each individual metatarsal, phalanx, and other bones with remarkable exactitude. Although his primary focus was on outline, he also added hatchings to indicate shading and volume. This page also includes two summary sketches of a skull drawn within numbered grid lines. A skull isolated in the upper left corner of page 3 is the most highly finished drawing in the notebook. In this virtuoso image, Johnson endowed the anatomical part with a palpable presence through his illusionistic modeling of the complex cranial structure.

By the time Johnson arrived in Düsseldorf, the twenty-five-year-old was already an accomplished draftsman who had achieved modest success making highly realistic crayon portraits of sitters in Washington, D.C., and Boston.[2] He went abroad to further his professional training and expand his artistic repertoire with the type of detailed genre scenes that were promoted by the Düsseldorf academy and were gaining popularity with American audiences. After a total of six years in Germany and Holland (see number 27), he returned to the United States, eventually settling in New York. As a mature artist, Johnson enjoyed critical acclaim for his skillfully painted narrative and figure subjects based on contemporary American life.

1. The artist inscribed "E Johnson / Royal Academy of Düsseldorf / Anatomical class. / 1849" on the front cover of this sketchbook. The best source on Johnson's career and studies abroad is Teresa A. Carbone and Patricia Hills, *Eastman Johnson: Painting America* (New York: Brooklyn Museum of Art in association with Rizzoli International Publications, 1999), 11–47.

2. The Brooklyn Museum also owns two of these portraits: acc. nos. 32.1717.1 and 32.1717.2.

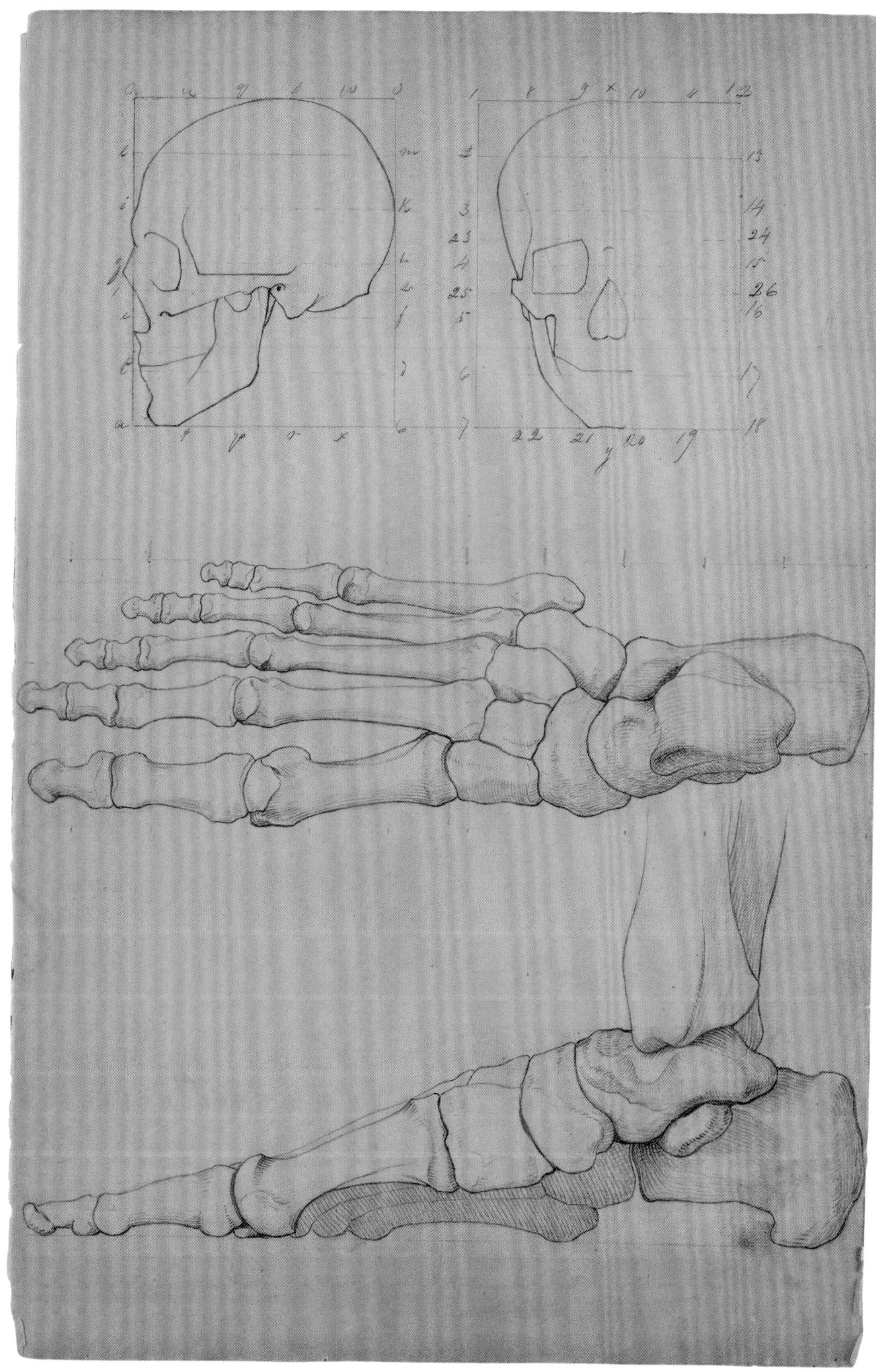

40.61, page 1

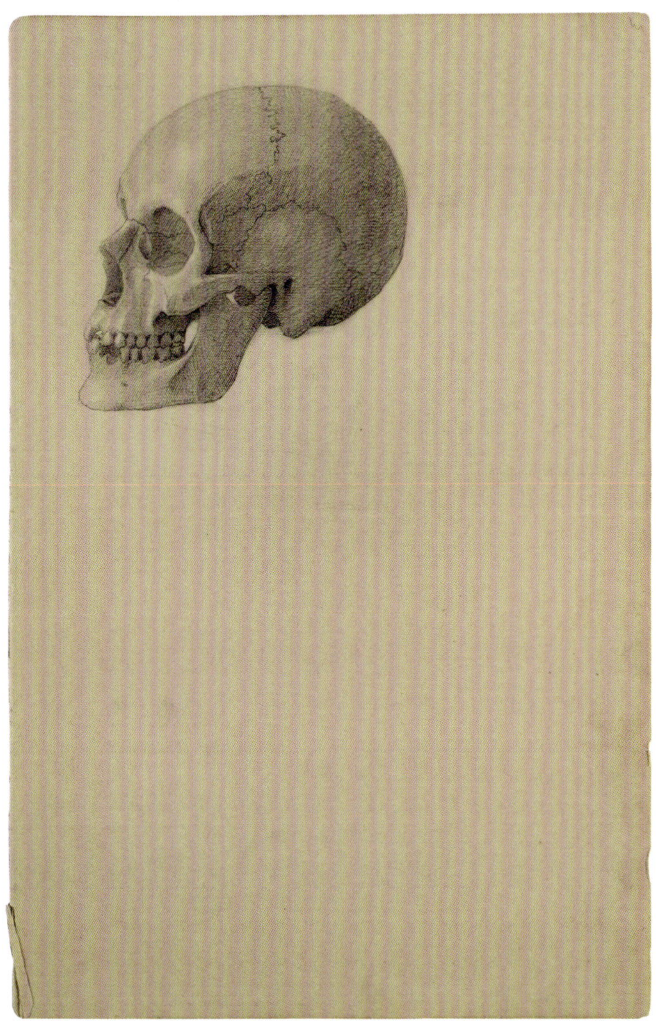

40.61, page 3

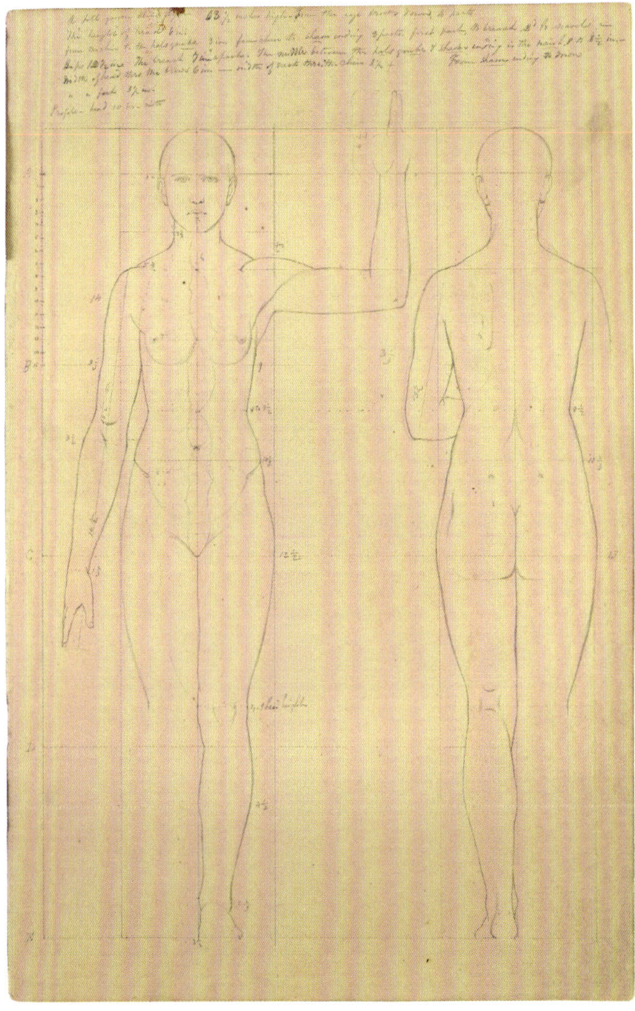

40.61, page 18

Daniel Huntington

American, 1816–1906

2 Skeleton Study, circa 1848

Black and red crayon and white chalk on beige, medium-weight, slightly textured wove paper, 20$\frac{5}{16}$ × 10$\frac{3}{8}$ in. (51.3 × 26.4 cm)
Gift of The Roebling Society, 68.167.3

3 Écorché (Figure Study of Musculature), circa 1848

Red, brown, white, and black crayon with graphite underdrawing on blue-green, medium-weight, slightly textured wove paper,
21$\frac{3}{4}$ × 14$\frac{15}{16}$ in. (55.2 × 37.9 cm)
Gift of The Roebling Society, 68.167.4

4 Nude Study, circa 1848

Black and white crayon on blue-green, medium-weight, slightly textured wove paper, 21$\frac{3}{4}$ × 15$\frac{1}{8}$ in. (55.2 × 38.4 cm)
Gift of The Roebling Society, 68.167.5

Although the circumstances of its creation are unknown, this suite of finely crafted figure drawings by the portraitist and history painter Daniel Huntington serves as a bravura demonstration of the artist's technical expertise as a draftsman, as well as his commitment to the academic mastery of human anatomy. The three sheets are based on the figure of a dancing faun from a Hellenistic sculpture, which Huntington likely knew from a plaster copy.[1] He represented this male nude, seen from behind and posed in a contrapposto stance, in progressively complete anatomical states: a skeleton, an écorché (a flayed body with the musculature exposed), and a fully fleshed figure. This layering effect is particularly evident in *Écorché* (number 3), in which the artist included faint outlines of the arm bones—the only part of the body not covered with red-hued muscles and tendons. In each drawing, Huntington illusionistically described the physical forms through his virtuoso handling of colored crayons and other media. He articulated the contours of individual bones in *Skeleton Study* (number 2), for instance, with precise lines and delicate hatch marks for shading, adding touches of white highlights and an outline of the figure in red. In the final study (number 4) Huntington created modulations of light and dark tones with soft strokes of white and black crayon, leaving the paper blank to provide the middle tones. As a group, these three works underscore a key principle of the academic tradition: knowledge of the body's underlying anatomical structure is fundamental to figural representation.

Born in New York to a socially prominent family, Huntington began his formal artistic training in 1835 with the artist-inventor Samuel F. B. Morse (1791–1872), a leading proponent of Grand Manner academicism and the first president of the National Academy of Design, and subsequently with the portraitist Henry Inman (1801–1846). At the time when Huntington made these drawings, in the late 1840s, he was a highly regarded painter and a leading character in New York's cultural world. Portraiture was his dominant output, but he also produced landscapes as well as historical and religious canvases with idealized figures inspired by his knowledge of Renaissance art gained during several trips to Europe. Huntington served as president of the National Academy of Design from 1862 to 1870 and again from 1877 to 1890. He was also a member of the Century Club (founded in 1847) and involved in the founding of the Metropolitan Museum of Art (1870). Throughout his long career, Huntington was perceived as the embodiment of the art establishment that more progressive American artists began rebelling against in the late nineteenth century.

1. The author thanks Marc Simpson for identifying the antique prototype for these drawings (the original of which is in the Galleria degli Uffizi, Florence). For information on artists' sources for anatomical study in the mid-nineteenth century, see Donald R. Thayer, "Early Anatomy Instruction at the National Academy: The Tradition behind It," *American Art Journal* 8, no. 1 (May 1976): 49–50.

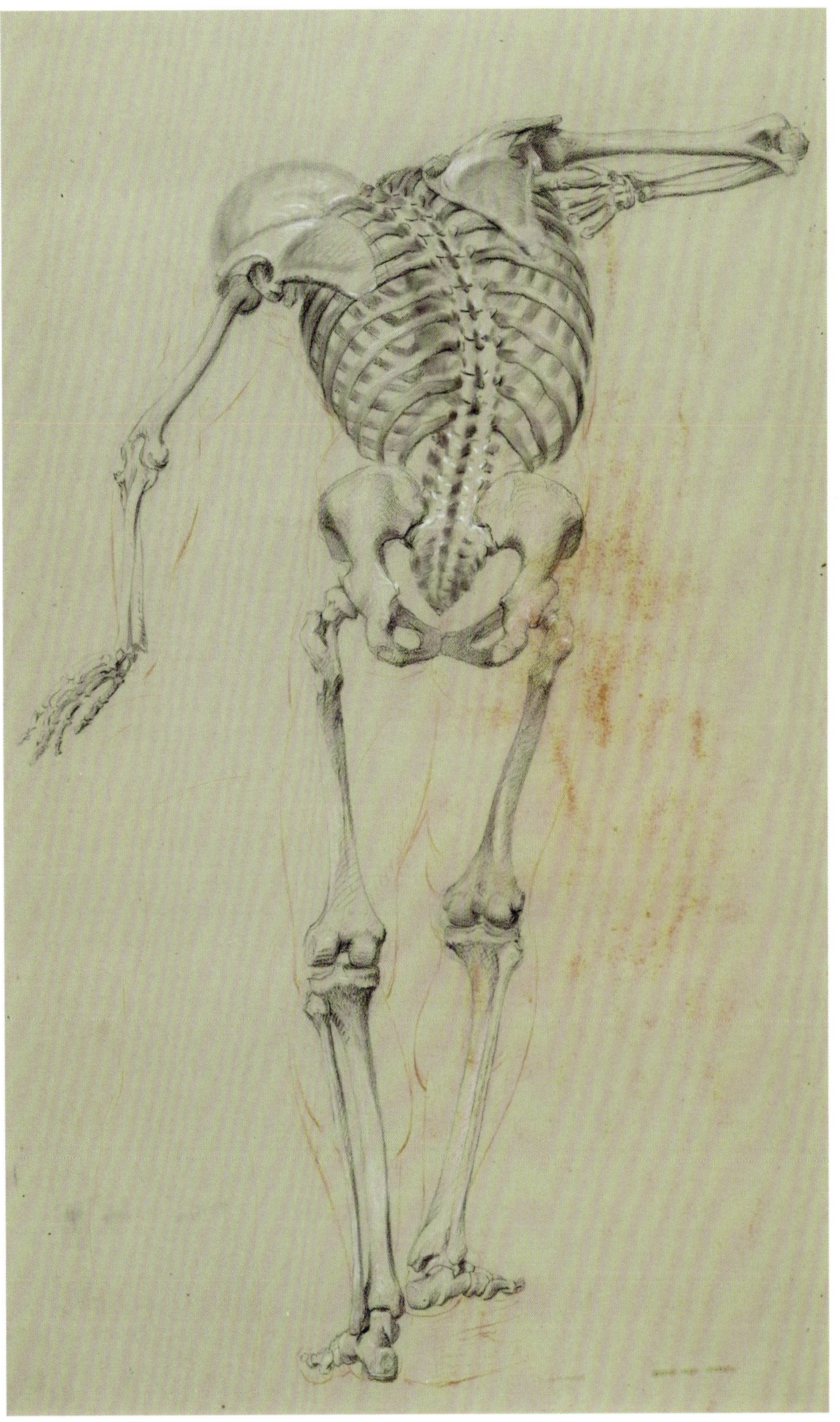

2

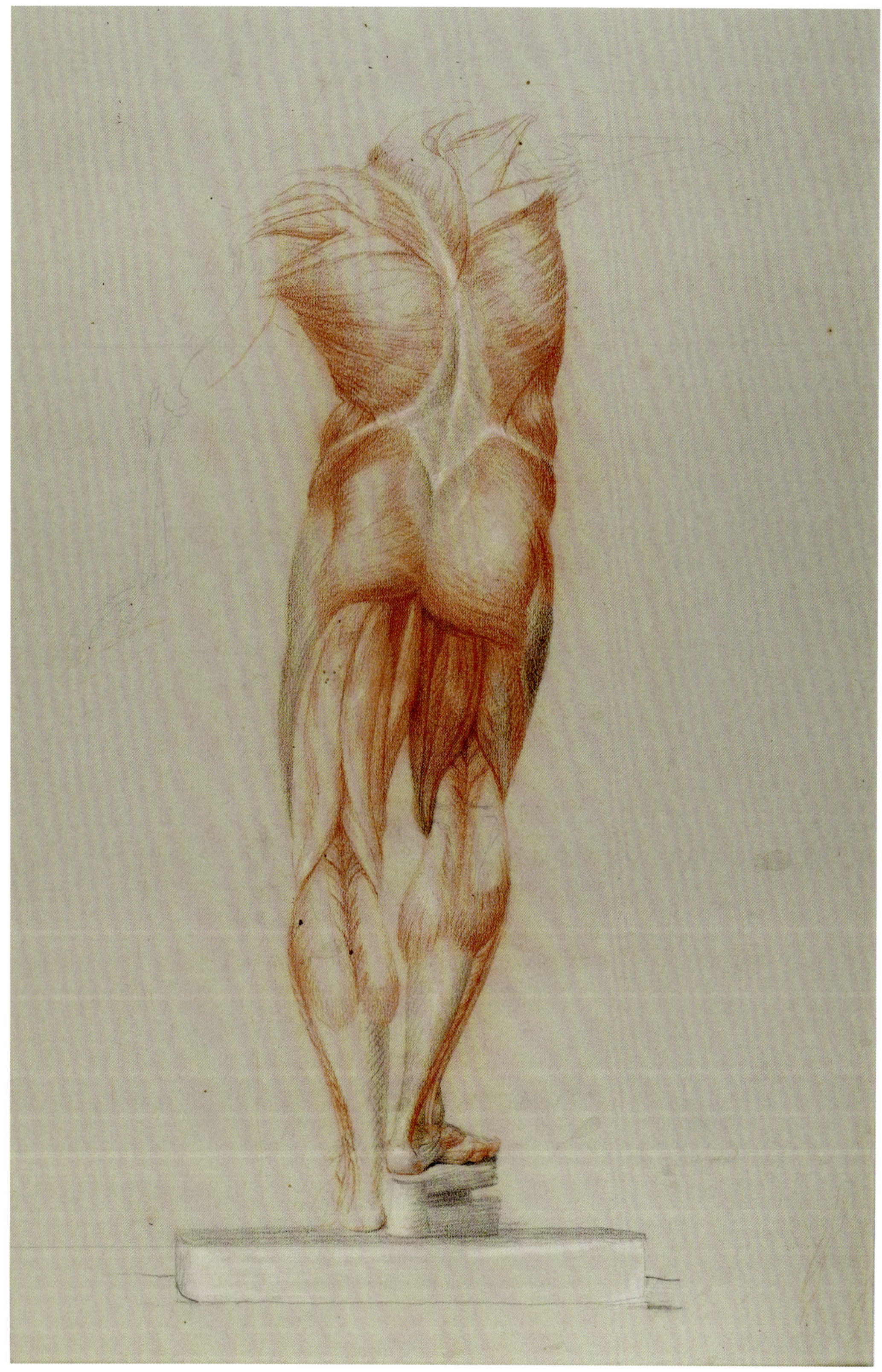

3

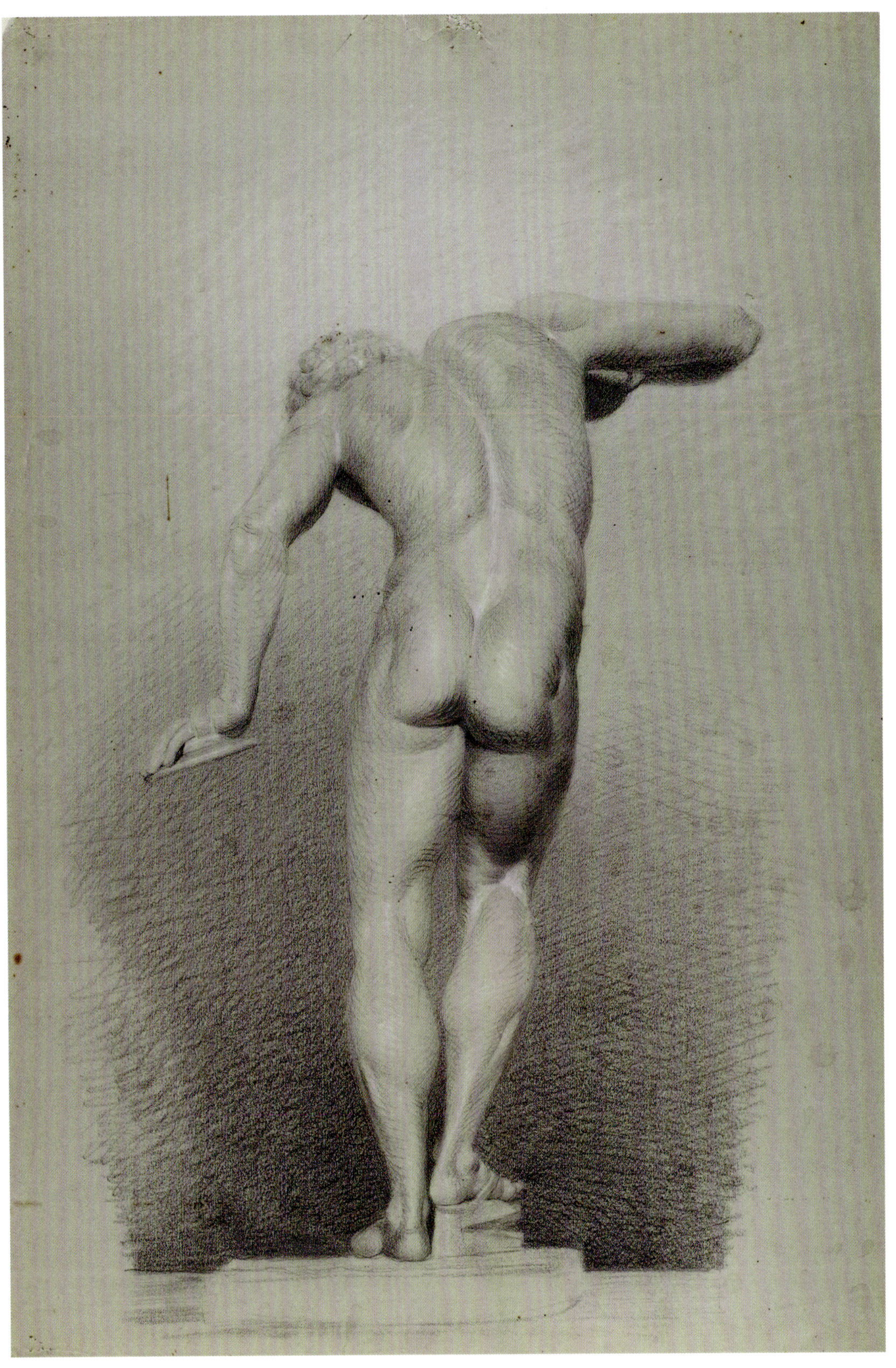

4

John Singer Sargent

American, born Italy, 1856–1925

5 Sketchbook, 1871–72

Graphite, charcoal, watercolor, and white chalk on paper, 9³⁄₁₆ × 11⅞ × ½ in. (23.3 × 30.2 × 1.3 cm)
Signed twice in graphite, across top of page 1: "John Sargent 1871." and "John Sargent- / [Mu]nich"
Gift of Bronson Binger, 1996.231

Best known as a high-society portraitist and master watercolorist, the cosmopolitan John Singer Sargent was also a consummate draftsman. Born in Florence, Italy, to wealthy expatriate American parents, Sargent drew prolifically and precociously throughout his youth, which was spent traveling around Europe with his family.[1] During these peregrinations, he received an informal artistic education by visiting the cultural treasures of the Old World. This sixteen-page sketchbook contains drawings of a variety of subjects from the family's stay in Germany in 1871–72, when Sargent was fifteen. Almost half of the images consist of his sketches of classical statuary from the famous plaster cast collection of the Albertinum in Dresden.[2] For example, page 14 features the full-length figure of the Aphrodite of Knidos and several head studies, and page 15 includes the Vipsania Agrippina, the Borghese Warrior, and a dancing maenad (from a relief attributed to Kallimachos), as well as marginal sketches of the hands of some of these figures. Although he had not yet received any formal academic training, Sargent embraced the standard practice of copying canonical works of art both to develop his hand and eye and to master the forms of human anatomy in its idealized state. For the graphite drawings on these two pages, he adopted a quick, linear style to capture the general contours of the classical models in broad strokes. In another copying exercise—the meticulously rendered head of Pan on page 8—Sargent focused on tonal modeling. He described the furrowed brow, curly hair and beard, and twisting horns of this demigod with a careful calibration of lights and darks to create depth and the illusion of volumetric form. This sketchbook also contains sketches of people, landscape elements, and animals—including a charming "portrait" of a camel (page 6)—as well as a watercolor painting of the pyramids (undoubtedly made from imagination or another image).

In 1873 Sargent began his academic study in Florence at the Accademia delle Belle Arti and then, from 1874 to 1878, in Paris at the École des Beaux-Arts and in the atelier of Charles Auguste Émile Durant, better known as Carolus-Duran (1837–1917). Another American student, J. Alden Weir (1852–1919), described Sargent's drawings as equal to those of the Old Masters.[3] By the late 1870s, Sargent was exhibiting paintings on both sides of the Atlantic and earning international recognition for his dashing portraits executed in the painterly realistic style of his mentor Carolus-Duran and Old Masters such as Diego Velázquez (1599–1660). Settling in England in 1886, Sargent continued his peripatetic travels throughout his life. In addition to his success in portraiture, Sargent was acclaimed for his landscape subjects, watercolors, and murals.

1. Several other youthful sketchbooks by Sargent can be found in the collections of the Fogg Museum, Harvard Art Museums, and the Metropolitan Museum of Art, New York.
2. The seed of this collection was the more than eight hundred plaster casts from the estate of the Neoclassical painter Anton Raphael Mengs (1728–1779).
3. Edward J. Nygren, *John Singer Sargent: Drawings from the Corcoran Gallery of Art* (Washington, D.C.: Smithsonian Institution Traveling Exhibition Service and Corcoran Gallery of Art, 1983), 15. Sargent won the highest award for drawing at the École des Beaux-Arts in 1877.

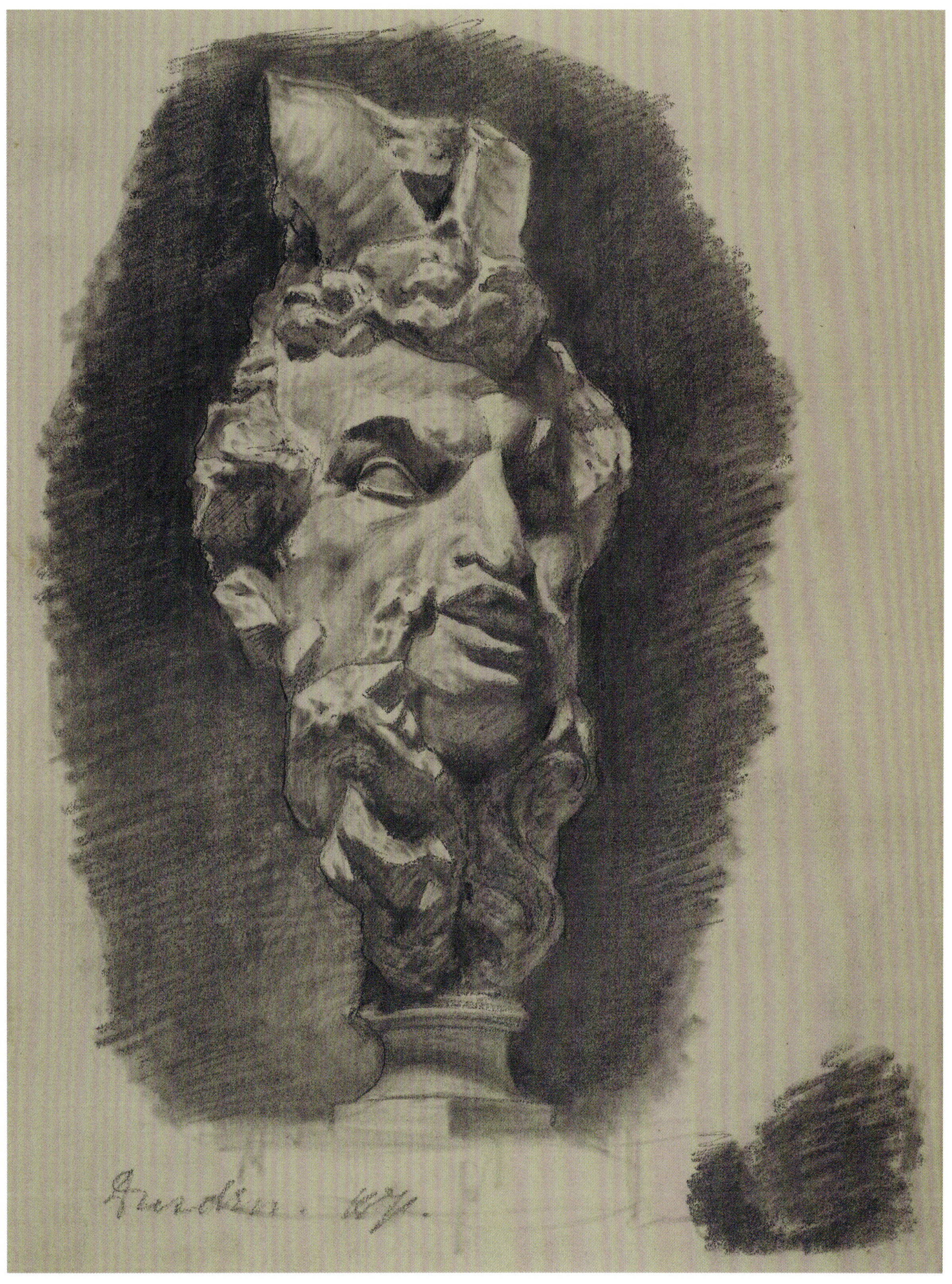

1996.231, page 8

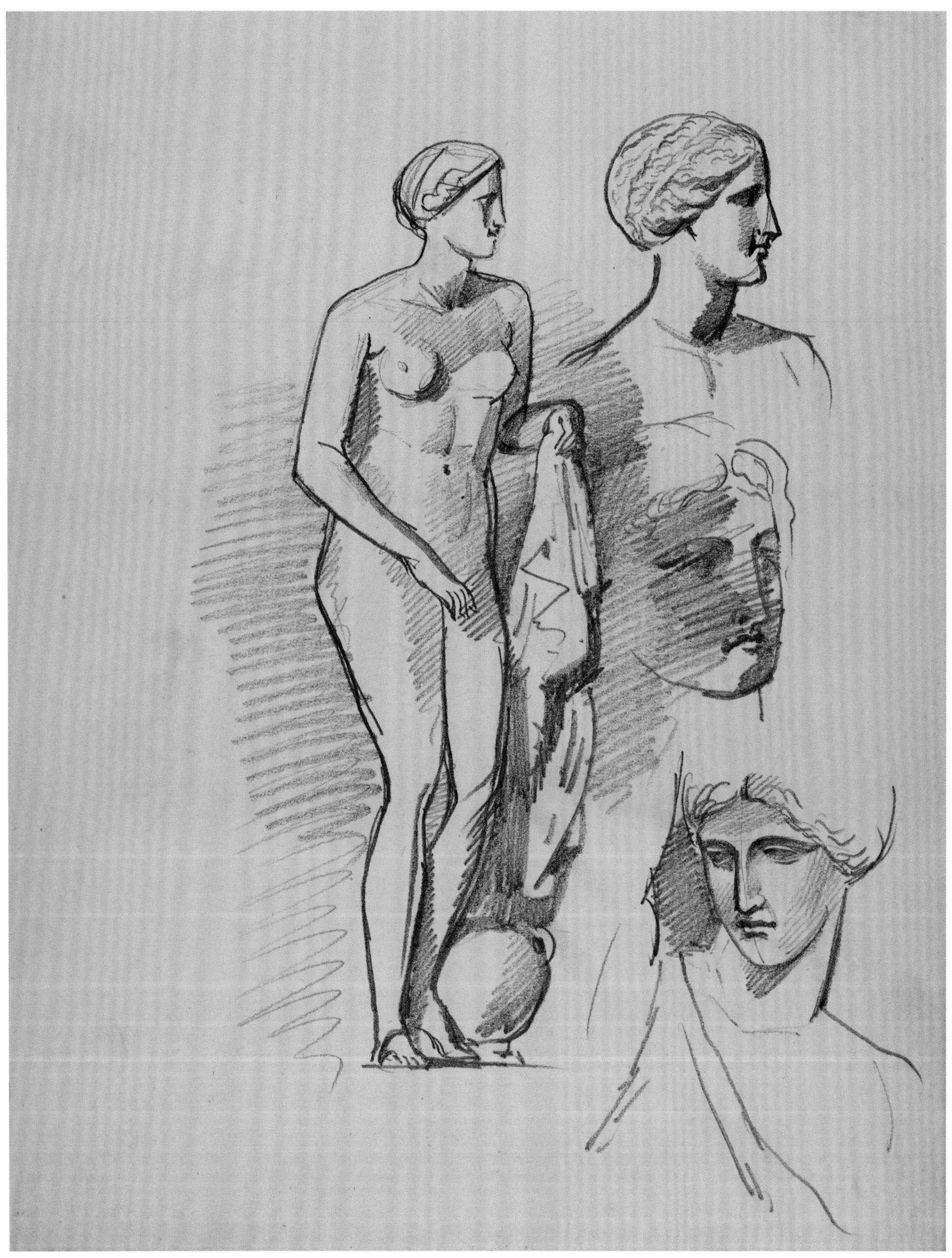

1996.231, page 14

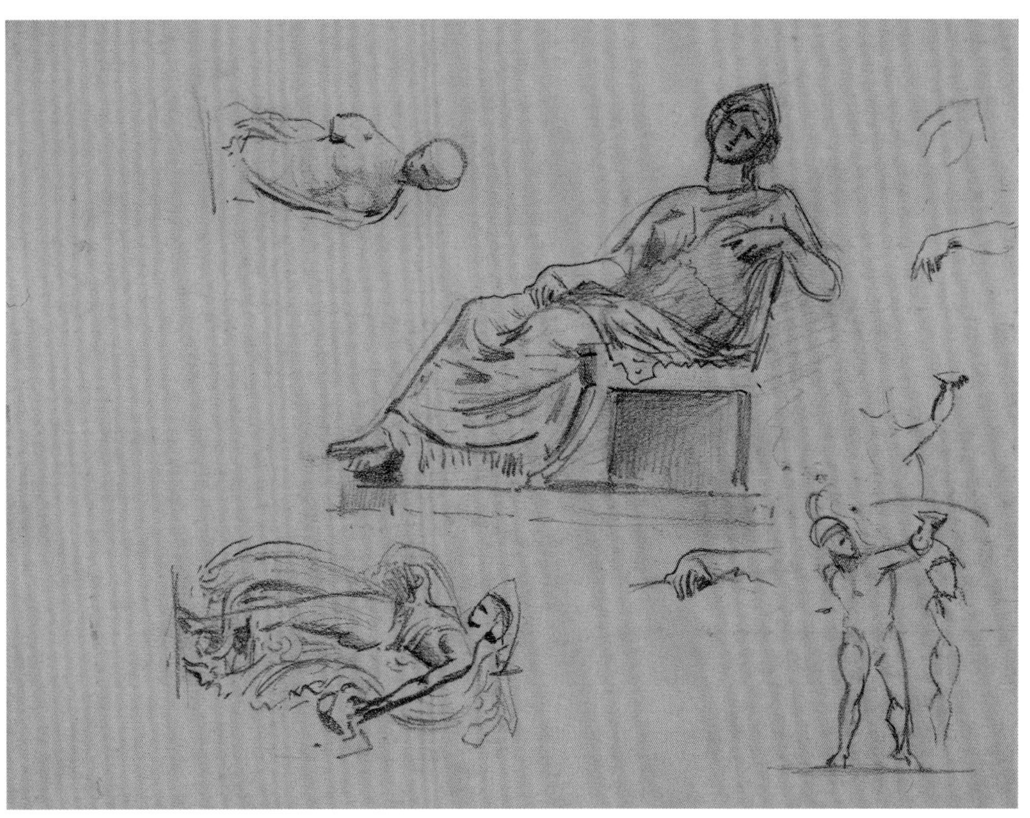

1996.231, page 15

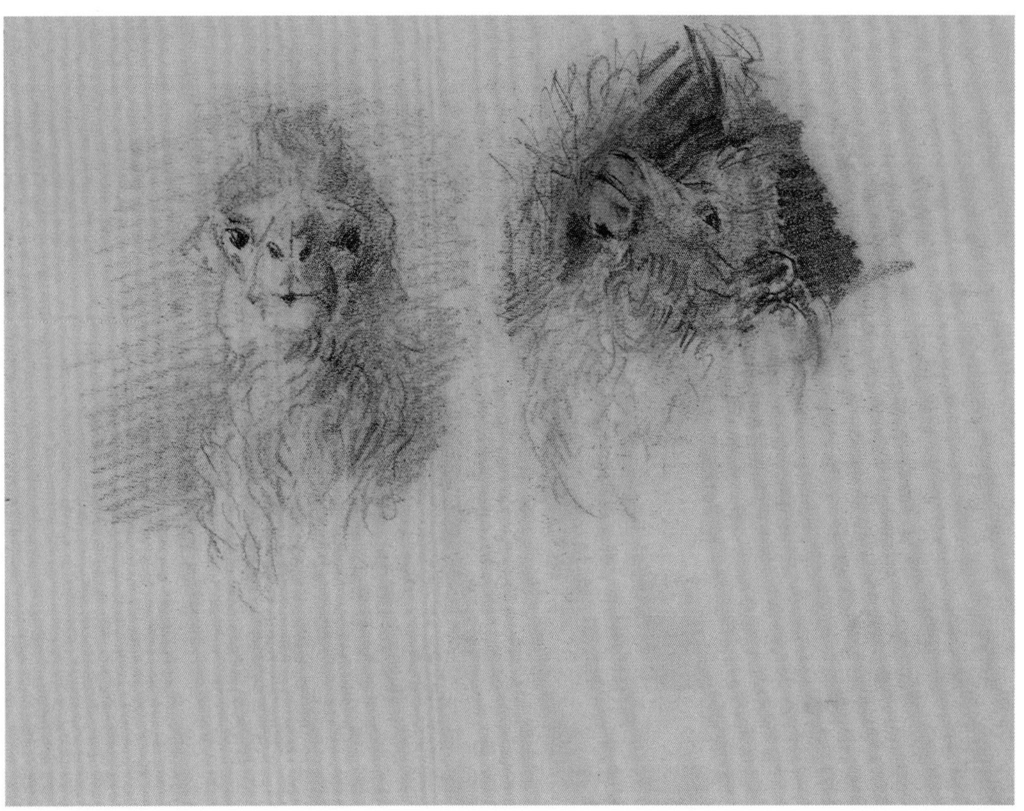

1996.231, page 6

Edward Hopper

American, 1882–1967

6 Male Nude, circa 1903–4

Charcoal (with possible additions of black crayon) on cream, moderately thick, moderately textured laid paper, 24 × 9⅝ in. (61 × 24.4 cm)
Gift of Mr. and Mrs. Morton Ostrow, 82.253.2

Edward Hopper created this accomplished drawing of a standing male nude in profile in **Robert Henri**'s life class at the New York School of Art about 1903–4, during a modeling session documented in a photograph (figure 1). Although Henri was not a conventional teacher or artist, he did promote anatomical study as a foundational tool for artists. He regularly used live models in the studio and classroom (see number 7), though he eschewed the traditional step of drawing from casts of antique statuary.

In this charcoal study, Hopper varied the density of his line and the application of his medium, from crisp outlines to smoky smudges, to define and model the forms of the male physique with great accuracy. The results of the artist's close observation are also evident in his treatment of the face, which captures both the model's individuality and his air of boredom as he holds the pose. The tiny, roughly sketched figure of a female nude in the upper right corner of the sheet injects a note of bawdy humor. Since social propriety prohibited mixed-sex modeling, the figure is an invention—perhaps intended to represent the interior thoughts of the artist or model. The angled forms in the loosely sketched background at left evoke the tilted easels of Hopper's classmates.

Born and raised in Nyack, New York, Hopper was a prolific and skilled draftsman from an early age. Rockwell Kent (1882–1971), a fellow student at the New York School of Art, recalled that Hopper could always be counted on to produce "an obviously brilliant drawing."[1] Hopper's graphic talents, exemplified by *Male Nude*, earned him a teaching position at the school in 1905 and, subsequently, a successful early career as an illustrator. Hopper also mastered oil, watercolor, and etching and became critically acclaimed for his realistically painted scenes of alienated urban dwellers and quiet New England landscapes.

1. Rockwell Kent, *It's Me O Lord: The Autobiography of Rockwell Kent* (New York: Dodd, Mead, 1955), 84.

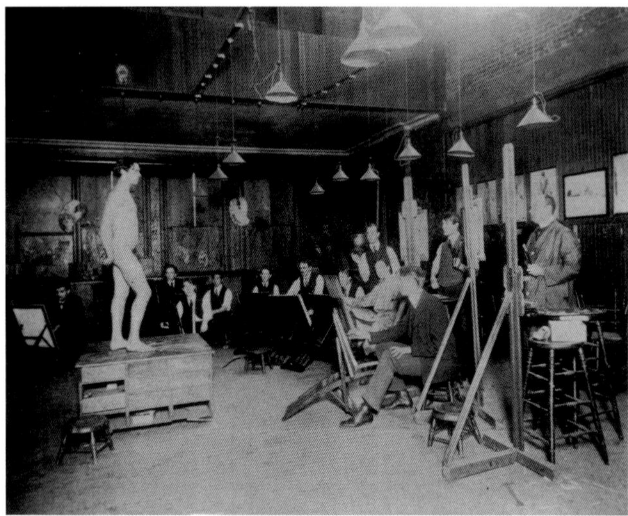

Fig. 1. *Robert Henri's Life Drawing Class at New York School of Art*, circa 1903–4. The Arthayer R. Sanborn Hopper Collection Trust, 2005. Photograph: Courtesy of The Frances Mulhall Achilles Library, Whitney Museum of American Art, New York. Edward Hopper is the first seated figure on the right.

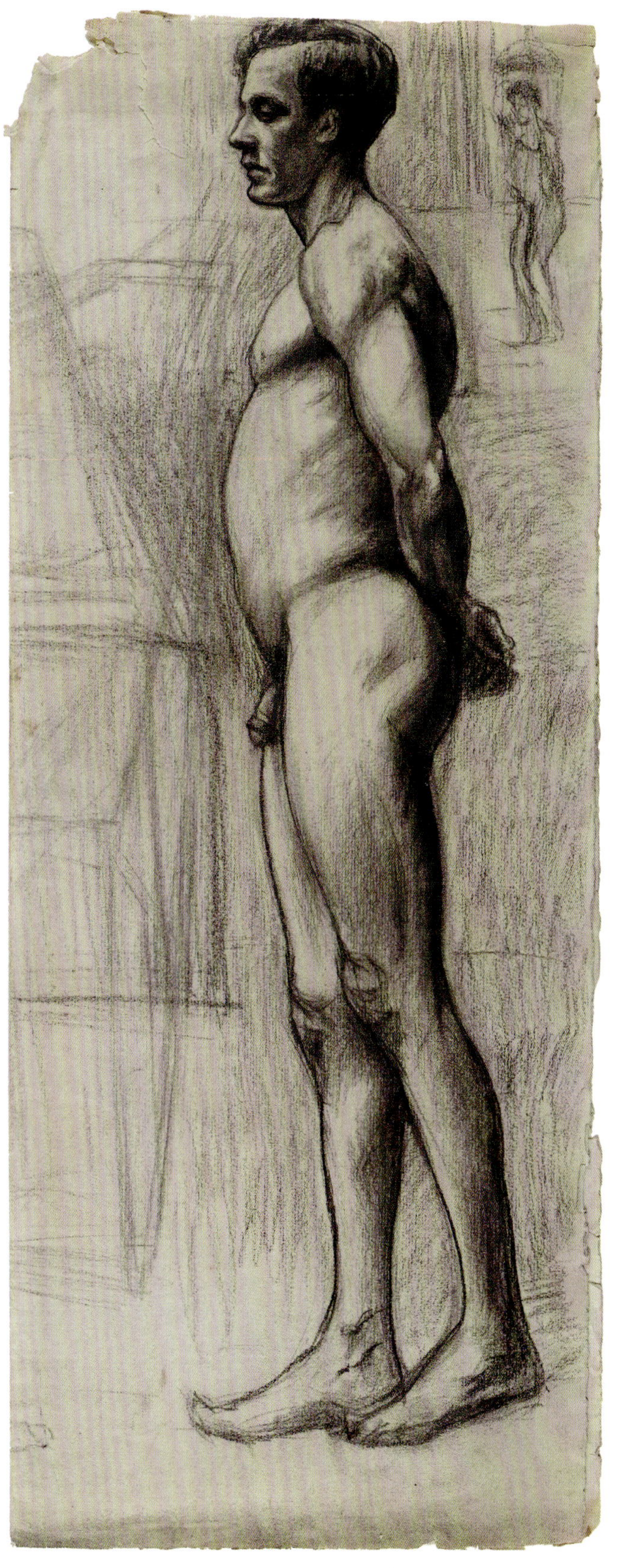

Robert Henri

American, 1865–1929

7 Nude Perched on Chair, circa 1910

Red crayon and graphite on cream, medium-weight, smooth wove paper, 12¹⁄₁₆ × 7¹⁵⁄₁₆ in. (30.6 × 20.2 cm)
Gift of Dr. and Mrs. Theodore Leshner, 76.127.11

In this quickly executed sketch, undoubtedly done from life, Robert Henri captured a nude female model balanced on a stool and hugging her legs to her chest while gazing over her shoulder. Using brick-colored crayon, he outlined her form with vibrant strokes—highlighting certain contours with a sharper line—and applied shading with smudged rubbings. More concerned with the overall impression than with anatomical precision, Henri rendered her hands and facial features in abbreviated fashion. The face, for instance, is a stylized heart shape dominated by large, staring eyes. Notwithstanding the spontaneity of execution and reductive treatment of human anatomy, the artist conveyed a sense of the body's volume. For example, he was able to suggest the fall of shadow and light by modeling one side of the nose with only a few soft strokes.

Although Henri painted few nudes—his oeuvre is dominated by vigorously brushed portraits and landscapes—he firmly believed in figure study as an important foundation for artists, a conviction rooted in his academic training at the Pennsylvania Academy of the Fine Arts in Philadelphia and at the Académie Julian in Paris. His style was strongly influenced by the frankness and dark palette of **Thomas Eakins**, the Realist painter and instructor who introduced a rigorous approach to anatomy into the Pennsylvania Academy's curriculum. (Although Henri arrived at the school in 1886, shortly after Eakins's infamous departure over the issue of study from the nude, the elder artist's legacy was still strong.) When Henri himself later became a teacher in New York, he regularly used live models in the classroom (see number 6). *Nude Perched on Chair* might be a demonstration piece he dashed off while teaching at the New York School of Art (1902–9) or at his Henri School (1909–12). In contrast to Eakins, Henri did not insist on scientific precision in rendering the human form. In one of his life classes, students spent half an hour simply observing a model and drew from memory the following hour, after the model had been dismissed.[1] He instructed students, "What you must express in your drawing is not 'what model you had,' but 'what were your sensations,' and you select . . . the [model's] traits that best express you."[2]

An inspiring and charismatic mentor, Henri encouraged his friends and students to rebel against the rigid artistic conventions upheld by the National Academy of Design by taking inspiration from contemporary life and pursuing individual means of expression. The leading figure of the Ashcan School of urban Realist painters, Henri was active in organizing exhibitions of progressive art.

1. William Innes Homer, *Robert Henri and His Circle* (Ithaca, N.Y.: Cornell University Press, 1969), 161.
2. Robert Henri, *The Art Spirit*, comp. Margery Ryerson (Philadelphia: J. B. Lippincott Company, 1923), 80.

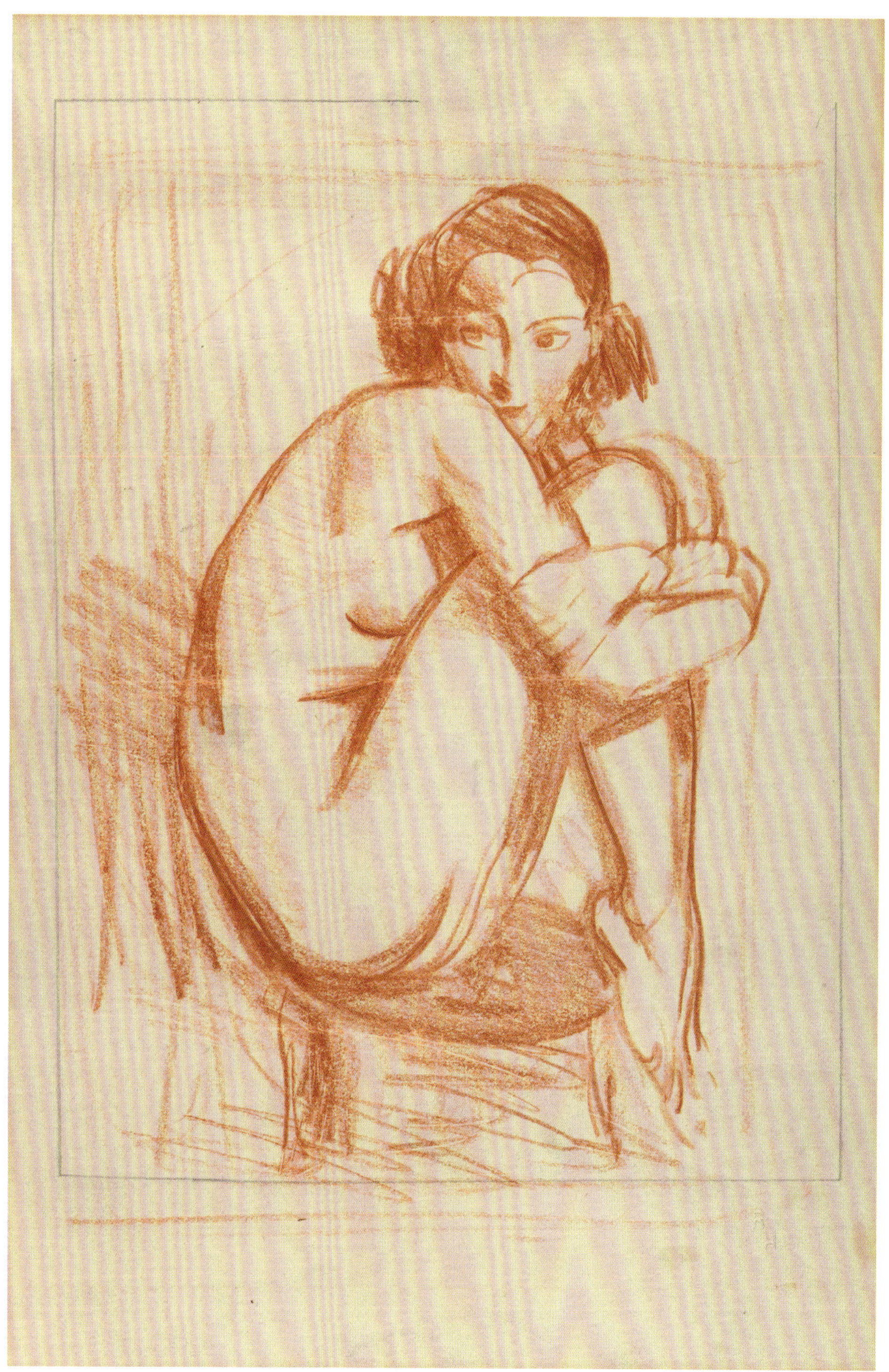

Arthur Bowen Davies

American, 1862–1928

8 **Nude,** undated

Pastel on beige Japanese laid paper mounted to wood-pulp board, 11 × 14½ in. (27.9 × 36.8 cm)
Gift of Frank L. Babbott, 25.713. © Estate of Arthur B. Davies

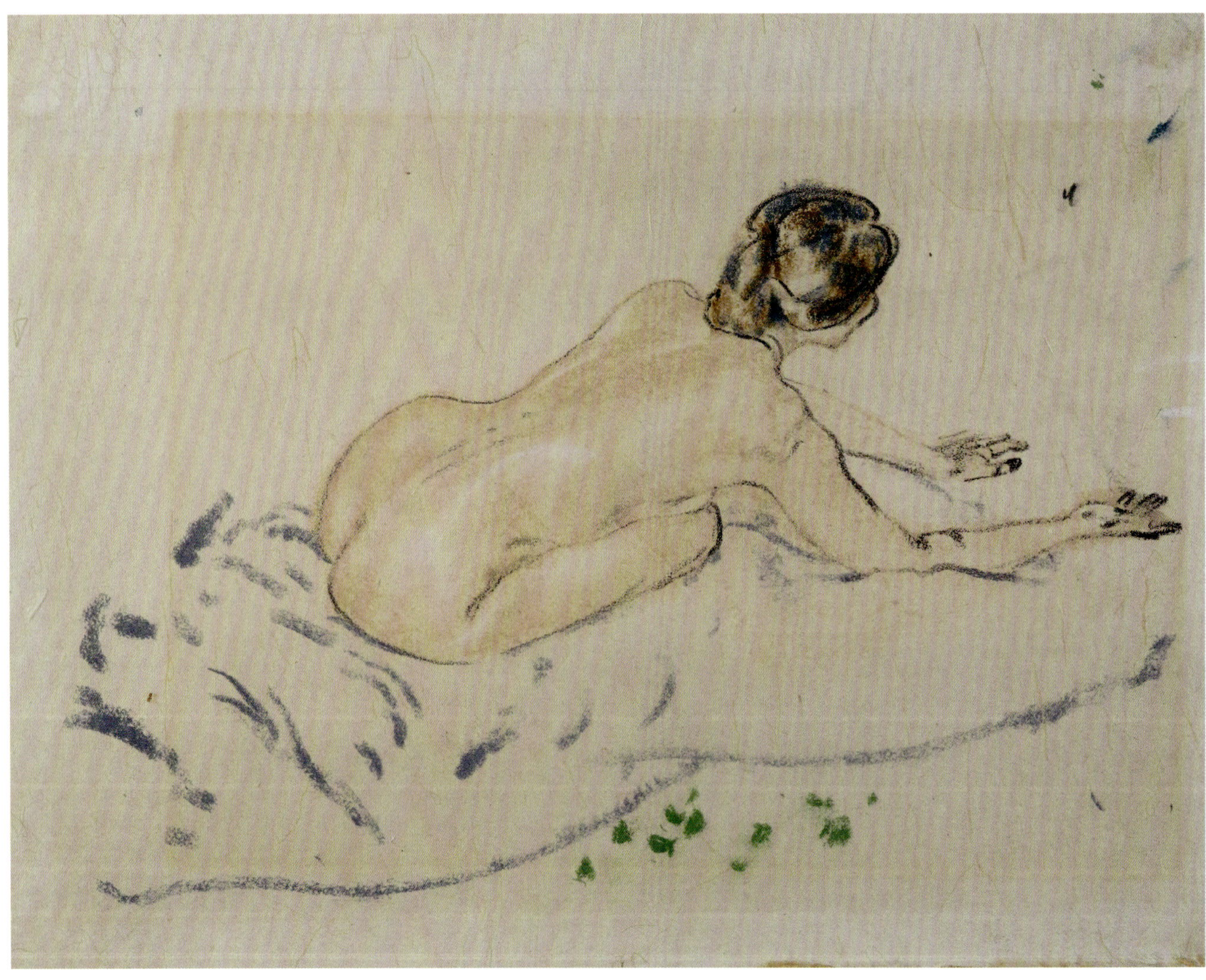

Throughout his career, Arthur Bowen Davies was drawn to the expressive potential of the female body. In various media, he depicted dancers and idealized women engaged in rhythmic movements. Although the model in this drawing appears in a static and somewhat awkward pose, she is nonetheless endowed with a nimble grace and lyrical beauty. Davies achieved these effects with his adroit handling of the pastel, capturing the undulating contours of her body with delicate black lines and subtly modulated flesh tones. In discussing Davies's art, the critic Royal Cortissoz stated, "I find it difficult to turn from the drawings, their charm is so haunting."[1] This particular drawing has the intimate quality of a domestic scene; a few cursory touches of blue and green pastel seem to describe bed linens. Given the figure's slender body type and physical grace, the model might have been Edna Potter, a dancer Davies met in 1902 and with whom he lived secretly in Manhattan for more than twenty years while supporting his estranged wife and their children in upstate New York.

Born in Utica, New York, Davies received his first formal art instruction in Chicago and then, after a stint as a draftsman for a civil engineering firm in the American Southwest and Mexico City, he moved to New York in 1887 and resumed his training at the Art Students League. He supported himself by producing illustrations for popular magazines. During the 1890s he began exhibiting his works and gained a loyal circle of patrons and admirers. The year 1895 was marked by the first of several trips he made to Europe. Davies developed a highly personalized and poetic style that drew inspiration from eclectic sources, including Old Master paintings and modern art. He became best known for his Symbolist pictures of ethereal landscapes populated with elegantly arranged figures. Active as an adviser to collectors, Davies also organized exhibitions of progressive art: he was the leading force behind the watershed Armory Show of 1913.

1. Royal Cortissoz, "Arthur B. Davies," in Duncan Phillips, *Arthur B. Davies: Essays on the Man and His Art* (Cambridge, Mass.: Riverside Press, 1924), 24.

Albert Sterner

American, born England, 1863–1946

9 Nude, 1916

Red and white chalk on off-white, moderately thick, moderately textured Japanese laid paper, 18⅛ × 15⅛ in. (46 × 38.4 cm)
Signed in red chalk, lower left: "Albert Sterner / 1916"
Gift of the artist, 29.1030

In this monochromatic nude study, Albert Sterner described the gently twisting form of his seated female model with quick, assured strokes, changing the pressure on his chalk stick to create varying values and textures of the sanguine color—from heavy, dark outlines to wispy, light touches. The speed of execution is evident in his schematic treatment of certain features, such as the woman's hair and foot and the cushion on which she sits. The overall effect is nevertheless one of palpable physicality. Sterner modeled the figure naturalistically, capturing the folds of skin at her waist and the pendulous weight of her breast.

An American citizen born in London, Sterner first studied drawing at the Birmingham Art Institute in England as a teenager and at the Académie Julian in Paris in 1886, under the instruction of the French painters Jules-Joseph Lefebvre (1834–1911) and Gustave Boulanger (1824–1888). Throughout his career, Sterner lived a cosmopolitan existence, spending several years in Chicago and New York as well as periods in European cities. He worked primarily as an illustrator for newspapers, magazines, and books. This commercial work honed his skills as a draftsman and brought him international acclaim but made it difficult for him to establish a reputation as a fine artist. Sterner's oeuvre was remarkably varied: he executed landscape, portrait, figure, and still-life subjects in paintings, drawings, watercolors, and lithographs. One critic evaluated his figure studies, done in an academic style, as follows: "As is the case with many artists of a high order of merit, Sterner turns to the nude to find the best theme for the embodiment of his powers. The truth and vigor of these studies are noteworthy."[1]

1. Martin Birnbaum, *Introductions: Painters, Sculptors, and Graphic Artists* (New York: Frederic Fairchild Sherman, 1919), 84.

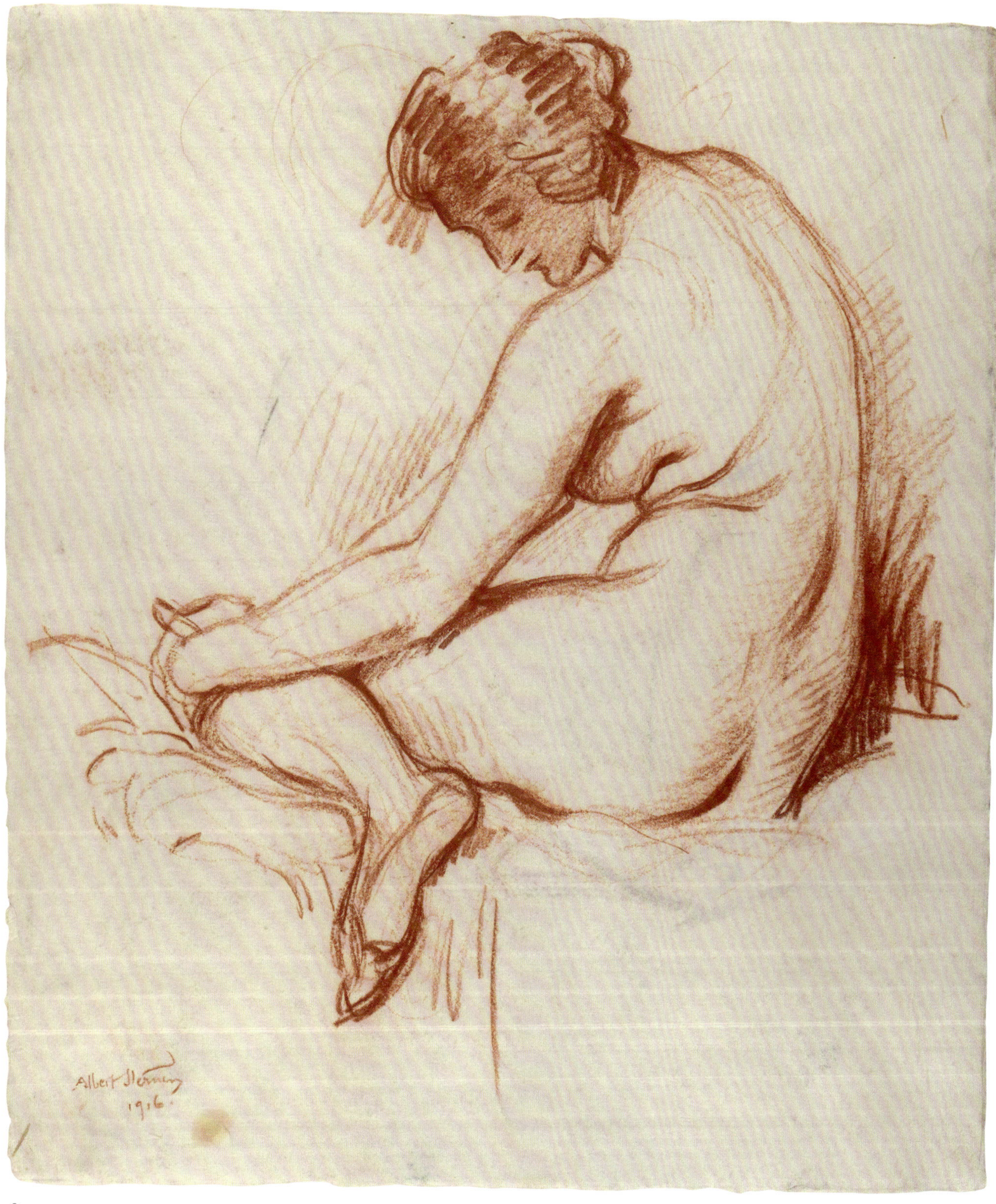
Albert Sterner
1916.

Max Weber

American, born Russia, 1881–1961

10 Composition with Four Figures, 1910

Charcoal and pastel on moderately thick, moderately textured laid paper, 24¼ × 18¼ in. (61.6 × 46.4 cm)
Signed twice in graphite and charcoal, lower right: "Max Weber 1910"
Dick S. Ramsay Fund, 57.17

11 Standing Figure, 1911

Blue-gray ink on tan, moderately thick, smooth wove paper, 14½ × 10½ in. (36.8 × 26.7 cm)
Signed in ink and graphite, lower right: "MAX WEBER / 1911"
Gift of the artist, 57.28

One of the first American modernists to embrace avant-garde innovations in European art, Max Weber made these two figure drawings during a period of stylistic experimentation after a three-year sojourn in Paris from 1905 to 1908. Born in Russia, he immigrated to New York with his family at age ten and later studied at the Pratt Institute in Brooklyn. Eager to continue his artistic training, Weber traveled to the French capital, arriving just in time to see the debut of the Fauves at the Salon d'Automne (1905) and the important Paul Cézanne (1839–1906) retrospective (1906). Weber immersed himself in his studies, enrolling in various classes and visiting the city's museums, where he could view art from around the world.[1] He also frequented the salon of Leo and Gertrude Stein, who hosted gatherings of vanguard artists and writers in their art-filled home. Through the Steins, Weber befriended Pablo Picasso (1881–1973) and Henri Matisse (1869–1954). Weber was one of several students who encouraged the latter to teach a class in 1907. When he returned to New York, he began producing work that reflected his Parisian experiences.

One such work is *Composition with Four Figures* of 1910, in which two standing female nudes and a seated woman are crowded into a rectangular composition with the face of a fourth figure—shown in profile—at upper left. This charcoal-and-pastel drawing embodies Weber's myriad aesthetic influences, particularly his sources in other figural art rather than the live model. In a style indebted to the partially abstracted nudes of Matisse and the early Cubist pictures of Picasso and Georges Braque (1882–1963), Weber rendered the human body as a series of blocky forms, faceted planes, and distorted proportions.[2] His directional hatchings, used to create modeling through the massing of light and dark tones, recall the thickly applied, patterned brushstrokes of Cézanne, while the masklike faces evoke African art, which was admired and collected by many vanguard artists, including Weber, in a phenomenon known as "primitivism."

Although these Cubist and primitivist elements are also evident in *Standing Figure*, when it is seen together with *Composition with Four Figures*, the two works demonstrate the range of Weber's early modernist experiments. In the more linear and lyrical treatment of the human body in *Standing Figure*, he rendered the female form in a simplified outline of curving contours and intersecting planes. He added minimal shading to suggest volume, but his primary concern was the exploration of abstract spatial relations rather than anatomical accuracy: thus, the figure's raised arm extends from the top of her breast, the fingers look like five dashes, and the left leg lacks a foot and terminates in twisting lines.

Initially, Weber's progressive style confounded American audiences, who were largely unfamiliar with contemporary developments in European art. In reviewing an exhibition of his work at Alfred Stieglitz's 291 gallery in 1911, one critic noted: "[Weber] has reverted to a rude sort of Aztec symbolism which seems to be without significance to any soul but himself. Grotesque profiles, enormous eyes, bodies joined like dolls, barbaric patterns in the landscapes—these are the elements of Mr. Weber's pictures and their ugliness is appalling."[3] Today, Weber is recognized for helping to alter the course of American art through his promotion of a modernist aesthetic.

1. Weber first enrolled at the Académie Julian but became frustrated with the emphasis on traditional drawing. Accustomed to the more progressive curriculum of Arthur Wesley Dow (1857–1922) at Pratt, he left the Julian to study at the Académie Colarossi and Académie de la Grande Chaumière.

2. As a specific source for Weber's *Composition with Four Figures*, John R. Lane suggests a drawing by Braque of three female figures from circa 1907 (current location unknown) that was reproduced in Gelett Burgess, "The Wild Men of Paris," *Architectural Record*, May 1910, which also included a quote from Braque: "To portray every physical aspect of an object . . . required three figures, much as the representation of a house requires a plan, elevation, and a section." Lane, "The Sources of Max Weber's Cubism," *Art Journal* 35 (Spring 1976): 232–33.

3. Joseph Edgar Chamberlain, "An Aztec Obsession," *New York Evening Mail*, Jan. 16, 1911, 8, also reprinted in *Camera Work*, no. 36 (Oct. 1911): 31.

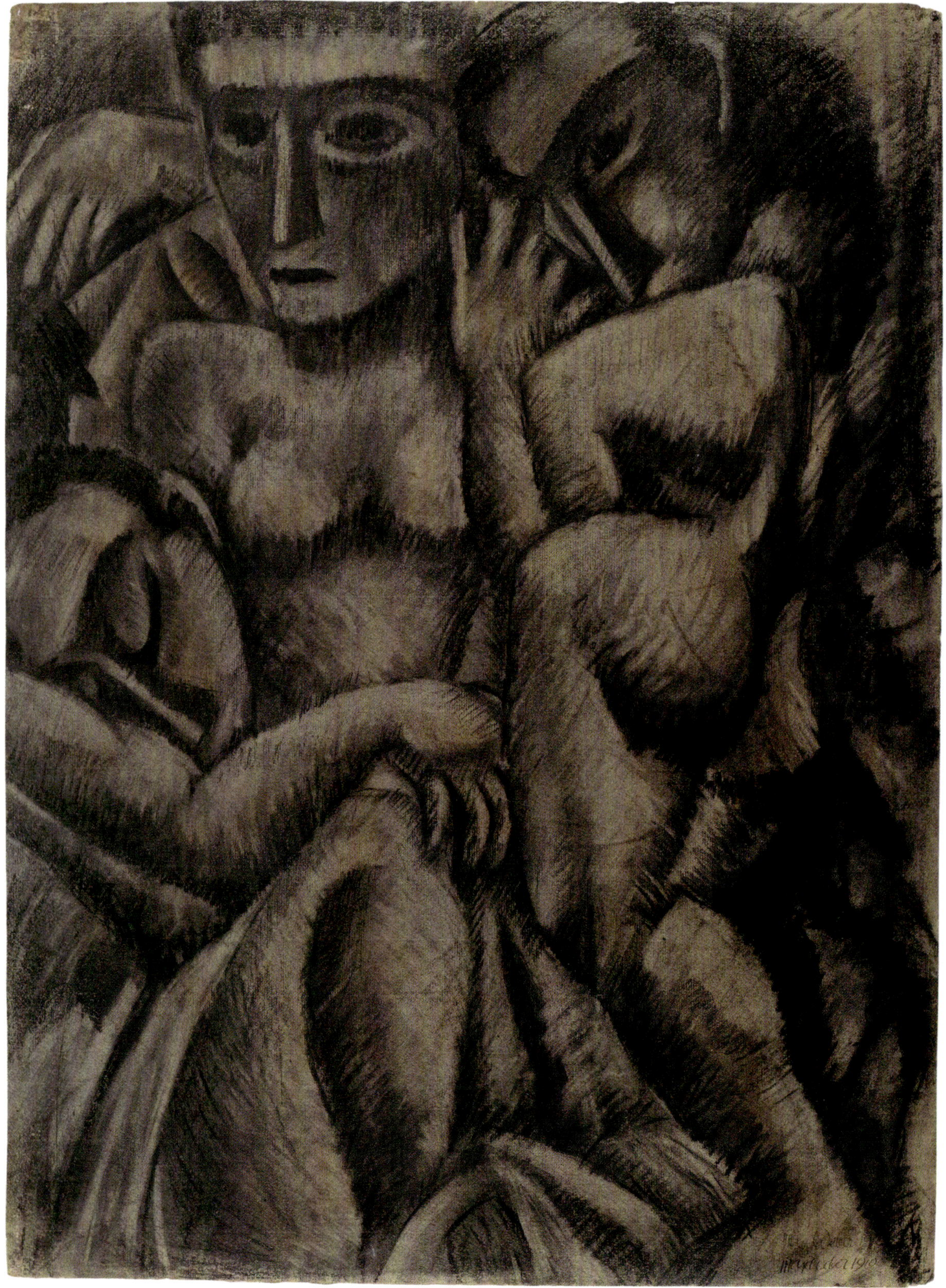

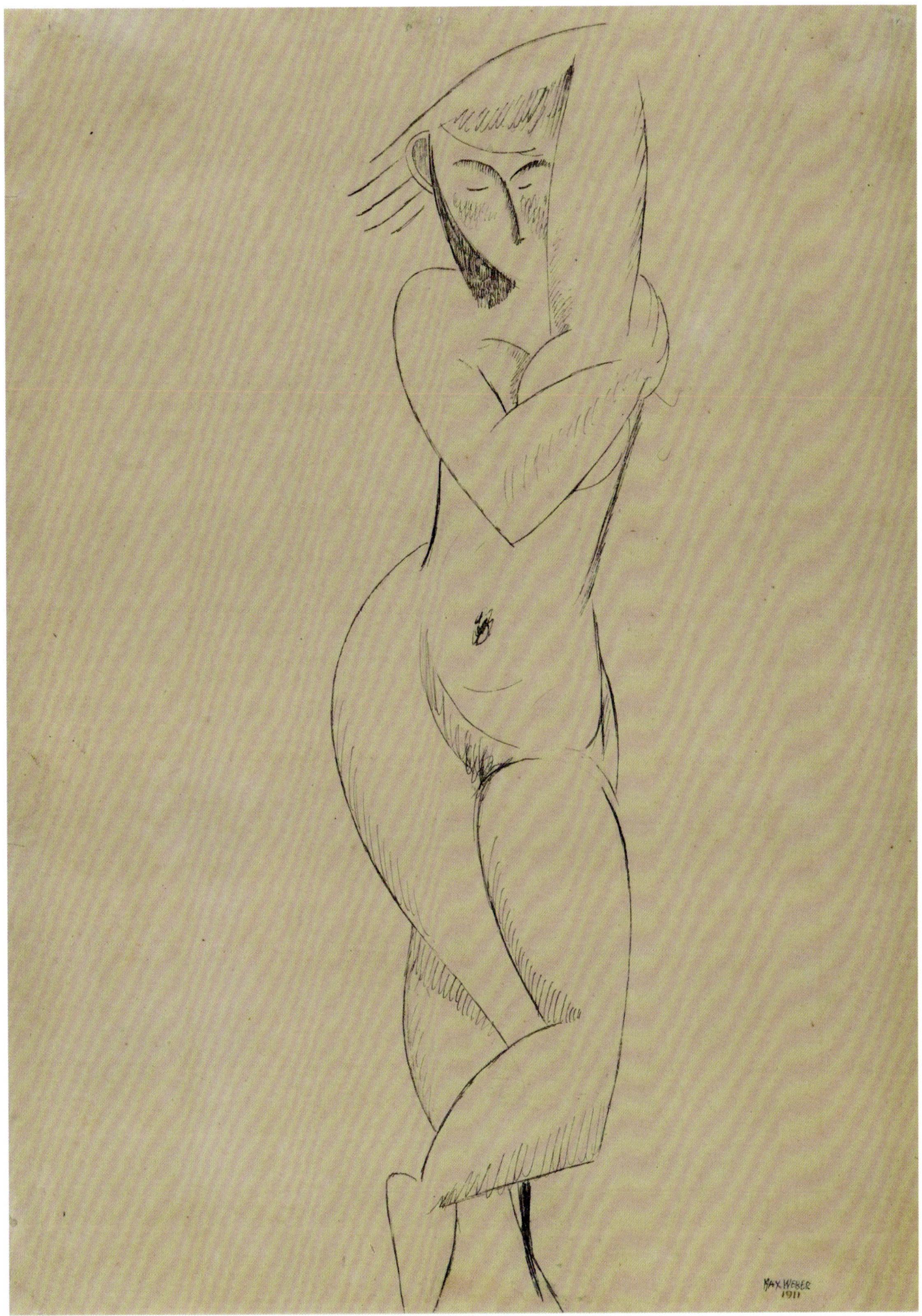

11

Abraham Walkowitz

American, born Siberia, 1878–1965

12 Abstraction, 1912

Graphite on cream, medium-weight, moderately textured laid paper, 19 × 12⅝ in. (48.3 × 32.1 cm)
Signed in ink, lower right: "A. WALKOWITZ 1912"
Gift of the artist, 39.655

Abraham Walkowitz's *Abstraction* evokes standing figures in an entangled embrace. The artist experimented with Cubist-inspired figuration by breaking down forms into faceted geometric shapes and adding soft hatchings to suggest shading and volume. This particular abstraction looks to contemporary art, as opposed to an academic cast or live model, and is reminiscent of Pablo Picasso's (1881–1973) *Standing Female Nude* (figure 2). Walkowitz would have been familiar with Picasso's drawing, which was purchased by Alfred Stieglitz (1864–1946) after its 1910 exhibition in Stieglitz's 291 gallery. In 1912 Walkowitz had his first exhibition at 291, which marked the beginning of his fruitful relationship with Stieglitz and the gallerist's circle of American modernists.

Walkowitz's *Abstraction* can be compared with **Max Weber**'s more representational *Composition with Four Figures* of 1910 (see number 10) in its fractured surfaces and tangled and at times illegible bodies. Through Weber, Walkowitz met important avant-garde artists during his 1906–7 studies in Europe, including Henri Matisse (1869–1954), Auguste Rodin (1840–1917), and Henri Rousseau (1844–1910), and familiarized himself with Weber's experiments in Cubism, which were influenced by such artists as Picasso, Georges Braque (1882–1963), and Robert Delaunay (1885–1941).

Like other members of the modernist camp at 291, Walkowitz believed that the artist must disregard or alter the laws of past artistic traditions. He valued the expression of emotion in an improvised manner and often created work with no particular subject in mind. In reviews of Walkowitz's first exhibition at 291, critics were divided between progressives, who supported American modernism, and conservatives, who favored traditional, academic art. The *New York Globe* proclaimed Walkowitz "as weird as the worst of them,"[1] while the *Sun* took a more admiring view: "Walkowitz does not hand us little bundles of ideas and impressions ready for instant assimilation. He stimulates us, the onlookers, to meet him part way, by the exercise of our imaginations. Was it not Baudelaire, speaking to a friend, who said in effect: 'When your imagination has traveled half way, to meet mine, as revealed in what I have written, then between us we have produced a masterpiece'?"[2]—CG

1. Arthur Hoeber, "Art and Artists,"
   New York Globe, Dec. 23, 1912, 10,
   quoted in *Camera Work*, no. 41
   (Jan. 1913): 26.
2. "Strong Work by a New Artist,"
   Sun (New York), Dec. 29, 1912, 15.

Fig. 2. Pablo Picasso (Spanish, 1881–1973). *Standing Female Nude*, 1910. Charcoal on paper, 19 × 12⅜ in. (48.3 × 31.4 cm). The Metropolitan Museum of Art, Alfred Stieglitz Collection, 49.70.34. © 2011 Estate of Pablo Picasso / Artists Rights Society (ARS), New York. Image: © The Metropolitan Museum of Art

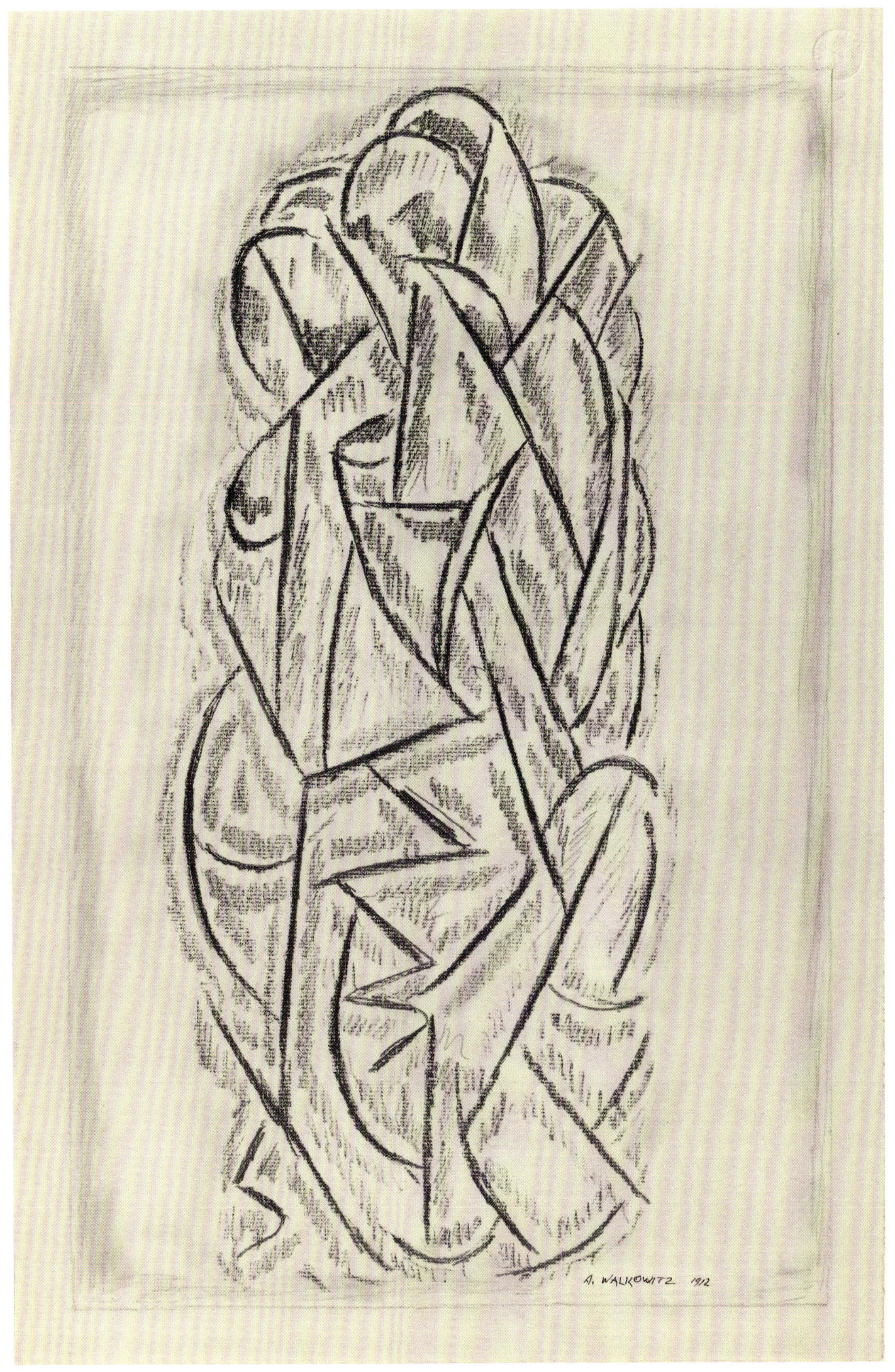
A. WALKOWITZ 1912

Bradley Walker Tomlin

American, 1899–1953

13 **Back,** circa 1925

Conté crayon and watercolor on beige, medium-weight, moderately textured laid paper with watermark, 11½ × 11⁵⁄₁₆ in. (29.2 × 28.7 cm)
Signed in graphite, lower right: "Tomlin"
Gift of Frank L. Babbott, 25.520

In this figure study, the future Abstract Expressionist artist Bradley Walker Tomlin captured the solidity of his seated female nude model, describing the contours of the woman's back with delicate tonal modulations created by dragging and rubbing a Conté crayon across the textured surface of the paper. He also hinted at an underlying abstract structure to the figure with lightly sketched Cubist planes that intersect on her lower back. The accents of watercolor in red, black, and green hues serve a decorative rather than representational function and further indicate Tomlin's interest in formal concerns. Here, he treated the female body as an object of aesthetic experimentation, not of anatomical study, using it to explore subtle contrasts of rounded volumes and flat surfaces, strong lines and smoky shadows, monochromatic tones and washes of color.

Back was one of the first of Tomlin's works to enter a museum collection. As such, it is a rare surviving example of his early oeuvre, since later in his career the artist destroyed many of his initial efforts.[1] Born in Syracuse, New York, he showed artistic promise at a young age. As a teenager, he studied sculptural modeling in the studio of Hugo Gari Wagner (life dates unknown) and then painting at Syracuse University. After graduating in 1921, Tomlin moved to New York City, supporting himself doing commercial illustration work. He began a lifelong practice of spending summers in Woodstock, New York, the site of an emerging artists' colony. In 1923 Tomlin visited Europe for the first time to continue his studies at the Académie Colarossi and the Académie de la Grande Chaumière in Paris. During this period, he made portraits, landscapes, and still lifes in a broadly realistic style that showed an eclectic range of influences, including American and European modernism. Tomlin was always a thoughtful artist who was willing to experiment, and the 1936–37 exhibition *Fantastic Art, Dada, and Surrealism* at the Museum of Modern Art in New York inspired him to reject figuration in favor of biomorphic forms in a decorative Cubist idiom. In the mid-1940s, he arrived at the abstract compositions of his mature style, for which he is best known. These works, in which dots, crosses, and other calligraphic shapes are arranged across the entire canvas, were acclaimed for their lyrical grace. With his friends Adolph Gottlieb (1903–1974), Philip Guston (1913–1980), Robert Motherwell (1915–1991), and others, Tomlin was an integral and respected member of the New York school of Abstract Expressionists until his untimely death in 1953.

1. See Jeanne Chenault, "Bradley Walker Tomlin: Early Paintings and Intimations," *Archives of American Art Journal* 14, no. 3 (1974): 7–13.

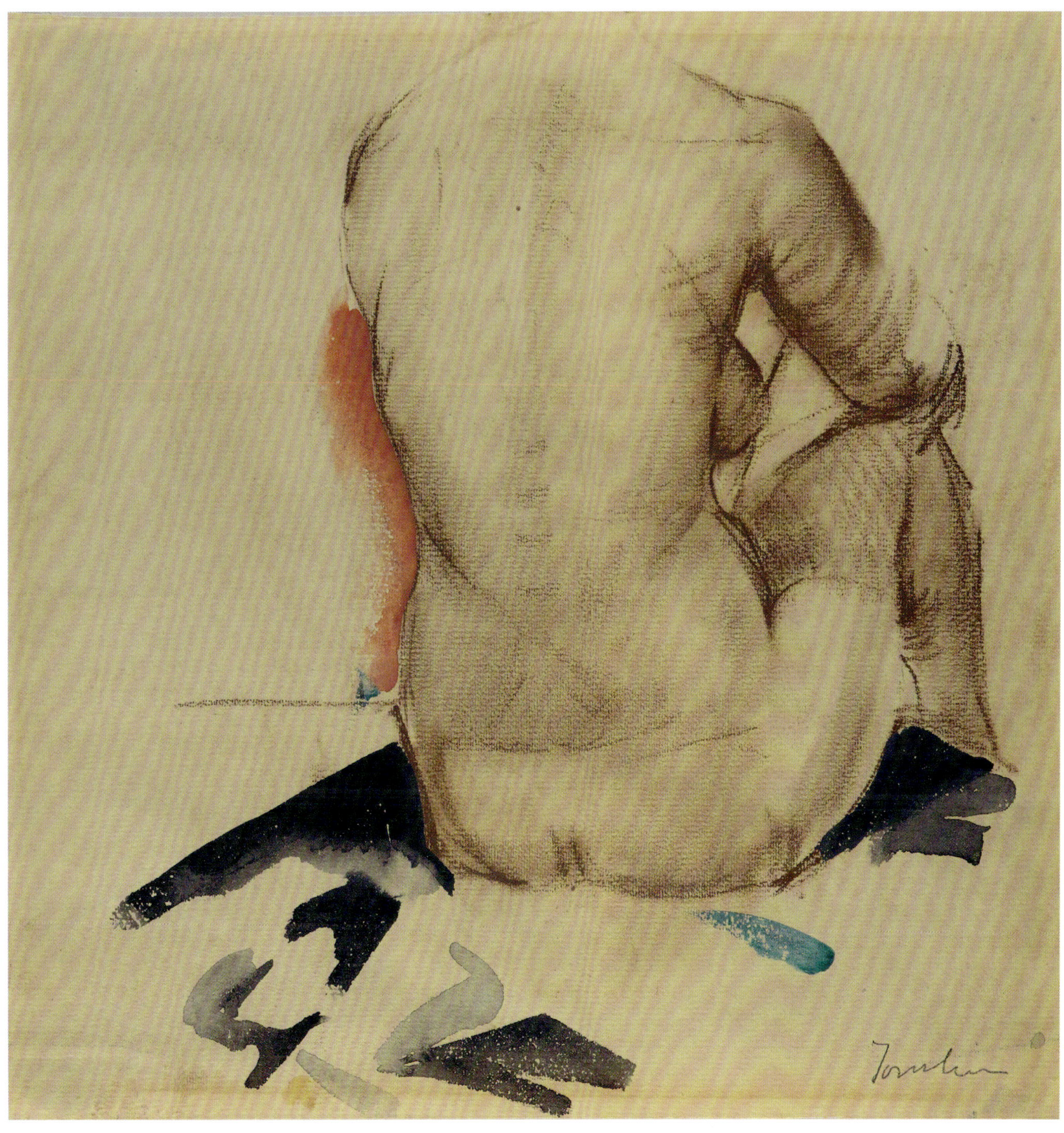

Gaston Lachaise

American, born France, 1882–1935

14 Back of a Nude Woman, 1929

Black ink on cream, medium-weight, slightly textured wove paper, 17⅞ × 12 in. (45.4 × 30.5 cm)
Inscribed and signed in graphite, lower left: "To Carl Zigrosser / G. Lachaise / 1929"
Gift of Carl Zigrosser, 38.183. © Estate of Gaston Lachaise

This exuberant drawing conveys the powerful energy and voluptuous eroticism of the female nude—a favorite subject of the sculptor Gaston Lachaise. Seen from behind, the woman sways her ample hips to the left in counterbalance to her extended right leg, which is draped with a scarf. Lachaise reduced the figure to an outline of sinuous curves rendered in assured, flowing strokes of black ink. Anatomical details are either minimal, such as the brief lines articulating the spine and shoulder blades, or subtly distorted, such as the continuous slope from the shoulder to the wrist and the relatively tiny feet. Instead of using traditional shading and modeling, the artist relied entirely on the expressive quality of line and silhouette to animate the figure. Note how he varied the density of ink—wispy and light in some areas, solid and heavy in others—by changing the pressure on his pen.

Lachaise's sculptures of monumental, buxom women earned him a place as one of the most important sculptors in the United States during the first half of the twentieth century. Although his drawings are generally not preparatory studies for his three-dimensional works, they evince the same preoccupation with the female body. Lachaise's muse was his beloved wife, Isabel Dutaud Nagle (1872–1957), who embodied his ideas about universal womanhood as an eternal life force. He met Nagle, who was married at the time, in Paris when he was a promising art student. Smitten with her majestic beauty and frustrated by his academic training, he determined to follow her across the ocean, settling first in Boston in 1906 and then in New York in 1912. After working in the studios of the sculptors Henry Hudson Kitson (1863–1947) and Paul Manship (1885–1966), Lachaise began exhibiting his own figural works, which presented a new feminine ideal that endowed the classical Venus type with modernist forms and earthy sexuality. The art critic Henry McBride reported that Lachaise was seeking "a new feeling of poetry that [he] found upon this side of the water when contemplating our American women. He says our women will do wonderfully to typify the extraordinary energy that most foreigners now admit is characteristic of American men and enterprise. It is this super-force in the women here that he tried to express in sculpture."[1] The first living artist to be accorded a retrospective exhibition at the Museum of Modern Art, New York (1935), Lachaise was also active in artistic and literary circles, particularly through his affiliation with the *Dial*, a monthly arts journal. He dedicated this drawing to the art critic, curator, and gallerist Carl Zigrosser.

1. Henry McBride, "Gaston Lachaise: Sculptor," *Fine Arts Journal* 36 (Mar. 1918): 54–55.

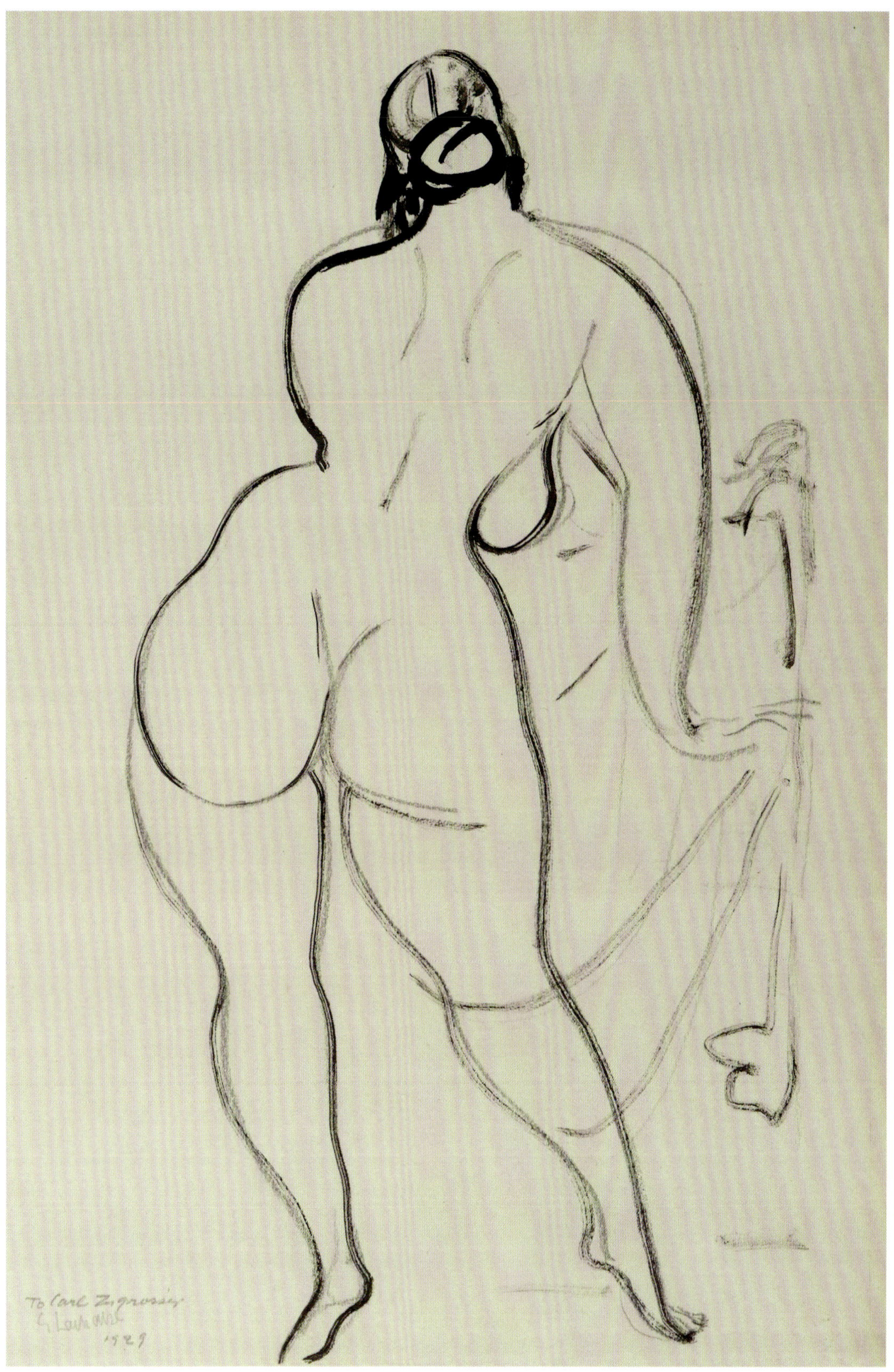

William Zorach

American, born Lithuania, 1887–1966

15 Seated Nude, 1930

Graphite on beige, medium-weight, moderately textured wove paper, 22⅞ × 16¾ in. (58.1 × 42.5 cm)
Signed in graphite, lower right: "William Zorach"
Gift of the collection of the Zorach children, 84.45.2. © The Zorach Collection, LLC

The human body played an integral role in the art of the sculptor William Zorach, and his oeuvre is dominated by imagery of the figure arranged in a variety of poses—reclining, kneeling, standing—and in groups. Although he embraced this traditional academic subject, his approach was distinctly modern in its reductive handling of anatomical forms. In this drawing, Zorach rendered the figure of a nude woman seated on a blanket-covered cushion as a simple, flattened outline with minimal modeling. Despite the schematic treatment, he articulated enough essential details—the model's collarbones, kneecaps, and the crease of her belly—to endow her body with a realistic sense of physicality and individuality. Zorach's skill as a draftsman is evident in his assured and expressive use of graphite. Slight undulations in the contours and variations in tone—created by changing the pressure on the pencil—emphasize the play of line against the broad expanses of blank paper.

Born Zorach Samovich in Lithuania, the artist immigrated with his family to Cleveland, Ohio, at age four and later changed his name to William Zorach. His early passion for drawing led to an apprenticeship in a commercial lithography shop during his teens. He also took art classes at the Cleveland School of Art and, after his 1908 move to New York, at the National Academy of Design. At both of these schools he excelled in academic life drawing.[1] In 1910 Zorach, like many artists of his generation, traveled to Paris—a trip that had a transformative effect on his art. While in France, he met his future wife, the artist **Marguerite Thompson (Zorach)**, as well as other modernist artists, and witnessed the vanguard developments in European art. Back in New York, Zorach rejected his academic training and adopted a painting style that combined the bright colors of Fauvism with the fractured forms of Cubism. His works were included in such landmark exhibitions as the Armory Show (1913) and the Forum Exhibition of Modern American Painters (1916). By 1922 he had largely abandoned painting for sculpture, a medium for which he felt a natural affinity. Zorach became a leading figure in the direct-carving movement. Throughout his career, Zorach continued to draw, and about 1920 he developed the characteristic crisp outline style seen in *Seated Nude* (see also numbers 43, 55).

1. Roberta K. Tarbell, *William and Marguerite Zorach: The Maine Years* (Rockland, Maine: William A. Farnsworth Library and Art Museum, 1979), 27.

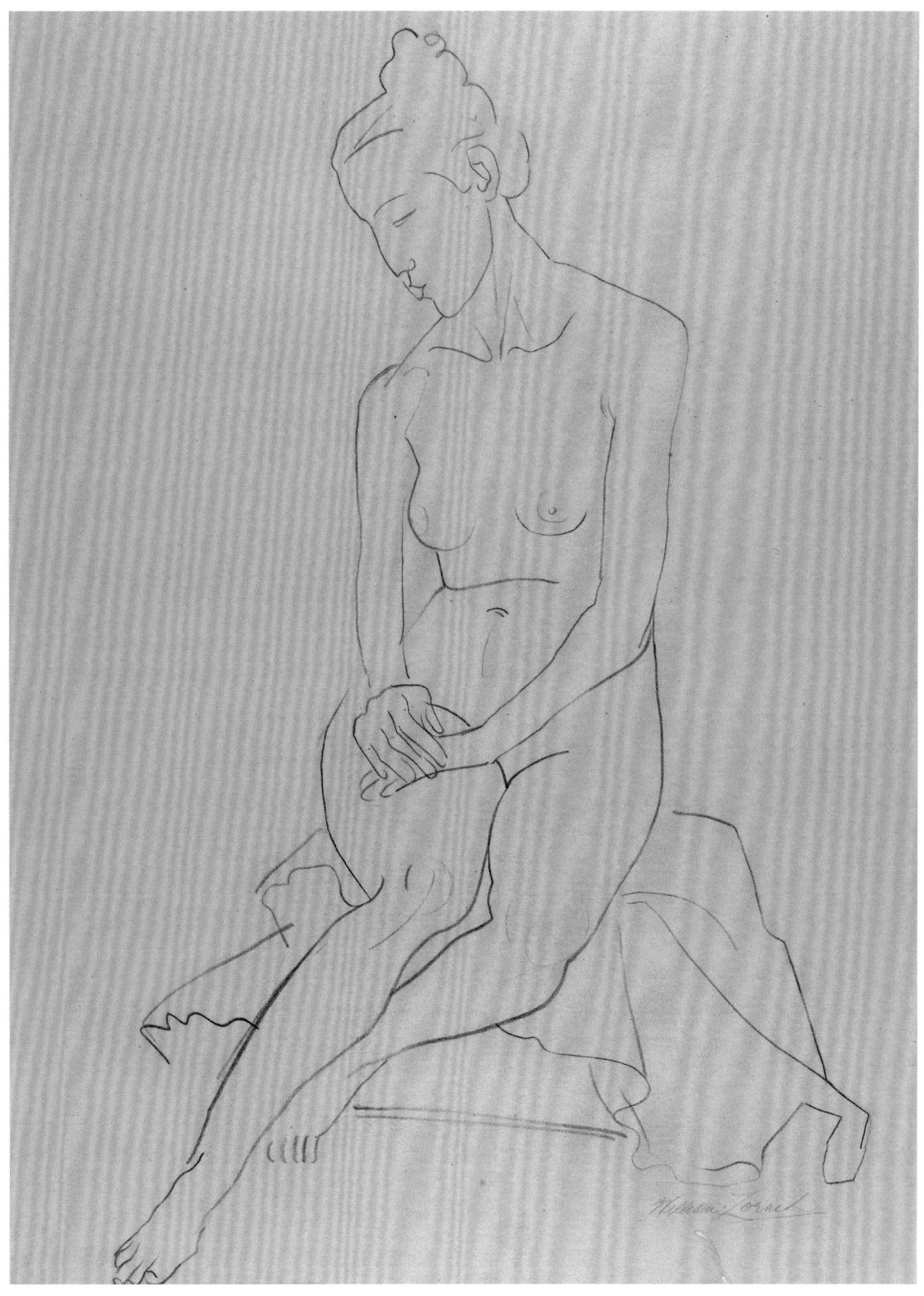

Louise Nevelson

American, born Russia, 1900–1988

16 Untitled (Standing Female Nude), circa 1932–34

Graphite on white, medium-weight, smooth wove paper, 16¹⁵⁄₁₆ × 13⅞ in. (43 × 35.2 cm)
Signed in graphite, lower center: "Nevelson"
Gift of Samuel Goldberg in memory of his parents, Sophie and Jacob Goldberg, and his brother, Hyman Goldberg, 78.277.4. © 2012 Estate of Louise Nevelson / Artists Rights Society (ARS), New York

From 1929 to 1934, Louise Nevelson created—almost compulsively—hundreds of drawings of the female nude, including this one done on a page torn from a spiral notebook.[1] Here, as is typical of this body of work, Nevelson drastically simplified the human form into a spare outline and distorted its anatomical proportions. The absence of detail and modeling, combined with the large areas of blank paper, emphasizes the flatness of the image. Notwithstanding this reductive treatment, the figure exudes energy by means of the thin, fluid quality of Nevelson's line and the expressive contours, particularly in the massive hips and bulbous thighs. Contemporary critics remarked on this vibrancy when the artist exhibited some of her female nudes, along with sculptural pieces, at A.C.A. Galleries in New York in 1936. One wrote: "[Nevelson] contributes twelve drawings which, despite their jagged, uneven line, oddly suggest strength and solidity."[2]

The period in which Nevelson made these drawings was a transitional one for her. Dissatisfied with the conventional role of wife and mother, she decided to leave her husband of ten years and began serious, full-time artistic training in New York City. Her independence caused financial hardship (exacerbated by the Great Depression), but it also brought exciting opportunities, professional stimulation, and camaraderie with other artists. At the Art Students League, she studied with Kenneth Hayes Miller (1876–1952); Hans Hofmann (1880–1966); and Kimon Nicolaides (1891–1938), who was particularly influential, encouraging students to tap into their intuitive feelings through drawing from memory and drawing without looking at the paper. Nevelson also took classes with the modernist sculptor **Chaim Gross** at the Educational Alliance Art School in 1933 (see number 19) and worked as an assistant to the Mexican muralist Diego Rivera (1886–1957) on his project for Rockefeller Center. Although Nevelson experimented with a range of media—drawings, paintings, and sculpture—in the 1930s she focused most intensely on drawing because, for her, it served as an emotional outlet and a source of personal strength. In subsequent decades, she turned primarily to sculpture and became best known for monumental, monochromatic wood assemblages constructed from objects found in the streets.

1. She sometimes created forty to fifty drawings of the female nude in a day. Laurie Lisle, *Louise Nevelson: A Passionate Life* (New York: Summit Books, 1990), 73.

2. Quoted in Arnold B. Glimcher, *Louise Nevelson* (New York: Praeger Publishers, 1972), 43.

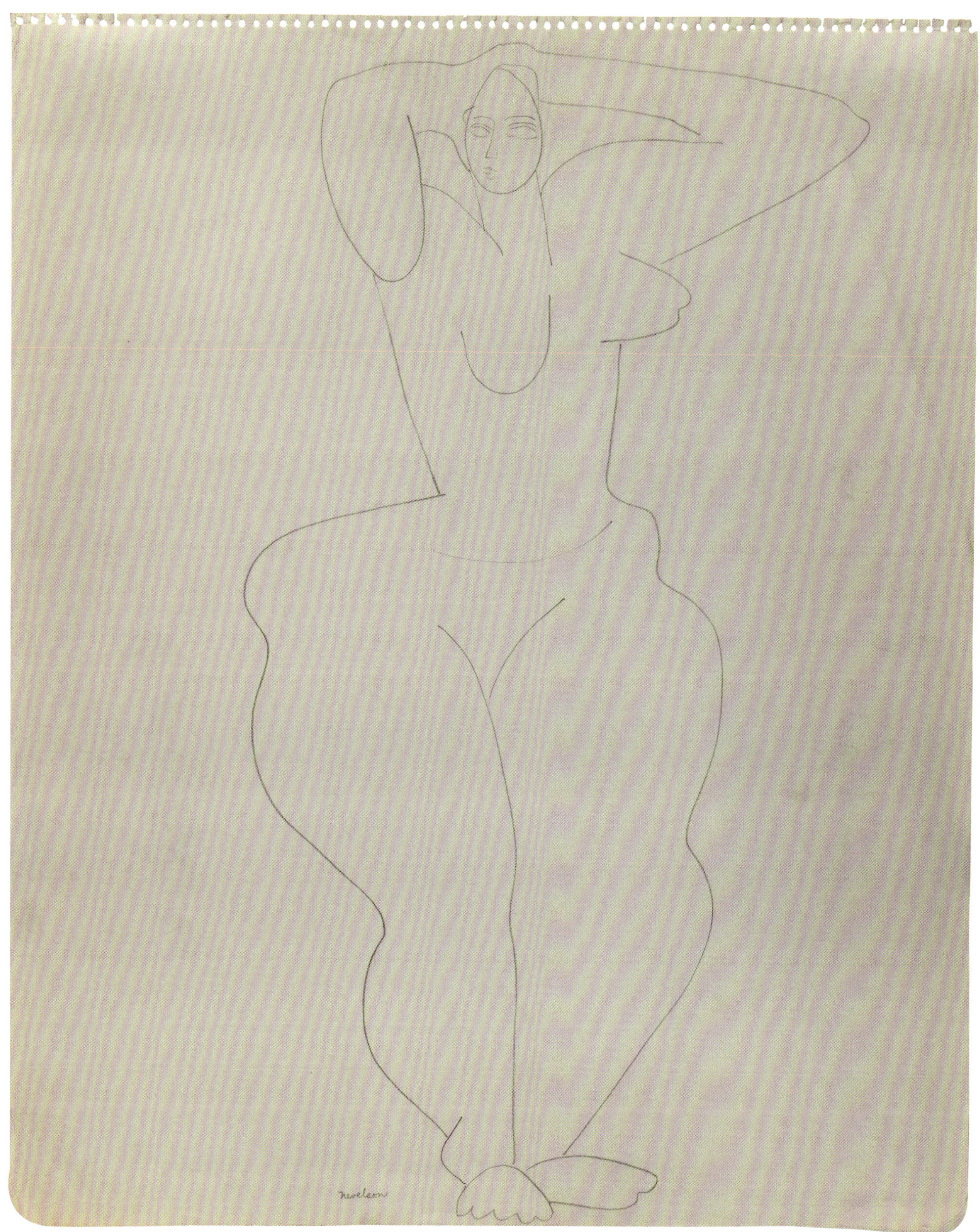

Isamu Noguchi

American, 1904–1988

17 **Bending Figure,** 1933

Black ink on gray-brown, moderately thick, moderately textured wove paper, 24⅛ × 20 in. (61.3 × 50.8 cm)
Signed in graphite, lower left: "ISAMU / '33"
Dick S. Ramsay Fund, 48.69.2. © The Isamu Noguchi Foundation and Garden Museum, New York / Artists Rights Society (ARS), New York

18 **Model,** circa early 1930s

Black ink on cream, thin, slightly textured paper, 22⅛ × 17⅜ in. (56.2 × 44.1 cm)
Signed in graphite, upper right: "Isamu / [artist's symbol of circle bisected by vertical line]"
Dick S. Ramsay Fund, 41.975. © The Isamu Noguchi Foundation and Garden Museum, New York / Artists Rights Society (ARS), New York

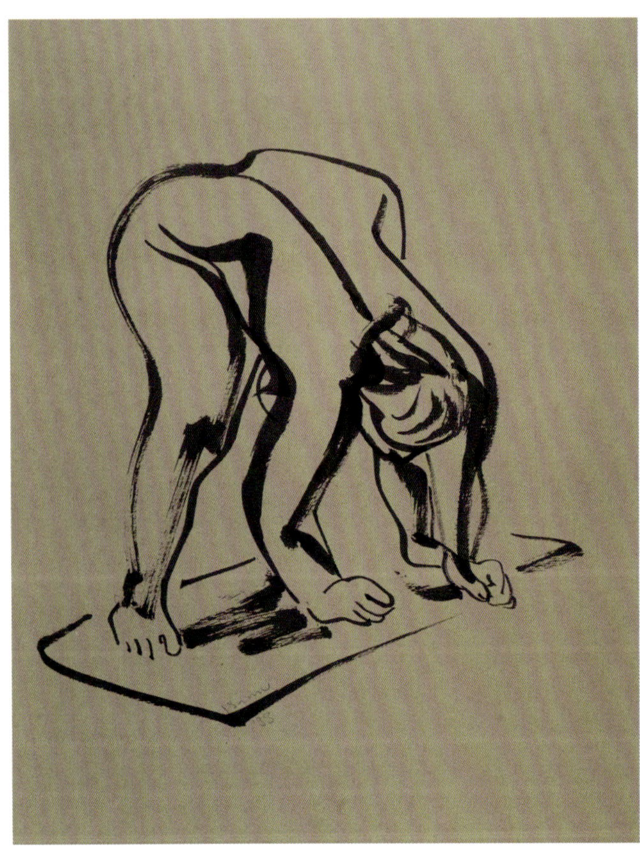

17

An artist who worked primarily as a sculptor, Isamu Noguchi generally used drawing as preparation for his three-dimensional creations, making small sketches and brief notations of his ideas. An exception within his graphic oeuvre is a series of about fifty monumental figurative drawings he made in the early 1930s based on his studies of traditional Chinese brush drawing in Beijing with the celebrated master Qi Baishi (1863–1957). These two examples represent a nude female (Noguchi also depicted men, parent-and-child groups, and a baby, using local models), but they differ markedly from each other in both technique and approach to figuration. In the more painterly *Bending Figure*, the artist applied the ink with a thick paintbrush to render the woman's form with long, serpentine lines and slashing strokes. By changing the pressure of his touch and twisting the tip of the brush, he varied the density and width of the black outlines over the course of each stroke. Such variations provide a suggestion of volumetric mass in an otherwise flattened and abstracted figure.

Whereas *Bending Figure* relies primarily on broadly swept, expressive contours, *Model* evinces a more intimate, contained, and deliberative quality. In this drawing, Noguchi traced the outline of the seated figure with a thin, delicate line and then added areas of cross-hatching to create a play of light and dark across the expanse of the model's back. For some reason, Noguchi did not articulate the right hand or left arm of his model; these omissions may be an indication of the experimental nature of these ink drawings as he tried out a new medium and its varied visual effects. His artistic skill and manual dexterity are evident in his deft manipulation of the unforgiving ink medium to create such different effects in these two drawings.

Born in Los Angeles to a Japanese father and an American mother, Noguchi spent much of his childhood in Japan before returning to the United States at age thirteen. He achieved early success sculpting portrait busts in a realistic academic style and then turned toward abstraction after seeing an exhibition of the modernist sculpture of Constantin Brancusi (1876–1957) in New York in 1926. The following year, Noguchi traveled to Paris and became Brancusi's studio assistant, absorbing lessons from his mentor in how to reduce organic motifs to their essential forms and familiarizing himself with other developments in the Parisian art scene. With the goal of bridging Western and Eastern cultural traditions, he traveled to Asia in 1931–32, studying brush drawing in China and traditional pottery in Japan. His mature sculptural work is characterized by abstract, often biomorphic forms; he also created outdoor sculpture environments, furniture, and set designs.

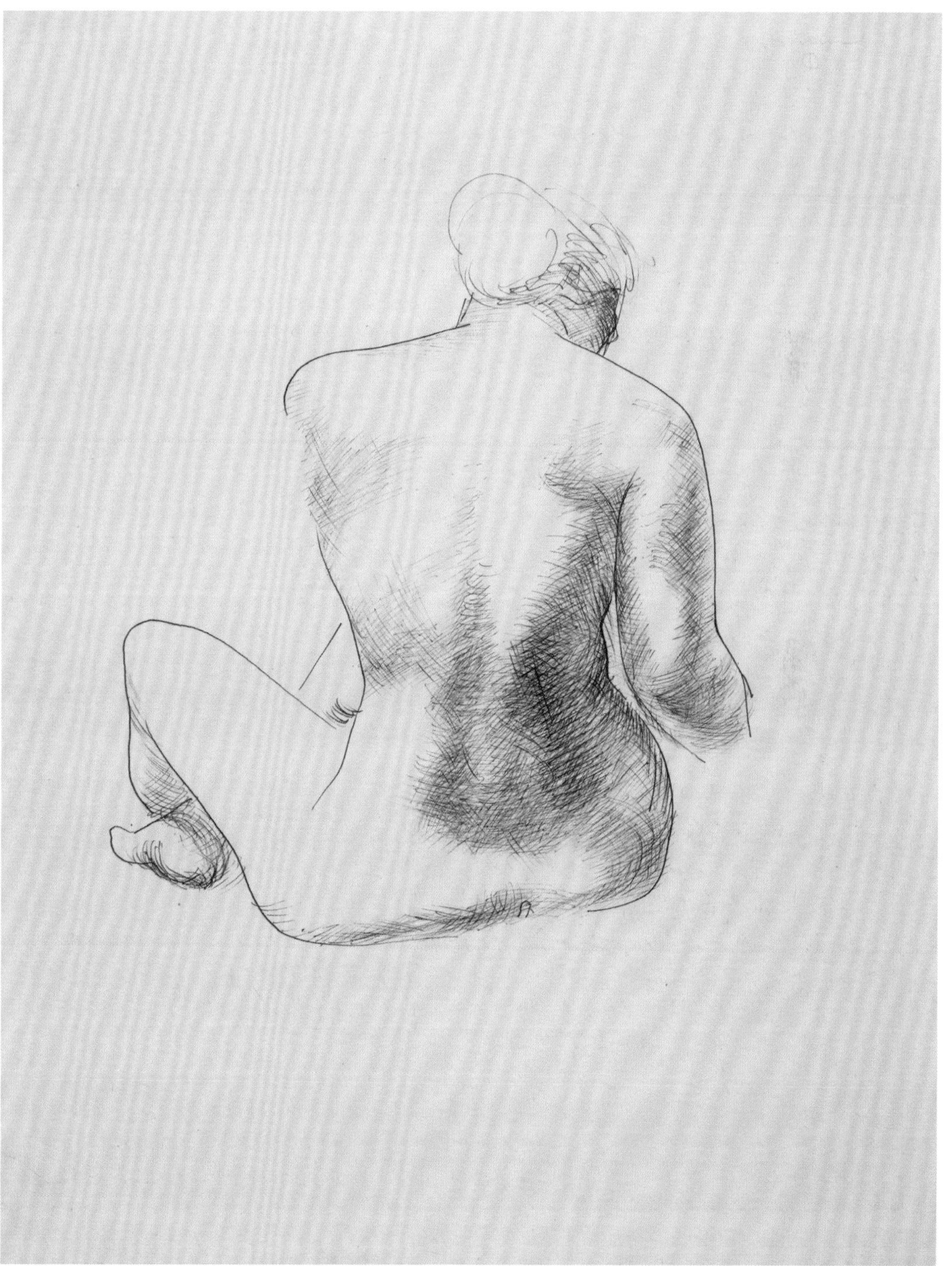

18

Chaim Gross

American, born Austria, 1904–1991

19 Study No. 1 for "Ballerina," circa 1940

Graphite on green-gray, medium-weight, moderately textured laid paper, 38 × 25⅚₆ in. (96.5 × 64.3 cm)
Signed in graphite, lower right: "Chaim Gross"
Designated Purchase Fund, 42.418. © Estate of Chaim Gross

Primarily known for his sculptures of the female figure—particularly nudes, mothers, and acrobats and other performers—Chaim Gross was also a prolific draftsman who sketched regularly in various media.[1] An integral part of his sculpting process, drawing helped him to capture the poses of his live models and to conceptualize the forms of three-dimensional works. This large graphite drawing is one of a series of preparatory studies for his wood sculpture *Ballerina* (Brooklyn Museum, acc. no. 40.874), commissioned by the Works Project Administration (WPA) as a demonstration of direct-carving techniques for audiences at the New York World's Fair, held from 1939 to 1940 (figure 3).[2]

Both the study and the finished sculpture reveal the artist's characteristic treatment of the human body, incorporating simplified modeling and distorted proportions—seen here in the ballerina's exaggeratedly thick legs and narrow waist. In the drawing, Gross delineated the figure with loosely sketched outlines, often making multiple strokes along the same contours, and then modeled the bulbous forms with contrasting areas of lights and darks. He created the shading with a combination of energetic hatch marks and looping scribbles, as well as rubbings with the side of the pencil. The dynamic quality of his line animates the figure, despite its static pose, and evokes the rough-hewn surface textures of many of the artist's sculptures.

After a difficult youth marked by persecution for his Jewish identity, the Austrian-born Gross immigrated to New York City in 1921. He took art classes at the Educational Alliance Art School and the Beaux-Arts Institute of Design, where he learned to appreciate the beauty of abstracted forms and sinuous lines from the sculptor **Elie Nadelman**. Both schools emphasized traditional techniques of drawing from life and modeling in clay. Gross also studied carving with Robert Laurent (1890–1970), joining him and other modernist sculptors in their advocacy of direct carving. His New York studio became a lively meeting place for artists, and he also enjoyed the camaraderie of the summer art colony in Provincetown, Massachusetts. His joyful figural sculptures and his affinity for the natural properties of wood, in particular, earned him widespread recognition and numerous public commissions throughout his career. Gross also taught at several venues, including the Brooklyn Museum Art School.

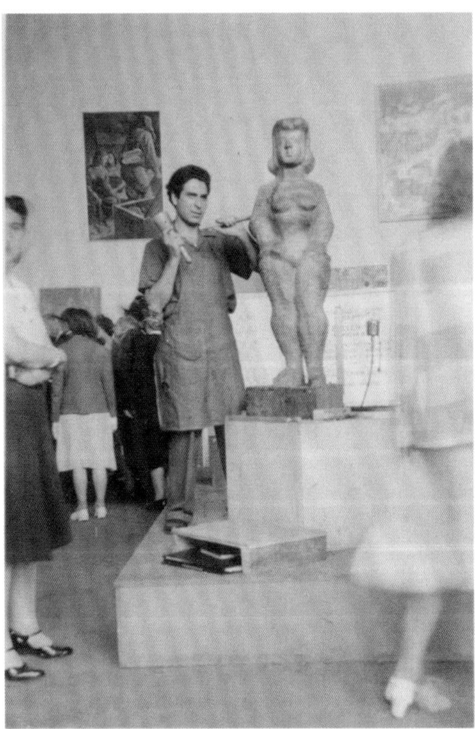

Fig. 3. *Chaim Gross Carving "Ballerina" at the New York World's Fair*, 1940. Renee and Chaim Gross Foundation, New York. © Estate of Chaim Gross. The drawing on the easel behind the artist may be the Brooklyn Museum's study featured here.

1. Roberta K. Tarbell, *Chaim Gross Retrospective Exhibition: Sculpture, Paintings, Drawings, Prints* (New York: Jewish Museum, 1977), 16.
2. Gross carved *Ballerina* in the lobby of the American Art Today building for nearly three months and was seen by an estimated 80,000 to 100,000 people. See "Goldfish-Like Privacy No Handicap to Sculptor," *New York Times*, Aug. 6, 1940, 22, and "Before 160,000 Eyes," *Art Digest* 15 (Oct. 1, 1940): 14. The Brooklyn Museum owns another preparatory study for *Ballerina*, acc. no. 42.417.

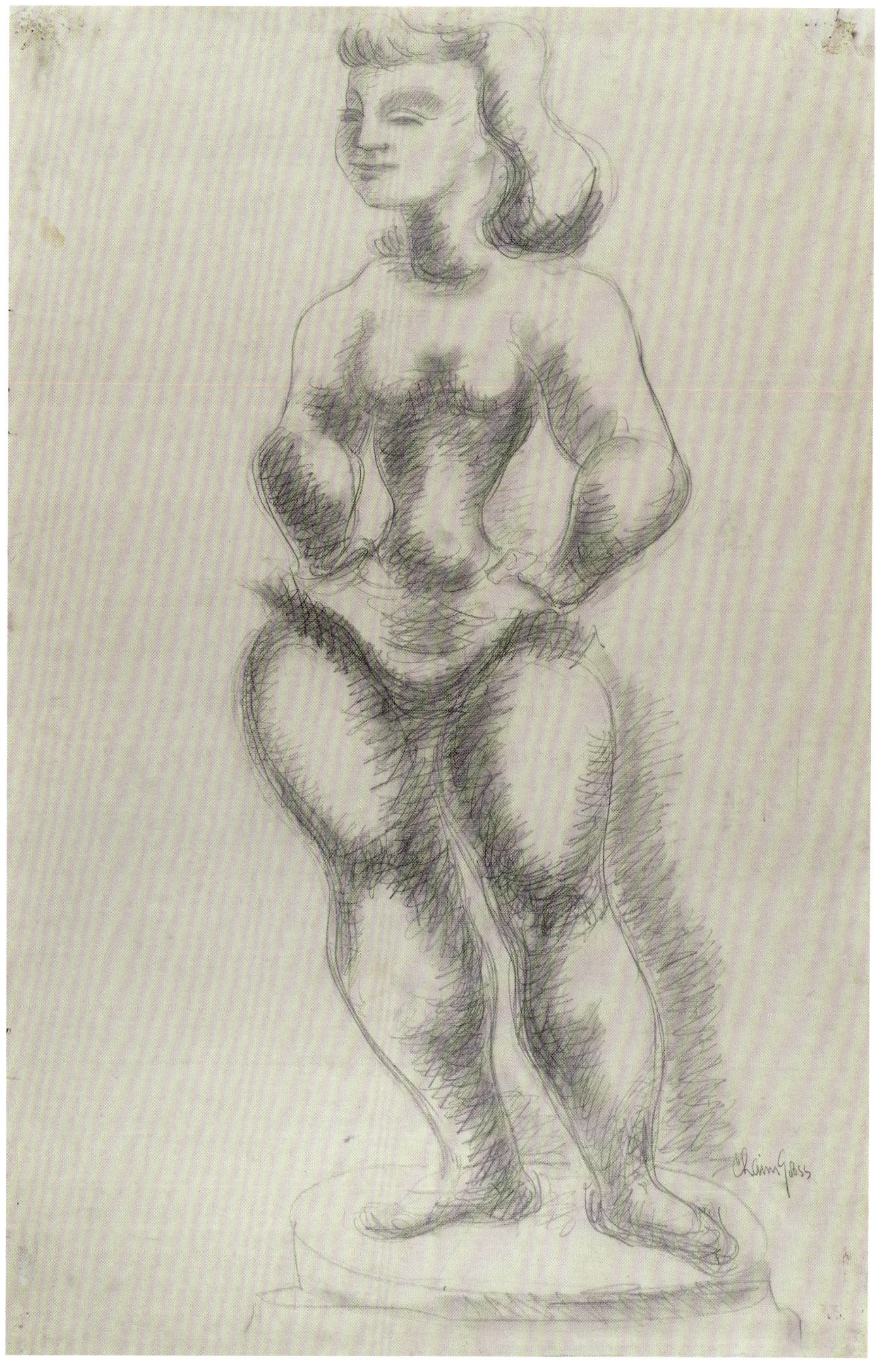

Abraham Walkowitz

American, born Siberia, 1878–1965

20 Dancing Figure (Isadora Duncan), undated

Black ink and graphite on cream, medium-weight, moderately textured wove paper, 8 × 3¹⁄₁₆ in. (20.3 × 7.8 cm)
Signed in ink, lower center: "A. Walkowitz"
Gift of the artist, 39.473a. © Estate of Abraham Walkowitz

21 Dancing Figure (Isadora Duncan), undated

Black ink and graphite on cream, medium-weight, moderately textured wove paper, 8 × 3⁷⁄₁₆ in. (20.3 × 8.7 cm)
Signed in ink, lower center: "A. Walkowitz"
Gift of the artist, 39.473b. © Estate of Abraham Walkowitz

22 Dancing Figure (Isadora Duncan), undated

Black ink and graphite on cream, medium-weight, moderately textured wove paper, 8 × 3³⁄₈ in. (20.3 × 8.6 cm)
Signed in ink, lower center: "A. Walkowitz"
Gift of the artist, 39.473c. © Estate of Abraham Walkowitz

These drawings are among the thousands by the American modernist Abraham Walkowitz depicting the revolutionary modern dancer Isadora Duncan (1877–1927), whom Walkowitz first saw perform in Paris in 1907. Duncan sought to express the harmony of body and soul through dance, embracing a philosophy that movement originated in the body's solar plexus as a central energy.[1] "Isadora is movement," Walkowitz explained. "I watched her dances, and I never had her pose, I just watched the movement, that's what makes the dance—the feeling, the movement, the grace."[2] While these abstract drawings suggest the forms of the dancer's head and limbs, their primary focus is the fluid shape of Duncan's tunic costumes inspired by classical sculpture and her expressive movement and energy. One drawing (number 20) conveys tension in the tight twist of the figure and drapery toward the body's core, while another (number 21) evokes a great release of energy in its suggestion of raised arms and an animated leg lift. In the third work (number 22), the figure, with lowered head, becomes more introspective as the drapery gently sweeps around her body. Walkowitz mounted these three drawings side by side, as if to suggest a narrative sequence akin to frames in a moving picture.

In a 1958 interview, Walkowitz stated, "I have done more Isadora Duncans than I have hair on my head."[3] He reproduced a selection of these drawings in his 1945 book, *Isadora Duncan in Her Dances*, in which one of Duncan's followers described his works as "the vision of Isadora as she danced in her inexpressibly musical way the reality of life, love, death, and all the myriad nuances leading to those final states."[4] To Walkowitz, Duncan "was a muse. She had no laws. She didn't dance according to rules. She created. Her body was music."[5] A founding member of the American Society of Independent Artists, which sought freedom from the traditional juried exhibition system of the National Academy of Design, Walkowitz admired Duncan's complete rejection of academic "laws" and "rules." In return, Duncan expressed her gratitude to the artist, stating, "Walkowitz, you have written my biography in lines without words."[6]—CG

1. See Isadora Duncan, *My Life* (New York: Boni and Liveright, 1927), especially page 75, for a discussion of Duncan's philosophy of movement.
2. Abraham Walkowitz, Oral History Interview, Dec. 8 and 22, 1958, Archives of American Art, Smithsonian Institution, quoted in Abram Lerner and Bartlett Cowdrey, "A Tape Recorded Interview with Abraham Walkowitz," *Archives of American Art Journal* 9, no. 1 (Jan. 1969): 15.
3. Ibid. Theodore Eversole claims that Walkowitz completed more than five thousand drawings of Duncan. See Theodore W. Eversole, *Abraham Walkowitz: New York Modern* (Cincinnati: T. W. Eversole, 2009), 62.
4. Maria-Theresa Duncan, "Isadora, the Artist: Daughter of Prometheus," introduction to Abraham Walkowitz, *Isadora Duncan in Her Dances* (Girard, Kans.: Haldeman-Julius Publications, 1945), unpag.
5. "A Tape Recorded Interview," 15.
6. Quoted in Martica Sawin, *Abraham Walkowitz, 1878-1965* (Salt Lake City: Utah Museum of Fine Arts, 1974), 10.

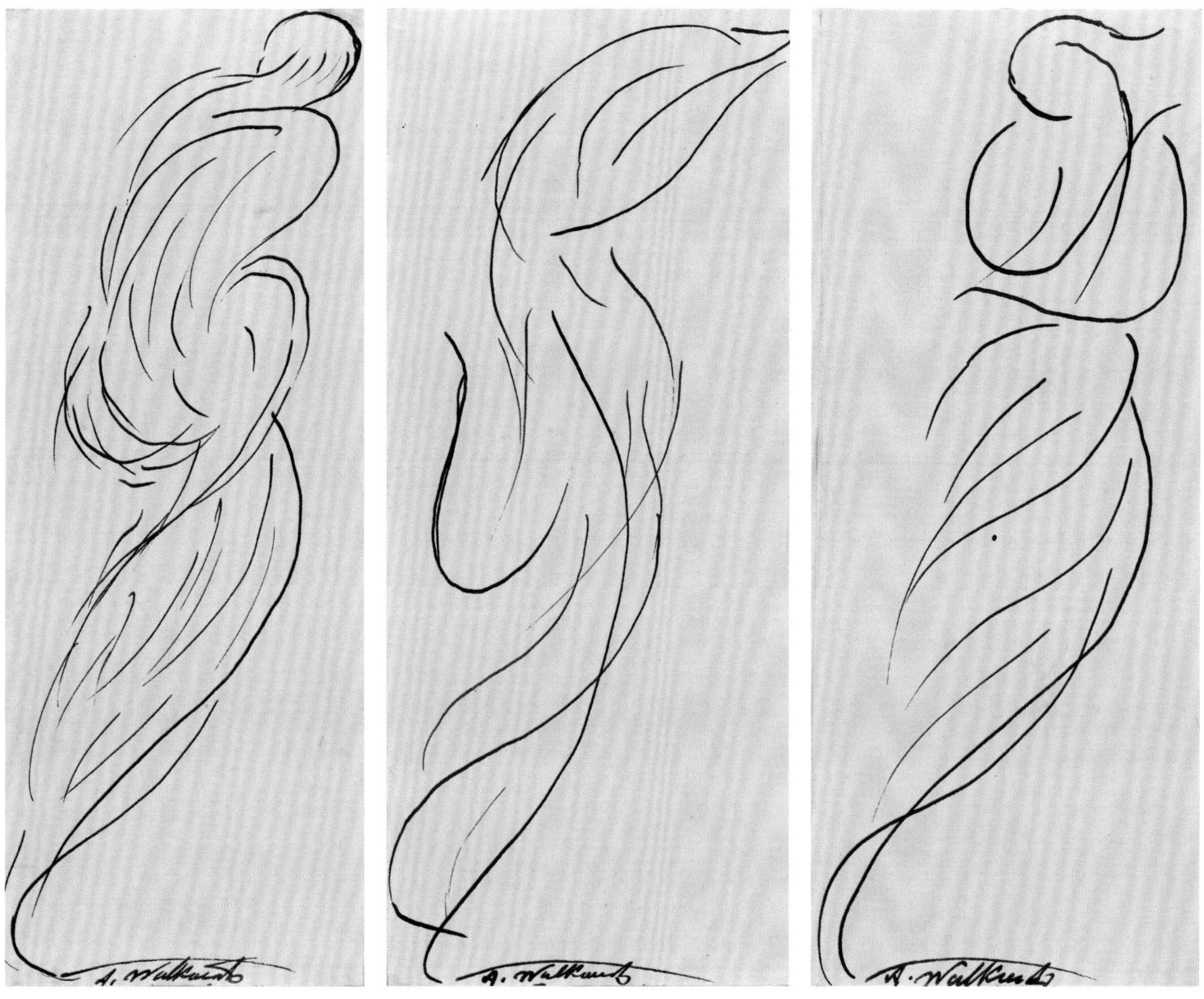

Richard Bruce Nugent

American, 1906–1987

23 Dancing Figures, circa 1935

Black ink and graphite on cream, moderately thick, moderately textured wove paper, 14¾ × 10½ in. (37.5 × 26.7 cm)
Gift of Dr. Thomas H. Wirth, gift of Frederick J. Adler, by exchange, bequest of Richard J. Kempe, by exchange, and gift of Abraham Walkowitz, by exchange, 2008.50.6. © Thomas H. Wirth

A dancer and performer himself, the African American artist Richard Bruce Nugent had a deep affinity for the expressive possibilities of the human body in motion, and he frequently represented dancers in his graphic art. In this work, two nude female figures, framed within a decorative border of tropical foliage, perform an intricate choreography of contrapuntal movements. Nugent depicted the dancers and plants as stylized, abstracted forms rendered in flat, black silhouettes, which he created by drawing outlines in graphite and filling them in with ink. His remarkable control of the liquid medium is evident not only in the sinuous shapes and precision of his contours but also in the thin white lines, created by reserving areas of the paper, that distinguish body parts within a silhouette. The stark contrast of black and white, as well as the schematic treatment of forms, adds to the dramatic visual impact of the image.

Dancing Figures reflects the silhouette aesthetic that emerged in the art of the Harlem Renaissance. This idiom drew from the stylized forms of African art as well as from the bold graphic designs of Winold Reiss (1886–1953), a German-born illustrator whose works appeared in Alain Locke's *The New Negro* (1925), a seminal compilation of African American art and literature, and other publications (figure 4). Both Nugent and Aaron Douglas (1899–1979), who studied with Reiss and was one of the leading Harlem artists of the day, began to explore this approach in 1925. For Nugent, the silhouette also had racial and personal significance, as suggested in his poem "Shadow" (1925), a verse of which reads: "Silhouette / On the face of the moon / Am I. / A dark shadow in the light. / A silhouette am I / On the face of the moon / Lacking color / Or vivid brightness / But defined all the clearer / Because / I am dark, / Black on the face of the moon."[1]

Born and raised in Washington, D.C., Nugent met many of the cultural luminaries of the African American community—including Locke, Langston Hughes, and W. E. B. Du Bois—through his socially well-connected family. After moving to New York in the 1920s, he became an active member of Harlem's vital cultural scene, contributing drawings and poems to many of the leading black publications. Nugent was also an openly gay artist who bridged the black world of the Harlem Renaissance and the gay community of bohemian Greenwich Village.[2]

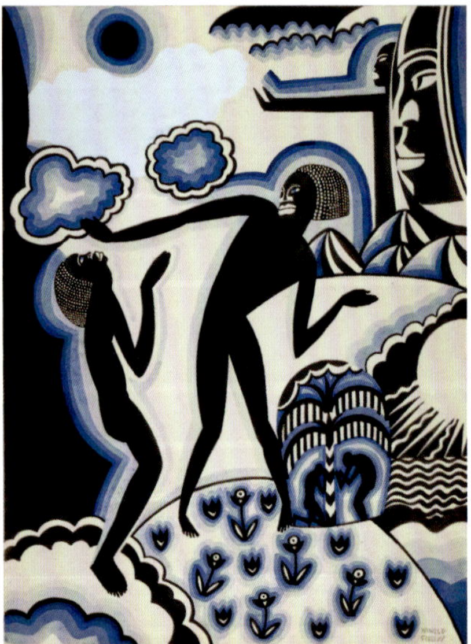

Fig. 4. Winold Reiss (American, born Germany, 1886–1953). *African Fantasy: The Awakening*, 1925. Ink, watercolor, and gouache on paper, 19¹³⁄₁₆ × 14¹⁵⁄₁₆ in. (50.3 × 37.9 cm). Smithsonian American Art Museum, Museum Purchase, 1989.3

1. Richard Bruce [Richard Bruce Nugent], "Shadow," *Opportunity* 3 (Oct. 1925): 296, reprinted in *Gay Rebel of the Harlem Renaissance: Selections from the Work of Richard Bruce Nugent*, ed. Thomas Wirth (Durham, N.C.: Duke University Press, 2002), 269.

2. Henry Louis Gates, Jr., foreword to *Gay Rebel of the Harlem Renaissance*, xii.

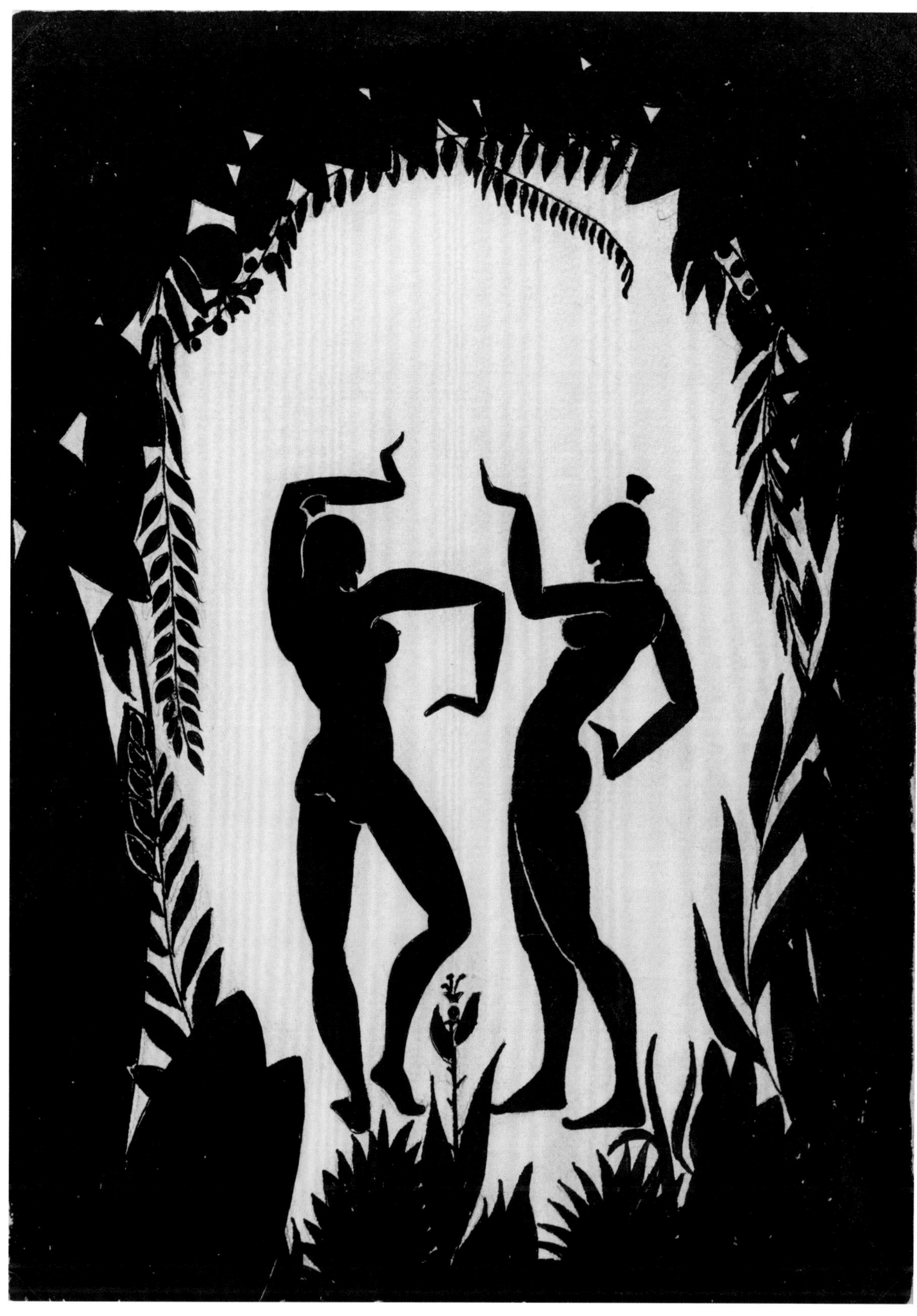

Max Weber

American, born Russia, 1881–1961

24 **The Dancer,** June 1946

Pastel on brown, moderately thick, rough-textured laid paper, 18³⁄₁₆ × 13¼ in. (46.2 × 33.7 cm)
Signed in graphite, lower right: "Max Weber / June 1946"
Gift from the collection of Hannelore B. Schulhof, New York, 87.46.1

Images of performers—dancers, musicians, actors—featured prominently in Max Weber's art as symbols of his own creative activity, as well as vehicles for his experimentations in the formal properties of line, form, and color. This drawing, a work from late in his career, represents the more abstract approach to figuration that he developed in the 1940s. He rendered the figure of a female dancer striding forward with her head thrown back as a series of intersecting, bold, dark outlines and radically simplified shapes. Despite the flat, reductive treatment of forms, Weber playfully captured the exuberance of the body in motion. The continuous line that traces an arc from her outstretched arm down to her foot is especially expressive. As Lloyd Goodrich observed about Weber's works in this period, "[His] line begins to have an independent life of its own, no longer merely definition of form but a living thing in itself, highly sensitive, vibrating, charged with feeling, and filled with intense energetic movement."[1] In *The Dancer*, the artist heightened the dynamic quality of his drawing with passages of brightly colored pastel—including pink, blue, green, white, and burgundy—that envelop the figure.

A pioneering American modernist, Weber spent a formative three years—from 1905 to 1908—in Paris. Initially enrolled in the Académie Julian, he quickly became frustrated with the conventional practice of drawing the figure from plaster casts and the emphasis on idealized classical forms. He left to study with the French Fauvist Henri Matisse (1869–1954), who provided live models. After Weber's return to New York, his paintings reflected the Cubist and primitivist influences of his European experience (see numbers 10, 11). His art evolved from more classicizing figures in the 1920s to the expressive, lyrical abstractions of such later works as *The Dancer*.

1. Lloyd Goodrich, *Max Weber Retrospective Exhibition* (New York: Whitney Museum of American Art, 1949), 53.

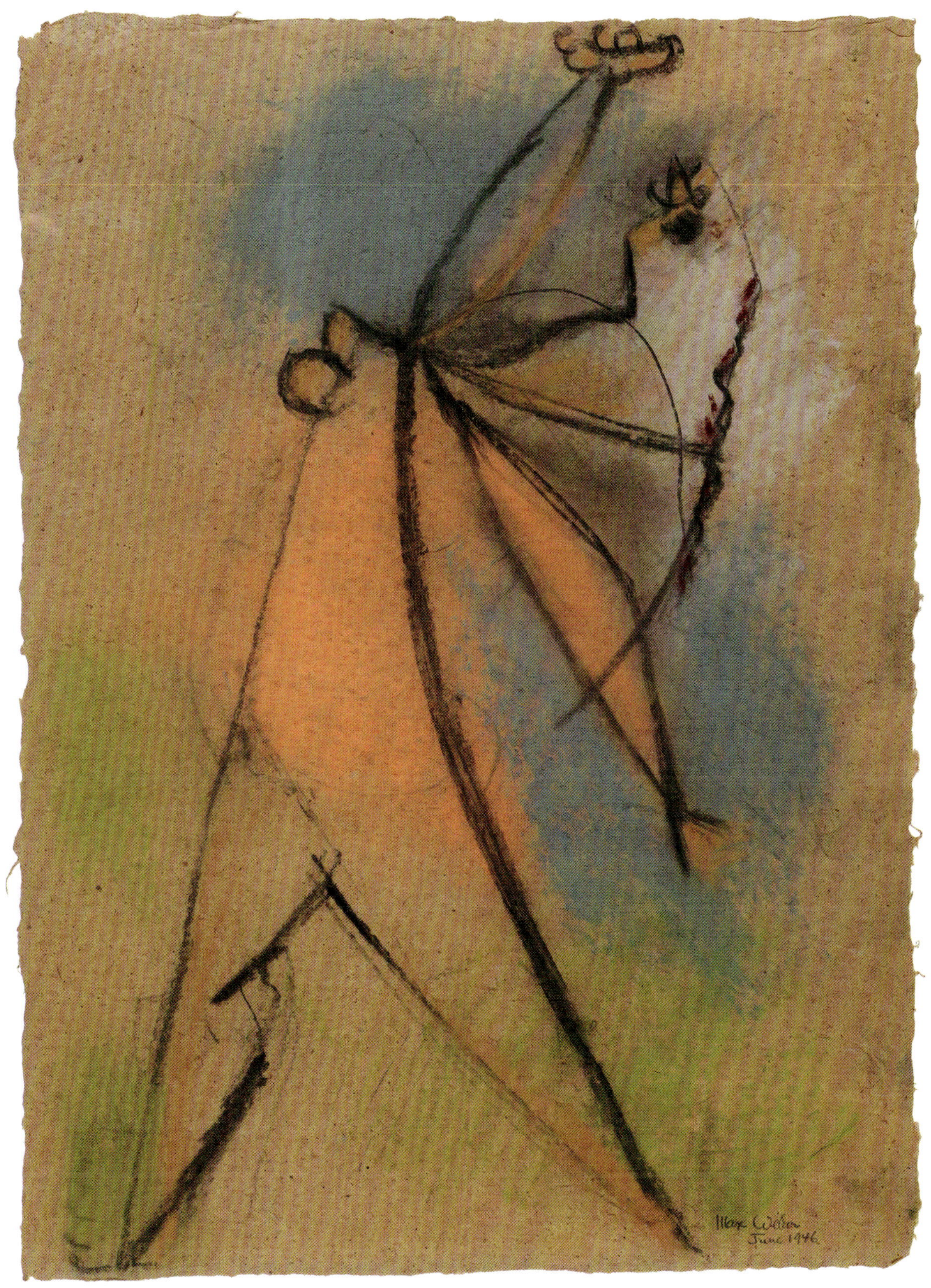

FASHIONING CHARACTER

Costume drawings have long served important and multi-faceted roles in American art—as technical exercises, as preparatory tools for works in other media, and as works of art in their own right. This section includes studies in which artists worked out the fall of drapery over the human figure. In the academic curriculum, artists advanced from portraying the nude body to depicting the clothed form. Mastering the illusionistic depiction of cloth over the body, as well as the relationship between the body's coverings and its underlying structure, was a fundamental component of artistic training.

In figural representation, costume adds not only a physical layer of material but also one of narrative content. Clothing helps to establish the identity of the subject, whether an actual individual in a portrait, a literary character, or a general type, such as a geisha girl or an idealized figure. Many of the drawings in this section feature peasants and other rural folk in humble attire, imagery that became invested with nostalgic associations about simpler, agrarian ways of life as the United States was increasingly urbanized over the course of the nineteenth century. Americans were fascinated not only with such rustic types but also with a range of social, ethnic, and cultural "others." This interest in the exotic and picturesque was fostered, in part, by the increased circulation of people, goods, and information around the globe. The late nineteenth-century phenomenon of japonisme, in which artists sought inspiration in Japanese subject matter and aesthetic style, was one such manifestation. "Exotic" types could also be found closer to home, including the denizens of urban ghettoes or modern New Women. In representing these casts of characters, artists used distinctive costume and other accessories to convey descriptive information about a figure—that is, to fashion a character's identity.

John Singleton Copley

American, 1738–1815

25 Studies for "Saul Reproved by Samuel for Not Obeying the Commandments of the Lord," 1797–98

Black and white chalk on blue, medium-weight, slightly textured laid paper, 12¼ × 14¼ in. (31.1 × 36.2 cm)
Purchased with funds given by Mr. and Mrs. Leonard L. Milberg, 1990.126.1a-b

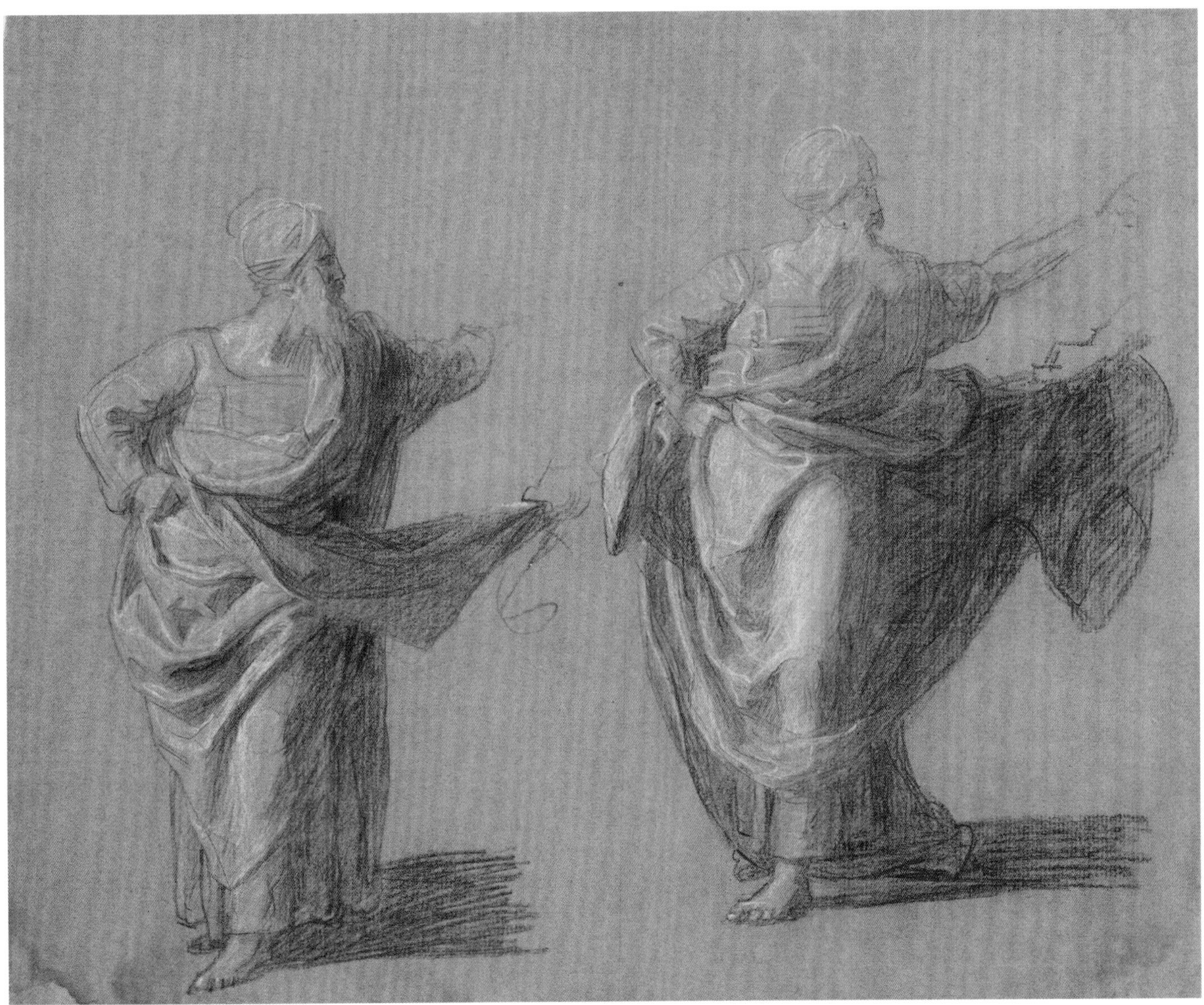

1990.126.1a (recto)

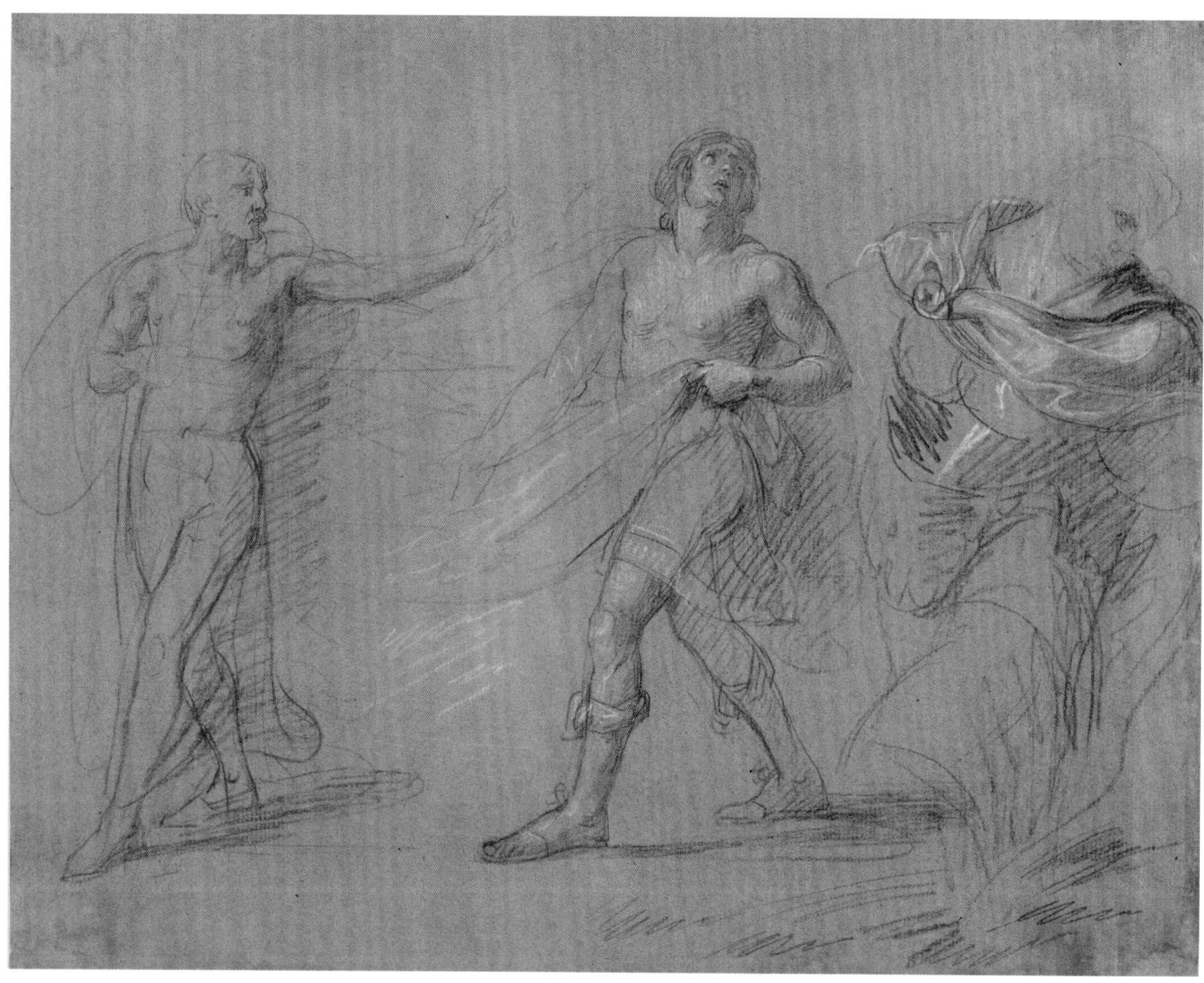

1990.126.1b (verso)

John Singleton Copley made this double-sided drawing in preparation for his canvas *Saul Reproved by Samuel for Not Obeying the Commandments of the Lord*, exhibited at the Royal Academy of Arts in London in 1798 (figure 5). The painting depicts a climactic moment from the Old Testament in which the prophet Samuel scolds Saul, king of Israel, who defied God's order to annihilate the enemy Amalekites by sparing their king and best livestock: "And as Samuel turned about to go away, [Saul] laid hold upon the skirt of his mantle, and it rent. And Samuel said unto him, The Lord hath rent the kingdom of Israel from thee this day" (1 Samuel 15:27–28). In the finished work, Samuel, at far left, delivers his admonition while pointing at Saul, who wears a red cloak and crown and is surrounded by his troops.

This sheet with figure studies in various levels of finish provides a fascinating glimpse into Copley's creative process. On the verso, he worked out the poses of his protagonists in three preliminary sketches, drawing the nude figures and then adding cursory details of their clothing. The two drawings of Saul indicate that, at this stage, Copley had not yet decided if he wanted to show him looking up or down. The recto shows two more advanced studies of Samuel, now fully clothed and with his dynamic, twisting pose established. Here, Copley experimented with different arrangements of the prophet's voluminous drapery, even including a loose indication of Saul's hand tugging a section of the mantle. (Neither image corresponds exactly to the final painting.) In both sets of studies, Copley used deft strokes of black crayon with touches of white chalk to model forms and drapery and to indicate shadows and highlights.

The most successful portraitist in colonial America, renowned for meticulously realistic, crisply delineated likenesses of his sitters, Copley left his native Boston in 1774 for London. Prompted by both political reasons and professional ambition, this move marked a major shift in his oeuvre. He adopted a more loosely brushed, painterly style and added history painting to his repertoire. In the Grand Manner tradition, history painting—monumental canvases with erudite and edifying themes drawn from history, mythology, the Bible, and literature—was considered the highest form of art, but there was little demand for the genre in America. Copley relied heavily on drawing to prepare for such complex, multifigural compositions, often gridding them for transfer to the canvas.[1]

1. For *The Siege of Gibraltar*, 1783–91 (Guildhall Art Gallery, London), one of his most elaborate pictures, Copley made more than eighty studies. See Jules David Prown, *John Singleton Copley*, vol. 2, *In England, 1774–1815* (Cambridge, Mass.: Harvard University Press, 1966), 322–37, 489–585. The one other known preparatory drawing related to *Saul Reproved by Samuel*, a study of the horse, is in the collection of the Addison Gallery of American Art, Phillips Academy, Andover, Massachusetts (acc. no. 1935.21).

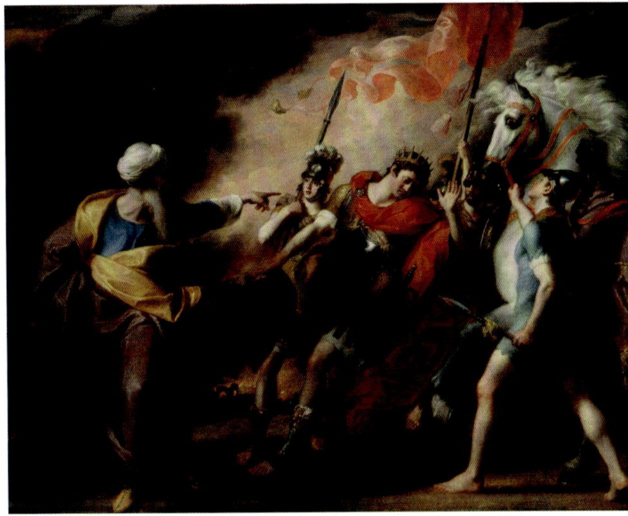

Fig. 5. John Singleton Copley. *Saul Reproved by Samuel for Not Obeying the Commandments of the Lord*, 1798. Oil on canvas, 67¾ × 85⅝ in. (172.08 × 217.49 cm). Museum of Fine Arts, Boston, Bequest of Susan Greene Dexter in memory of Charles and Martha Babcock Amory, 25.99. Photograph: © 2011 Museum of Fine Arts, Boston

Thomas Sully

American, born England, 1783–1872

26 Figure Studies, circa 1830s

Iron gall ink and watercolor on beige, medium-weight, moderately textured antique laid paper, 8¹³⁄₁₆ × 11½ in. (22.4 × 29.2 cm)
Signed in graphite, lower right, on verso: "T. Sully"
Gift of the American Art Council, 1990.102.1a-b

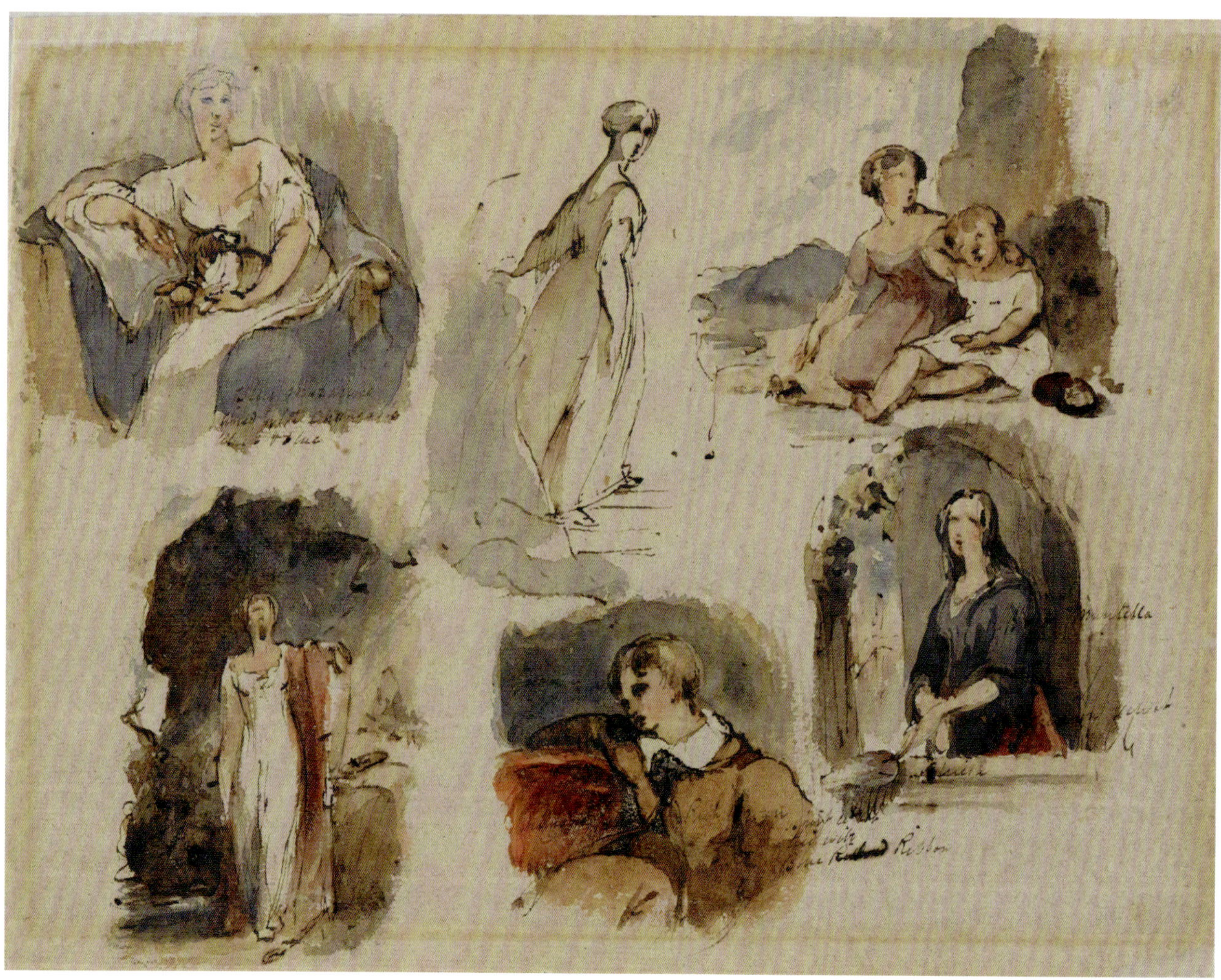

1990.102.1a (recto)

This double-sided page of sketches by Thomas Sully contains vignettes of figures wearing varied costumes and displaying a range of postures and gestures. Using the loose strokes of ink and layered washes of watercolor typical of his sketching practice,[1] Sully quickly captured the figures in soft colors and elegant poses. These idealized women, tender interactions between mothers and children, and male portrait studies are types Sully frequently used in his sentimental and flattering portraits. This sheet is significant for the way it demonstrates Sully's artistic process. Three vignettes on the verso are completed primarily in ink, capturing only rough outlines of the figures. Sully applied monochrome washes to build shading and volume in other studies on the sheet, including the top center of the recto and bottom center of the verso, completing his sketches with various hues of watercolor and additional color notations (many of which are obscured by the washes).

Sully spent most of his successful career in Philadelphia as a painter of portraits and fancy pieces. The sketch at the top center of the recto of this sheet was the prototype for his 1838 full-length portrait of Queen Victoria of England (The Metropolitan Museum of Art, New York), who had recently taken the throne.[2] By adjusting the figure's head to a more upright position and adding a crown and regal costume, Sully effectively transformed the sketch into an elegant painted depiction of the young queen. The ink-and-watercolor sketch at the lower left of the recto has been identified as a possible model for Sully's full-length portrait of Mrs. Reverdy Johnson, circa 1840 (Princeton University Art Museum, Princeton, New Jersey).[3] —CG

1. Theodore E. Stebbins, Jr., *American Master Drawings and Watercolors: A History of Works on Paper from Colonial Times to the Present* (New York: Harper and Row, 1976), 82.
2. Carrie Rebora Barratt, *Queen Victoria and Thomas Sully* (Princeton, N.J.: Princeton University Press, 2000), 45–46. Sully had used a version of this pose in his portrait *Rebecca Mifflin Harrison McMurtrie and Her Son, William* of 1818 (Westmoreland Museum of Art, Greenburg, Pennsylvania).
3. E. Maurice Bloch, *Faces and Figures in American Drawings* (San Marino, Calif.: Huntington Library and Art Gallery, 1989), 82.

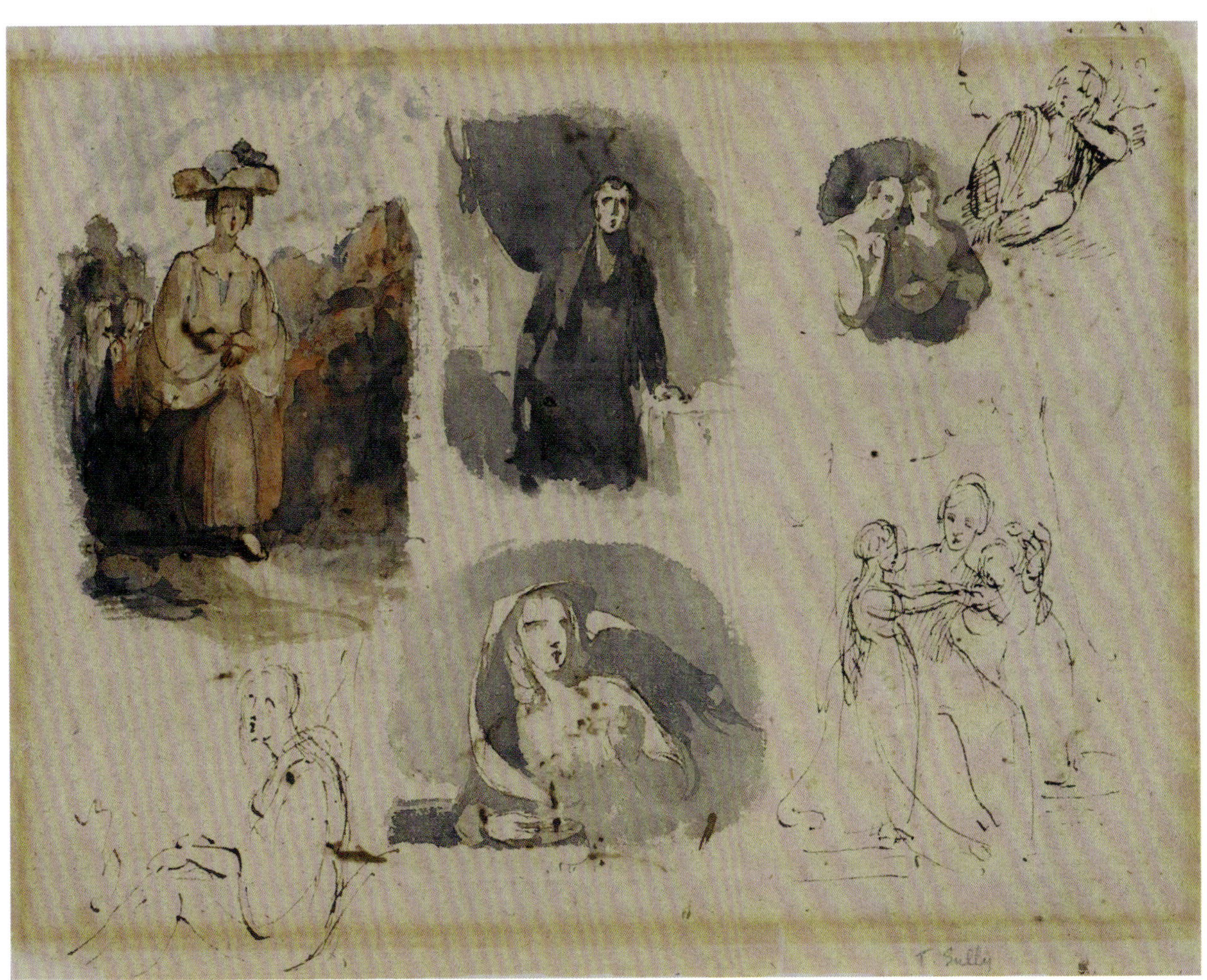

1990.102.1b (verso)

Eastman Johnson

American, 1824–1906

27 **Three Dutch Figures,** circa 1852

Graphite, watercolor, and white chalk on brown, medium-weight, moderately textured wove paper, 6½ × 10⅞ in. (16.5 × 27.6 cm)
Signed in graphite, lower left, on recto: "E.J."
Purchased with funds given by Mr. and Mrs. Leonard L. Milberg, 1990.101.6a-b

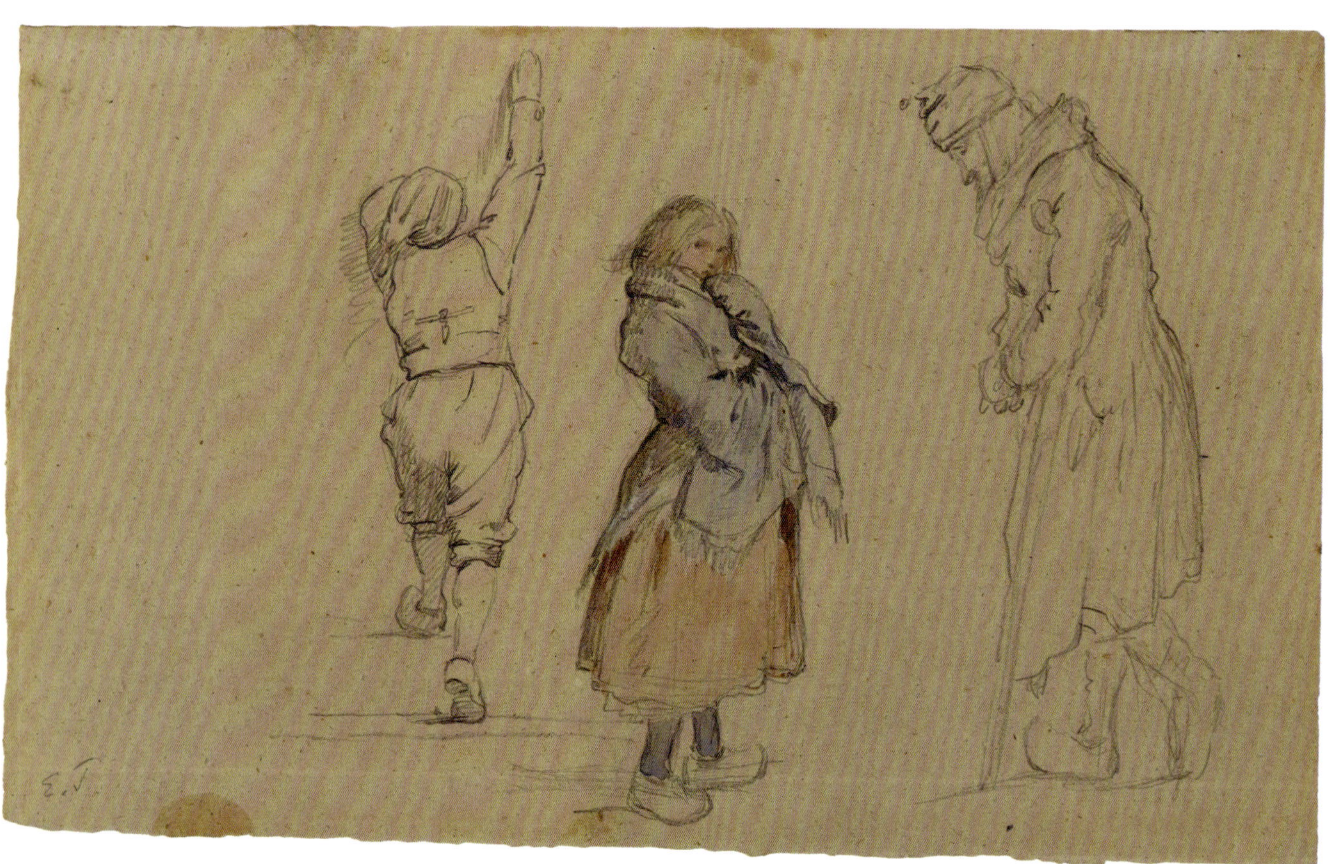

1990.101.6a (recto)

This sheet contains preparatory figure studies for *Doorway of a Castle in Winter*, circa 1852 (private collection), an oil painting that was a collaboration between Eastman Johnson and his friend and fellow American painter Louis Rémy Mignot (1831–1870).[1] For this genre scene, Mignot created the setting—a section of the rugged stone facade of a castle and a gnarled old tree dotted with snow—and Johnson painted the three peasants gathered around the arched entrance in search of alms. Based closely on the drawing, these figures include a boy viewed from behind in the act of climbing the stairs to knock on the door, a girl wrapping a cloak tightly around her body while looking out at the viewer, and an old man in profile who leans on a crutch

with hands clasped and head bowed in a gesture of supplication. In the drawing, Johnson captured their various poses and humble clothing with sketchy graphite lines, often making multiple passes over an area before finalizing the contours with darker outlines. He realized the figure of the girl more fully, in color, by applying thin washes of watercolor. The loose, energetic quality of his line enhances the nervous desperation and bedraggled appearance of the beggars. The verso of the sheet contains a similarly executed graphite sketch of a peasant woman carrying a basket of produce on her head; she does not appear in *Doorway of a Castle*.

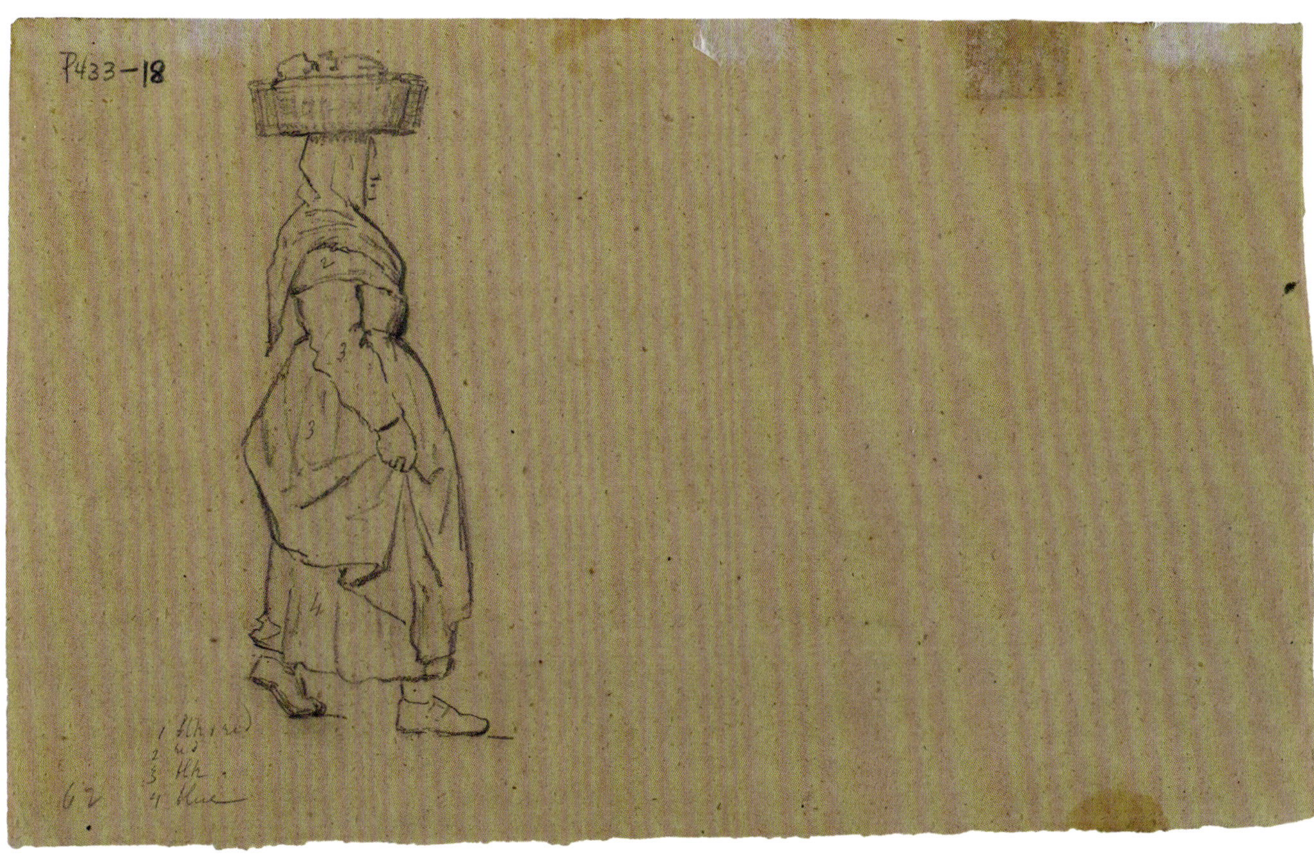

1990.101.6b (verso)

Johnson and Mignot worked on this painting while they were living in The Hague in Holland. Actively involved in the local art community, they embraced the contemporary revival of seventeenth-century Dutch genre painting. Johnson's rustic peasants recall the figure types who populated such works. He arrived in Holland in 1851, after a two-year stay in Düsseldorf (see number 1), and spent a productive four-year period studying the examples of Dutch masters, including Rembrandt van Rijn (1606–1669), and producing original compositions. Johnson's mature work, in which he depicted genre scenes of contemporary American life, was influenced by the chiaroscuro effects and richly painted realism of the Dutch tradition.

1. For an illustration, see Teresa A. Carbone and Patricia Hills, *Eastman Johnson: Painting America* (Brooklyn: Brooklyn Museum of Art in association with Rizzoli International Publications, 1999), 22.

Peter Frederick Rothermel

American, 1817–1895

28 Sketchbook, 1857

Graphite with touches of ink and watercolor on cream, medium-weight, slightly textured wove paper, 5¹¹⁄₁₆ × 8⅝ × ⅜ in. (14.4 × 21.9 × 1 cm)
Signed "PFR" on multiple pages
Purchase gift of Mr. and Mrs. Leonard L. Milberg, 1997.129

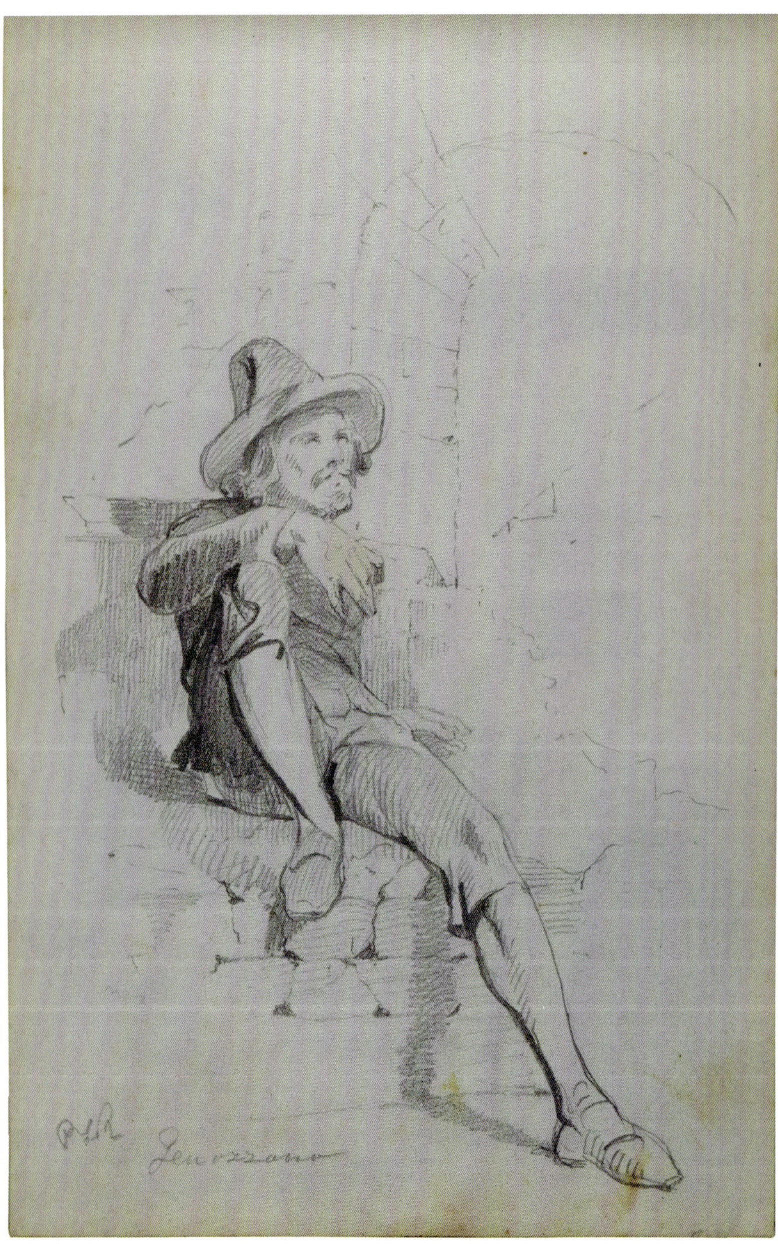

1997.129, page 11

Peter Frederick Rothermel used this forty-two-page sketchbook primarily during an extended stay in Genazzano, Italy, about forty miles east of Rome. The artist included sketches of the town's streets and citizens, studies of architecture and sculpture, a panoramic landscape, and historical compositions, as well as a list of painting subjects with potential prices. He captured the costumes and manners of Italian peasants in several highly finished figure studies (pages 11 and 27 verso). In one image, a man leans comfortably against a lightly sketched stone wall with one leg gracefully extended, while in another, a young woman carefully lifts her skirt to avoid the wet street after a rain. Such picturesque characters were popular with nineteenth-century American artists traveling in Italy and with their audiences.

The loosely drawn historical studies include narratives about Petrarch and the blind schoolmaster and Johannes Gutenberg with his first printed impression. One such image, inscribed "Robbing Titian's Studio While He was Dying / Titian's Death" (page 39), depicts the alleged story of thievery following the death of the famous Venetian Renaissance painter (circa 1488–1576) from bubonic plague.[1] Rothermel's sketchy style captures the chaos of the scene as Titian's possessions are raided and his paintings are removed from the walls and easels. Although no source has been found for the image, it was possibly done after a nineteenth-century painting, reflecting a Romantic view of Titian's life and works typical of the period.[2]

After training with the portrait painter Bass Otis (1784–1861) in Philadelphia, Rothermel traveled between 1856 and 1859, visiting London, Paris, Germany, northern Italy, and finally Rome and Genazzano, where he stayed for two years. To fund his travels, the artist obtained commissions, which he fulfilled with paintings completed abroad.[3] Rothermel was best known for his Grand Manner history paintings, with subjects akin to that of Titian's Death. History painting was never as successful in the United States as it was in Europe, however, and Rothermel's paintings seemed old-fashioned by the late 1850s, when the landscape paintings of the Hudson River School and genre pictures of everyday scenes were popular in America.—CG

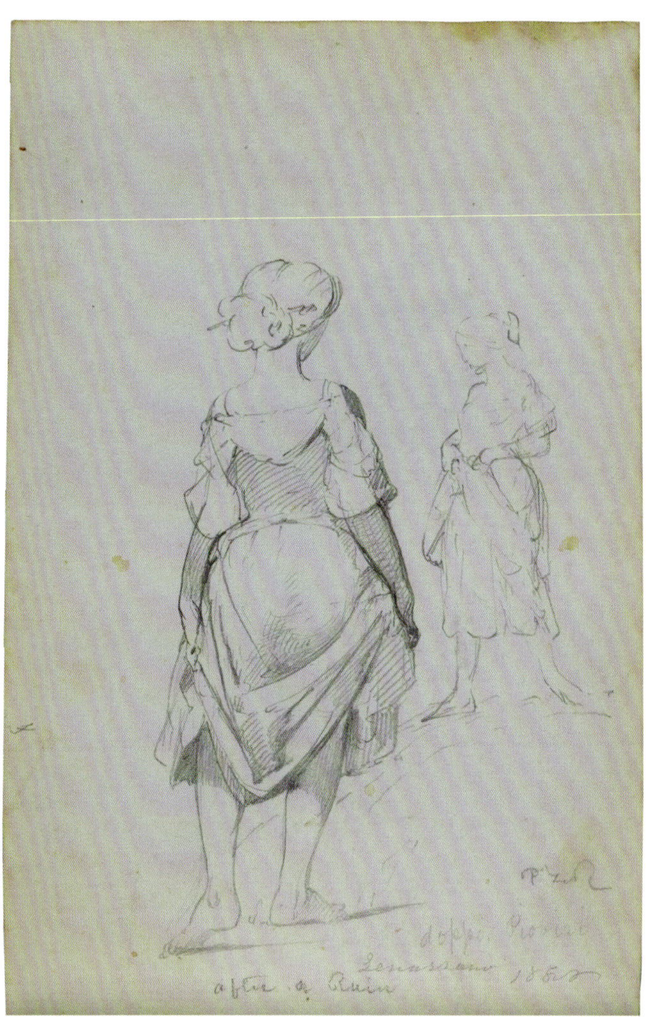

1997.129, page 27 verso

1. See E. Tietze-Conrat, "Titian's Workshop in His Late Years," *Art Bulletin* 28, no. 2 (June 1946): 46, and Mark Hudson, *Titian: The Last Days* (New York: Walker Publishing Company, 2009), 290. The author thanks Elinor Richter for suggesting this latter source.

2. See, for example, the 1849 engraving after *Titian's Studio, Venice* (New York Public Library), which depicts the unveiling of Titian's latest creation and the wealth of decoration and paintings in Titian's possession.

3. Mark Thistlethwaite, *Painting in the Grand Manner: The Art of Peter Frederick Rothermel (1812–1895)* (Chadds Ford, Pa.: Brandywine River Museum, 1995), 17–18. The artist's birth year is most likely 1817, although it has also been cited as 1812 (by Thistlethwaite and others) and 1814. As Thistlethwaite notes, James Vansyckle agreed to pay Rothermel $1,200 annually for three years to produce between two and four paintings each year.

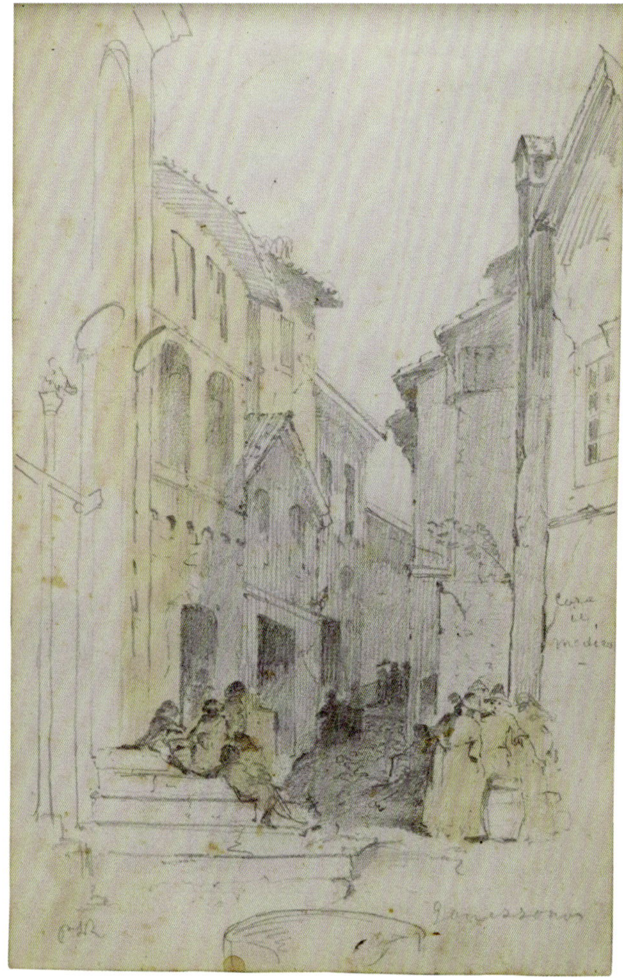

1997.129, page 7

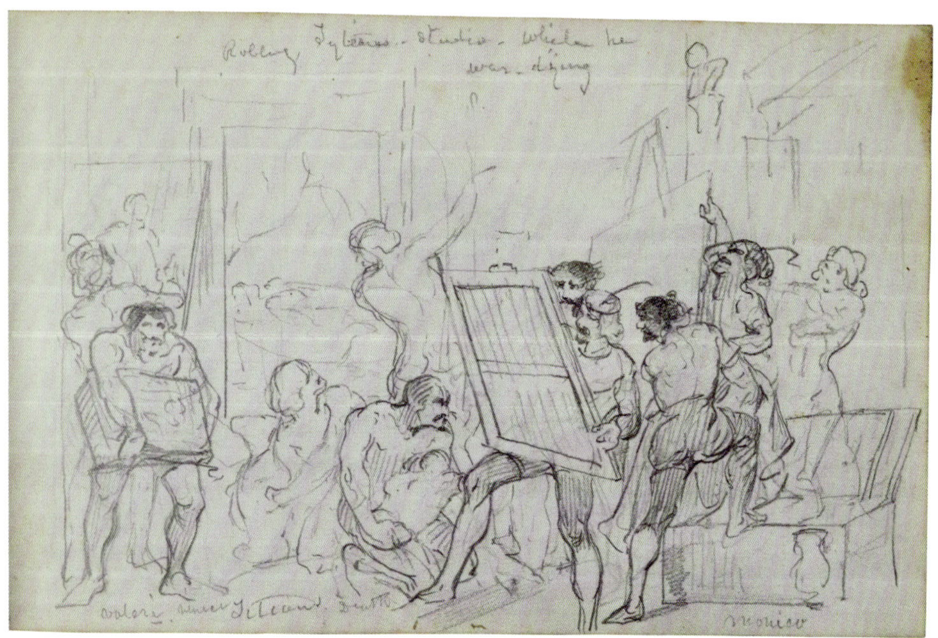

1997.129, page 39

Winslow Homer

American, 1836–1910

29 Girl Seated on a Rail Fence, circa 1878

Graphite with opaque white washes on beige, medium-weight, slightly textured wove paper, 6¹¹⁄₁₆ × 8¹⁄₁₆ in. (17 × 20.5 cm)
Frederick Loeser Fund, 28.210

30 Two Girls in a Field, 1879

Graphite on cream, moderately thick, rough-textured wove paper, 9¹³⁄₁₆ × 8⁵⁄₁₆ in. (24.9 × 21.1 cm)
Signed in graphite, lower right: "W. H – '79"
Frederick Loeser Fund, 28.211

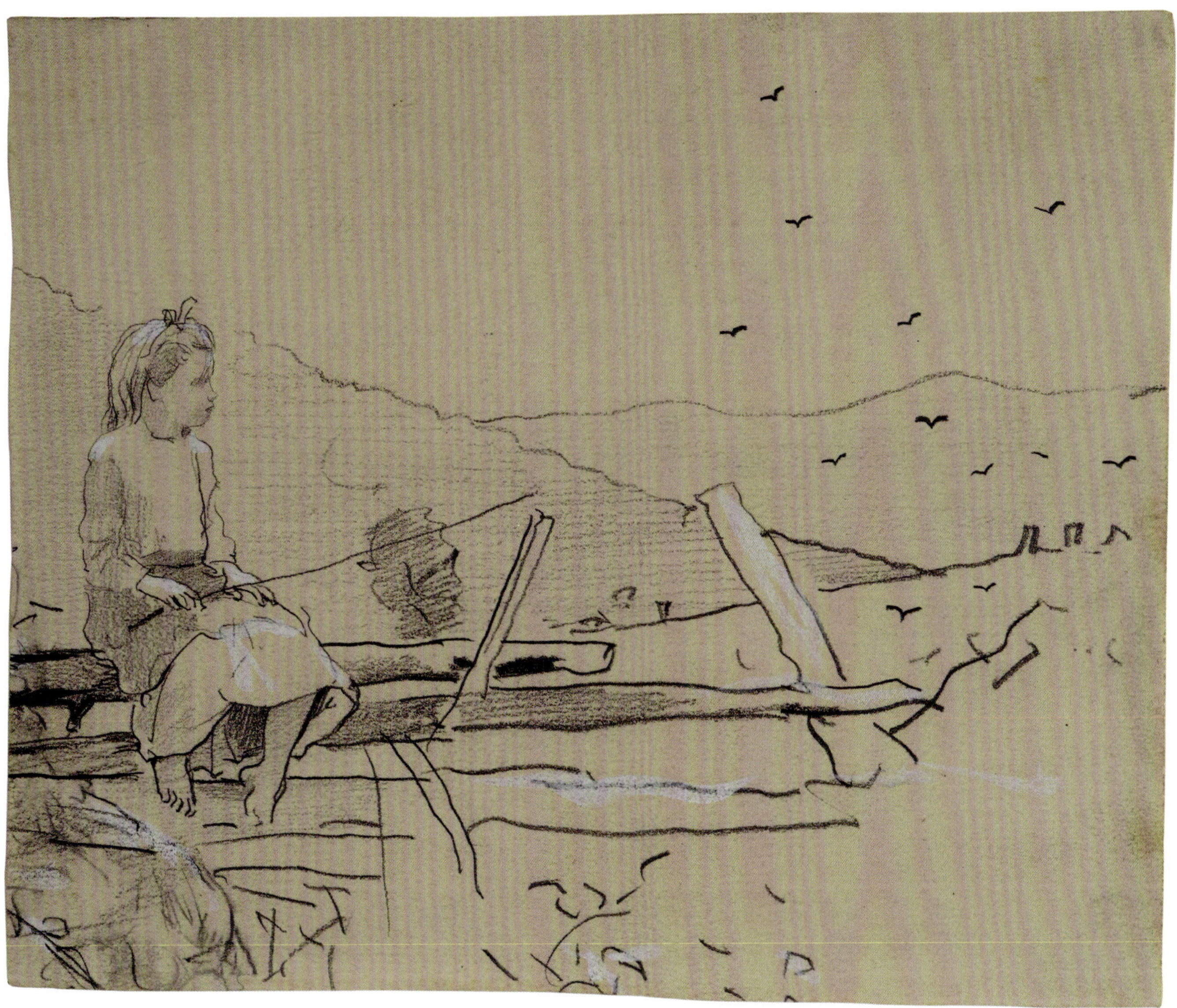

Girl Seated on a Rail Fence and *Two Girls in a Field* belong to the large body of drawings, watercolors, and paintings inspired by Winslow Homer's visits to Houghton Farm during the summers of 1878 and 1879. Located in Mountainville, New York, approximately sixty miles north of New York City, this farm was the country residence of Lawson Valentine, a prosperous manufacturer of paints and varnishes who was the artist's childhood friend and loyal patron. Most of the works in this series feature rural youths in an idyllic landscape, as can be seen in these two examples: in one, a young girl sits on a fence in front of a background of rolling hills; in the other, two older girls huddle together eating fruit from a nearby tree. Each figure wears a rustic costume consisting of a plain dress with a pinafore and a straw hat or bonnet. Homer most likely made these drawings outdoors, using local youngsters and children of fellow houseguests as models. His images have the immediacy and expressivity of quickly executed sketches. In both works, he captured the overall impression of the scene with nimble strokes of graphite, varying the darkness of his lines and applying loosely scribbled hatch marks to create tonal variations; he also added a few touches of white wash to *Girl Seated on a Rail Fence* to suggest highlights from the sun. Homer simplified the sitters' faces and other features and described natural motifs in a kind of pictorial shorthand; for instance, the birds flying over the fields in *Girl Seated on a Rail Fence* are rendered as V shapes, and the trees in *Two Girls in a Field* are abbreviated to a few branches.

By the late 1870s, Homer was well established as an artist of great originality who depicted scenes of contemporary American life in a realistic style. Rural children, shown at play and performing their chores, had regularly appeared in his art, from his earliest illustrations for popular magazines (such as *Harper's Weekly* and *Every Saturday*) to his recent paintings, watercolors, and drawings. During the post–Civil War period, representations of barefoot country boys and "Little Bopeeps" (such as the ones depicted in these two drawings) were embraced by American audiences.[1] The vogue for such images was fueled by a growing sense of optimism after the difficulties of war, as well as nostalgia for pastoral life in the face of rampant industrialization and urbanization. Homer's pictures are generally devoid of the overt sentimentality that characterized such popular imagery of children, however. Both *Girl Seated on a Rail Fence* and *Two Girls in a Field* possess a contemplative, even ambiguous quality. In the former, the little girl stares off into the distance in a mood of quiet reverie, and in the latter, the young friends appear physically close yet emotionally distant and withdrawn from each other.

1. A critic used this term when describing Homer's shepherdess type. See "The Water Color Exhibition," *Sun* (New York), Feb. 16, 1879, 3. In some of his images from Houghton Farm, where sheep were raised, Homer used a stylized, Rococo shepherdess costume (including a laced-front bodice and crook)—a departure from the more realistic, everyday clothing in these drawings.

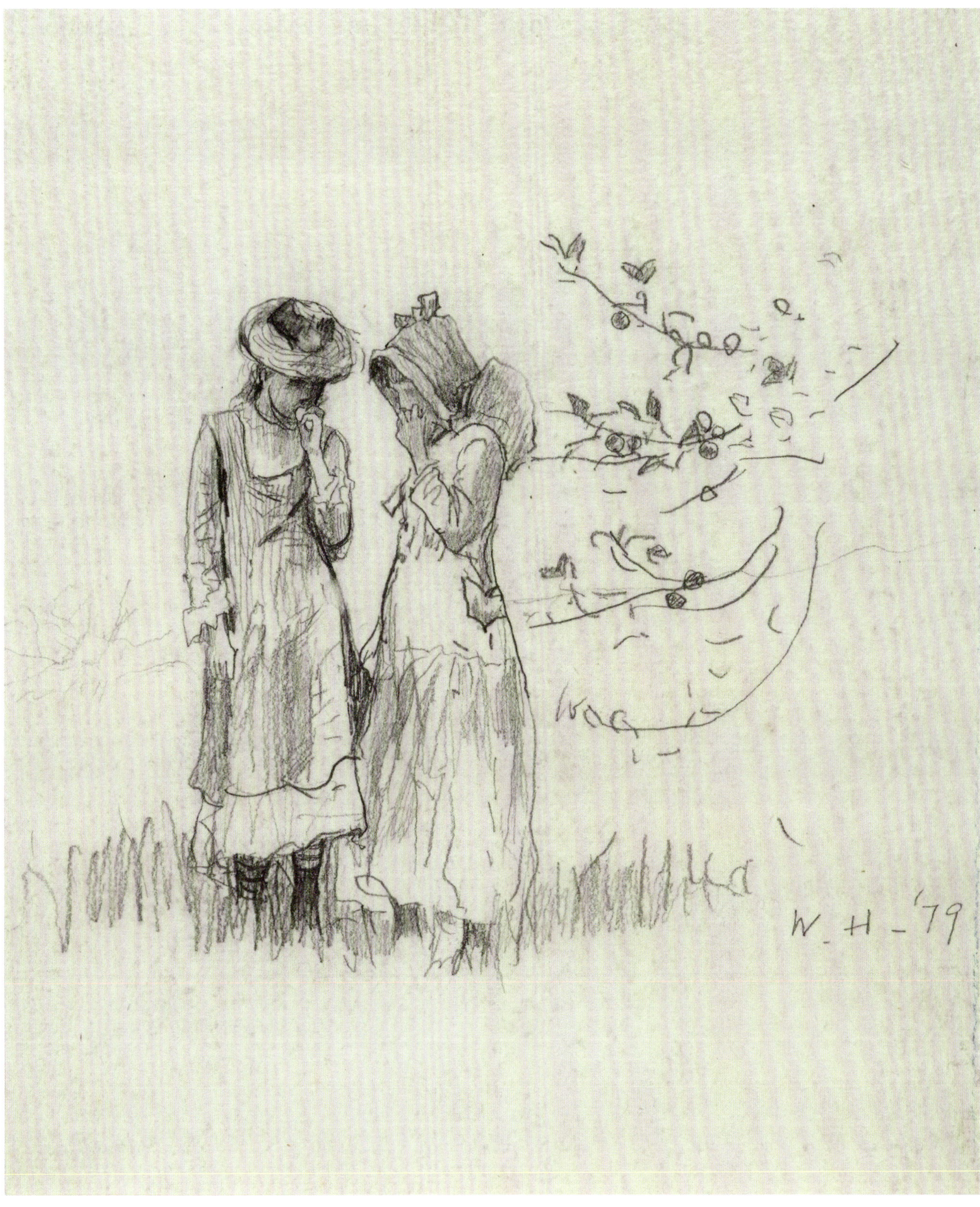

W. H. - '79

Robert Frederick Blum

American, 1857–1903

31 **Waiting for Aaron,** 1880

Carbon-based inks and washes on cream, moderately thick, moderately textured laid paper, 15¹³⁄₁₆ × 11¹⁵⁄₁₆ in. (40.2 × 30.3 cm)
Signed in ink, lower right: "Blum / .1880."
Caroline H. Polhemus Fund, 15.521

In this enigmatic figure drawing, Robert Blum depicted a seated young woman peeping out from under the wide brim of a poke bonnet, a style of hat that was popular during the first half of the nineteenth century. A low-backed dress, shawl, parasol, and gloves complete her fanciful historical costume. Seen from behind in a three-quarter view, her body forms an elegant C-shaped curve as she slouches on a bench while turning her head to the side. The contrast between this wilted pose and the intensity of her gaze creates a narrative tension—perhaps the anticipation suggested by the title, *Waiting for Aaron*.[1] Blum enhanced the energy of the figure with jagged, sketchy contours and varied handling of the ink from dark, solid lines to transparent, loose washes. He added further emphasis and mystery by fully articulating the upper portion of the woman's body but only faintly describing the bottom section of her skirts and the bench—forms that seem to dematerialize into the blankness of the paper.

The subject of this drawing has not been determined, but the work was possibly a commissioned illustration, perhaps one that ultimately was not used.[2] In 1880 Blum was at the outset of a career that would encompass a wide range of media (painting, watercolor, etching, pastel, illustration, and mural decoration) and subjects (particularly picturesque exotic figures; see number 35). Born in Cincinnati, he apprenticed in a commercial lithography shop while taking art classes at various schools. Blum became one of the "Duveneck Boys" who gathered around Frank Duveneck (1848–1919), a Munich-trained artist who worked in a broadly brushed, realistic style. Another important influence was the work of the Spanish painter Mariano Fortuny Marsal (1838–1874), known for highly detailed costume subjects. After further study in Philadelphia, Blum moved in 1878 to New York, where he earned a living as an illustrator for *Scribner's Monthly* and *St. Nicholas* and became actively involved in artistic circles. He rejoined the "Duveneck Boys" in Venice in 1880 and met James McNeill Whistler (1834–1903), whose "art for art's sake" philosophy and japonisme-inspired style had a profound impact on the younger man's art. The asymmetry of the composition, subtle tonal variations, and expressive use of line in *Waiting for Aaron* recall Whistler's etching style. Blum continued to travel throughout the remainder of his career and became a highly respected figure in the New York art world, involved in numerous artists' organizations and showing in many exhibitions.

1. *Waiting for Aaron* was inscribed in an unknown hand on the sheet to which this work was attached when the Museum acquired it in 1915.
2. Bruce Weber suggested that *Waiting for Aaron* might have been made as an unpublished illustration for Laura F. Richards, "Day-Dreams," *Scribner's Monthly* 7, no. 12 (Oct. 1880): 945; Blum's illustrations for the poem about a young girl fantasizing about a fairy prince—with no mention of an Aaron—differ markedly from the Brooklyn Museum's drawing, however, in terms of the girl's age and the drawing style. E-mail correspondence with author, May 29, 2010. *Waiting for Aaron* was reproduced without commentary and erroneously identified as a pencil sketch in a posthumous exhibition review, "Interesting Memorial Exhibition of Robert Blum's Paintings and Drawings—Fine Specimens of Mural Decoration," *New York Times*, Feb. 2, 1913, SM15.

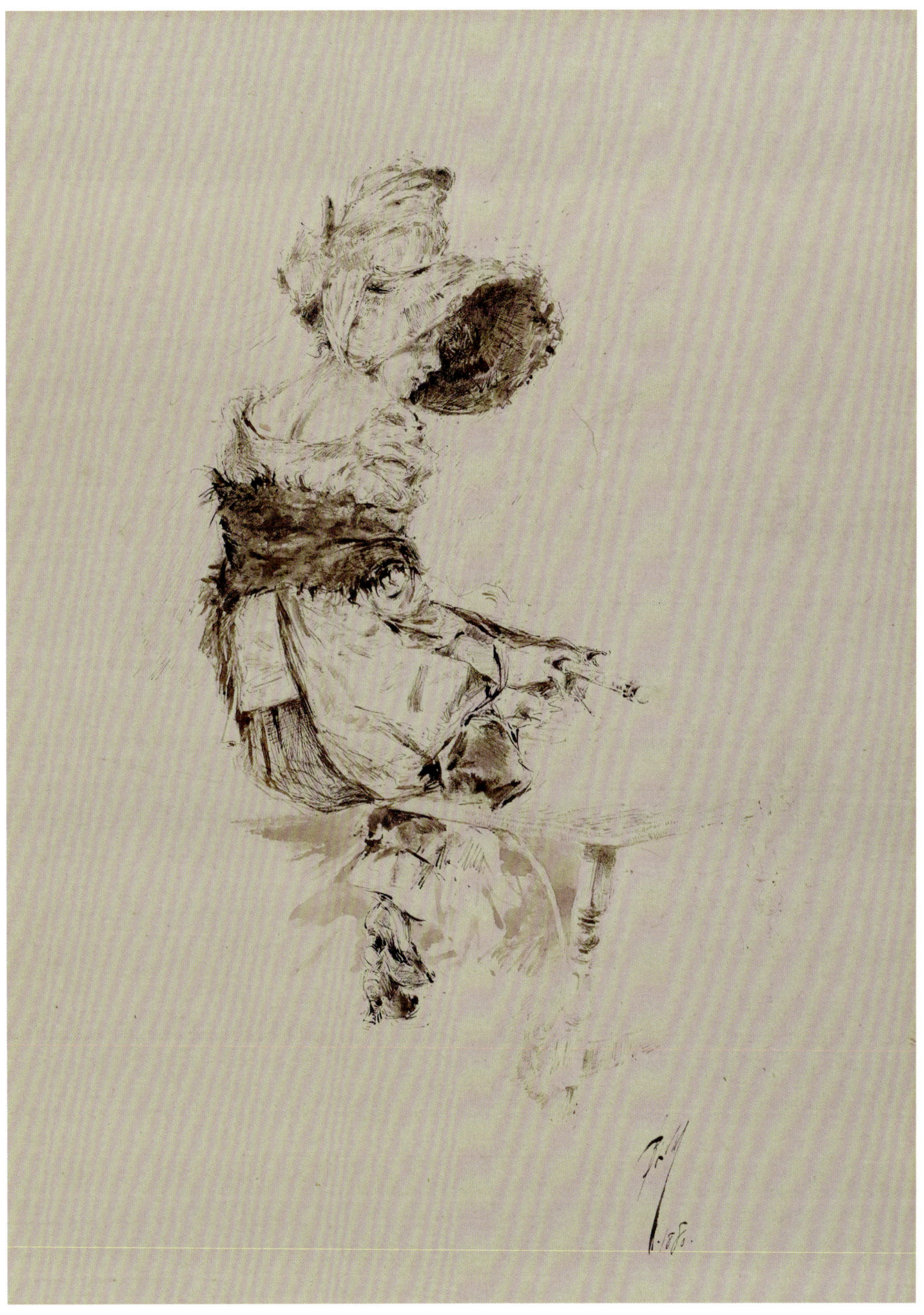

Daniel Ridgway Knight

American, 1839–1924

32 Peasant with Water Jug (Study for "The Well"), circa 1880

Graphite on brown, medium-weight, slightly textured wove paper, 10⅛ × 7⅛ in. (25.7 × 18.1 cm)
Signed in graphite, lower left: "D R K"
Purchased with funds given by Mr. and Mrs. Leonard L. Milberg, 1989.29.2

This work served as a preparatory study for Daniel Ridgway Knight's *The Well*, 1880, a sentimental painting depicting an encounter between a peasant boy and girl at a stone well set in a verdant landscape (figure 6).[1] Here, he focused on the young woman, delineating every detail of her figure and costume with assured graphite lines. (A few cursory scribbles provide a shorthand suggestion of the background.) Delicate passages of shading indicate the effects of light and shadow and endow her with a convincing three-dimensionality. Her body is gently bowed forward by the weight of the water jug she holds behind her back. The artist was sensitive to both the aesthetic and anecdotal impact of this pose—the girl's elegant, serpentine contour pulls her toward the young man in *The Well* and conveys an attitude of coy shyness.

Drawing had long played an important role in Knight's art. Despite growing up in Philadelphia in a pious Quaker household where art was forbidden, the young Knight made pen-and-ink copies of imagery he found in books in the library of the Franklin Institute. The quality of these drawings convinced his family to allow him to pursue a painting career.[2] He studied at the Pennsylvania Academy of the Fine Arts in Philadelphia and subsequently in Paris, at the École des Beaux-Arts, under Alexandre Cabanel (1823–1889), and in the atelier of Charles Gleyre (1808–1874). His academic training emphasized solid draftsmanship and the crucial function of preparatory drawings in the creative process. Knight settled permanently in France in 1871 and became highly successful with picturesque paintings of peasants, such as *The Well*, which were popular with European and American patrons. Critics regularly took note of his excellent draftsmanship, and one commentator described his studio in Poissy, "with its piles of studies and its portfolios bursting with sketches."[3] For these studies, he hired local residents to pose for him wearing rustic costumes that he provided.

1. Knight reproduced the drawing in an enlarged format on the surface of his canvas, using it as a guideline for the painted image. This underdrawing is visible with the infrared vidicon. See the entry on *The Well* in Teresa A. Carbone, *American Paintings in the Brooklyn Museum: Artists Born by 1876* (New York: Brooklyn Museum in association with D Giles, London, 2006), 2:733.

2. Harold T. Lawrence, "Daniel Ridgway Knight, Painter," *Brush and Pencil* 7 (Jan. 1901): 194–96.

3. Theodore Child, "Daniel Ridgway Knight," *Art Amateur* 12 (Apr. 1885): 105. On page 106, this article reproduces another preparatory sketch (current location unknown) for *The Well*, a more complete study including both figures and the setting; the girl is much less detailed than the figure in the Brooklyn Museum's drawing.

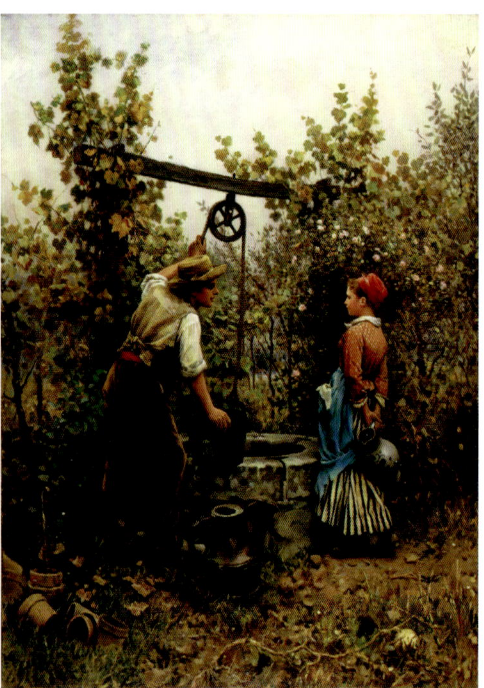

Fig. 6. Daniel Ridgway Knight. *The Well*, 1880.
Oil on canvas, 39⁵⁄₁₆ × 28¹⁵⁄₁₆ in. (99.9 × 73.5 cm).
Brooklyn Museum, Gift of Mr. and Mrs. William E. S. Griswold, 41.980.62

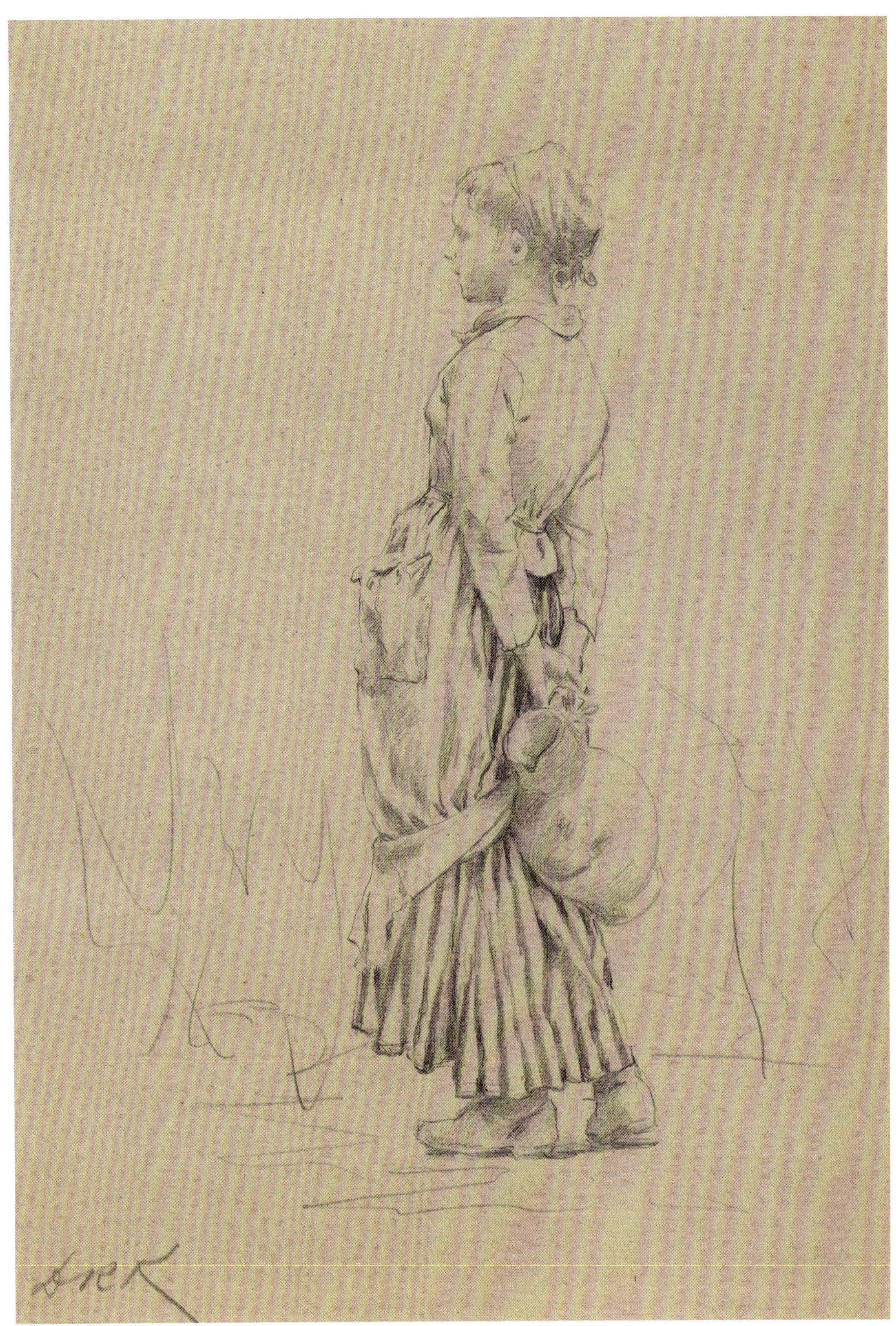

John La Farge

American, 1835–1910

33 Study for the "Sealing of the Twelve Tribes" Window, circa 1889

Graphite on yellow, translucent, smooth-textured wove paper, 16⅜ × 8 in. (41.6 × 20.3 cm)
Signed in graphite, lower right: "J Lafarge"
Gift of George D. Pratt, 13.1063

A preparatory study for a stained-glass window, this stunning graphite drawing represents a scene from the Bible's book of Revelation in which an angel places seals on the foreheads of God's faithful servants—"a hundred and forty and four thousand of all the tribes of the children of Israel" (7:4)—to designate them for salvation at Judgment Day. John La Farge distilled this event into two pairs of figures arranged within the confines of the window's shape, outlined in the drawing as a narrow rectangle with a pointed arch at the top and a triangular reserve at the bottom. In the lower section of the image, an angel marks a woman holding her hands in prayer, while above, an already chosen couple embraces and looks skyward. A few sketchily described clouds in the background establish the heavenly setting. Notwithstanding the simplicity of his design, La Farge enlivened the composition through expressive variations in pose and drapery. The figures twist and turn in dynamic contrapposto stances and are wrapped in heavy robes that gather, tuck, and flow around their bodies. Using a very fine pencil, he delineated the general contours and then modeled forms with thin hatch lines in varying size and density—a technique that produced a subtle range of gray tonalities. Darker passages, such as the shadows under a figure's chin or in deep drapery folds, consist of heavier massings of hatch marks, while the brightest highlights are areas of the paper left untouched. The resulting image is one of great beauty and refinement: the robed figures have both a convincing volumetric presence and a delicate, ethereal quality.

A cosmopolitan and multitalented artist, La Farge is best known for his decorative work—particularly stained glass and mural painting—in the American Renaissance style. Drawing played a crucial role in such projects.[1] Although he was a master colorist, he initially conceived of a design in line, not color; he likened a monochromatic drawing to the skeletal support of a stained-glass window (without its colored panes).[2] The Brooklyn Museum's drawing is the final study for the *Sealing of the Twelve Tribes* window, installed in the transept of Trinity Church in Buffalo, New York (figure 7). La Farge made this design on speculation with the intention of exhibiting the window at the 1889 Exposition Universelle in Paris to showcase some of his innovative stained-glass techniques, including the use of opalescent glass. He found a patron in Charlotte Sherman Watson, the widow of a prominent Buffalo banker, who commissioned *The Sealing of the Twelve Tribes* in memory of her mother and aunt. Although reluctant to delay its installation in Buffalo, Watson let La Farge send the window to Paris, where it won him a Cross of the Legion of Honor from the French government.[3]

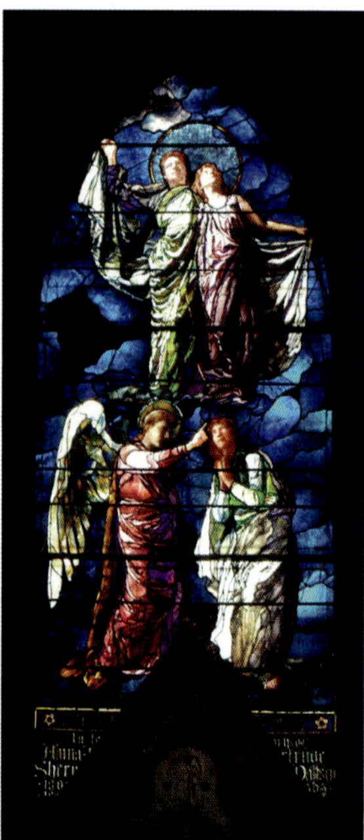

Fig. 7. John La Farge. *The Sealing of the Twelve Tribes (Anna M. Sherman and Gretchen Van Daltsen Memorial Window)*, 1889. Stained glass, 168 × 64 in. (426.7 × 162.6 cm). Located in north transept of Trinity Church, Buffalo, New York

1. In 1908 he destroyed several thousand preparatory sketches and studies for decorative projects. *Dessins américains des collections nationales de 1760 à 1945 (American Drawings in the French National Collections from 1760 to 1945)* (Paris: Réunion des Musées Nationaux, 1991), 48.
2. La Farge's thoughts on drawing are recorded in Royal Cortissoz, *John La Farge: A Memoir and a Study* (Boston: Houghton Mifflin Company, 1911), 192.
3. For additional information about this commission, including excerpts of the correspondence between the artist and patron, see H. Barbara Weinberg, *The Decorative Work of John La Farge* (New York: Garland Publishing, 1977), 397–400. An additional study for the *Sealing of the Twelve Tribes* window is at the Metropolitan Museum of Art, New York (acc. no. 1971.180.146).

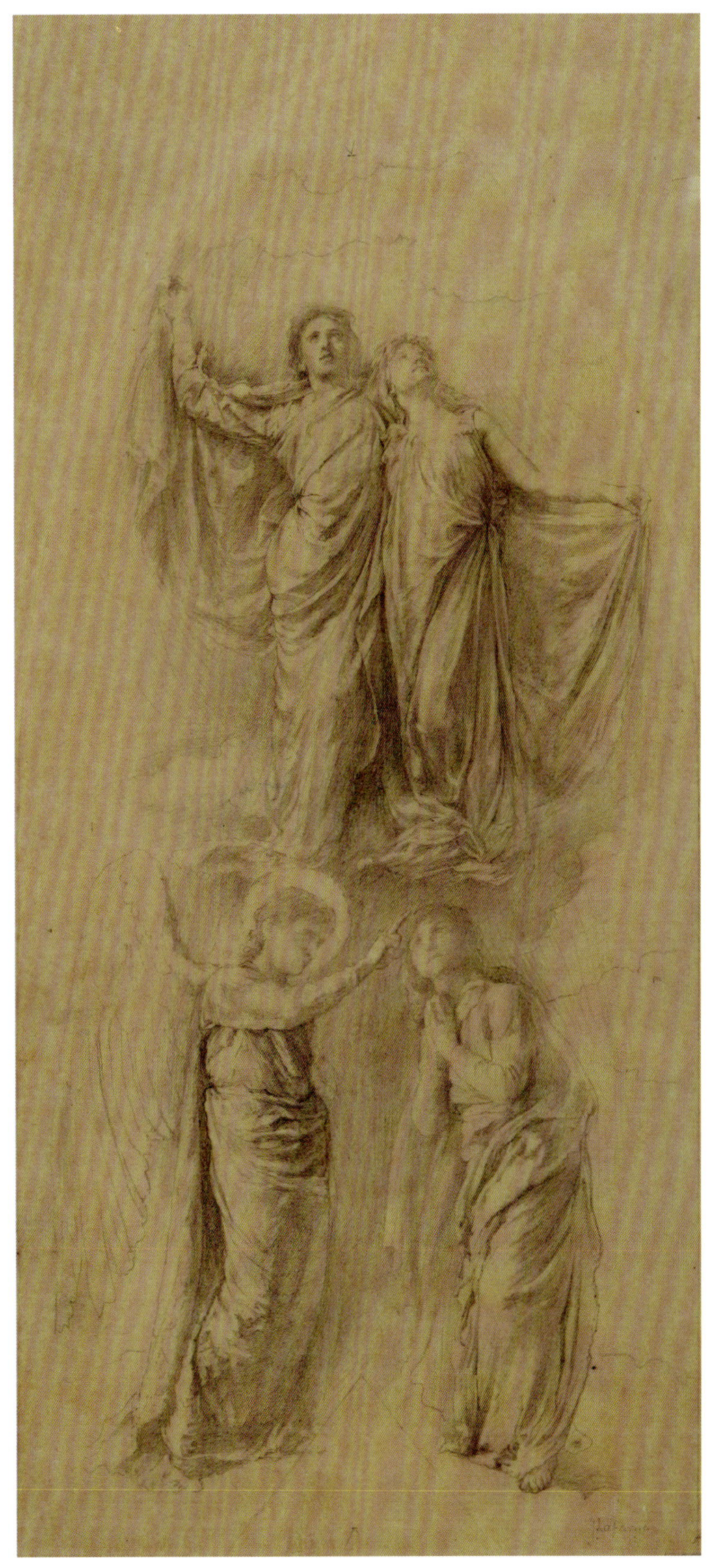

Elihu Vedder

American, 1836–1923

34 Bound Angel, 1891

White chalk and black Conté crayon on bluish green, moderately thick, slightly textured wove paper, 11½ × 8⅞ in. (29.2 × 22.5 cm)
Signed in Conté crayon, lower right: "18 V 91"
Bequest of William H. Herriman, 21.482

Depicting a personification of the human soul as a nude female angel, this highly finished drawing is a study for *Soul in Bondage* (figure 8), an allegorical picture about the conflict of the soul. Elihu Vedder's daughter described the painting's subject as follows: "[The soul] is in darkness because she is turned from the light, and lightly bound because she may free herself as in each hand she holds the emblem of either good or evil, in the butterfly and the serpent."[1] Although Vedder rendered the angel's idealized body as fettered and immobile, he suggested an active inner life by portraying her in an attitude of contemplation—head tilted back, eyes closed, and brow slightly furrowed. There are minor variations between the drawing and the finished painting, most notably in the background. In the study, the angel appears on the shore of an expansive body of water with a setting sun in the distance. This liminal position between land and sea implies the undetermined fate of the soul. For *Soul in Bondage*, Vedder changed the surroundings to the foot of a stone staircase and the atmosphere to a swirling vortex that symbolizes a life's journey. (The emblematic butterfly and snake are also absent in the drawing.)

Bound Angel exemplifies Vedder's technical prowess as a draftsman, as well as his practice of making preparatory drawings for his paintings (see also number 64).[2] Using deft strokes of white chalk and black Conté crayon, he rendered the forms of the angel and landscape with a powerful sense of illusionism. This work and its related painting also typify Vedder's oeuvre in their classicizing treatment of the human figure and their visionary Symbolist subject matter.

Born in New York, the artist spent much of his career as an expatriate living in Italy, although he maintained ties with the United States through regular visits, exhibitions, and commissions for decorative murals. Vedder's greatest international success was his design and illustrations for the 1884 edition of Edward FitzGerald's English translation of *Rubáiyát of Omar Khayyám*, a book of verse about the transience of human life written by the twelfth-century Persian astronomer, mathematician, and poet. The book, which sold out within six days, secured Vedder's fame as an artist of great aesthetic and poetic sensibilities. *Bound Angel* resembles his *Rubáiyát* images in figural style, esoteric theme, and emotional expressiveness.

1. Carrie Vedder to her mother, Caroline Vedder, Mar. 27, 1892, quoted in Regina Soria, *Elihu Vedder: American Visionary Artist in Rome (1836–1923)* (Rutherford, N.J.: Fairleigh Dickinson University Press, 1970), 338.

2. A preparatory drawing for *Soul in Bondage* that resembles the finished picture more closely is in the collection of the Addison Gallery of American Art, Phillips Academy, Andover, Massachusetts (acc. no. 1931.45).

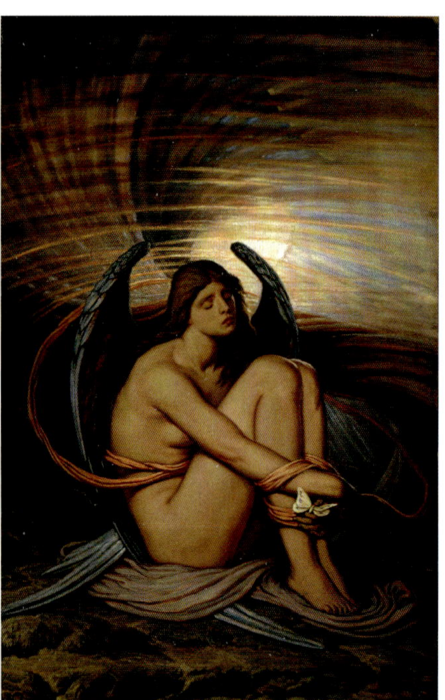

Fig. 8. Elihu Vedder. *Soul in Bondage*, 1891–92. Oil on canvas, 37¹³⁄₁₆ × 24 in. (96.1 × 60.9 cm). Brooklyn Museum, Gift of Mrs. Harold G. Henderson, 47.74

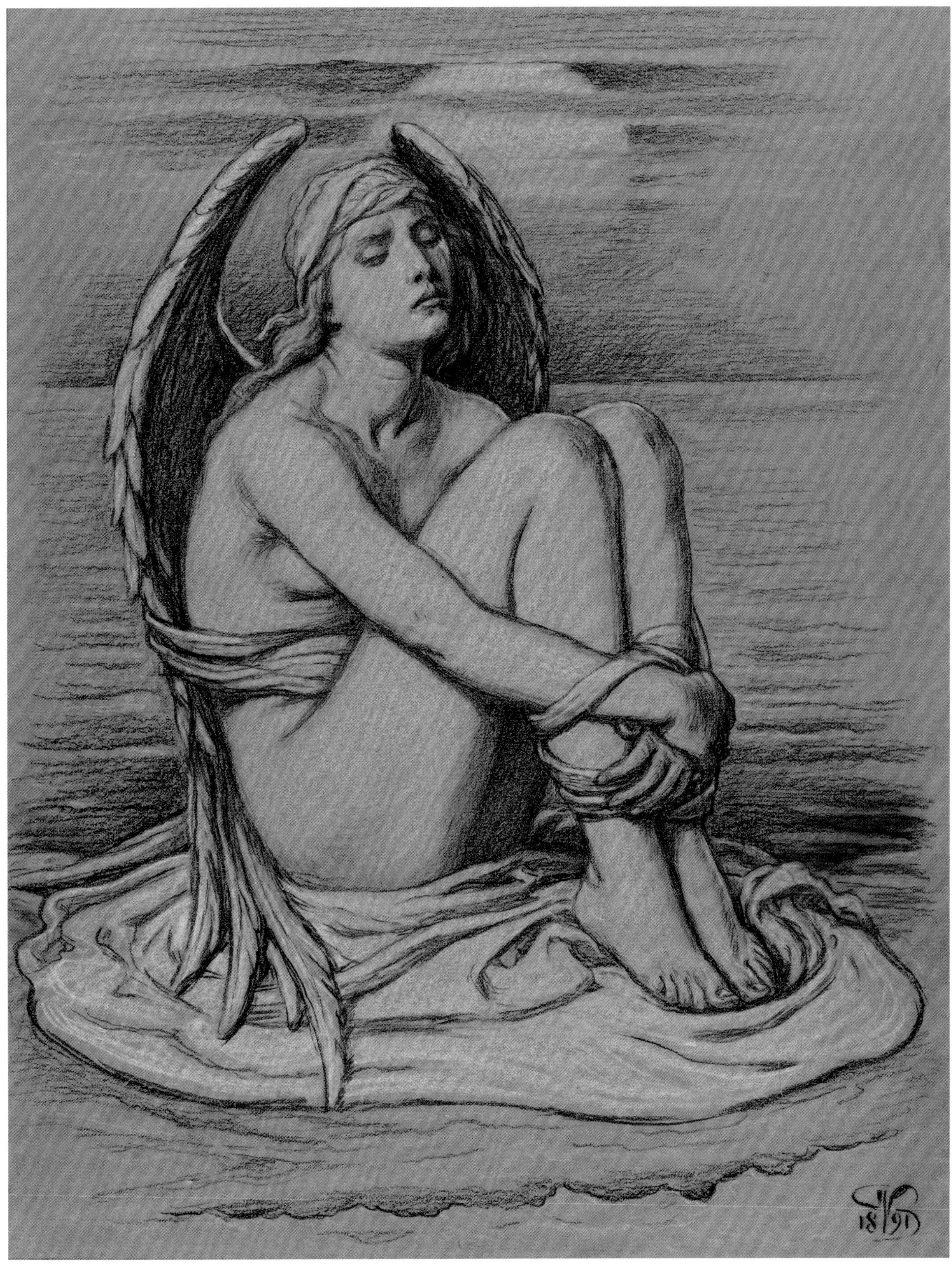

Robert Frederick Blum

American, 1857–1903

35 Woman in a Japanese Costume, circa 1890–92

Pastel on thick paper with a mauve-gray textured ground, mounted to paper board and attached to a wood strainer,
28⅝₁₆ × 22⅜ in. (71.9 × 56.8 cm)
Gift of Henrietta Haller, 11.525

This drawing combines two of Robert Blum's artistic interests—Japanese culture and the pastel medium. Like many American and European artists of the late nineteenth century who participated in a phenomenon known as japonisme, Blum incorporated the motifs and aesthetic principles of Japanese art in his work. His engagement with Japan also included direct experience: he traveled to the island nation in 1890–92, recording his observations about the people and landscapes in various media. Blum was also a leading proponent of the American revival of pastel, which had rarely been used in the country's fine art outside eighteenth- and early nineteenth-century portraiture (see numbers 45, 46). In 1882 he founded the Society of Painters in Pastel with **William Merritt Chase**, **J. Carroll Beckwith**, and others, and served as the organization's president. These pastelists embraced the medium for its portability; pure, vibrant colors; and feathery Impressionist-inspired surface textures. Through several exhibitions held between 1884 and 1890, the society helped to foster greater experimentation with the medium among artists and new appreciation for its distinctive properties among collectors and the public. Blum's interest in both pastel and Japanese aesthetics had been fostered by his friendship with the American expatriate James McNeill Whistler (1834–1903), whom he met in Venice in 1880.

As in this drawing, which most likely dates from his trip to Japan, Blum regularly depicted kimono-clad women in his art, in part to capitalize on the popular Western fascination with the exotic geisha type.[1] Leaving the lower portion of the figure unfinished, the artist masterfully crafted his image through soft, modulated touches of pastel for the facial details and looser strokes for the voluminous folds and colorful patterns of the costume. One critic, in reviewing a memorial exhibition of Blum's work, aptly captured the sensuous effects of his pastels: "One thinks of silky surfaces, of the down on the peach, and the bloom on the plum; one is reminded of things that are luscious and piquant in flavor and that appeal to nothing deeper than the senses. How charming they are, these soft, enchanting strokes of color that show us a pretty Geisha girl or a flower that blooms in the Spring with the same impersonal and dainty blitheness."[2]

1. Several of Blum's images of geisha were reproduced as illustrations to Colgate Baker's story "The Heart of a Geisha," *Metropolitan Magazine* 20 (July 1904): 419–28.

2. "Interesting Memorial Exhibition of Robert Blum's Paintings and Drawings—Fine Specimens of Mural Decoration," *New York Times*, Feb. 2, 1913, SM15.

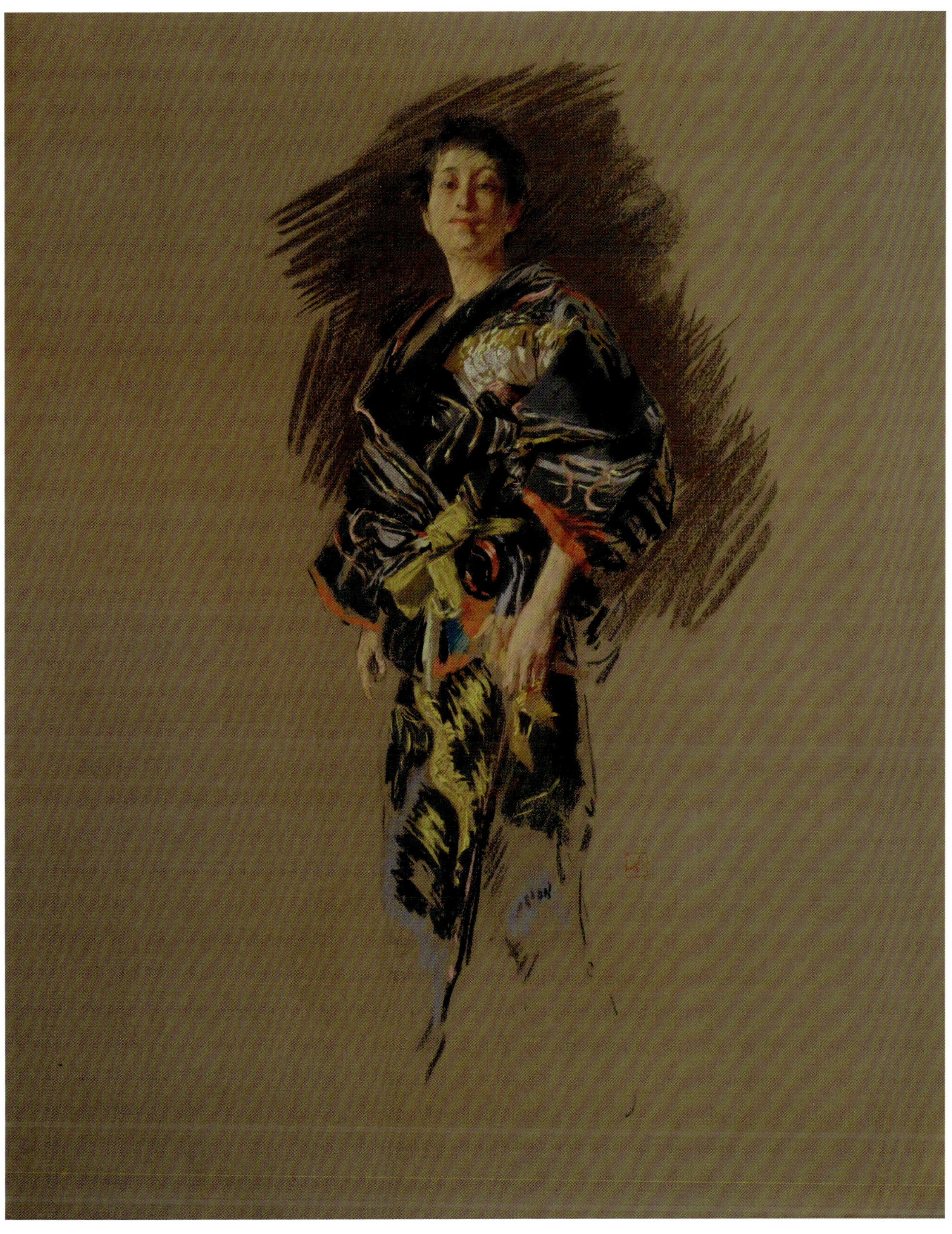

Edward Penfield

American, 1866–1925

36 Sketch of a Spanish Man, 1906

Watercolor and graphite on off-white, medium-weight, moderately textured wove paper, 11½ × 7¾ in. (29.2 × 19.7 cm)
Gift of the Enoch Pratt Free Library, 61.36.1

37 Sketch of a Spanish Man, 1906

Watercolor and graphite on off-white, medium-weight, moderately textured wove paper, 11⁵⁄₁₆ × 7¹¹⁄₁₆ in. (28.7 × 19.5 cm)
Gift of the Enoch Pratt Free Library, 61.36.2

Beginning in the late nineteenth century, many American artists and their audiences were fascinated with the exotic appeal of Spain and its culture.[1] Created during Edward Penfield's 1906 trip through Spain, these two drawings were most likely studies for the artist's travelogue *Spanish Sketches*.[2] The full-length profiles capture the scruffy character of the male subjects through their colorful work shirts, patched pants, and bearded faces. Using a controlled graphite outline and watercolor applied in flat washes, Penfield endowed these Spaniards with a realism and frankness that add an appealing sense of authenticity. Despite the simple and rugged appearance of these working men, the artist also recognized their dignity, evident in their proud bearing. Recounting a story of his guide, Fernando, who is pictured in *Spanish Sketches* and may be one of the men depicted in these drawings, Penfield wrote: "He had dropped his humble demeanor and stooped pose, and held his head in a lordly manner, for he was . . . a man of capital spending his money, and commanding the proper courtesy from the shopkeeper. . . ."[3]

The linearity and flattened colors of these two studies are reminiscent of the artist's best-known works: his Art Nouveau posters of the 1890s for *Harper's Weekly* executed in a style inspired by Japanese prints and the lithographs of the French artist Henri de Toulouse-Lautrec (1864–1901).

Although the drawings shown here were not reproduced in *Spanish Sketches*, the book includes almost thirty narrative illustrations by Penfield featuring similar characters (figure 9). Penfield's chapter "Between Towns in Spain" appeared with full-color illustrations in *Scribner's Magazine* before the full travelogue was published as a book.[4] According to *Scribner's*, "Mr. Penfield was especially interested in the droll and picturesque human aspects of the country, and Spain proved a surprisingly rich field."[5]

Penfield trained at New York's Art Students League in 1890 and created his earliest paintings in an Impressionist style. He first published work in *Harper's Weekly* in 1891, creating posters that appealed to the middle- and upper-class men and women who made up the readership for such literary periodicals. Penfield continued to work for *Harper's* until 1901, when he began to devote his time to illustrating for his own and other publications, including *Scribner's*.—CG

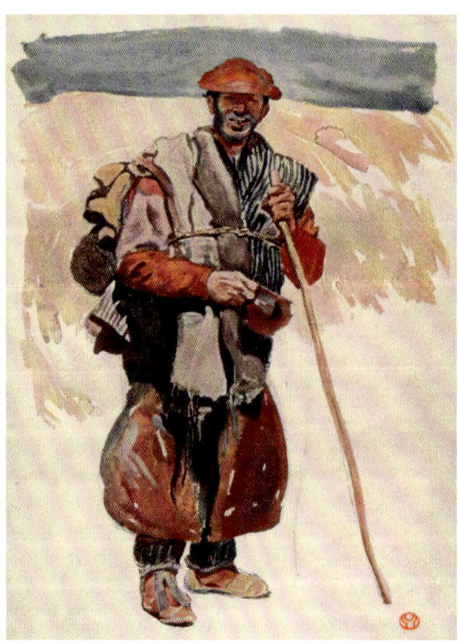

Fig. 9. Edward Penfield. *A Spanish Tramp*, reproduced from Edward Penfield, *Spanish Sketches* (New York: Charles Scribner's Sons, 1911), page 39. Arts and Architecture Collection, Miriam and Ira D. Wallach Division of Art, Prints and Photographs, The New York Public Library, Astor, Lenox and Tilden Foundations

1. H. Barbara Weinberg, "American Artists' Taste for Spanish Painting," in Gary Tinterow and Geneviève Lacambre, et al., *Manet/Velázquez: The French Taste for Spanish Painting* (New York: Metropolitan Museum of Art, 2003), 259.
2. Edward Penfield, *Spanish Sketches* (New York: Charles Scribner's Sons, 1911). The Brooklyn Museum received these drawings mounted in an album with sixteen other Spanish sketches, mostly figures, street scenes, and interior views. It is unknown who compiled the album and when.
3. Ibid., 13–14.
4. Edward Penfield, "Between Towns in Spain," *Scribner's Magazine* 40, no. 4 (Oct. 1906): 441–51. A portion of Penfield's account of travels in Holland had similarly been published in the magazine. Edward Penfield, "The Magenta Village," *Scribner's Magazine* 40, no. 1 (July 1906): 25–33.
5. "Magazine Notes," *Scribner's Magazine* 39, no. 6 (June 1906): 46. This item advertised Penfield's forthcoming "Between Towns in Spain."

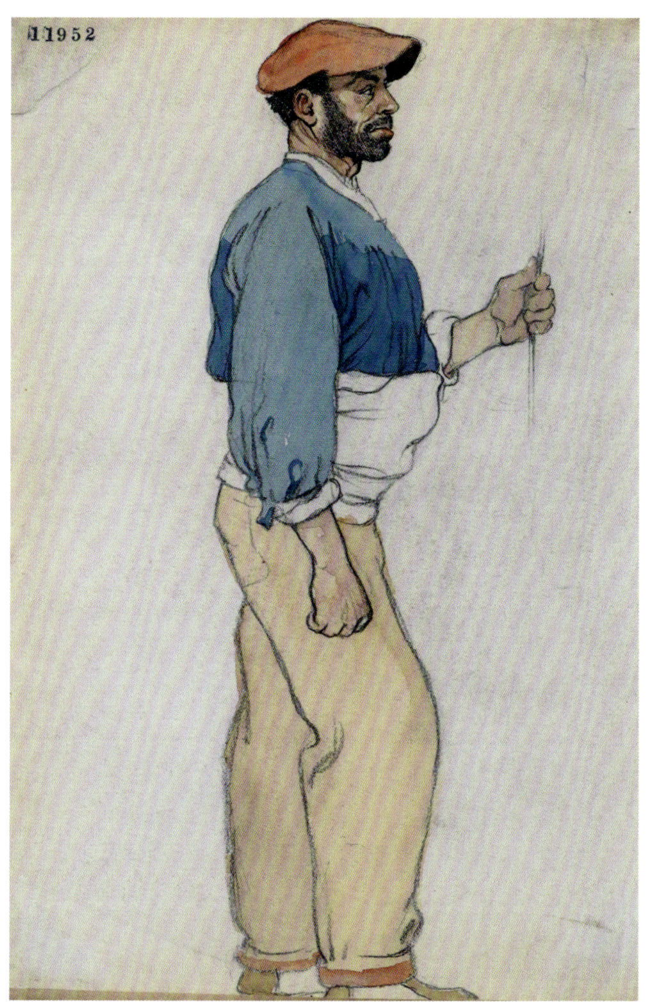

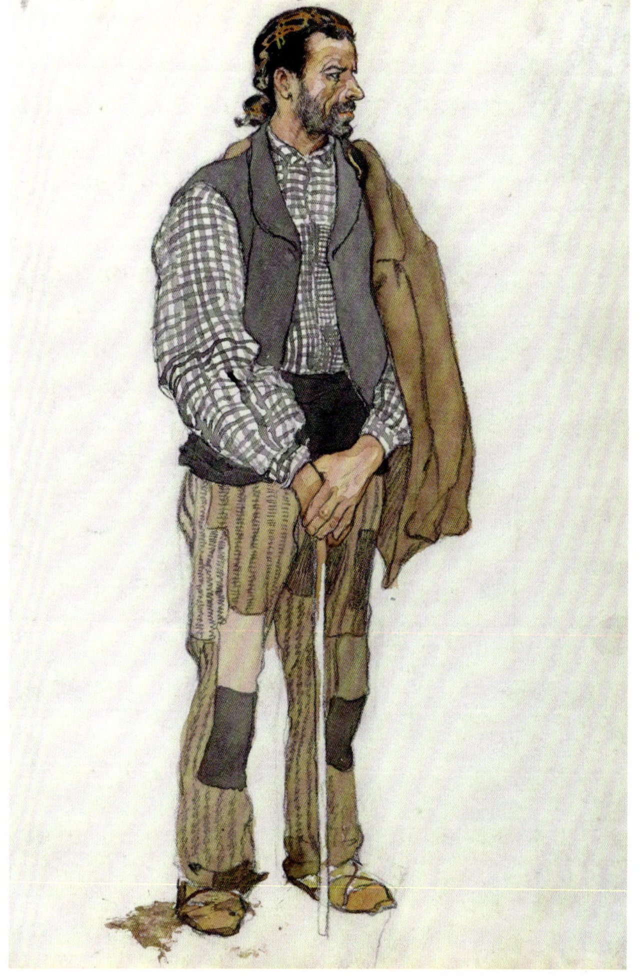

Edward Hopper

American, 1882–1967

38 Standing Female Figure, 1900

Black ink and graphite on beige, thick, smooth wove paper,
22⁹⁄₁₆ × 14⁵⁄₁₆ in. (57.3 × 36.4 cm)
Signed in ink, lower right: "E Hopper / .1900."
Gift of Mr. and Mrs. Morton Ostrow, 84.306.6

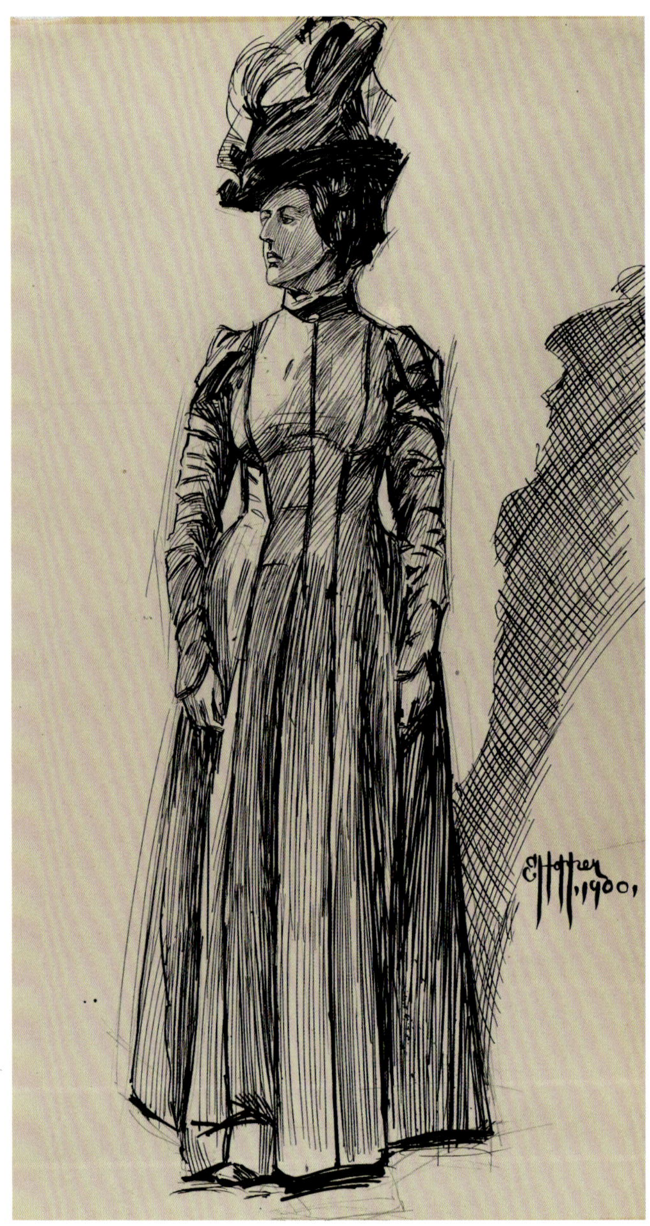

Edward Hopper drew prodigiously from a young age, teaching himself to draw in pen and ink by copying pictures from books and magazines. His graphic abilities led his parents to encourage him to pursue a career as an illustrator, and in 1899 he enrolled at the Correspondence School of Illustration in New York. This drawing dates from his time there, although the circumstances surrounding its creation are unknown; it could be either a class assignment or an independent exercise. With its linear style characterized by bold outlines, strong tonal contrasts, and parallel hatchings for shading, *Standing Female Figure* has the appearance of period illustrations, particularly the immensely popular Gibson Girl imagery of **Charles Dana Gibson** (see number 53).

Hopper first sketched his subject in graphite and then worked over this initial drawing in black ink, using lines of varying thickness to create darker and lighter passages. Wearing a long coat, tailored in a fashionable cut with puffed sleeves and high collar, and a large hat, this matronly woman faces the viewer while looking off to the left. Hopper provided no narrative details, yet he endowed his character with a formidable presence through the solidity of her form, the stiffness of her bearing, and the plainness of her dress.

Ambitious to become a painter, Hopper left the Correspondence School after one year and transferred to the New York School of Art, where he studied with the legendary teachers **William Merritt Chase**, **Robert Henri**, and Kenneth Hayes Miller (1876–1952) (see number 6). Hopper's early training as an illustrator came in handy at the outset of his career, when professional success eluded him. For more than a decade, beginning in 1906, he did commercial illustration for popular and trade publications—work he found frustrating but financially expedient.[1] In the 1920s Hopper earned critical recognition as a painter, etcher, and watercolorist for his realistic images of urban life and New England landscapes. Throughout his mature career, the modern American woman—often depicted alone and lost in thought—was featured prominently in his art.

1. For a good summary of Hopper's career and his illustration work, see Gail Levin, *Edward Hopper: A Catalogue Raisonné*, vol. 1, *Edward Hopper: Perspectives on His Life and Work; Illustrations* (New York: W. W. Norton & Company in association with Whitney Museum of American Art, 1995).

George Benjamin Luks

American, 1867–1933

39 Figure of a Man—Back View, undated

Black Conté crayon on off-white, medium-weight, smooth wove paper, 10⅛ × 8³⁄₁₆ in. (25.7 × 20.8 cm)
Dick S. Ramsay Fund, 58.43.3

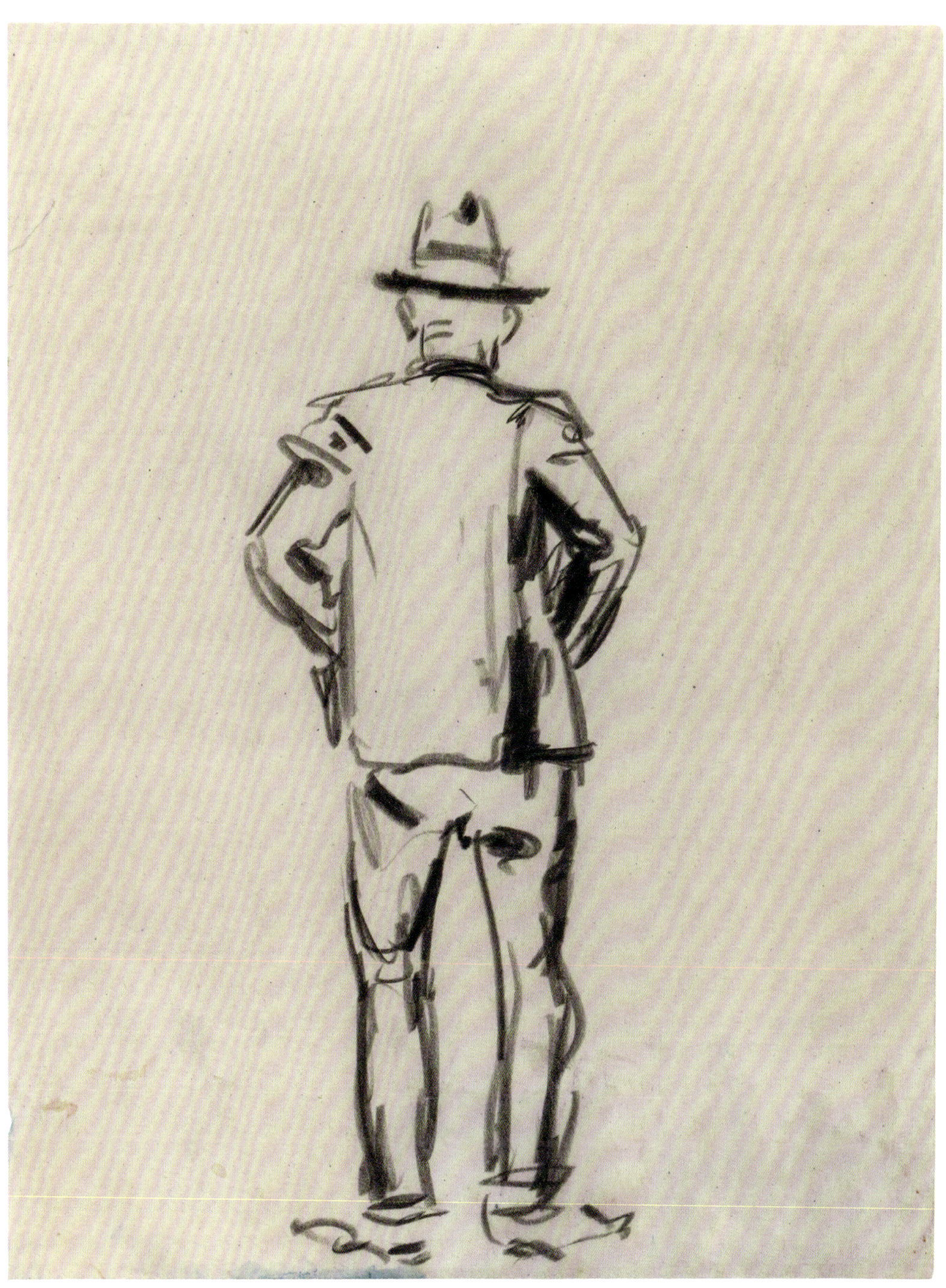

In this drawing, the urban Realist George Benjamin Luks captured a man standing on the street, seen from behind, with quick, lively strokes of his crayon. Expressive lines and scribbles describe the figure's static, hands-on-hips pose and the general contours of his clothing. Although Luks treated forms cursorily, he conveyed a sense of the character's individuality through such details as the bunched fabric of the sleeves, the creased skin at the back of the neck, and the distinctive profile of the fedora. The man's stance suggests an attitude of curiosity as if he—like the artist—has stopped to observe some urban spectacle. Luks constantly roved the bustling streets of New York City, sketching along the way on any available piece of paper, including small scraps, envelopes, menus, and bills. The subject of this drawing was undoubtedly one of the city's denizens whom Luks observed on his frequent perambulations (see also number 71).

Born in Williamsport, Pennsylvania, Luks began his training in 1884 with drawing classes at the Pennsylvania Academy of the Fine Arts in Philadelphia. He temporarily abandoned his artistic pursuits to perform in a traveling vaudeville act with his brother until 1889, when he went to Germany and enrolled in the Düsseldorf Royal Academy. Luks quickly became dissatisfied with academic practice and embarked on an independent exploration of art in various European cities. Back in Philadelphia, he began working as an illustrator for various newspapers, where he honed his skills as an astute observer of modern life and a recorder of quick, on-the-spot sketches. He befriended John Sloan (1871–1951), **William Glackens**, and other illustrators in the orbit of the charismatic and progressive artist **Robert Henri**. At Henri's encouragement, Luks moved in 1896 to New York, where he earned recognition for his illustration work and his popular comic strip *Hogan's Alley*. In 1902 he began devoting himself to painting, depicting unvarnished urban subjects in broadly rendered pictures. The rejection of one of Luks's portraits from a National Academy of Design exhibition prompted Henri to rebel against the art establishment and, in 1908, to form the group the Eight, also called the Ashcan School. As one of these progressive artists, Luks embraced the city's grittier side in both his art and his life. A rowdy, hard-drinking, and aggressive personality, he died on the street from injuries suffered in a barroom brawl.

— • ● • —

Benjamin Osro Eggleston

American, 1867–1937

40 Little Girl Holding an Apple, 1927

Graphite on cream, moderately thick, very smooth wove paper, 10⅛ × 11¹⁄₁₆ in. (25.7 × 28.1 cm)
Signed in graphite, lower left: "BENJAMIN EGGLESTON / 1927"
Dick S. Ramsay Fund, 75.187

Conveying more than just an accurate physical likeness, this charming sketch of an African American youth also suggests a forceful personality and implies a narrative. Holding an apple in one hand, the girl glares to the left with a worried, furrowed brow and determined set to her mouth. The viewer can imagine that she is gathering her wits and steeling her resolve as she prepares to confront some challenge—perhaps other children trying to take her apple. Benjamin Osro Eggleston used quick and assured strokes of a pencil to delineate the details of her appearance and modest outfit, including her solidly modeled facial features, the woolly texture of her cropped hair, and the plaid pattern of her skirt.

By 1927 Eggleston was well established as a painter of idealized portraits and Tonalist landscapes, but he retained his facility with sketching from life that he had gained during his early work as a staff artist for the *Minneapolis Tribune* (1886–87). He settled in Brooklyn in 1890 and, over the next several decades, participated actively in exhibitions and artists' organizations, including the Salmagundi Club and the Brooklyn Art Club (later renamed the Brooklyn Society of Artists, of which

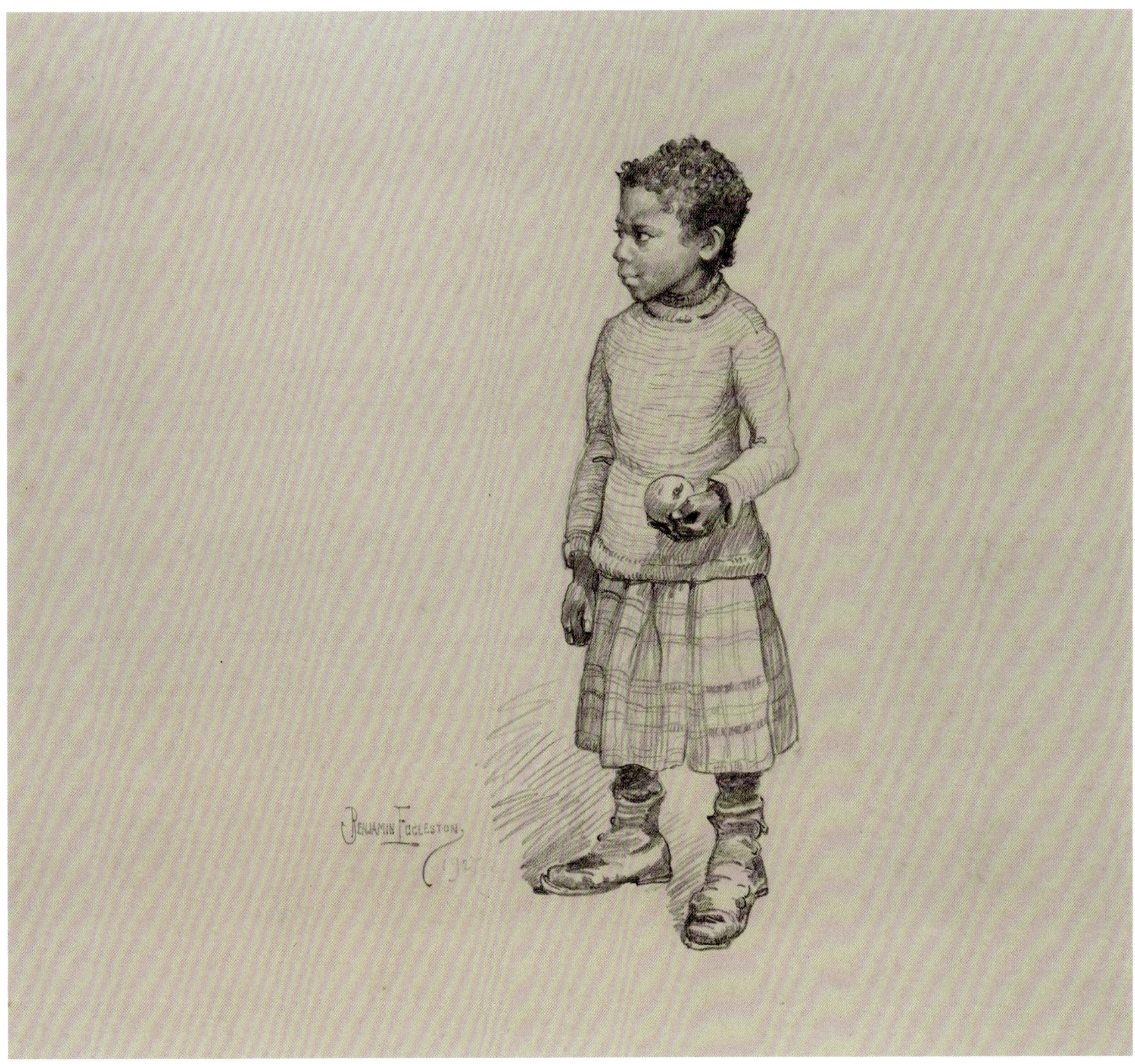

he was president from 1903 to 1927). As a sign of his local prominence, his obituary called him the "dean of Brooklyn artists."[1] A 1928 article reported that Eggleston, lamenting that his portrait subjects were generally wealthy people, "expressed grief at being unable to paint the intriguing types he meets on the street and in the subway."[2] The young girl depicted in this drawing may be one such "intriguing type" whom the artist encountered while out and about in the city and captured in a rapidly executed sketch.

1. "Benj. Eggleston Dies; Was Dean of Borough's Artists," *Brooklyn Daily Eagle*, Feb. 16, 1937, 13.
2. "Brooklyn Artist Prefers to Paint Very Young Pretty Girls or Time-Mellowed Old Ladies," *Brooklyn Daily Eagle*, May 10, 1928, sec. 1, p. 2A.

Raphael Soyer

American, born Russia, 1899–1987

41 **Two Dancers,** circa 1935–40

Pastel on gray wove paper, 24¼ × 18⅛ in. (61.6 × 46 cm)
Signed in graphite, lower right: "RAPHAEL SOYER"
Museum Collection Fund, 40.85. © Estate of Raphael Soyer

During the 1930s, the Social Realist Raphael Soyer began regularly depicting intimate interior scenes populated by solitary or small groups of nude or partially undressed women, as in this pastel. Identifiable as a dancer by her form-fitting shorts, one of the women here leans casually against the corner of a screen and stares wistfully into space, while the other figure, with her back turned toward the viewer, is engaged in the act of dressing. The two seem to have an easy familiarity that allows them to share a comfortable silence, yet their lack of direct interaction adds a note of melancholy to the scene and evokes the alienation of modern life. Soyer's cool palette of mostly blues, pinks, and grays and the pastel medium's soft edges and textures heighten the mood of introspective quietude.

For Soyer, the female body was a subject that provided an opportunity to explore both aesthetic and emotional concerns. As he explained, "A female figure to me is a very deep and mysterious thing, and I feel very comfortable with the female nude. . . . Even when it's not beautiful, the female figure is more expressive than a man's."[1] His respect for and personal connection with his models—indeed, he befriended many of the dancers, artists, and other women who posed for him—are evident in his individualized treatment of their appearance. Soyer's figures were inspired by his fascination with the images of ballet dancers and bathers by Edgar Degas (1834–1917).

Although Soyer did not adopt the daring croppings and unusual vantage points of the French Impressionist, he did experiment with formal design in *Two Dancers*, where the strong geometries of the screen, architectural elements, and striped shirt of one of the dancers contrast with the curving forms of the female body.

Throughout his career as a painter, draftsman, and printmaker, Soyer created his realistic and sensitive portrayals of a broad range of urban dwellers, including dancers, working men and women, derelicts, and his own artistic circle. During his youth in Russia, his father, a Hebrew scholar, fostered his love of art and encouraged him to draw. The family immigrated to the United States in 1912 and settled in New York. Soyer studied art at the Cooper Union, the National Academy of Design, and the Art Students League, usually taking evening classes because he had to work odd jobs to help support his family. The success of his first exhibition in 1929 allowed him to devote himself full-time to his art.

1. Raphael Soyer, interview by Israel Shenker, "Raphael Soyer: 'I Consider Myself a Contemporary Artist Who Describes Contemporary Life,'" *Artnews* 72 (Nov. 1973): 57.

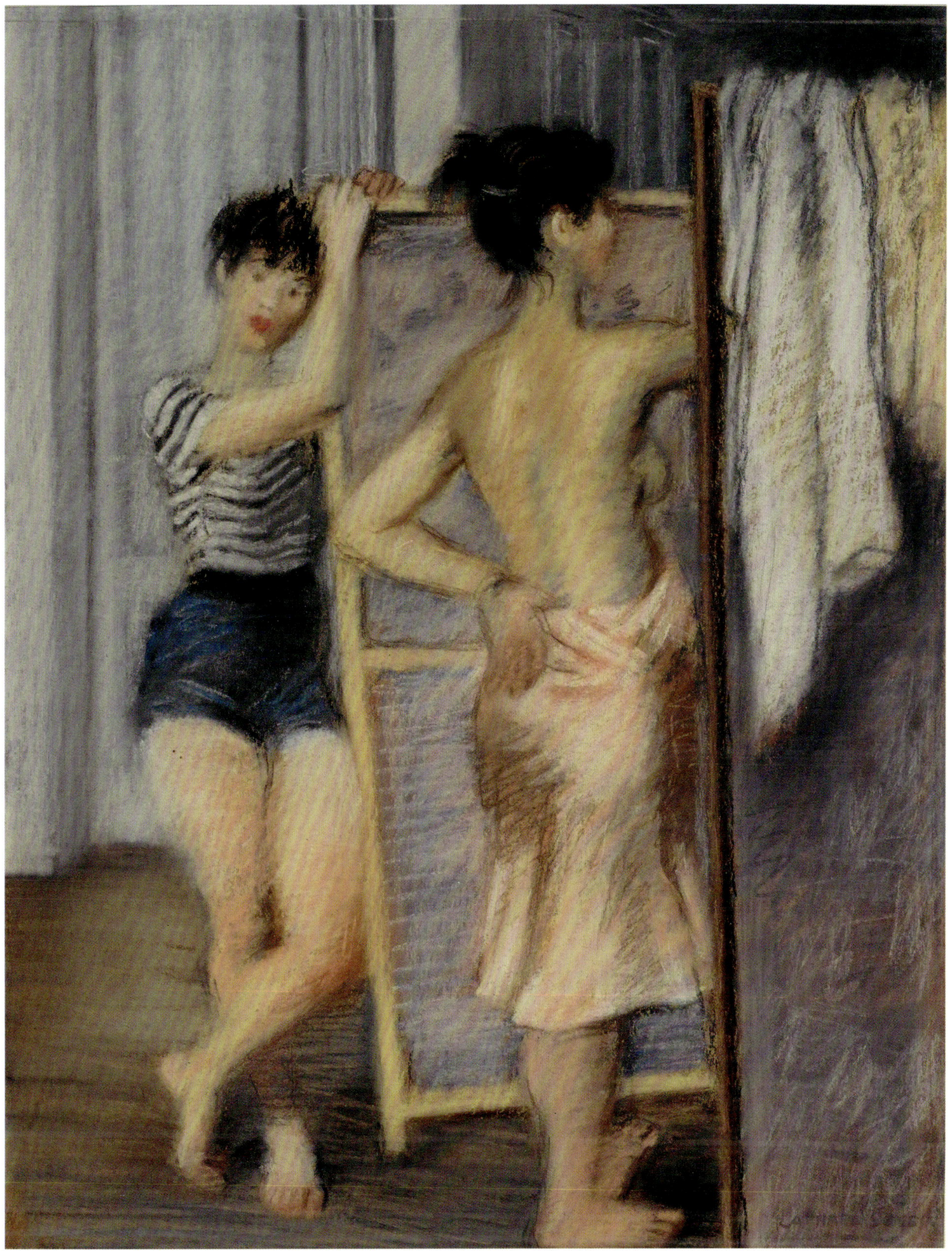

Kahlil Gibran

American, born Lebanon, 1883–1931

42 The Burden, 1919

Watercolor and graphite on medium-weight, cream wove paper, 11¹⁄₁₆ × 8⁹⁄₁₆ in. (28.1 × 21.7 cm)
Signed in graphite, lower right: "K. G. / 1919"
Gift of Mrs. Frank L. Babbott, 21.277

This enigmatic drawing depicts a nude female figure carrying an infant atop her head. The group, in turn, appears to be suspended in space between a pair of large, disembodied hands. Kahlil Gibran modeled the bodies of the mother and child with graphite and then colored them in with flesh-toned watercolors. While the hands have the same bold outline as the figures, they are drawn solely in graphite and have a network of lightly sketched, frenetic scribbles both within and beyond their borders. The disparity of scale between the figural group and the hands, as well as the contrast between colored and monochromatic forms, adds to the otherworldly character of this image.

Throughout his career as a Symbolist artist and writer, Gibran was deeply concerned with the transcendence of the soul and the universal experiences of love, spirituality, and the life cycle. *The Burden* is typical of his imagery in its emphasis on the human body, juxtaposition of disparate elements, and allusive, poetic content. Published without explication in a collection of his drawings in 1919,[1] this work suggests themes of the responsibilities of motherhood and the omnipresence of a divine agent guiding human endeavors. Gibran rendered the mother figure with a somewhat androgynous physique and obscured her face in shadow, making her a symbol of humankind. His powerful treatment of anatomy led contemporary critics to compare Gibran's work with that of the Renaissance masters Leonardo da Vinci (1452–1519) and Michelangelo Buonarotti (1475–1564), while the expressive character of his line was likened to the style of the French sculptor Auguste Rodin (1840–1917), with whom Gibran studied in Paris in 1908–10. One reviewer noted that Gibran's female figures in tinted drawings such as *The Burden* "have undeniable beauty."[2]

Born in a rural village in Lebanon, Gibran immigrated to Boston at age twelve. Impressed by his artistic talents and lyrical sensibilities, the Pictorialist photographer F. Holland Day (1864–1933) took the youth under his wing, introducing him to Boston's intellectual elite (many of whom became patrons) and helping to launch Gibran's literary and artistic career. After attending college in Beirut and studying art in Paris, Gibran settled in New York. He remained active in international cultural circles and was celebrated for a uniquely imaginative vision that blended Arabic and Western traditions. His novel *The Prophet* (1923) became one of the all-time best-selling books in the United States.[3]

1. *Twenty Drawings by Kahlil Gibran*, with an introductory essay by Alice Raphael (New York: Alfred A. Knopf, 1919), unpag.
2. Glen Mullin, "Blake and Gibran," *Nation*, Apr. 10, 1920, 482. This article was a review of *Twenty Drawings by Kahlil Gibran* (see n. 1 above).
3. Patricia Jobe Pierce, "Kahlil Gibran," in American National Biography online, www.anb.org (accessed Nov. 15, 2011).

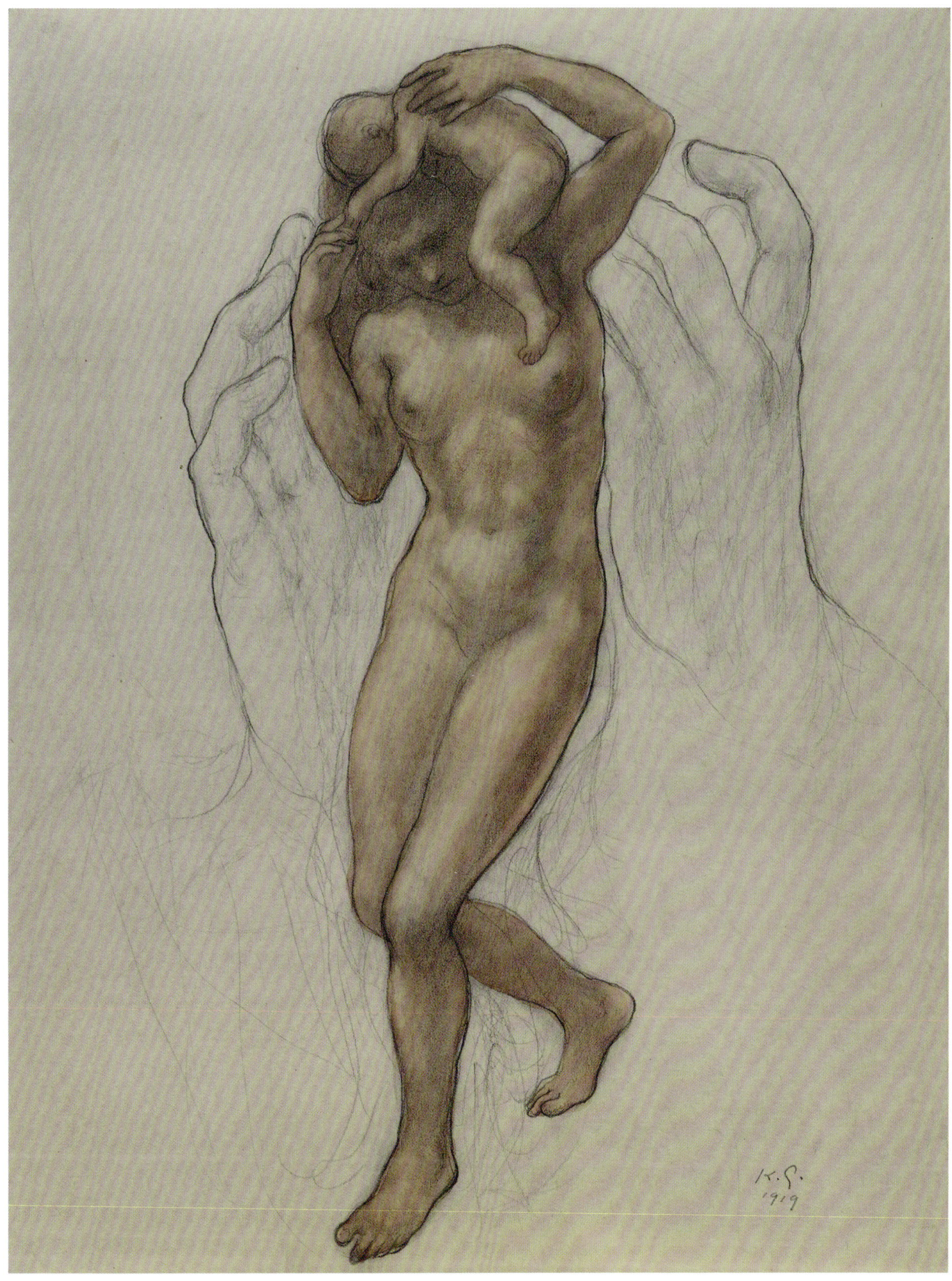

William Zorach

American, born Lithuania, 1887–1966

43 Dahlov Reading, circa 1930

Graphite on cream, thin, slightly textured wove paper, 11$\frac{1}{16}$ × 8$\frac{1}{2}$ in. (28.1 × 21.6 cm)
Signed in graphite, lower right: "William Zorach"
Gift of William Bloom, 84.46.21. © The Zorach Collection, LLC

A devoted family man, the modernist sculptor William Zorach regularly used his wife, the artist **Marguerite Zorach**, and their two children as a source of artistic inspiration. As he explained, "To hire a model and sit down to work has no meaning to me. My children, my wife, the animals I know, the people who enter my life—things that are deeply a part of me and in which I see a relationship to life . . . these are my material."[1] In this tender, informal portrait, he depicted his daughter Dahlov (born 1917), easily recognizable by her long hair with straight bangs, engaged in a casual activity in their home.[2] Wearing a plain sweater, breeches, and Oxford shoes, she sits on a couch with a book open on her lap. Zorach conveyed her complete absorption in her reading not only through her self-contained pose (she does not acknowledge the artist or viewer) but also through his treatment of forms. In his characteristic drawing style of the period, he reduced her figure to an outline of single graphite lines with minimal modeling, including only a few passages of feathery shading on her legs and elsewhere (see also numbers 15, 55). In addition, he distorted her torso, particularly where the legs meet the hips, and flattened the spatial relationships between the figure, couch, and background wall. The resulting effect is that Dahlov appears to merge with her environment.

After initial training in Cleveland and New York, Zorach traveled to Paris in 1910–11. There he gained familiarity with avant-garde currents in European art, including Fauvism and Cubism, and met Marguerite Thompson, whom he would marry in 1912, a year after they returned to New York. He first gained recognition for his richly colored paintings that displayed a range of modernist influences, but in the early 1920s, he turned most of his efforts to sculpture, becoming one of the earliest American sculptors to embrace direct carving. He also continued to make works on paper—drawings, watercolors, and prints. Figures, especially family members and mother-and-child groups, featured prominently in his oeuvre.

1. Artist's statement, in William Zorach, *William Zorach* (New York: American Artists Group, 1945), unpag.

2. Dahlov Zorach Ipcar became a painter and illustrator of children's books.

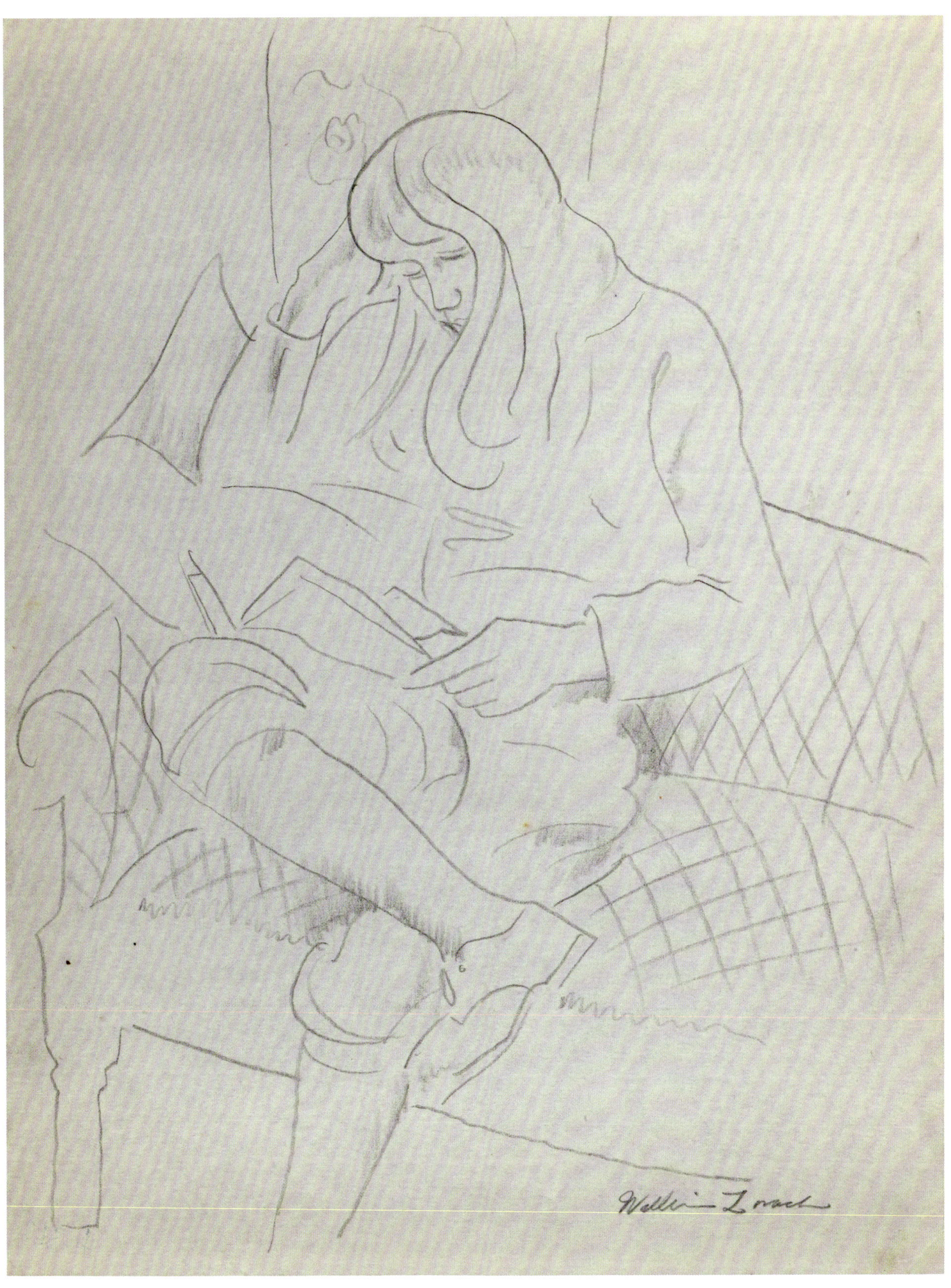

Louis (George Louis Robert) Bouché

American, 1896–1969

44 The Three Sisters, 1918

Graphite on cream, moderately thick, moderately textured laid paper, 24³⁄₁₆ × 18⅞ in. (61.4 × 47.9 cm)
Inscribed and signed in graphite, across bottom: "—THE THREE SISTERS—L. BOUCHÉ 1918—"
Gift of Miss Ettie Stettheimer, 45.121

This highly finished group portrait by the modernist Louis Bouché, primarily known for his still lifes and portraits, exemplifies the artist's interest in Cubism, particularly in the flattened and faceted forms of the faces, bodies, and clothing of the sitters. The multitude of patterns and textures of the room, including the lace curtains, demonstrates Bouché's knack for depicting interiors, which led one critic to describe this phase of his career as the "Nottingham Lace Period," referring to a lacemaking center in Victorian England.[1] Depicting his friends the three Stettheimer sisters—Caroline (Carrie, 1869–1944), Henrietta (Ettie, 1875–1955), and Florine (1871–1944), the well-known modernist painter—Bouché imbued each with unique characteristics (figure 10). Florine, at left, stands confidently with arms folded. Carrie is elegantly seated at center, wearing a large cameo necklace and daintily holding a teacup, while Ettie leans playfully on the back of her sister's chair, a sly smile forming at her lips. A small toy horse at lower right, whose meaning is lost to the modern viewer, may have held some personal significance for the artist and sitters. The landscape view through the window most likely references the sisters' time in Switzerland, where they lived until the outbreak of World War I. Their mother, Rosetta Stettheimer, with whom the sisters resided and who was frequently depicted in Florine's paintings, probably appears in Bouché's drawing in the small framed photograph placed on the dresser.

The Stettheimers often hosted extravagant private salons and were friendly with major figures in the New York art world, including the artists Marcel Duchamp (1887–1968), Francis Picabia (1879–1953), and **Marsden Hartley**. Fashionable in their dress, they also adorned their Manhattan home with unusual and whimsical furniture—often designed by Florine—and materials such as lace, artificial flowers, and even cellophane.[2] Known for their unconventional lifestyle, none of the three sisters married. Each pursued her own interests: Florine was a painter, Ettie a writer, and Carrie a hostess and creator of a dollhouse replica of the Stettheimer home (Museum of the City of New York).

Born in New York, Bouché moved with his mother in 1909 to Paris, where he pursued artistic training. In 1915 he returned to New York and studied at the Art Students League. An excellent draftsman, Bouché also completed paintings and murals and later taught at the Art Students League and the National Academy of Design.[3]—CG

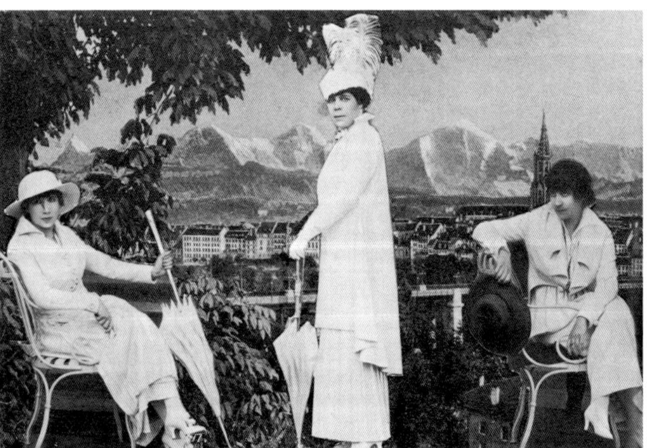

Fig. 10. Photocollage of Stettheimer sisters, circa 1914. Formerly collection of Kirk Askew, Jr.; current location unknown. From left to right: Florine, Carrie, and Ettie

1. Ilene Susan Fort and Michael Quick, *American Art: A Catalogue of the Los Angeles County Museum of Art Collection* (Los Angeles: Los Angeles County Museum of Art, 1991), 352–53.
2. Cécile Whiting, "Decorating with Stettheimer and the Boys," *American Art* 14, no. 1 (Spring 2000): 35–36. Florine in particular had a love of draped lace, like many artists in the 1910s who were influenced by that decorative style of the Victorian period.
3. Bouché's drawing skills are praised in Robert Morris Coffin, *An American Show* (Cincinnati: Cincinnati Art Museum, 1946), 6.

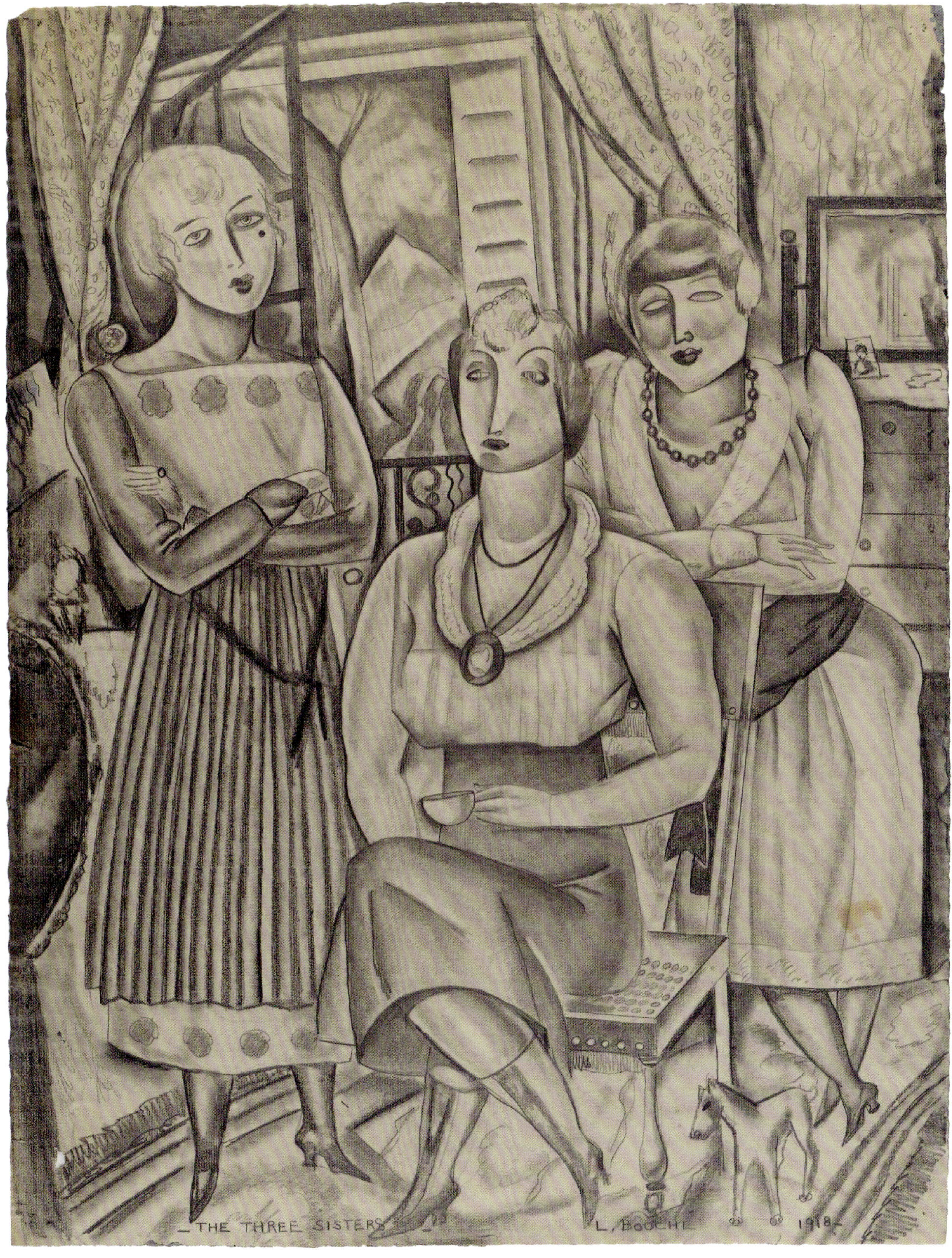
THE THREE SISTERS
L. BOULHE   1918_

PORTRAYING PERSONALITIES

Throughout the history of American art, portraiture was an important—sometimes the dominant—genre of artistic production. The nature of drawing makes it well suited to portraiture. A drawing can be made with more ease, speed, and economy than an oil painting or a sculpture, and graphic media can achieve a wide range of pictorial effects. Furthermore, the intimacy of the process of drawing a portrait—the close physical proximity of artist and sitter and the collaborative interaction between them—often enhances the sense of immediacy and presence evoked by the likeness.

This section explores various kinds of portraits, including formal commissions of specific individuals, casual images of personal acquaintances, and idealized depictions of generalized types, as well as symbolic or emblematic portraits. Most appear in a conventional bust-length format, capitalizing on the age-old assumption that the face constitutes the body's most idiosyncratic and expressive register. As a representation of an individual, a portrait functioned not only to record appearance but also to signify social identity, moral character, mood, and personality. Many artists used a naturalistic style to convey accurately the material facts of a sitter's distinctive physiognomy and fleeting facial expression, while others manipulated the subject's image through idealization or abstraction, or added symbolic elements to express additional information about a person's character.

Charles Balthazar Julien Févret de Saint-Mémin

French, 1770–1852, active in America 1793–1814

45 James Alexander Fulton of Mount Erin, circa 1808

Black crayon, pastel, charcoal, and white chalk on laid paper coated with pink opaque watercolor and pastel mounted to wood-pulp board,
21⁵⁄₁₆ × 15¼ in. (54.1 × 38.7 cm)
Museum Collection Fund, 30.1104

46 Elizabeth Bland Mayo Fulton of Powhattan Seat, circa 1808

Charcoal, black crayon, red and white chalk, and pastel on laid paper coated with pink opaque watercolor and pastel mounted to wood-pulp board,
21½ × 15⁷⁄₁₆ in. (54.6 × 39.2 cm)
Museum Collection Fund, 30.1105

These two drawings are among the more than 120 portraits the French émigré and itinerant artist Charles Balthazar Julien Févret de Saint-Mémin executed during a stint in Richmond, Virginia, in 1807–8. His visit coincided with the sensational trial of Aaron Burr for treason, an event that drew scores of visitors (and potential patrons) to the state capital. The sitters here are James Alexander Fulton (1774–1823), an Irishman who immigrated to Baltimore, and his new wife, Elizabeth Bland Mayo Fulton (1782/88–1848), the daughter of a prominent Virginia family. Around the time that their portraits were drawn, the couple established their own plantation, Mount Erin, next to the Mayo family's seat outside Richmond on the Saint James River.

As is typical of Saint-Mémin's oeuvre, the sitters appear in bust-length profiles (designed to face each other when the portraits were hung) on pink-painted paper. This layer of tinted gouache not only adds color to the drawing but also provides a rough surface texture, or tooth, for holding the powdery pastel medium.[1] Saint-Mémin achieved his remarkably precise realism in part through the aid of a physiognotrace, a mechanical device developed in Europe in the 1780s that allowed the artist to trace a silhouette of the head quickly and accurately. After establishing the outline, he added the details of the sitter's face and clothing by hand in colored media—mostly black and brown, with touches of white. His proficiency as a draftsman is evident in the way he varied the application of the medium to describe different forms, materials, and textures, such as Elizabeth's wispy curls, the white muslin of her fashionable Empire-style dress, and the velvety black fabric of her husband's jacket.

A member of a prominent French family and a former military officer, Saint-Mémin immigrated to the United States to escape the violence of the French Revolution. His known artistic oeuvre consists of nearly a thousand profile portraits he drew while in America from 1793 to 1814.[2] Traveling to New York, Philadelphia,

Charleston, and other cities to make likenesses of the social elite (George Washington and Thomas Jefferson were among his prominent sitters), Saint-Mémin became the most renowned profile portraitist of the period. The eighteenth-century vogue for profile portraits was influenced by Neoclassical taste on both sides of the Atlantic—apparent, for instance, in Wedgwood portrait medallions (figure 11)—as well as by Johann Kaspar Lavater's ideas on physiognomy, a popular pseudoscientific notion that a person's character was manifest in the shapes of his or her facial features.

1. See Marjorie Shelley, "The Craft of American Drawing: Early Eighteenth to Late Nineteenth Century," in Kevin J. Avery, *American Drawings and Watercolors in the Metropolitan Museum of Art*, vol. 1, *A Catalogue of Works by Artists Born before 1835* (New York: Metropolitan Museum of Art, 2002), 41.
2. The best source on Saint-Mémin is Ellen G. Miles, *Saint-Mémin and the Neoclassical Profile Portrait in America* (Washington, D.C.: National Portrait Gallery and the Smithsonian Institution Press, 1994). In addition to the original drawings, Saint-Mémin offered his clients etched copies of their portraits and frames painted with black and gold borders. The frames on the Brooklyn Museum's drawings are original.

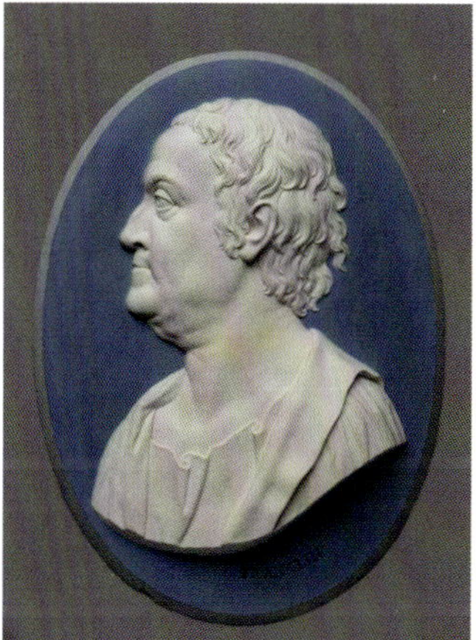

Fig. 11. Modeled by William Hackwood (died 1836). Manufactured by Wedgwood & Bentley (Etruria, Staffordshire, England, 1768–80). *Portrait Plaque of Benjamin Franklin*, 1777–79. Jasperware, 10⁷⁄₈ × 8 in. (27.6 × 20.3 cm). Brooklyn Museum, Gift of Emily Winthrop Miles, 57.180.4

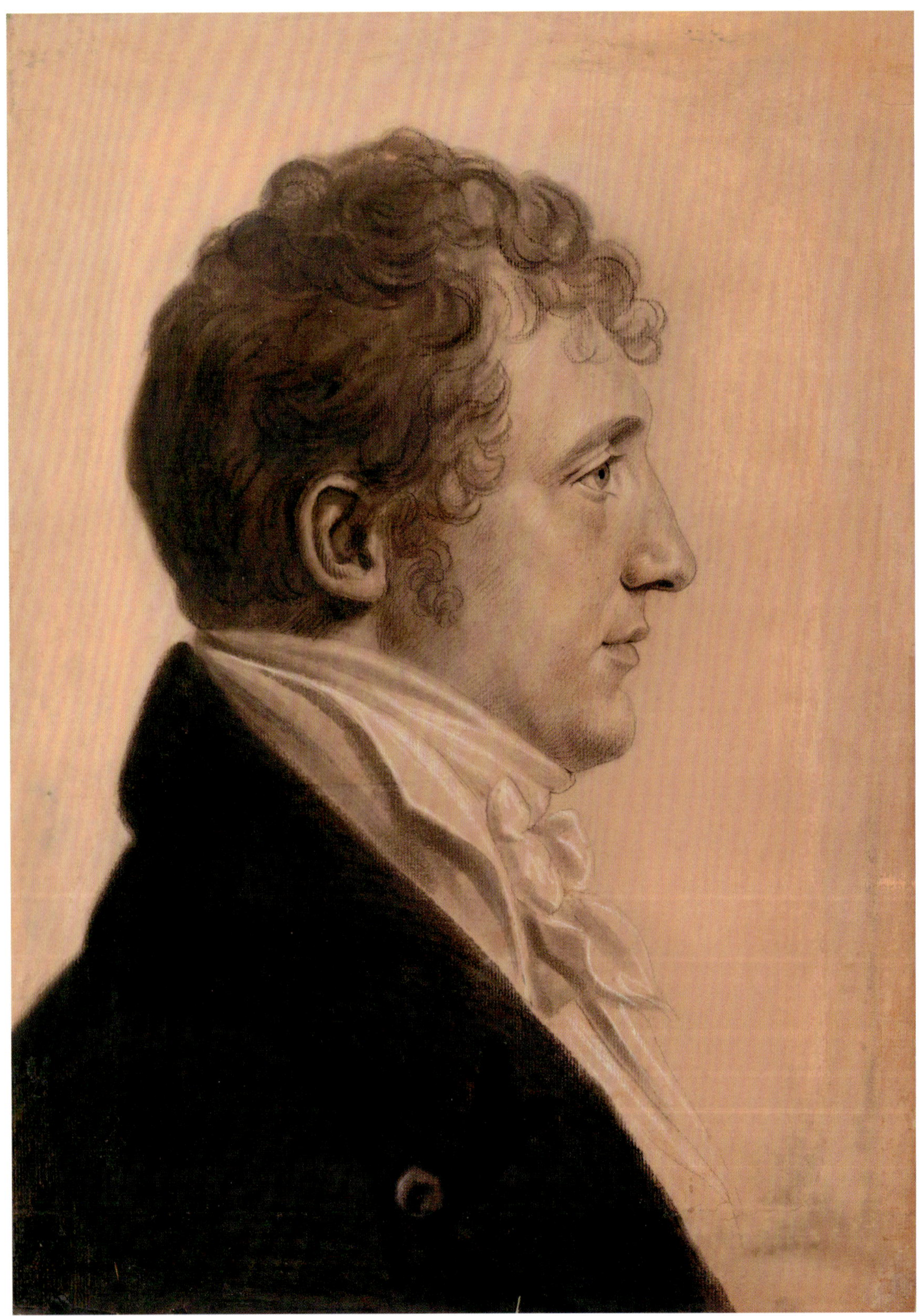

45

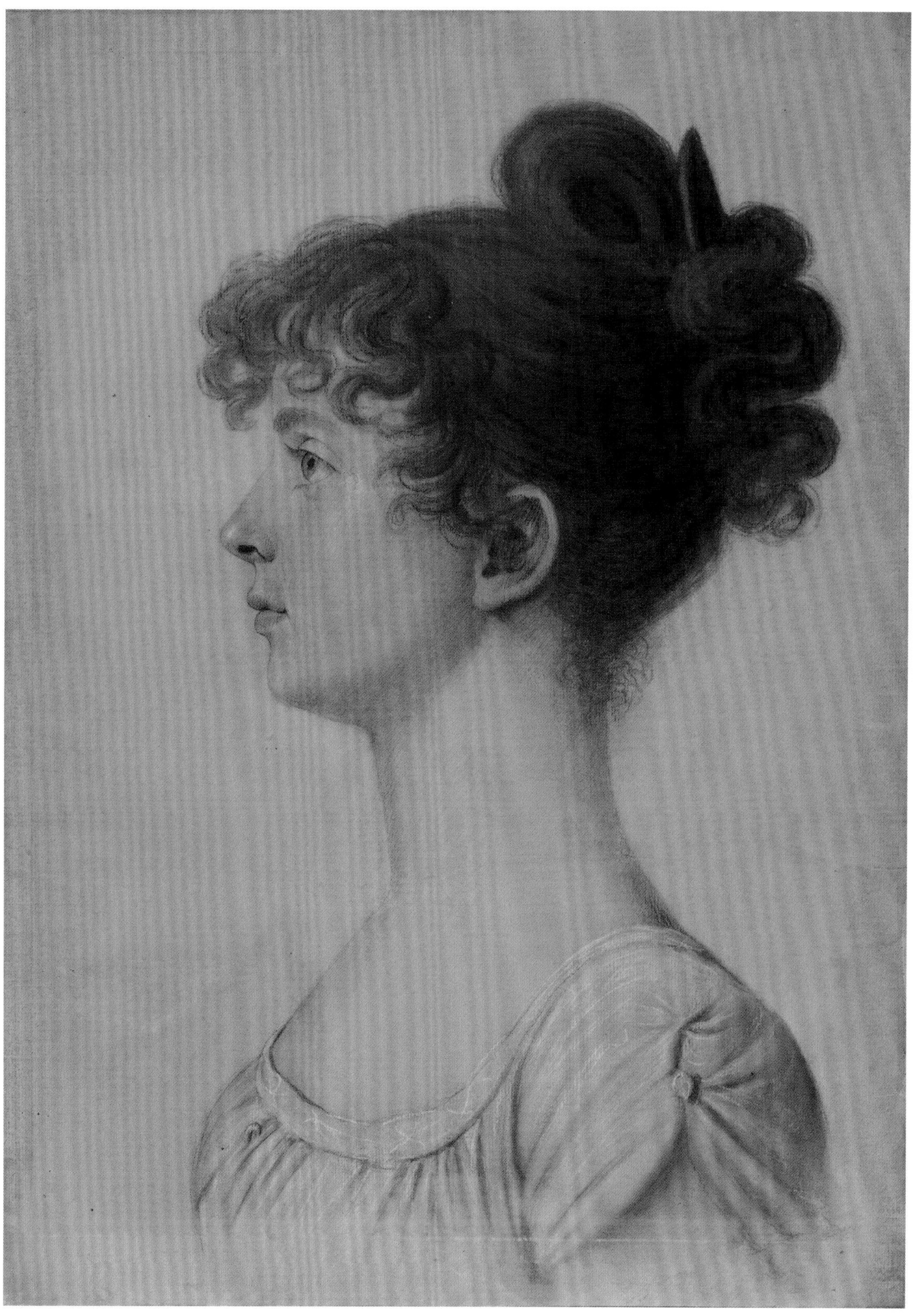

46

William Merritt Chase

American, 1849–1916

47 **Sketchbook,** 1872

Graphite and black, red, and white Conté crayon on cream and tan, medium-thick, slightly textured wove paper, 11⅞ × 9⁷⁄₁₆ × ¹¹⁄₁₆ in. (30.2 × 24 × 1.7 cm)
Signed in graphite, inside front cover: "Will. M. Chase. / 3 Neuhauser Sr. / Kunst Academy / München"
Gift of Newhouse Galleries, Inc., 29.27.11

In 1872 William Merritt Chase traveled to Europe to continue his formal training. He considered the academies in both Paris and Munich—at the time, the most popular choices among American students—and selected the latter, in part because he feared that the bohemian atmosphere in Paris would distract him from his work.[1] Shortly after enrolling at Munich's Royal Academy in the fall, Chase filled this twenty-four-page sketchbook with drawings, mostly of portrait heads, in various media. There are also figure studies (including partial figures) from nude and costumed models and other artistic exercises. A spread (pages 2–3) containing male heads exemplifies Chase's talents as both a draftsman and a portraitist. Using a combination of firm outlines and loose diagonal strokes, he quickly yet accurately described the distinctive appearance of each man—the beak nose of one, the bushy sideburns of another. The informal nature of these portraits, the intense downward gaze of many of the figures, and the hint that some of them have an arm outstretched (as if reaching toward an easel) suggest that Chase's subjects are his fellow students captured at work in the classroom, like the young man shown drawing on page 8. On page 9, Chase depicted the head of a studio model, who appears in several drawings, and made a sketch of a foot, which he later scribbled over. This "portrait" study has the individualized specificity of those on pages 2–3 but is rendered primarily through tone. Chase modeled the forms of his sitter's face by manipulating

tonal values from rich darks to bright lights, with the paper providing the lightest tone. The strong contrasts in this image are typical of the style associated with the Munich academy—a style inspired by such Baroque masters as Rembrandt van Rijn (1606–1669), Diego Velázquez (1599–1660), and Frans Hals (circa 1581–1666). Chase would become the most successful American practitioner of this brand of vigorous and loosely worked Realism (see number 48).

During his five years in Munich, Chase was part of a close-knit community of artists, including his fellow Americans Walter Shirlaw (1838–1909), Frank Duveneck (1848–1919), and **John Henry Twachtman**, who shared living quarters, met almost every evening in their favorite bar, traveled together in the summers, and painted portraits of one another. Chase also won several awards for his draftsmanship and garnered a prestigious portrait commission from his instructor Karl Theodor von Piloty (1826–1886), the Royal Academy's director and a prominent history painter.

1. He later recalled, "I could saw wood in Munich instead of frittering in the Latin merry-go-round [of Paris]"; quoted in Ursula Frohne, "'A Kind of Teutonic Florence': Cultural and Professional Aspirations of American Artists in Munich," in *American Artists in Munich: Artistic Migration and Cultural Exchange Processes*, ed. Christian Fuhrmeister, Hubertus Kohle, and Veerle Thielemans (Berlin: Deutscher Kunstverlag, 2009), 77.

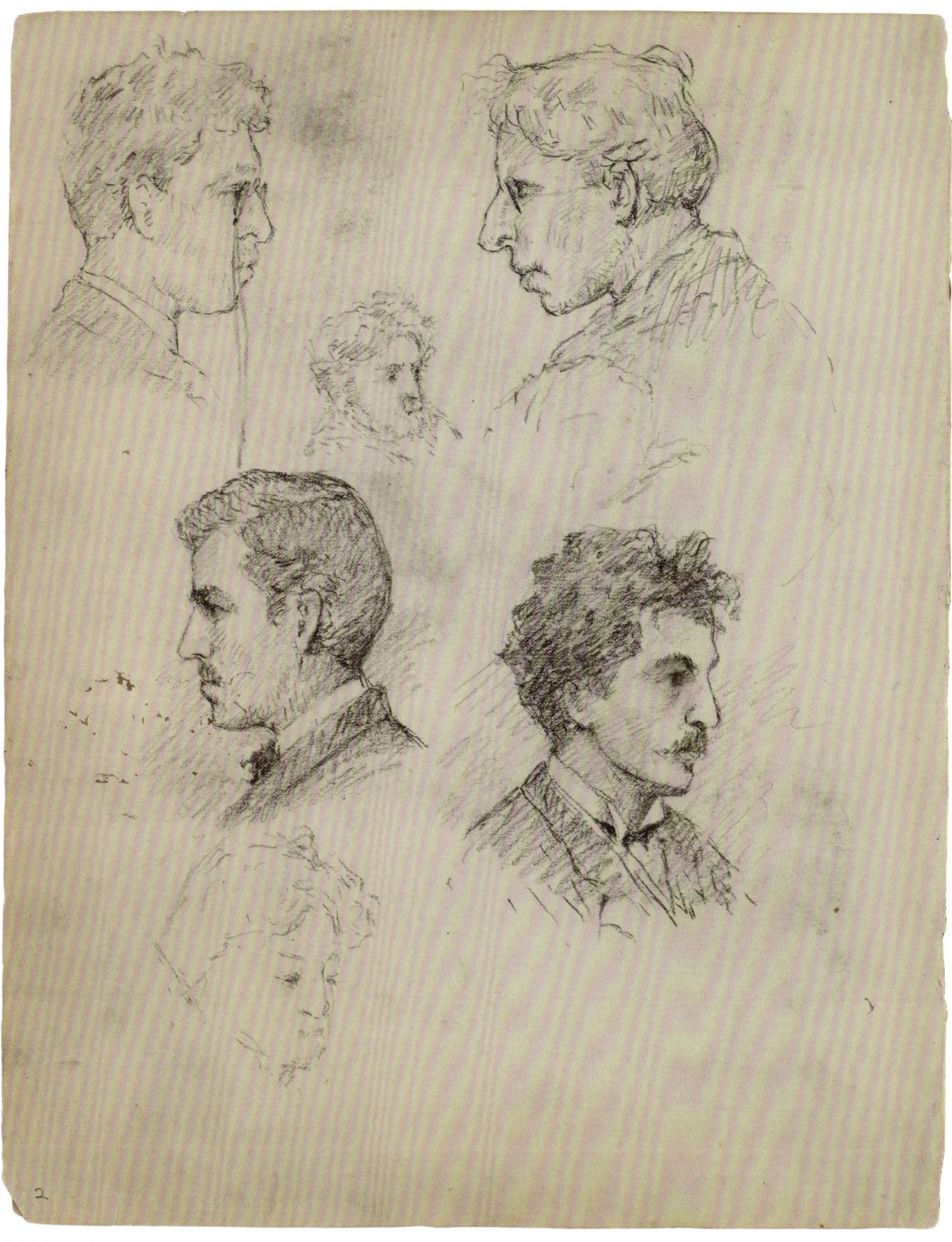

29.27.11, page 2

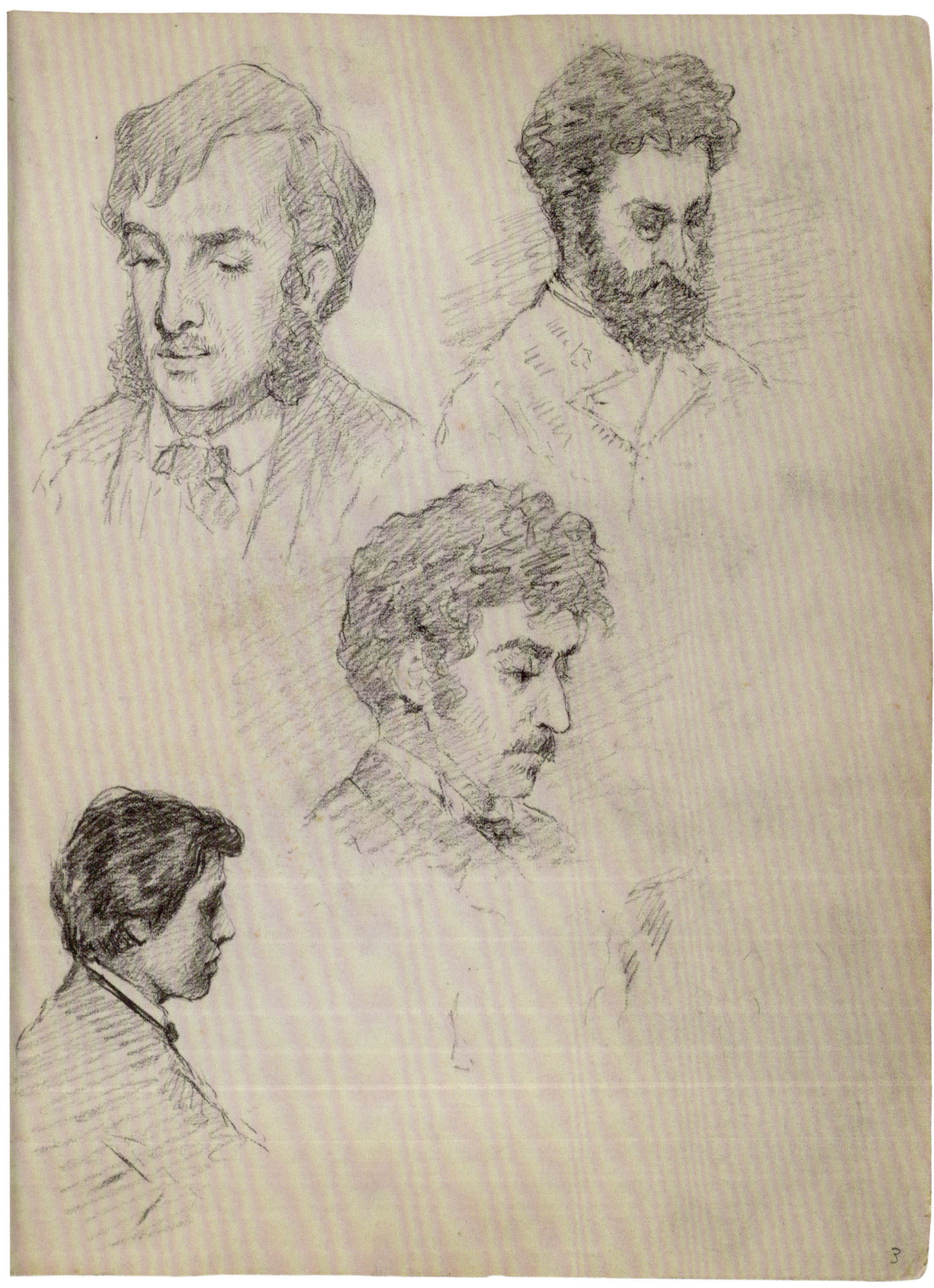

29.27.11, page 3

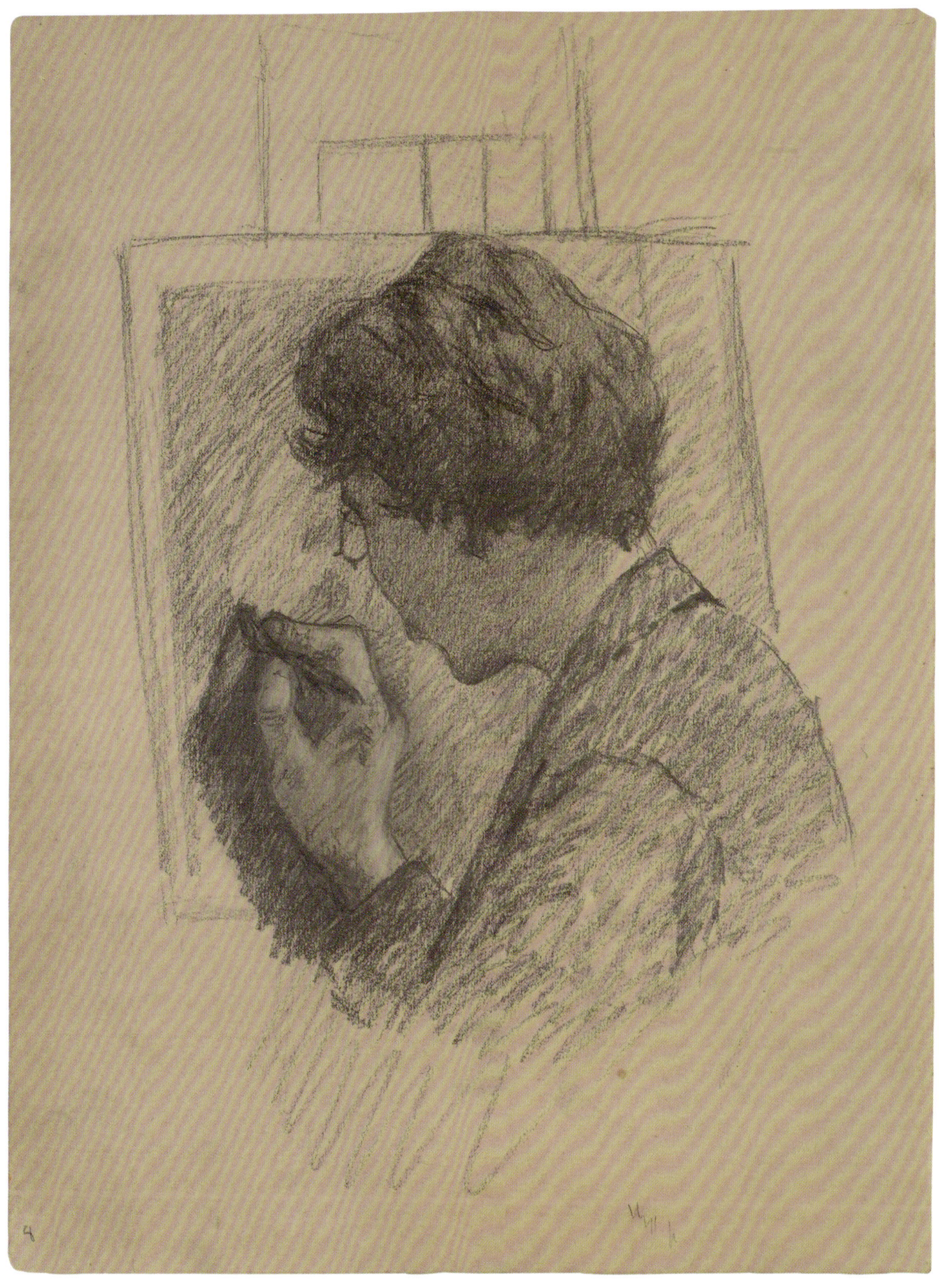

29.27.11, page 8

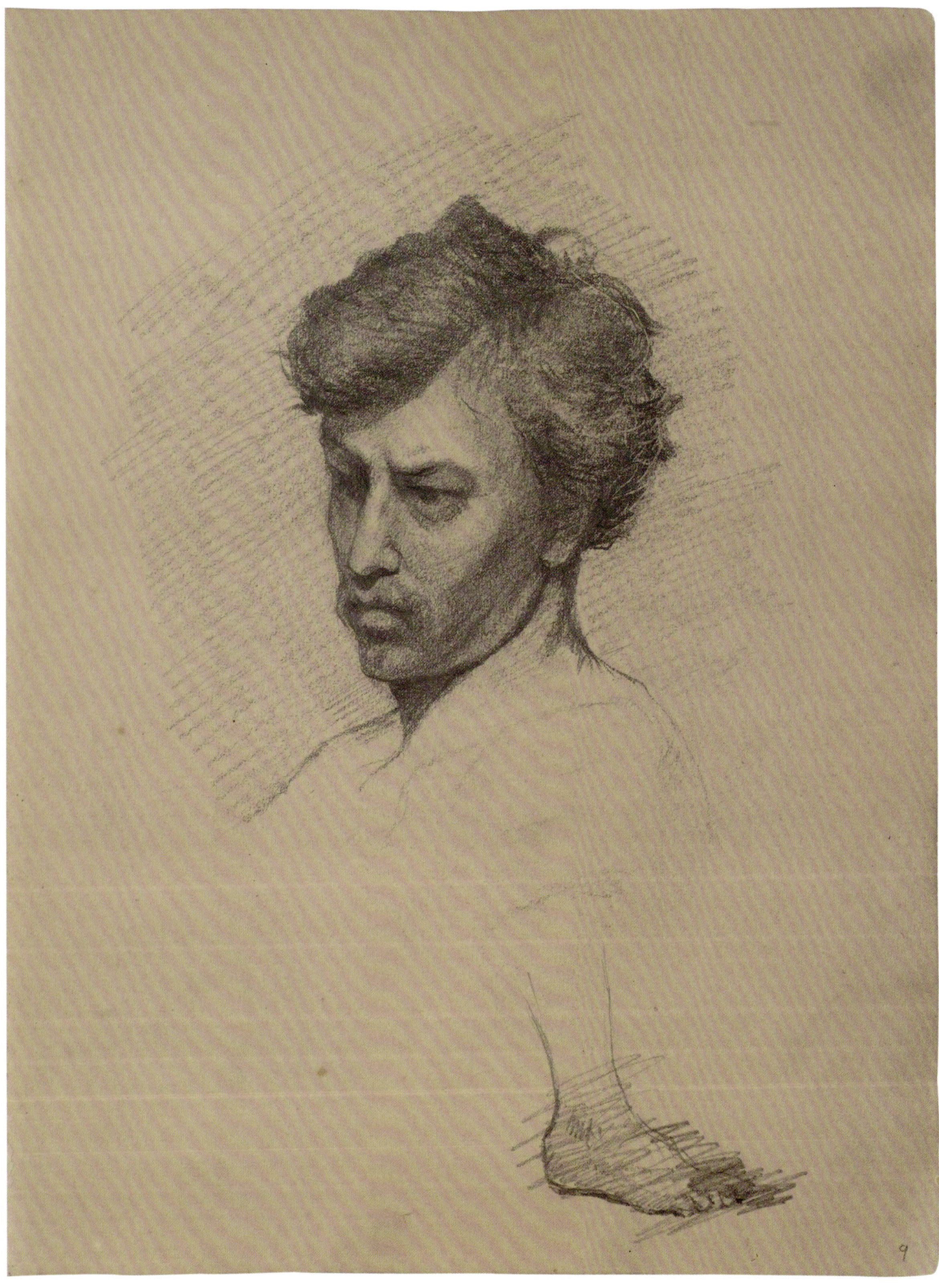

29.27.11, page 9

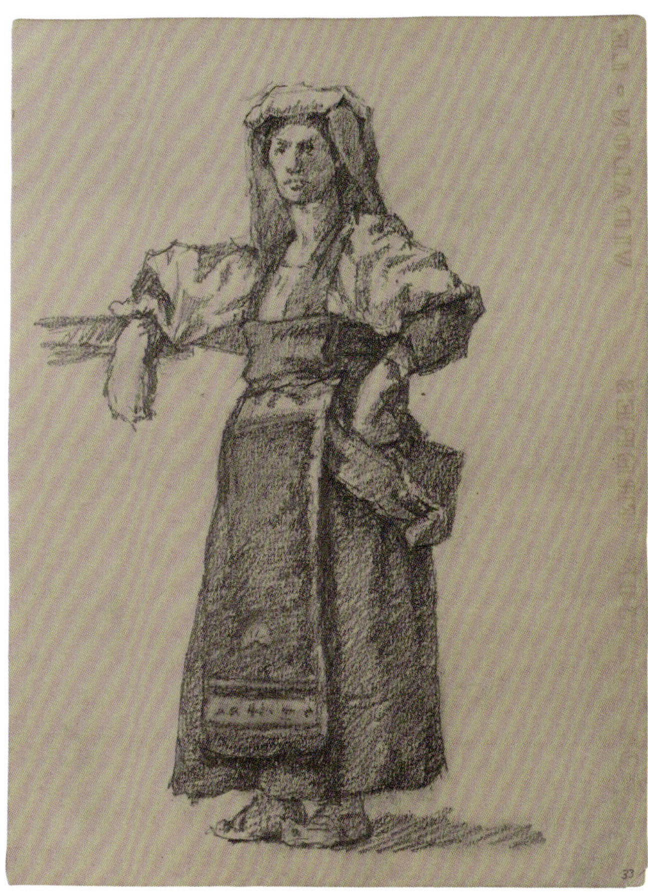

29.27.11, page 33

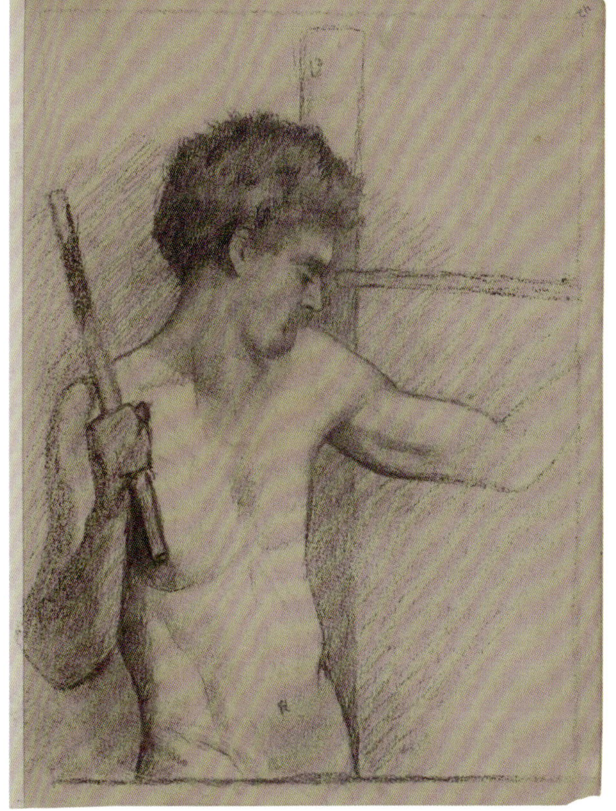

29.27.11, page 42

William Merritt Chase

American, 1849–1916

48 Self-Portrait Studies, circa 1886

Brown ink on off-white, medium-weight, moderately textured laid paper, 11½ × 16½ in. (29.2 × 41.9 cm)
Gift of Newhouse Galleries, Inc., 29.27.12

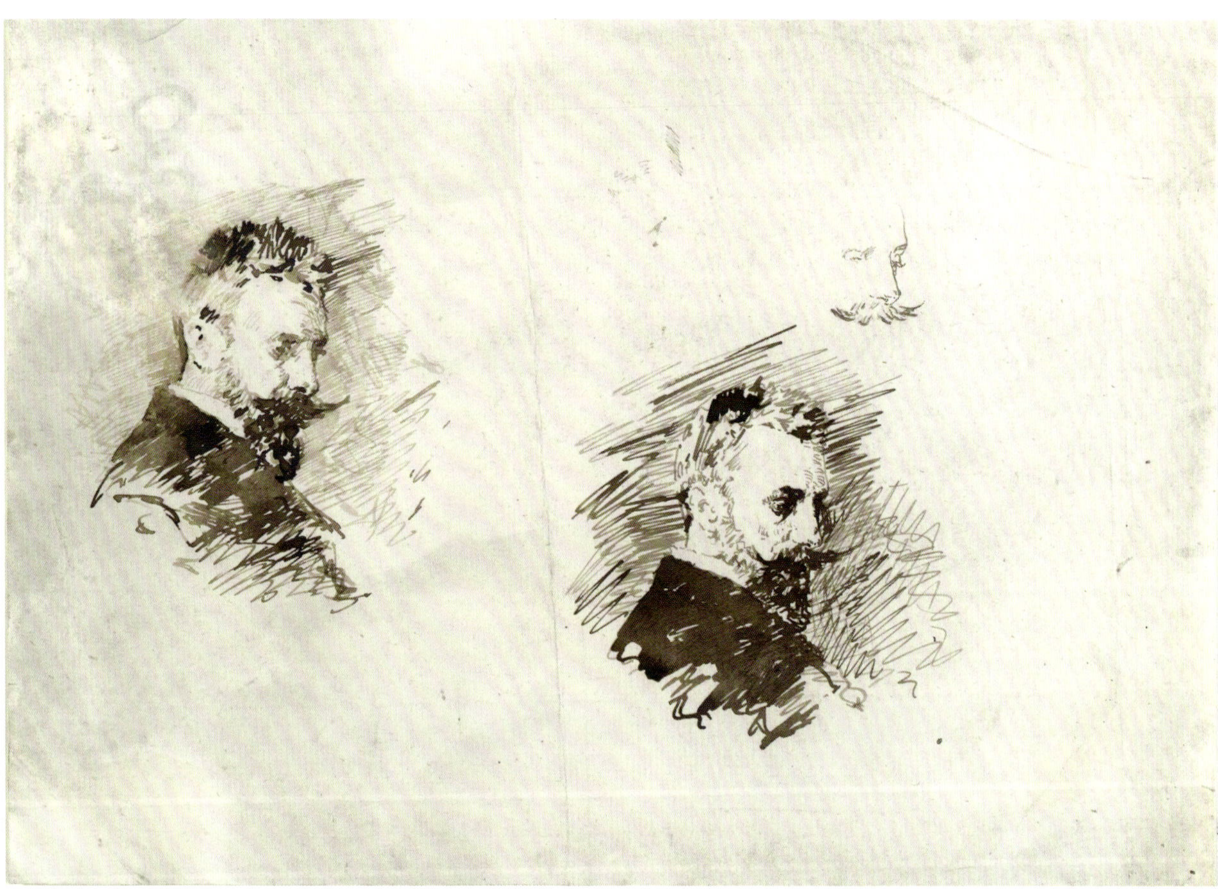

Here readily recognizable by his long, straight nose, cropped hair, pointy beard, and upturned mustache, William Merritt Chase most likely made these ink studies in preparing a self-portrait for black-and-white reproduction in S. G. W. Benjamin's 1886 book *Our American Artists*.[1] Chase rendered his likeness with short, tight lines and freer strokes and washes. He varied the concentration of the ink to create lighter and darker tones and experimented with slightly different effects in the two primary images, particularly in the coat and background shading. (He also included a partial sketch of his face, at the upper right.) With the head turned in profile and the eyes slightly downcast, the portraits exude an air of quiet introspection, in contrast to the gregarious personality and dashing presence for which the artist was well known. With the exception of pastels, drawings are relatively rare in Chase's oeuvre, and most date from his studies in Munich (see number 47). He generally did not make preparatory studies for his paintings, preferring to work directly with oil.[2]

Born in Indiana, Chase received his early training from a local portraitist in Indianapolis and during a brief stint at the National Academy of Design in New York (1869–70). In 1872 he enrolled in the Royal Academy in Munich, where he took classes in drawing (from plaster casts and live models), painting, and composition and joined the city's convivial community of American artists.

During his six-year sojourn abroad, he sent pictures to exhibitions in the United States and began to earn critical acclaim for his richly textured, realistic style. Back in New York in 1878, Chase established a large, lavishly appointed studio that displayed his cosmopolitanism through objets d'art that he had accumulated in Venice. His studio became the most famous artist's space in America, the subject of articles and his own pictures.[3] Throughout the remainder of his highly successful career, Chase created portraits, figural compositions, still lifes, and landscapes in oil and pastel, although his dark Munich-inspired palette was eventually eclipsed by brighter hues inspired by Impressionism. He was a leading figure in the New York art world and an active participant in professional organizations, including the Society of American Artists, formed in 1877 by progressive artists seeking an alternative to the conservative National Academy of Design, where Chase also served as president from 1885 to 1896. A devoted teacher, he held posts at the Art Students League and several other schools, including two he founded, the Chase School of Art (later the New York School of Art) and the Shinnecock Summer School of Art (see number 92).

1. S. G. W. Benjamin, *Our American Artists* (Boston: D. Lothrop and Company, 1886). The self-portrait, which appears on page 57, is very similar but not identical to the Brooklyn Museum's studies; the location of the original drawing for the printed image is currently unknown.
2. The catalogue raisonné estimates that Chase made 150 drawings in media other than pastel, but that number does not include this sheet and ten other drawings as well as the sketchbook (number 47) in the Brooklyn Museum's collection.
3. Ronald G. Pisano, *The Complete Catalogue of Known and Documented Work by William Merritt Chase (1849–1916)*, vol. 4, *Still Lifes, Interiors, Figures, Copies of Old Masters, and Drawings* (New Haven, Conn.: Yale University Press, 2010).
3. For a succinct discussion and image of Chase's studio, see Teresa A. Carbone, *American Paintings in the Brooklyn Museum: Artists Born by 1876* (New York: Brooklyn Museum in association with D Giles, London, 2006), 1:365–67.

— • ◉ • —

Charles Sprague Pearce

American, 1851–1914

49 Study for "The Beheading of Saint John the Baptist," circa 1881

Charcoal on cream, medium-weight, moderately textured laid paper, 6⅛ × 7 in. (15.6 × 17.8 cm)
Signed in charcoal, lower left: "CSP" [in monogram]
Inscribed in charcoal, lower left: "Fragment"
Gift of Sidney M. Katz, 85.243.2

The striking beauty of this small charcoal study by the American expatriate Charles Sprague Pearce belies its gruesome subject matter—the imminent decapitation of Saint John the Baptist at the behest of King Herod. In the manner of his teacher, the French academic painter Léon Bonnat (1833–1922), Pearce modeled his forms primarily through tone rather than line. By rubbing the side of a charcoal point against the paper and by varying the pressure to modulate the tone, he achieved gradations of lights and darks and soft, hazy edges. In addition, the textured surface of the paper, visible in the horizontal lines from the laid-paper mould, gives this drawing a rich, velvety quality.

Pearce undoubtedly used a live model to aid him in describing the saint's head and upper torso with anatomical accuracy. This naturalism is particularly evident in John's protruding collarbone and the bags under his eye. The artist also captured the personality of the martyr. Although his body is bent over and his arms pinned back, John lifts his head and stares straight ahead in an attitude of calm stoicism and unshakable faith in the face of death.

Like many American artists who came of age in the late nineteenth century, Pearce studied in Paris. He settled permanently in France, specializing in portraits, genre scenes of peasants, and history paintings—often with exotic orientalist subjects—rendered in a realistic academic style. The Museum's drawing was made as a study for his monumental work *The Beheading of Saint John the Baptist*, 1881 (figure 12),[1] which depicts the saint kneeling at the feet of his executioner in a prison cell. Exhibited in both France and the United States, this canvas—one of the artist's best-known works during his lifetime—garnered awards (including an honorable mention at the 1881 Paris Salon) but mixed reviews. The anatomical precision manifest in Pearce's preparatory drawing was not necessarily appreciated in the painting; one critic faulted it for being overly literal: "The science displayed is almost too great, indeed, since it is greater than the artistic instinct which should control it. The modeling is so realistically done that the picture as such is injured."[2]

1. The Art Institute of Chicago acquired the painting in 1882; in 1950 the museum deaccessioned it and gave it as a gift to Mundelein College, now part of Loyola University in Chicago. Loyola has no record of the work. The author thanks Sarah E. Kelly, Henry and Gilda Buchbinder Associate Curator of American Art, The Art Institute of Chicago, and Jonathan Canning, Martin D'Arcy Curator of Art, Loyola University Art Museum, for their help in trying to find this painting.

2. "Art in Philadelphia," *New York World*, Nov. 28, 1881, 2, quoted in Mary Lublin, *A Rare Elegance: The Paintings of Charles Sprague Pearce* (New York: Jordan-Volpe Gallery, 1993), 20.

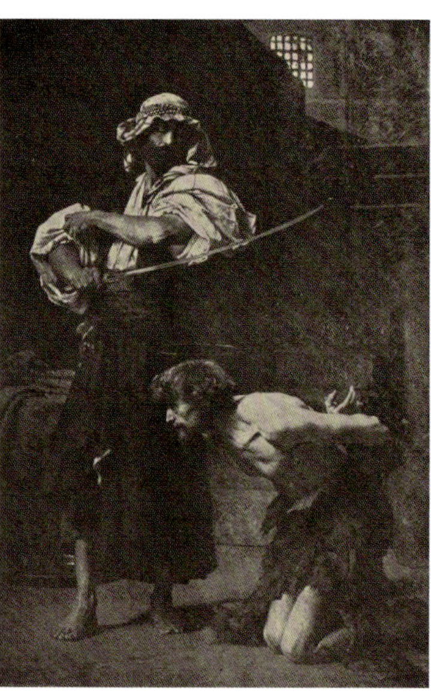

Fig. 12. Charles Sprague Pearce. *The Beheading of Saint John the Baptist*, 1881. Oil on canvas. Current location unknown. Reproduced from Charles Francis Browne, "The Permanent Collections in the Museum of the Art Institute of Chicago, VII: American Paintings," *Brush and Pencil* 2 (Sept. 1898): 253. Arts and Architecture Collection, Miriam and Ira D. Wallach Division of Art, Prints and Photographs, The New York Public Library, Astor, Lenox and Tilden Foundations

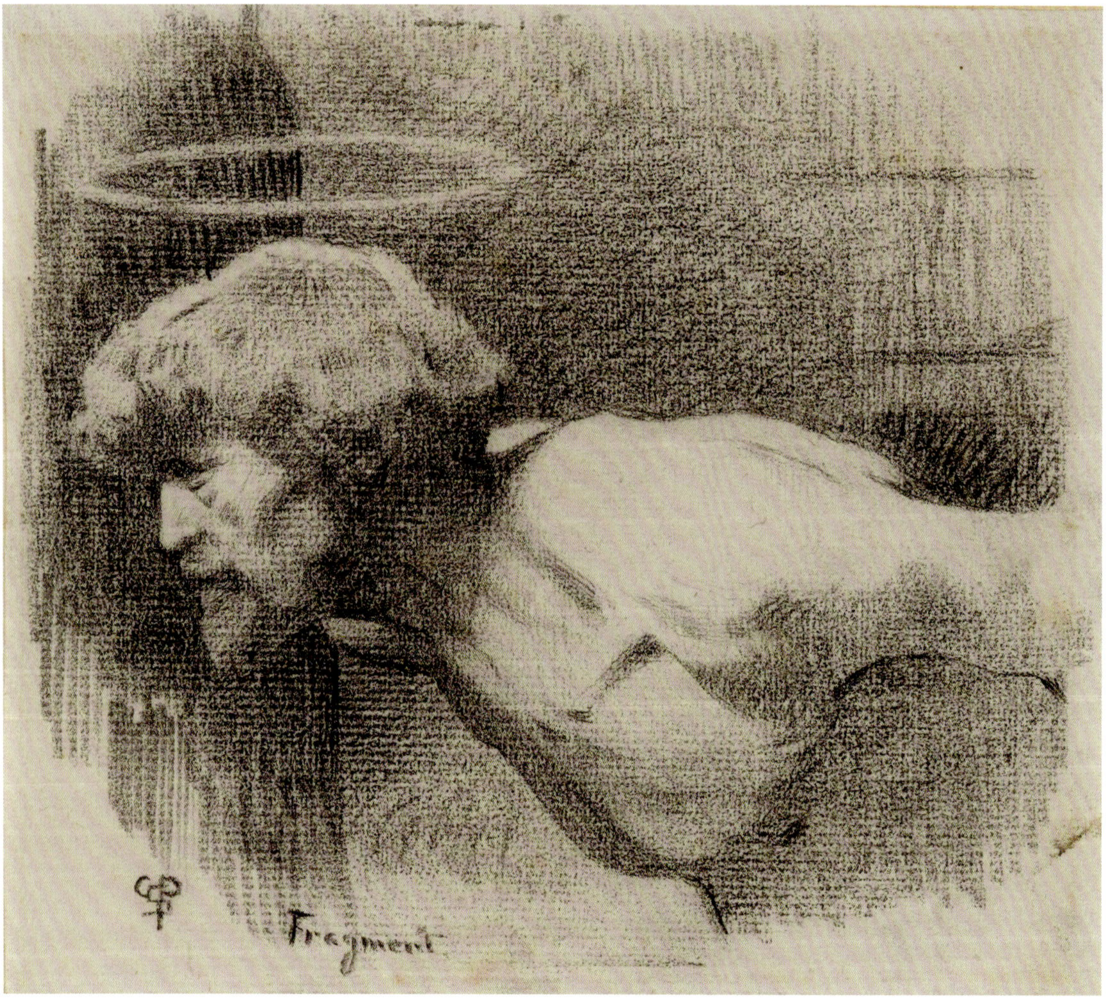

Henry Mosler

American, born Silesia, 1841–1920

50 Portrait of the Artist's Daughter, January 17, 1883

Graphite on beige, medium-weight, slightly textured wove paper, 6³⁄₁₆ × 4⁵⁄₈ in. (15.7 × 11.7 cm)
Signed and inscribed in graphite, lower right: "Henry Mosler / 17.1.83 Paris."; lower left: "to dear Edith"
Joseph F. McCrindle Collection, 2009.20.5

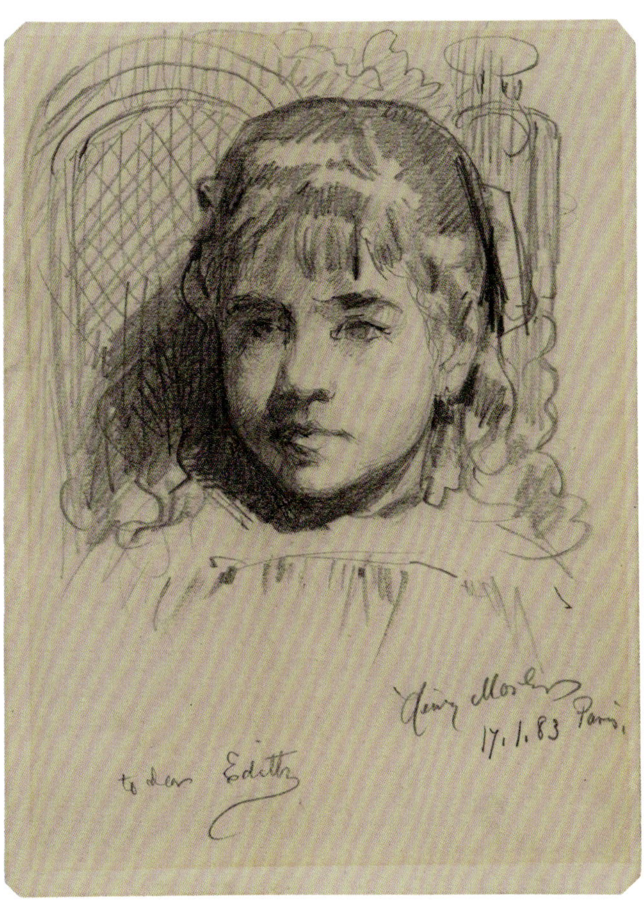

Portrait of the Artist's Daughter displays Henry Mosler's tender relationship with his daughter Edith (born mid- to late 1870s). Edith and her mother and siblings were frequent subjects of Mosler's paintings. In this quick sketch, completed while the family was living in Paris, Mosler rendered the fine wisps of Edith's curly hair, her large eyes, and the soft curve of her chin. She sits primly, properly dressed and groomed, but her sidelong gaze hints that she is longing for the posing session to end.

This portrait is typical of Mosler's "study heads," a method he learned during his training with Alexander von Wagner (1838–1919) in Munich. Through such sketches, artists familiarized themselves with the heads and faces of a small number of models so as to experiment with different techniques. As his family continued to grow, Mosler used this "study head" practice to improve his portraiture, creating intimate studies such as this drawing. Arriving in Munich in 1875, Mosler also studied at the Royal Academy under Karl Theodor von Piloty (1826–1886), a specialist in history painting and the rendering of accurate period costumes. Although genre scenes of American and European subjects remained Mosler's artistic focus, portraits and "study heads" made up a significant part of his oeuvre.

In interviews conducted during his lifetime, Mosler claimed to have been born in New York City, but his birthplace was actually Troplowitz, Silesia.[1] In 1849 the family moved to Cincinnati, where Mosler began his art career as a wood engraver and then as an illustrator for *Harper's Weekly* during the Civil War. Mosler returned to Europe in 1863 to further his artistic study and continued to divide his time between the two continents for the remainder of his career.—CG

1. Mosler Family Tree, Mosler File, American Jewish Archives, Hebrew Union College–Jewish Institute of Religion, Cincinnati; and Florence Finch Kelly, "The Art of Henry Mosler," *Broadway Magazine*, Sept. 1907, 727. These are cited in Barbara C. Gilbert, *Henry Mosler Rediscovered: A Nineteenth-Century American-Jewish Artist* (Los Angeles: Skirball Museum/ Skirball Cultural Center, 1995), 17.

Minerva Josephine Chapman

American, 1858–1947

51 **Woman in Profile,** undated

Charcoal on cream, medium-weight, moderately textured laid paper with two watermarks, 22⅛ × 16¾ in. (56.2 × 42.5 cm)
Gift of Mr. and Mrs. Morse G. Dial, Jr., 77.272. © Estate of Minerva Josephine Chapman

Minerva Chapman crafted this bravura bust-length portrait of a woman seen from behind with an intuitive understanding of the properties of the powdery charcoal medium applied to textured paper. After outlining the sitter's facial features with a thin line, the artist modeled the forms primarily through sfumato or smoky effects with subtle variations in tone. Reserved areas of paper produce brighter passages and white highlights. Chapman focused her attention on the face, paying careful attention to such details as the precise contour of the nose, the intricate forms of the ear, and the folds of skin in the neck; the hair and fringed kerchief are more broadly described. The sitter is unidentified, but certain resemblances to Chapman herself (figure 13)—especially the full cheeks and strong nose—hint that the work may be one of the artist's self-portraits, which she executed in various media.

Despite its powerful naturalism, the portrait limits the viewer's insight into the sitter's personality and character: the woman literally turns away from the observer and gazes off to the side of the composition. Her facial expression is inscrutable, although she has a contemplative air that suggests she is lost in her own thoughts. Here Chapman subordinated portraiture's conventional dictates of revelation to a sense of privacy and psychological interiority.

Chapman's career coincided with a dramatic growth in the number of professional female artists in the late nineteenth century, when women gained access to advanced artistic training and exhibition opportunities. Raised in Chicago, she attended various academies in Chicago, Munich, and Paris, including the Parisian school of the plein air painter Charles Lasar (1856–1956), which attracted many female students. Although she spent much of her professional life in Paris, she participated actively in exhibitions and artists' organizations in the United States and garnered international acclaim. She was best known for her work in miniature painting, the focus of her artistic output after 1900.[1] A prolific and dedicated artist, Chapman also produced landscapes, still lifes, and portraits in other media. The relatively free handling of charcoal in this drawing represents a departure from the meticulous detail and controlled technique required in her miniatures.

1. Chapman made more than 181 tiny paintings (mostly portraits) in oil on canvas or watercolor on ivory. Paul J. Staiti, *Minerva J. Chapman* (South Hadley, Mass.: Mount Holyoke College Art Museum in association with the National Museum of Women in the Arts, 1986), 14.

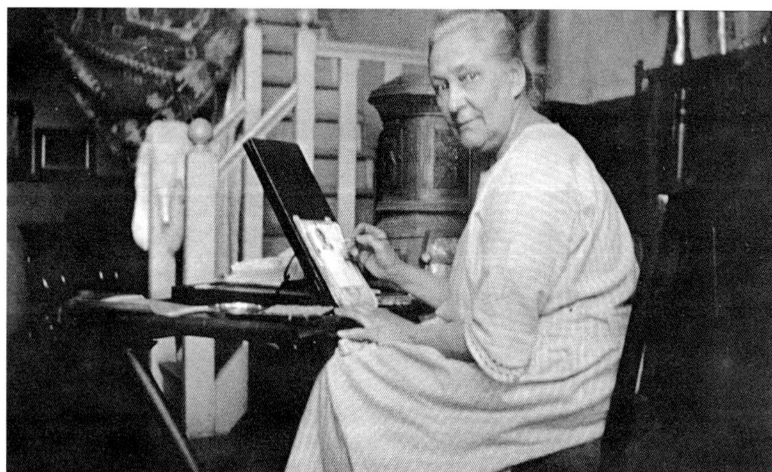

Fig. 13. *Minerva Chapman Painting in Her Studio/Home, Palo Alto, California*, circa 1938. Collection of Mary Dial. © Estate of Minerva J. Chapman. Reproduced from *Minerva J. Chapman: A Retrospective Exhibition* (Washington, D.C.: Adams, Davidson Galleries, 1971), page 9

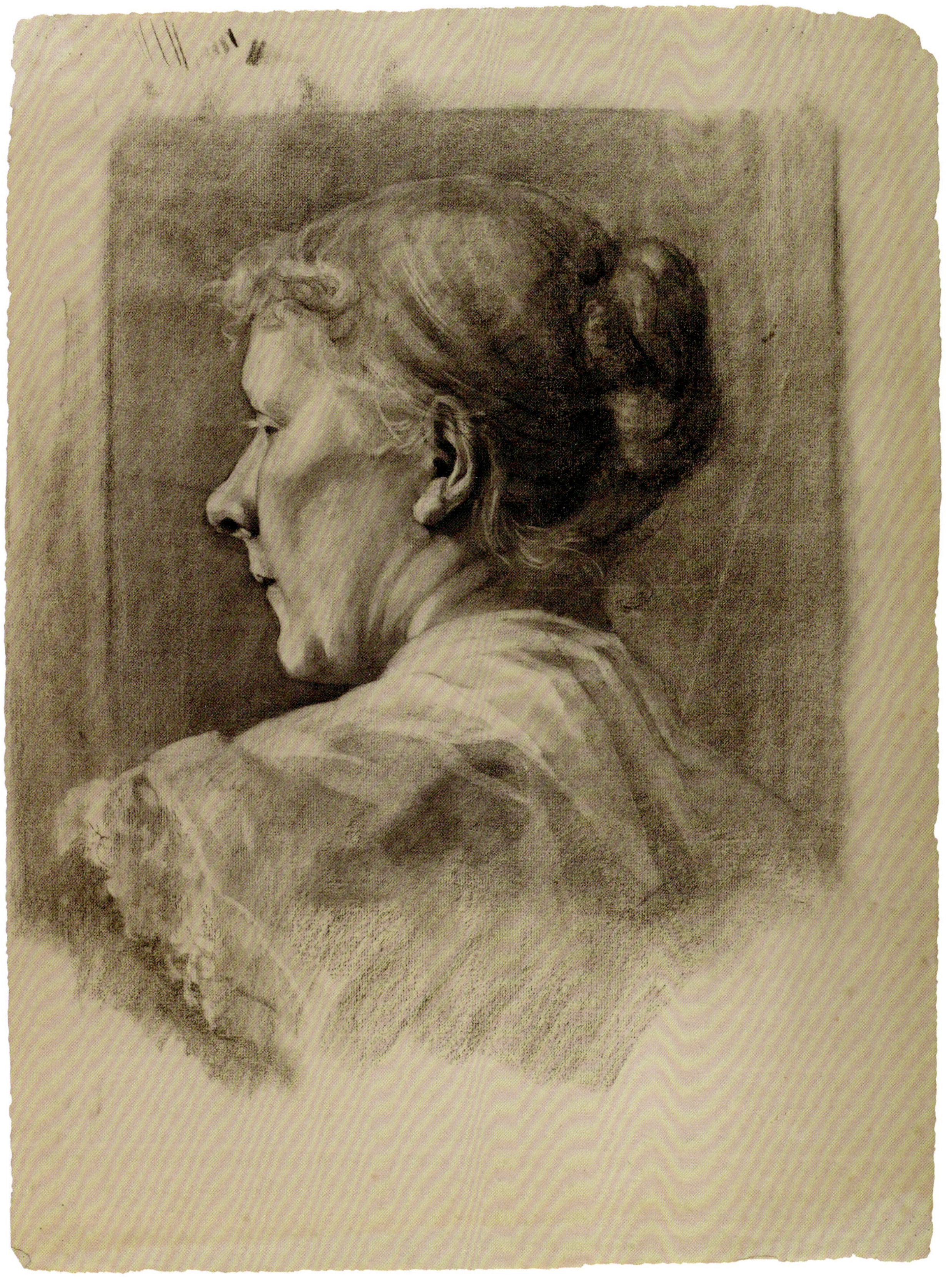

J. Carroll Beckwith

American, 1852–1917

52 Portrait of Minnie Clark, circa 1890s

Charcoal and pastel on blue-fibered, medium-weight, moderately textured laid paper, 22⅜ × 18¼ in. (56.8 × 46.4 cm)
Signed in charcoal, upper left: "CARROLL BECKWITH"
Gift of J. Carroll Beckwith, 17.127

In his tender portrait of Minnie Clark (life dates unknown), executed in black charcoal with accents of colored pastel, J. Carroll Beckwith gracefully modeled his sitter's facial features with a sensitivity that captures the hardworking model's beauty and strength. Beckwith's loose handling of the medium in the high-collared dress and in the almost illegible interior space, including part of a framed picture, focuses attention on the more detailed rendering of the young woman's direct gaze, strong jaw, and soft lips. Clark, "the queen of professional models in this country," was portrayed by many artists, including Thomas Wilmer Dewing (1851–1938) (figure 14).[1] She began posing for Beckwith about 1890, quickly becoming the artist's favorite model and a close companion and daughter figure to Beckwith and his wife, Bertha.[2]

Best known as the face of the original "Gibson Girl," Clark appeared in **Charles Dana Gibson**'s famous and widely emulated illustrations of fashionable, young, middle-class women, images that set the standard for feminine beauty in that period (see number 53). Beckwith's more naturalistic and humanizing representation of Clark stands in great contrast to this idealized Gibson Girl type. Some competition emerged between the two artists over Clark's modeling time, and in March 1892 Beckwith confided in his diary, "I had Minnie Clark to pose this afternoon. She is certainly the finest model I ever saw and I do not blame Gibson for keeping her entirely to himself."[3] Beckwith, who took a strong interest in Clark's well-being, believed that Gibson had more than a professional interest in the young woman.[4]

Primarily known for his Impressionist-inspired portraits and genre scenes, Beckwith began training in the Paris atelier of Charles Auguste Émile Durant, better known as Carolus-Duran (1837–1917), in Paris alongside **John Singer Sargent**. Disappointed in the lack of drawing instruction, Beckwith decided to supplement Carolus-Duran's teachings with enrollment at the École des Beaux-Arts and additional drawing lessons. When he returned to New York in 1878, Beckwith was hired to teach drawing at the Art Students League. For the remainder of his career, the artist and instructor strongly believed "that the hand should first be taught to be the skilled servant of the mind and the eye. . . . This trade mastery should permit him or her then, and only then, to essay a certain degree of original expression, but still under the guidance of a recognized authority."[5]—CG

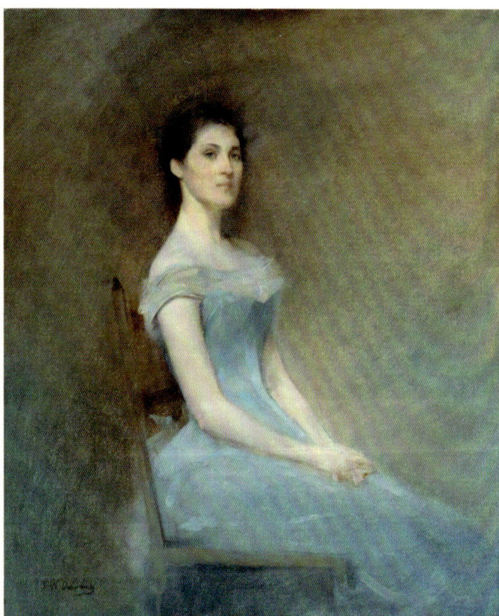

Fig. 14. Thomas Wilmer Dewing (American, 1851–1938). *Figure of a Girl in Blue (Portrait of Miss Minnie Clark)*, circa 1892. Oil on canvas, 36⅜ × 29¼ in. (93.4 × 74.3 cm). University of Michigan Museum of Art, Ann Arbor, Gift of Mr. Raymond C. Smith, 1968/2.68

1. Robert Howard Russell, "How Charles Dana Gibson Started," *Ladies' Home Journal*, Oct. 1902, 8, quoted in Daniel Delis Hill, *Advertising to the American Woman, 1900–1999* (Columbus: Ohio State University Press, 2002), 92.

2. Throughout his diary, Beckwith mentioned his affection for Clark and her importance to his work. At his summer home in Onteora, New York, on July 14, 1896, he wrote to Clark asking her to visit, claiming that he could not get to work without her. On September 19, 1899, he wrote, "Were Minnie our own daughter we could not do more for her or work harder"; J. Carroll Beckwith Papers, National Academy of Design, New York.

3. Diary entry, Mar. 19, 1892, ibid.

4. Ibid., Jan. 6, 1894: "[Minnie Clark] is certainly one of the finest models I ever knew and I do not blame Dana Gibson for falling in love with her." See also David Slater, "The Fount of Inspiration: Minnie Clark, the Art Workers' Club for Women, and Performances of American Girlhood," *Winterthur Portfolio* 39 (Winter 2004): 229–58.

5. J. Carroll Beckwith, "Right Art Training. Carroll Beckwith Advises Americans to Follow the French," *New York Times*, Aug. 5, 1917, E2.

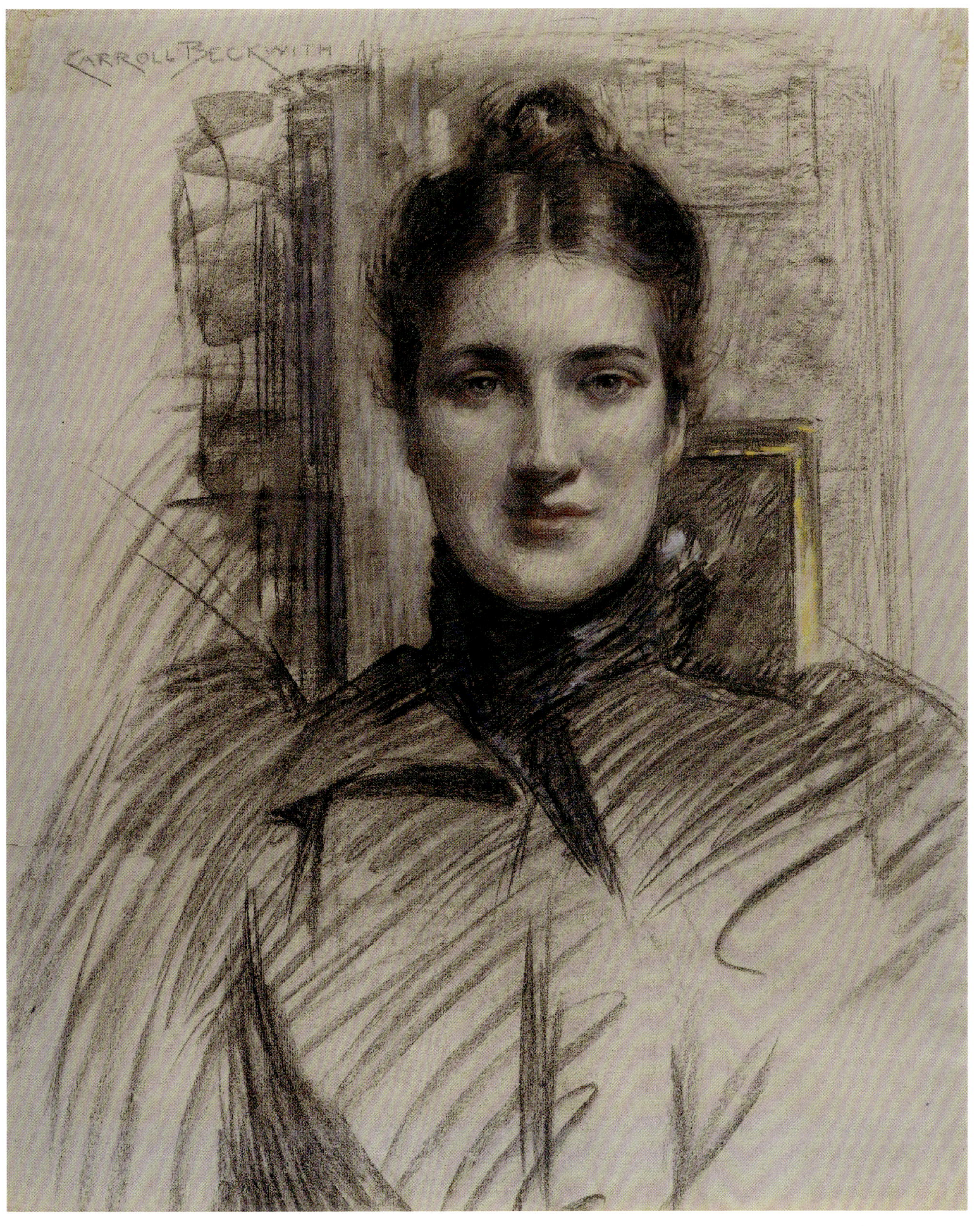

Charles Dana Gibson

American, 1867–1944

53 Young Woman Struck with Cupid's Arrows, circa 1900

Black ink on cream, medium-weight, slightly textured wove paper, 10 × 12 in. (25.4 × 30.5 cm)
Gift of Michael Cohen, 69.85

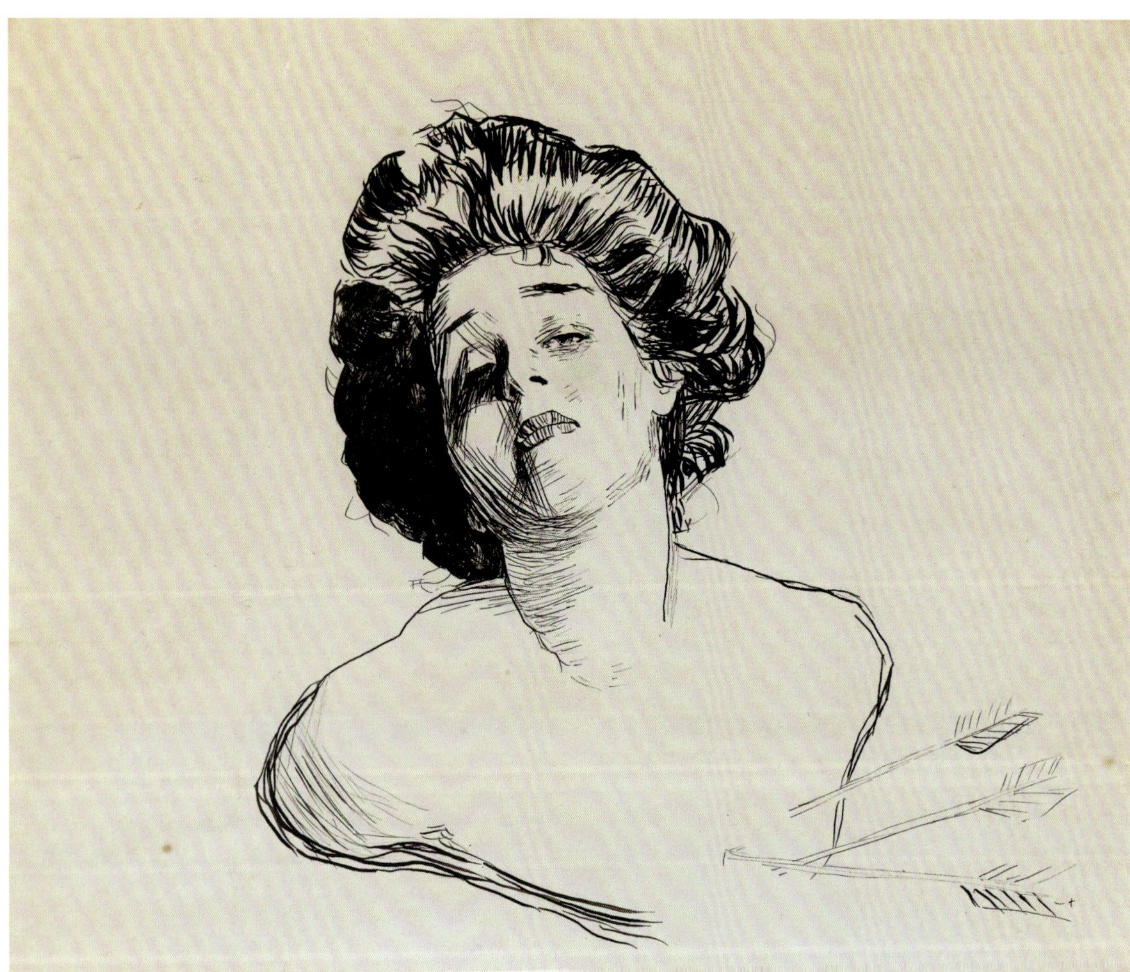

This drawing, by the immensely popular and influential illustrator Charles Dana Gibson, exemplifies the artist's mature style. Most likely a study for one of his well-known "Gibson Girl" illustrations, it portrays a young woman who has been struck by three arrows, with her head thrown back as if in ecstasy and her heavy eyelids barely open. The allusion to Cupid suggests that this is a symbolic portrait of a woman in love. Gibson often depicted themes of romance between the sexes. This image is rendered primarily in simple outline with only light cross-hatching around the woman's face to create shading, a technique that focuses attention on her rich, inky black hair and the graceful lines of her neck and shoulders. Gibson's illustrations benefited from the revival of pen-and-ink drawing in the late nineteenth century, and his style became the most emulated of the time.[1]

The Gibson Girl was an attractive and youthful middle-class woman who became the ideal of feminine beauty, and her clothing and hair became the standard style, imitated by women throughout the country. Embodying the modern American woman who was making gains in education and professionalism, she was often depicted as dominating her male companion or exasperated by society's standards. It is believed that Minnie Clark (life dates unknown), also the subject of the Brooklyn Museum's portrait by **J. Carroll Beckwith** (see number 52), served as the original model for the Gibson Girl. Although she lived in poverty as an artist's model, Clark became the icon for American female beauty and independence in the 1890s.

After studying in New York, London, and Paris, Gibson submitted his first drawing in 1887 to *Life* magazine. He soon became a regular contributor and eventually the magazine's editor, and also contributed to other major publications in New

York. Gibson produced his Gibson Girl and equally attractive and confident "Gibson Man" illustrations until the outbreak of World War I, when he began illustrating patriotic propaganda and focusing on oil painting.—CG

1. Henry C. Pitz, "Charles Dana Gibson: Delineator of an Age," in Edmund Vincent Gillon, *The Gibson Girl and Her America: The Best Drawings of Charles Dana Gibson* (New York: Dover Publications, 1969), ix.

Elie Nadelman

American, born Poland, 1882–1946

54 **Head,** undated (possibly 1920s)

Graphite on cream, thin, smooth wove paper, 11 × 8½ in. (27.9 × 21.6 cm)
Gift of Virginia Zabriskie, 1997.202.2. © Estate of Elie Nadelman

Although primarily known as a sculptor of elegantly stylized figures, Elie Nadelman was also an accomplished draftsman. His drawings generally parallel his sculpture in subject matter and style, reflecting his shifts from proto-Cubist fragmentation to reductive classicism to idiosyncratic mannerist distortions. Female heads—both individualized portraits and idealized types—appeared regularly in his oeuvre. This delicately sketched graphite image of a woman's head in profile most likely falls into the latter category. In this work, Nadelman's main emphasis is on outline and the planar flatness of the picture surface. He radically abstracted the features into essentialized shapes, representing the ear as a curved line, the lips as two parallel hatches, and the upper profile from forehead to nose as a continuous straight edge. There is no modeling of the rounded masses of the face and no physiognomic detail (not even an eye).

Nadelman rendered this image with light, flowing strokes of his pencil, often going over an area several times as if experimenting with his line. The drawing's spontaneous

quality suggests that it might be a quick preliminary study for one of his many sculptures of the female head. In those three-dimensional works, Nadelman also simplified human anatomy and often styled the hair as seen here, in an updo with a roll across the forehead (figure 15). In its shape and pose (with sharply uptilted chin), however, the drawing's head does not closely resemble any of the sculptural versions.

Born in Warsaw, Nadelman studied at the Warsaw Art Academy for four years before traveling to Munich, where the city's collections of classical sculpture made a deep impression on him. He moved to Paris in 1904 and began exhibiting his works to great acclaim and becoming involved in vanguard cultural circles. The outbreak of World War I drove Nadelman to New York. His success continued in America, where he enjoyed the support of key promoters of modernism, including Alfred Stieglitz and Gertrude Vanderbilt Whitney. Nadelman became particularly interested in American folk art, and in the 1920s he increasingly devoted his efforts to collecting.

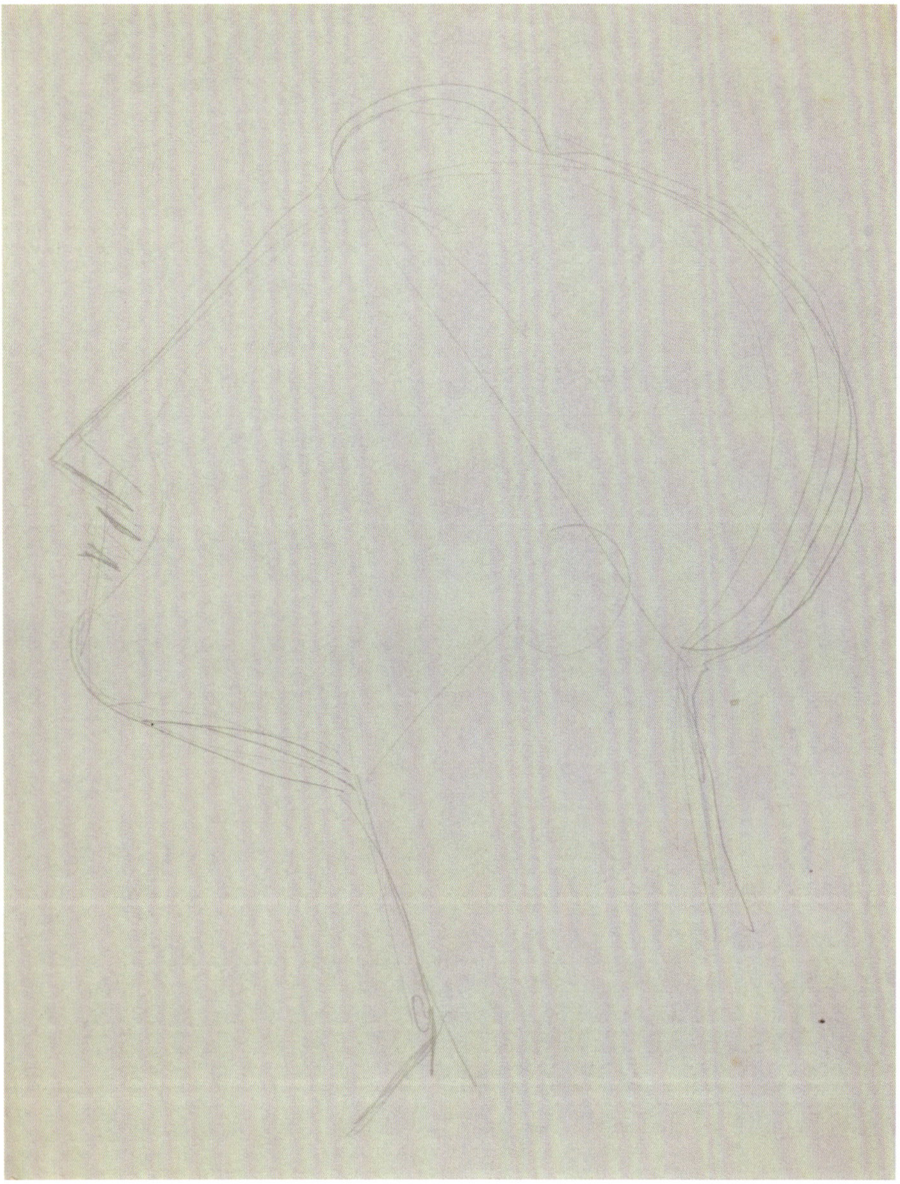

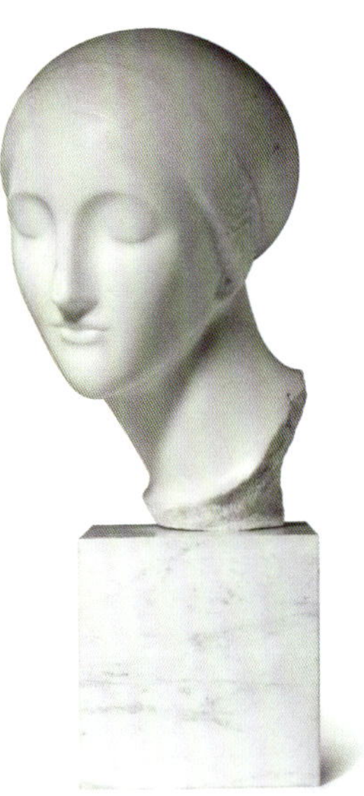

Fig. 15. Elie Nadelman. *Early Ideal Head (La Mystérieuse)*, circa 1916–17. Marble, height 7½ in. (19.1 cm). Private collection. Photograph: © Christie's Images / The Bridgeman Art Library

William Zorach

American, born Lithuania, 1887–1966

55 Profile of a Woman's Head, undated

Graphite on cream, medium-weight, smooth wove paper, 11⅞ × 8⅞ in. (30.2 × 22.5 cm)
Signed in graphite, lower left: "William Zorach"
Gift from the collection of Estelle and Jay Sam Unger, 1996.161.3. © The Zorach Collection, LLC

Like many modernist artists, William Zorach embraced a reductive approach to representation, distilling a motif to its essential forms and eliminating unnecessary details. In portraiture, this approach emphasizes the most distinctive aspects of a sitter's appearance but also reduces the amount of available visual information. Zorach's graphite drawing of an unidentified woman wavers between these competing effects of individualization and generalization. Using minimal, assured strokes of the pencil, the artist delineated the sitter's profile and long tresses—a style that he adopted in many of his drawings, beginning in the late 1910s (see also numbers 15, 43). He added a few lighter touches to suggest facial features and long, undulating strokes to describe the flowing hair. Overall, his linear style flattens the head and emphasizes the two-dimensionality of the image and the picture plane.

The gestural immediacy of Zorach's lines conveys the sense that this image is a spontaneous record of his creative impulses and thought processes. He acknowledged this documentary function of drawing: "Drawing is very important. It is the means whereby I capture the fleeting beauty of movement and gesture and make available for future use my observation and sensitivity to life around me."[1] The link between the artist's mind and hand was also paramount in Zorach's artistic process for his sculpture, the work for which he is best known. He was one of the leading American practitioners and proponents of direct carving, or working hands-on with the medium.

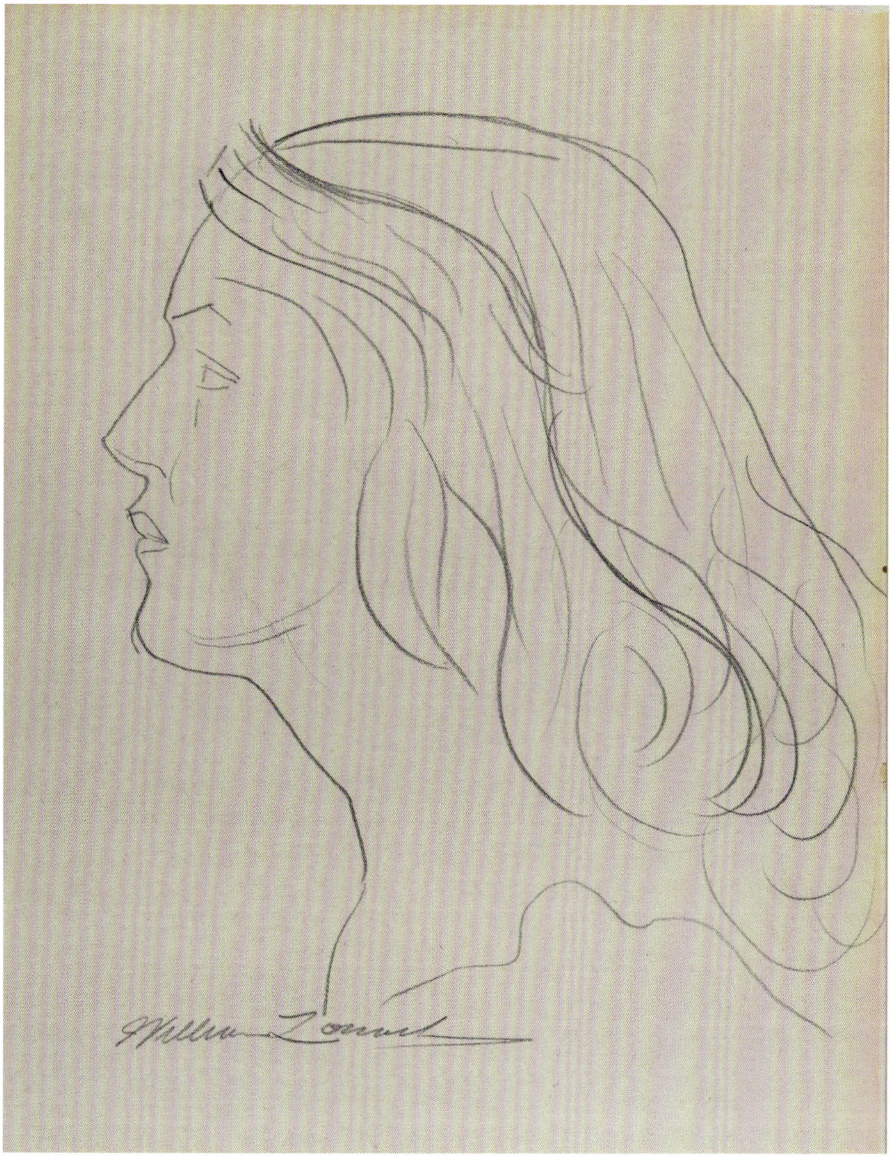

In preparation for a career as a painter, Zorach studied at art schools in Cleveland and New York, mastering academic draftsmanship. Early in his career, he supported himself as a commercial lithographer, further developing his facility with drawing. An eye-opening sojourn in Paris in 1910–11 led to a decade of artistic experimentation with progressive styles and various media, including oil painting, watercolor, printmaking, and drawing. By 1922 Zorach had largely abandoned painting for sculpture. Working primarily in wood and stone, he sculpted figural and animal subjects in a mildly abstracted, naturalistic style. Zorach continued to draw throughout the remainder of his career, often in relation to his sculptural work.

1. William Zorach, *Zorach Explains Sculpture: What It Means and How It Is Made* (New York: American Artists Group, 1947), 61.

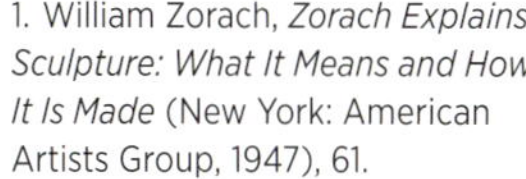

Marguerite Thompson Zorach

American, 1887–1968

56 **Marianne Moore,** circa 1925

Graphite on beige, medium-weight, smooth wove paper, 11 × 8½ in. (27.9 × 21.6 cm)
Gift of Mr. and Mrs. Tessim Zorach, 80.87. © The Zorach Collection, LLC

In this portrait drawing, Marguerite Zorach captured the distinctive appearance of the modernist poet Marianne Moore (1887–1972) in a spare outline. The sitter is easily recognizable by her slender face and neck, elongated fingers, and typical mannish dress, consisting of a loose jacket over a wide-collared shirt and cravat (figure 16). Using thin, economical pencil strokes, Zorach reduced forms into flattened planes and simplified shapes. Notwithstanding its abstracted quality, the portrait crackles with personality, conveyed through Zorach's use of expressive lines and physical distortions, particularly in the exaggeratedly long fingers and slight asymmetry of the face.

This drawing most likely dates to February 1925, when Moore and her mother visited Zorach's Greenwich Village studio to sit for a painted double portrait (National Portrait Gallery, Smithsonian Institution, Washington, D.C.).[1] Although the oil painting is more realistically modeled, both portraits depict Moore wearing the same clothing (though she wears the hat only in the drawing) and posed rigidly in a chair whose armrest terminates in a rounded knob. At the time of this sitting, Moore's career was on the rise: she had just won the Dial Award for Literature for *Observations* (1924), a book of verse that secured her reputation as an innovative force in American letters.[2] Zorach and Moore had first met in 1916 through mutual friends in New York's vanguard cultural circles. The poet greatly admired Zorach's richly colored paintings and embroideries, using them as the source of inspiration for her poem "In the Days of Prismatic Color" (1923).[3]

Raised in California, Zorach spent a formative four years studying art in Paris (1908–11), where she became familiar with the latest currents in European art and met many progressive artists, including **William Zorach**, whom she married in 1912. Settling in New York, she developed her own style influenced by the angular forms of Cubism and the vivid hues of Fauvism. She continued to work in a modernist idiom throughout her career, creating landscape and figural imagery in paintings, prints, and embroidered textiles. Both Zorachs were actively involved in the art scene, and their home served as a regular meeting place for artists and writers.

1. *Marianne Moore and Her Mother* is dated 1919, but art historians agree that this date is incorrect and that the painting was executed in 1925. See Linda Leavell, *Marianne Moore and the Visual Arts* (Baton Rouge: Louisiana State University Press, 1995), 37–40, especially 40n60.

2. Zorach published another portrait drawing of Moore to accompany a review of the poet's work; see William Carlos Williams, "Marianne Moore," *Dial* 79 (May 1925): 393.

3. See Leavell, *Marianne Moore and the Visual Arts*, 148–51.

Fig. 16. Nicolas Sarony Studio. *Marianne Moore*, 1924. Photograph, 8 × 5⅞ in. (20.3 × 14.9 cm). Rosenbach Museum and Library, Philadelphia, 2006.5116/MM XII:03:03a

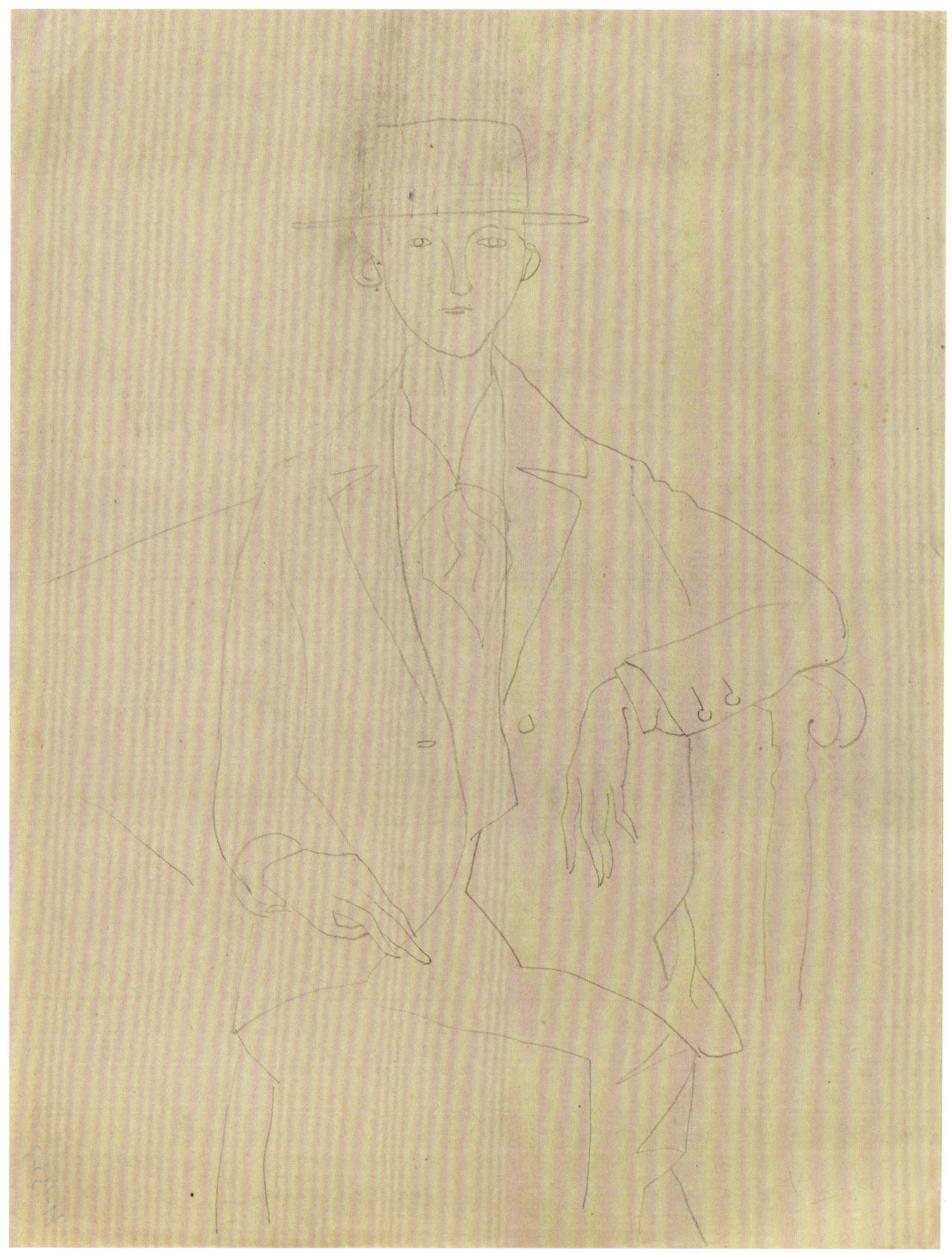

George Copeland Ault

American, 1891–1948

57 Girl's Head, 1927

Graphite on cream, moderately thick, slightly textured wove paper, 15⅝ × 13⁵⁄₁₆ in. (39.7 × 33.8 cm)
Signed in graphite, lower right: "G. C. Ault '27."
Gift of Maurice Vanderwoude in memory of Louise Ault, 81.250.1

Like many modernist portraits, George Copeland Ault's *Girl's Head* displays dynamic tensions between illusionistic three-dimensionality and the flat surface of the paper, between representation and abstraction, and between individualization and idealization. It portrays an austere, schematized head of an unidentified young woman, shown in three-quarter profile. Truncated at the neck, the head floats against a plain background, taking on an ethereal quality, yet the girl's physiognomy is distinctive enough to suggest she was an actual person rather than a generic or idealized type. Ault reduced the forms of the head into schematized shapes: the hair, for example, appears as a single helmetlike mass, with only a few discrete lines to indicate bangs. The hard-edged, relatively dark outline of the figure's silhouette and the broad areas of blank paper across her cheek emphasize the flatness of the paper support, while the modulated shading created with the side of the pencil endows the subject with a volumetric, almost sculptural presence.

Born in Cleveland, Ohio, into a prosperous manufacturing family, Ault spent much of his childhood in London, studying art at the Slade School and St. John's Wood Art School. The family returned to the United States in 1911, and by 1922 Ault had established himself as a painter in New York City. He worked primarily in a Precisionist style that reduced urban and industrial forms into pristine, simplified geometries (see number 107). Ault's pictures are distinguished from those of Charles Sheeler (1883–1965) and other Precisionists by their lyrical and mysterious mood. This quality was informed by his exposure to Surrealism on a 1924 trip to Paris and by his personal struggles with poor health, depression, alcoholism, and the tragic loss of several family members. Ault primarily depicted urban scenes, rural landscapes, and still lifes, only occasionally exploring the human figure. Although its subject matter is atypical, *Girl's Head* exemplifies his extraordinary skill as a draftsman. One contemporary critic praised Ault's drawings for "exhibit[ing] a sensitiveness of tone and quality."[1]

1. This critic was reviewing an exhibition of Ault's paintings, watercolors, and drawings at the Downtown Gallery (*Head of a Girl* was not included). "Downtown Gallery," *New York Herald Tribune*, Nov. 25, 1928, sec. 7, p. 10.

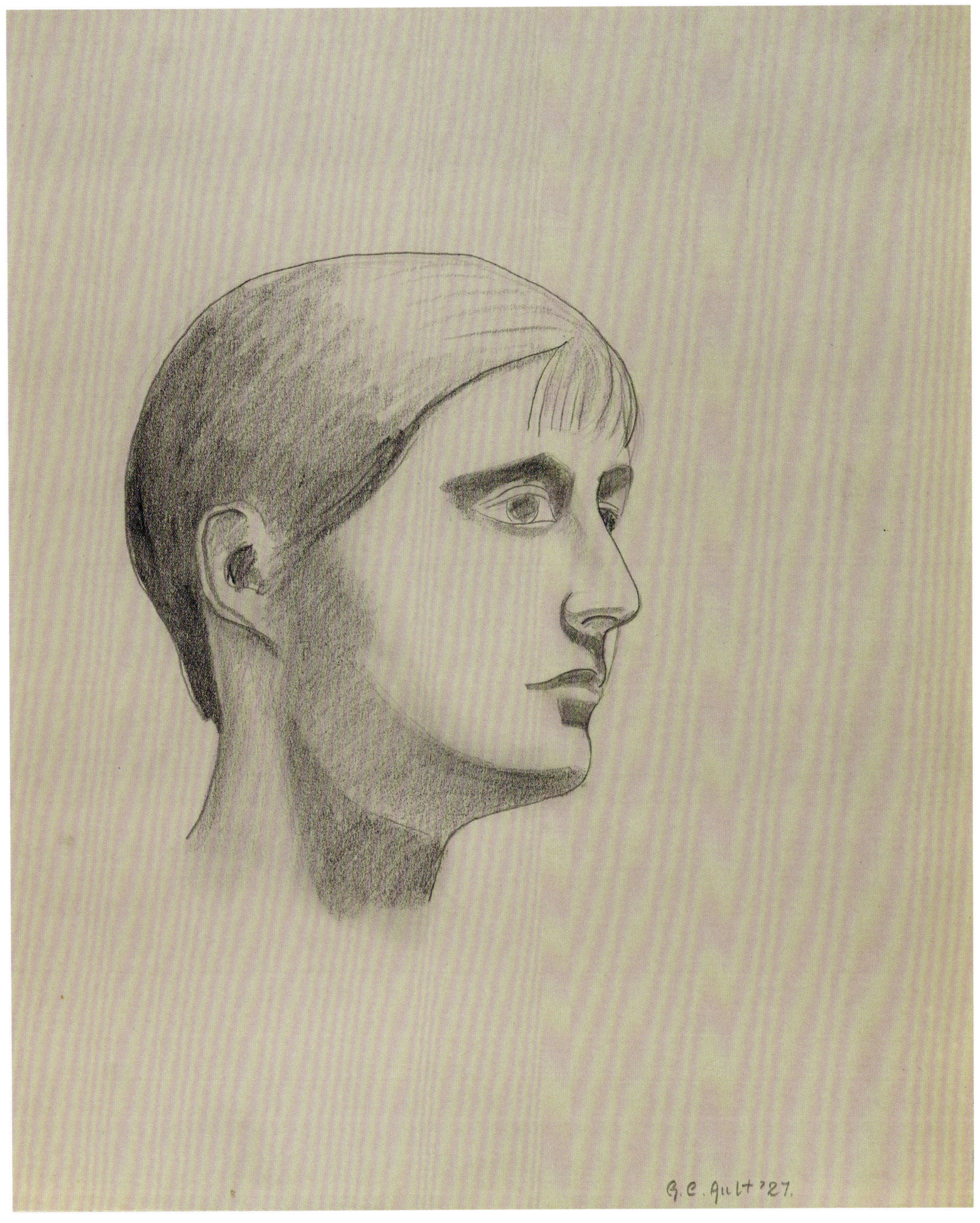

Stefan Hirsch

American, born Germany, 1899–1964

58 Siamese Cat, circa 1940

Charcoal on cream, thin, smooth wove paper, 17 × 14 in. (43.2 × 35.6 cm)
Signed in graphite, lower right: "Hirsch"
Gift of Janis Conner and Joel Rosenkranz, 2008.69. © Estate of Elsa Rogo and Stefan Hirsch

This elegantly spare drawing appears to be a quickly executed sketch of a Siamese cat caught in the moment between stasis and motion. With a delicate touch and minimal modeling, Stefan Hirsch used a combination of fuzzy charcoal lines and rubbings to capture the contour and distinctive markings of the animal as it stared intently at an unseen object off to the left while lifting a paw preparing to swipe at something. Forms are suggested with abbreviated strokes and sketchy passages that in some areas, such as the cat's haunch and back foot, approach abstraction. Hirsch also integrated broad passages of blank paper into his design, even leaving gaps in the cat's outline that are completed in the viewer's imagination. This drawing's expressive characterization of feline curiosity and grace indicates personal familiarity with the subject. Indeed, Hirsch and his wife, the artist Elsa Rogo (1901–1996), owned cats, and *Siamese Cat* may be a portrait of a beloved pet.[1]

Born in Germany to American parents, Hirsch spent his childhood in Europe, where he had access to great collections of traditional fine art and was exposed to progressive developments in contemporary art. After settling in New York in 1919, he was drawn into the modernist circle of Hamilton Easter Field (1873–1922), an artist, teacher, collector, and critic whose home in Brooklyn and summer school in Ogunquit, Maine, served as regular gathering places for vanguard artists. Hirsch worked in a range of artistic styles, exploring different subjects, including early Cubist experiments, Precisionist industrial scenes, Social Realist murals, and late abstractions. In the 1930s he increasingly devoted his efforts to teaching, championing artistic individuality with his students at Bennington College (1934–40), the Art Students League (1940–46), and Bard College (1942–61).

1. Hirsch's voluminous correspondence with Elsa and their friends contains numerous references to their cats. See, for example, Richard Wistar to Hirsch and Rogo, July 22, 1931, box 1, "Correspondence Personal, 1930s" folder; Mollie Friedman to Hirsch and Rogo, Sept. 22, 1937, box 1, "Correspondence Personal, 1930s" folder; and Hirsch to Rogo, Feb. 26, 1945, box 2, "Correspondence, 1945" folder; all Stefan Hirsch and Elsa Rogo Papers, 1926–1985, Archives of American Art, Smithsonian Institution.

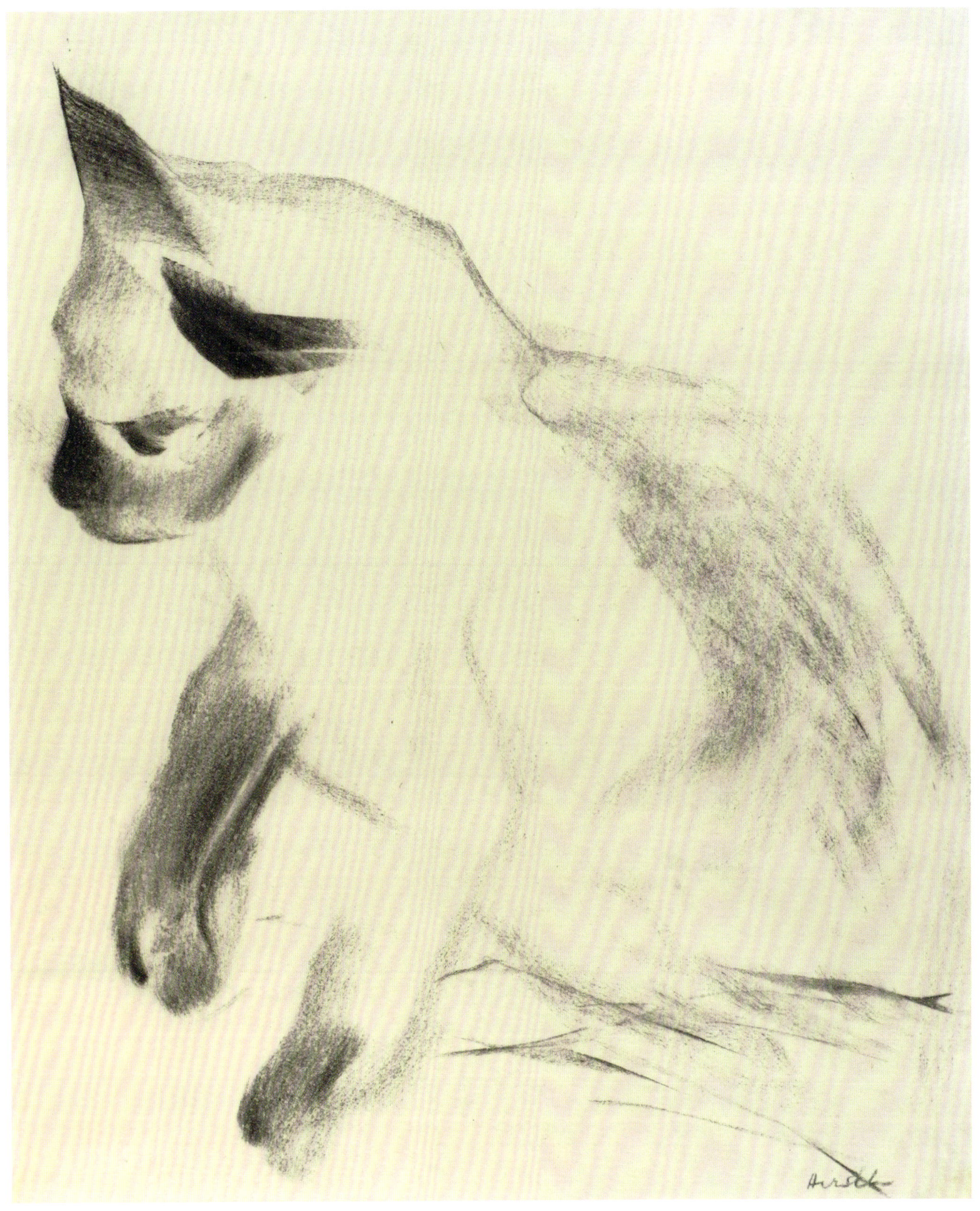

Yasuo Kuniyoshi

American, born Japan, 1893–1953

59 Baby and Toy Cow, 1921

Black ink on off-white, moderately thick, moderately textured wove paper, 14½ × 10⅞ in. (36.8 × 27.6 cm)
Signed in ink, lower center: "KUNIYOSHI 21"
Bequest of Edith and Milton Lowenthal, 1992.11.22

Born in Japan, the modernist artist Yasuo Kuniyoshi immigrated in 1906 to the United States, where he remained for the rest of his life. He keenly felt the pull of both his native culture and his adopted one and sought in his art "to combine the rich traditions of the East with my accumulative experiences and viewpoint of the West."[1] *Baby and Toy Cow* is one of a series of more than sixty ink drawings that Kuniyoshi made between 1921 and 1925, at the outset of his professional career in New York. It depicts an imaginative arrangement of disparate elements—an infant crawling on a blanket decorated with natural forms, a rattle drum with a yin-and-yang symbol, a tiny sailboat, and a cow pull toy—set against a roughly egg-shaped black ground. Given the autobiographical significance of these items, the drawing constitutes a symbolic portrait of the artist. Children and, especially, cows appeared with great frequency in Kuniyoshi's art of this period. As he recalled, "I was painting cows and cows at that time because somehow I felt very near to the cow. . . . You see I was born, judging by the Japanese calendar, in a 'cow year.' According to legend I believed my fate to be guided, more or less, by the bovine kingdom."[2] The cow toy in this drawing also recalls American folk art, which Kuniyoshi avidly collected, and refers, along with the sailboat, to his summers in Ogunquit, Maine. The rattle drum and its yin-and-yang motif nostalgically evoke his childhood in Japan.[3]

Like the iconography, the medium and style of *Baby and Toy Cow* allude to both Japanese and Western culture. The tipped-up perspective and asymmetrical composition—with large areas of the sheet left blank—suggest a Japanese aesthetic, while the figural distortions are indebted to developments in American and European modernism. Similarly, the artist drew on the long tradition of ink drawing in Eastern art, yet he manipulated the medium in unconventional ways.[4] Using a brush and a pen, he varied the application of his ink from broad washes to thin lines to create a wide variety of textures and tones. Despite his remarkable facility with this medium, Kuniyoshi focused his efforts primarily on painting after 1925, earning international acclaim for landscape, still-life, and figural subjects rendered in his typical hybridized and highly idiosyncratic style.

1. Yasuo Kuniyoshi, quoted in *Yasuo Kuniyoshi* (New York: American Artists Group, 1945), unpag.
2. Yasuo Kuniyoshi, "East to West," *Magazine of Art* 33, no. 2 (Feb. 1940): 75–77.
3. See Gail Levin, "Between Two Worlds: Folk Culture, Identity, and the American Art of Yasuo Kuniyoshi," *Archives of American Art Journal* 43, nos. 3–4 (2003): 8.
4. Jane Myers, "Independent Creations: Kuniyoshi's Ink Drawings of 1921–25," in Myers and Tom Wolf, *The Shores of a Dream: Yasuo Kuniyoshi's Early Work in America* (Fort Worth, Tex.: Amon Carter Museum, 1996), 57–58.

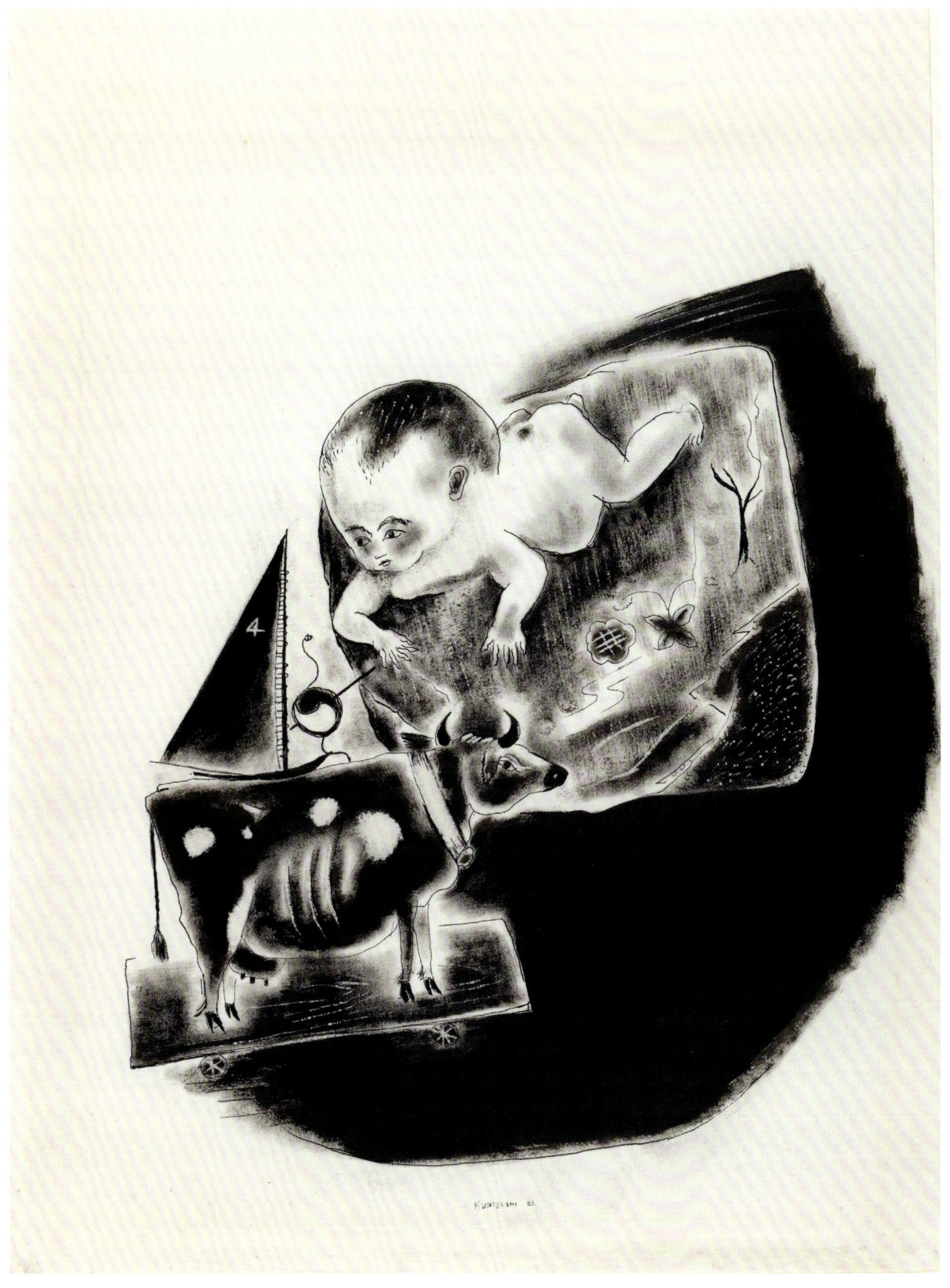

Violet Oakley

American, 1874–1960

60 Portrait of Mrs. J. Monroe Hewlett, 1937

Red, white, and black chalk (possibly Conté crayon) on beige, moderately thick, moderately textured wove paper, 15¹¹⁄₁₆ × 11¹¹⁄₁₆ in. (39.8 × 29.7 cm)
Signed in charcoal, lower right: "VIOLET OAKLEY / ROME, 1937"
Gift of the Monroe and Estelle Hewlett Collection, 53.197

Violet Oakley used colored chalks—primarily brick red with touches of black and white—to create this striking bust-length portrait of Estelle Rodgers Hewlett (1890–1967). The artist concentrated on the sitter's face, realistically modeling the distinctive features and wavy bob with a combination of sharp lines and soft smudges. (By contrast, just a few sketchy strokes describe the body.) Hewlett confronts the viewer with a direct gaze and self-assured expression. The turn of her head, while her body faces right, emphasizes the long, sinuous curve of her neck and gives her a poised, almost haughty, air. Oakley further enlivened the portrait by adding a white dot in each eye, suggesting a spark of inner life and intelligence.

According to the inscription at lower right, Estelle Rodgers Hewlett sat for her portrait in Rome in 1937. Little is known about her, except that she was the second wife of the New York architect and muralist James Monroe Hewlett (1867–1941), who served as the director of the American Academy in Rome from 1932 to 1935. It is likely that he knew Oakley—one of America's most famous mural painters—through their shared professional circles before his 1924 marriage to Estelle Rodgers.[1]

Raised in a cosmopolitan and artistic family, Oakley began her career as an illustrator in Philadelphia. She took up mural painting about 1900 and, over the next several decades, garnered numerous prestigious commissions as well as acclaim as the first woman artist to achieve success in this male-dominated field. In addition to her large-scale mural work in the American Renaissance style, she designed stained-glass windows and made hundreds of portrait drawings and paintings. Oakley was also actively involved in artists' organizations and campaigned for international disarmament and women's rights in both the United States and Europe.[2]

1. Hewlett was a member and president (1919–21) of the Architectural League of New York, which awarded Oakley a medal of honor in painting in 1916. They were both members of the National Society of Mural Painters and had colleagues in common, including the architect Frank Miles Day (1861–1918), who collaborated with Oakley on the Charlton Yarnall house in Philadelphia (1910–11) and was a founder of the American Academy in Rome.

2. For a succinct discussion of Oakley's life and place in American art, see Patricia Likos Ricci, "Violet Oakley: American Renaissance Woman," *Pennsylvania Magazine of History and Biography* 126 (Apr. 2002): 217–48.

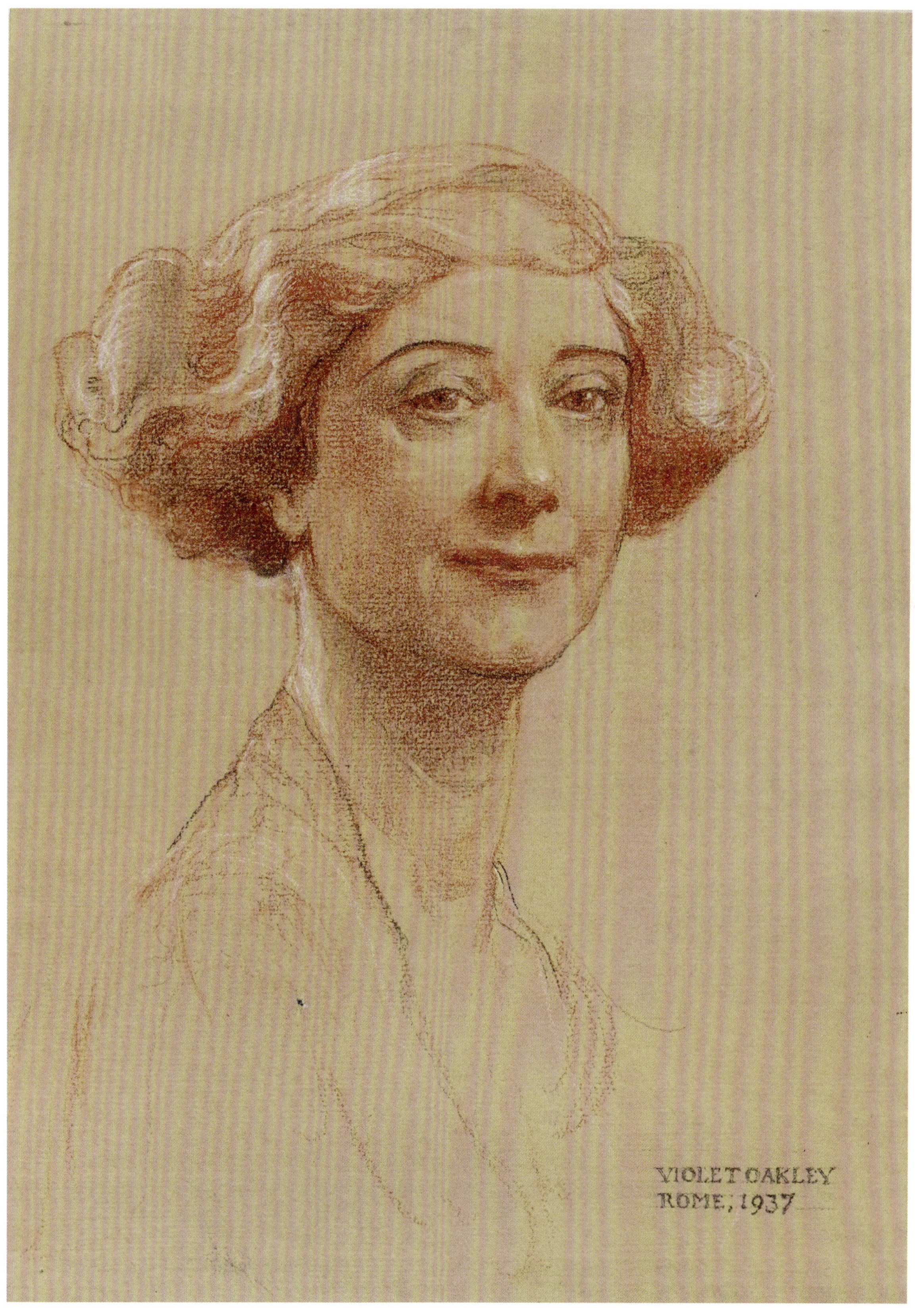
VIOLET OAKLEY
ROME, 1937

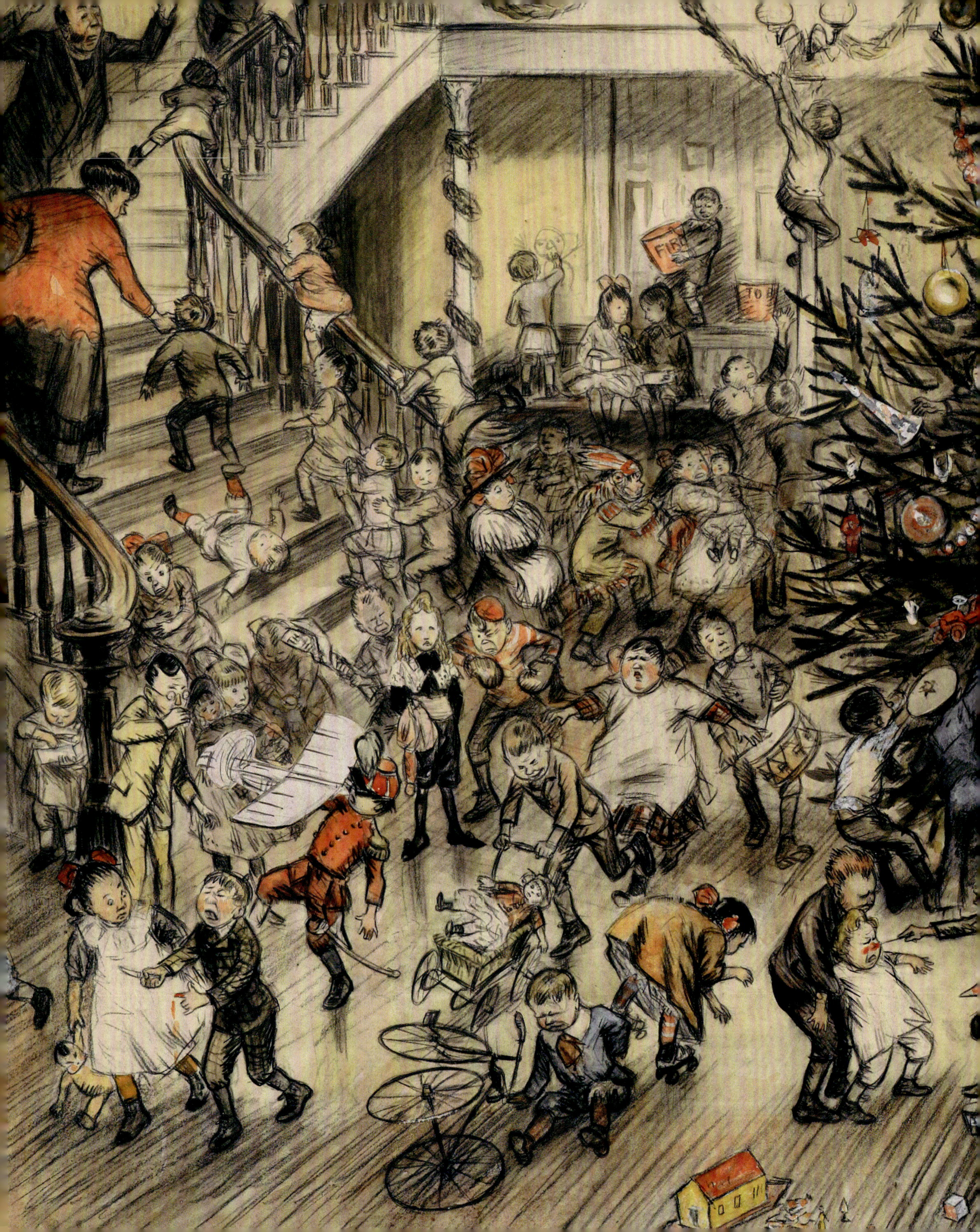

TELLING TALES

The drawings in this section relate stories through a combination of characters, setting, and action. Narrative pictures present the artistic challenge of conveying an anecdote through pictorial means in a way that is both easily legible and aesthetically engaging. In traditional academic training, artists generally advanced from figure drawing to the composition of multifigural, didactic images. Drawings played an important role as preparatory studies for the orchestration of pose, gesture, lighting, objects, and other components in the complex narrative paintings of the Grand Manner tradition—idealized and moralizing pictures depicting events from history, religion, and literature.

The middle decades of the nineteenth century witnessed the rise of genre painting in the United States. Widely popular with audiences and often humorous in nature, such scenes of everyday life deployed regional stereotypes and stock characters such as the yeoman farmer, country bumpkin, or rugged frontiersman. Later in the century, as many artists adopted a Realist approach to recording contemporary life, they found anecdotal interest in the lives and experiences of actual people and used drawings to capture their spontaneous observations.

Illustrations that accompanied written texts constitute another category of narrative drawings in this section. With the rapid expansion of the publishing industry and reproductive technologies in the second half of the nineteenth century, many artists found work in commercial illustration, making images for magazines, newspapers, and books consumed by tens of thousands of Americans. In all these diverse types of narrative drawings—preparatory academic studies, genre subjects, and popular illustrations—artists generally used a style rooted in naturalism to convey their tales clearly, while still manipulating formal elements and revealing details for expressive effect.

OPPOSITE:
William Glackens, *Merry Christmas (Yuletide Revels)*, circa 1910.
Detail of number 72

Benjamin West

American, 1738–1820

61 Know Thy Self, 1768

Iron gall ink and washes, carbon-based ink, and oil impasto and washes on ivory, moderately thick, moderately textured laid paper, 18¾ × 25½ in. (47.6 × 64.8 cm)
Signed in ink, lower right (on face of pedestal): "Benjn. West 1768—"
Inscribed in ink, in center (on face of bench): "Know thy self"
Brooklyn Museum Collection, X1042.40

This enigmatic wash drawing was created at the beginning of the London career of Benjamin West, the first American-born artist to achieve international fame. Raised in rural Pennsylvania, the precocious West received early encouragement from cultured benefactors, who recognized that artistic opportunities were limited in colonial America and funded his studies in Italy (1760–63). Under the tutelage of Anton Raphael Mengs (1728–1779) and Gavin Hamilton (1723–1798), West studied the works of Old Masters, became a proficient draftsman, and, like many of his contemporaries, embraced the period taste for Neoclassicism. Stopping in London on his way home, West decided to remain in England, where he specialized in history painting—large, multifigural compositions depicting themes from classical antiquity, the Bible, and literature—and rose to prominence as historical painter to King George III and second president of the Royal Academy of Arts.

Depicting an assembly of men arranged in small conversational groups within an open-air architectural setting, *Know Thy Self* most likely represents West's preliminary conception for a never-realized historical canvas. He used a limited palette to delineate the figures, structures, and other decoration with crisp ink outlines and to model forms with tonal washes. The drawing's subject remains obscure, but Marilyn Kushner convincingly interpreted *Know Thy Self* as an allegory about the Royal Academy, established in London as a professional organization for artists in 1768—the same year that West, a founding member, executed this drawing.[1] His composition alludes to Raphael's (1483–1520) Renaissance masterpiece *The School of Athens*, a fresco in the papal apartments at the Vatican that portrays an imaginary gathering of Western civilization's distinguished philosophers, including Plato and Socrates.[2] West's "school" is similarly set in a classicized structure, and his learned men are from different historical epochs, with some figures wearing classical togas and others donning eighteenth-century wigs and robes.[3] Both the title, *Know Thy Self*, alluding to an injunction attributed to the ancient Greek oracle at Delphi, and the bust of Minerva (Athena), the classical goddess of wisdom, in a niche on the right wall provide symbolic references to intellectual pursuits. A bright spotlight illuminating the center of the composition further dramatizes the theme of enlightenment. In *Know Thy Self*, West conveyed his commitment to Neoclassical styles and ideals and presented a vision of the Royal Academy as a noble community engaged in productive dialogue with the great cultural traditions of the past.

1. Marilyn Kushner, former Curator of Prints, Drawings, and Photographs at the Brooklyn Museum and currently Curator and Head, Department of Prints, Photographs, and Architectural Collections, New-York Historical Society, presented this interpretation in "Benjamin West Rediscovered at the Brooklyn Museum," a paper delivered with Antoinette Owen in the panel "Determining Authenticity and the Implications for Art History," College Art Association's 85th Annual Conference, New York, Feb. 18, 1997. The author is indebted to Kushner for generously sharing her ideas about this drawing.

2. West, who was dubbed "the American Raphael" and who named his first-born son after the Renaissance master, saw *The School of Athens* of 1509–10 in Rome (Stanza della Segnatura, Vatican) and might also have known the 1755 copy painted by his mentor Mengs (Victoria and Albert Museum, London).

3. Kushner argued that the combination of antique and modern attire anticipates West's revolutionary introduction of period-appropriate costume in history painting (in lieu of the conventional and generic classical garb), as seen in his sensational canvas *The Death of General Wolfe*, 1770 (National Gallery of Canada, Ottawa).

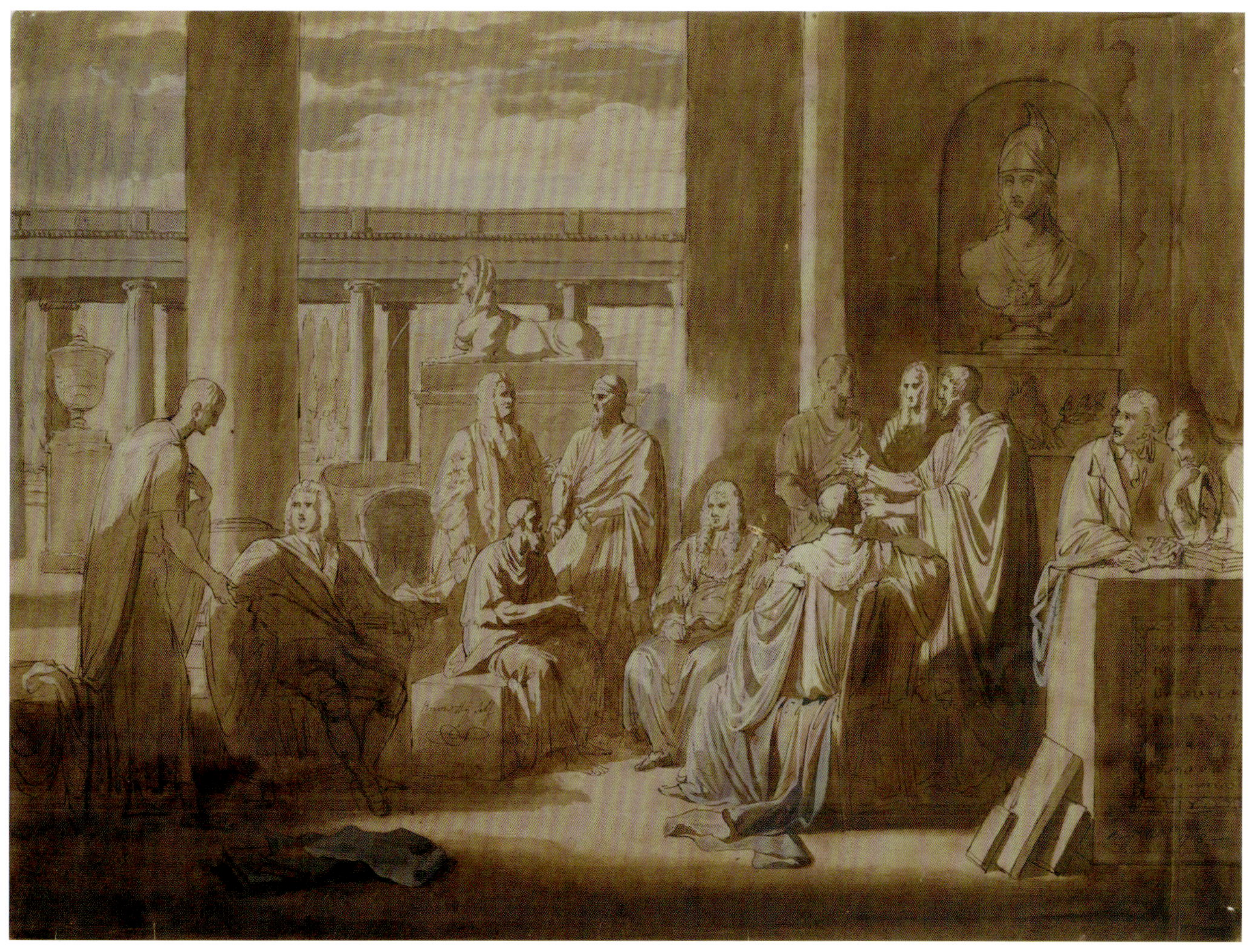

Constantine Hertzberg

American, born Germany, 1833–1919

62 A Drawing Lesson, 1865

Black ink on cream, thick, smooth wove paper, 10⁹⁄₁₆ × 6¾ in. (26.8 × 17.1 cm)
Signed and inscribed in ink, in center, on verso: "Composed and <u>Drawn with the Pen</u>. by Constantine Hertzberg. / Prof of Drawing and Perspective in the Brooklyn Polytechnique Institute and in / the Cooper Union. / August 1865."
Gift of Mrs. Tom Cochran, 19.186

A Drawing Lesson, by Constantine Hertzberg (also spelled Herzberg), depicts a male instructor and two female students, both of whom are seated and hold pencil to sketch pad. One student looks up at her teacher as he points into the distance, possibly demonstrating the rules of perspective. Hertzberg balanced the distant landscape with the intimacy of the immediate scene by enclosing his figures within a frame of two trees. He rendered the flowers and leaves with exacting precision, differentiating between the tones and textures of each species. The gradation in tonality, used to create a hazy atmosphere as the landscape recedes behind the figures, demonstrates the artist's skill as a draftsman.

In 1865, when this drawing was completed, Hertzberg was teaching drawing and perspective at the Cooper Union School of Design for Women in New York.[1] He was also a part-time drawing instructor at the all-male Polytechnic Institute of Brooklyn. *A Drawing Lesson* is possibly an autobiographical depiction of Hertzberg's Cooper Union teaching position; it also provides telling commentary on artistic training and gender in the latter half of the nineteenth century in the United States. Significantly, the lesson takes place outside rather than in a classroom studio, since Hertzberg's female students were encouraged to sketch *en plein air*—a practice promoted by Thomas Cole (1801–1848) and Asher B. Durand (1796–1886), leading figures of the Hudson River School of landscape painting. In a related drawing, Hertzberg depicted a group of male artists sketching outdoors and enjoying the picturesque surroundings (figure 17). A flamboyant dandy strolls along the path, while three of his companions lounge beneath the trees. The male artists' sketching trip appears to be a casual, everyday experience, in contrast to the female students' carefully contrived outing with a male supervisor and prim dog seated beside them. Although women continued to face many social and educational restrictions in the mid-nineteenth century, this period witnessed the rise of the professional female artist, for whom drawing was a key part of artistic training rather than merely a genteel, amateur accomplishment.

In 1852, at the Royal Saxon Academy of Fine Arts in Dresden, Hertzberg trained with (Adrian) Ludwig Richter (1803–1884), whose work focused on Romantic and fantastic depictions of local German landscapes. Richter's influence can be seen in Hertzberg's decorative, stylized treatment of nature in *A Drawing Lesson*.—CG

1. In the Brooklyn City Directory for 1865–66 (when this drawing was completed), Hertzberg listed his profession only as teacher, not as artist.

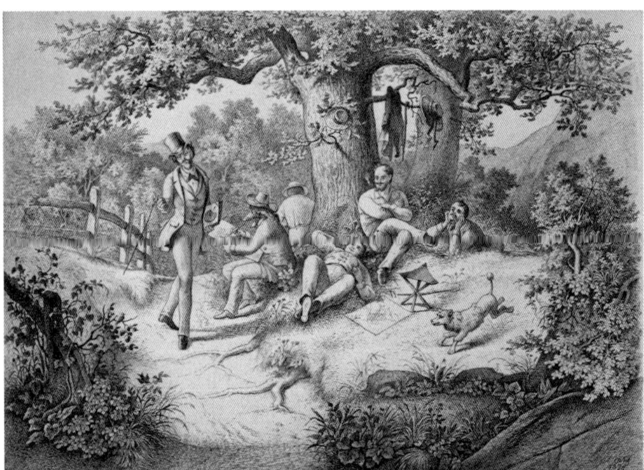

Fig. 17. Constantine Hertzberg. *Artists Sketching*, 1871. Pen and ink on paper, 6⅞ × 9¹⁵⁄₁₆ in. (17.5 × 25.3 cm). Museum of Fine Arts, Boston, Gift of Maxim Karolik for the M. and M. Karolik Collection of American Watercolors and Drawings, 1800–1875, 60.1072. Photograph: © 2011 Museum of Fine Arts, Boston

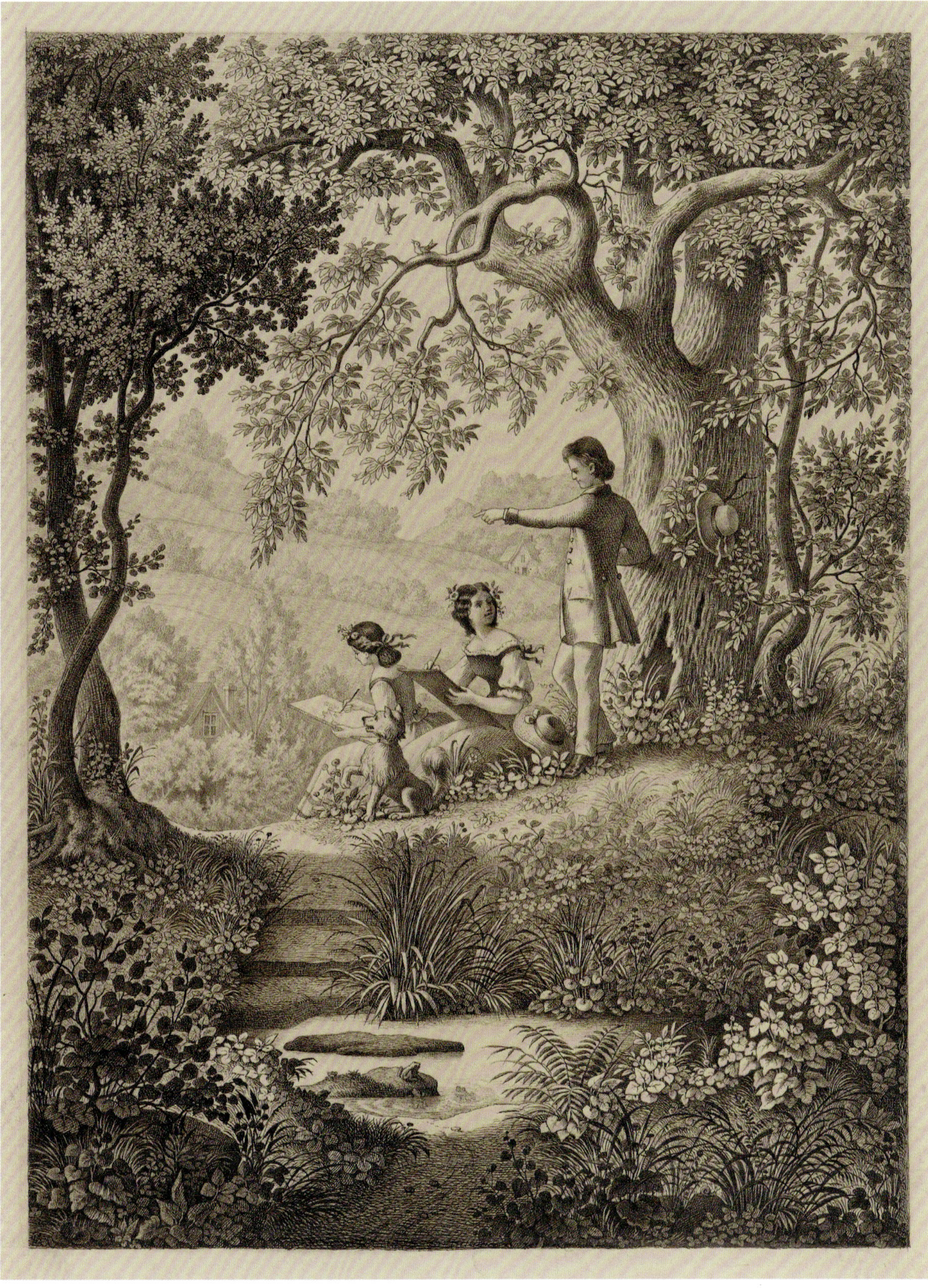

Felix Octavius Carr (F. O. C.) Darley

American, 1822–1888

63 The Leech and His Patient, illustration for *The Scarlet Letter*, circa 1878

Brown-black ink with graphite underdrawing on cream, thick, very smooth, highly calendered wove paper, 16⅟₁₆ × 22¼ in. (40.8 × 56.5 cm)
Signed in ink, lower left (on pipe): "F O C Darley"
Gift of William A. White, 15.484

Executed in the spare linear style that characterizes the work of F. O. C. Darley, this ink drawing was reproduced in an 1878 illustrated edition of Nathaniel Hawthorne's *Scarlet Letter* (originally published 1850), set in seventeenth-century Puritan Boston.[1] Notwithstanding the economy of Darley's line—figures and objects are rendered in thin ink outlines with minimal modeling—he convincingly tells his tale through an abundance of anecdotal details. *The Leech and His Patient* depicts the scene in which Roger Chillingworth, Hester Prynne's long-lost husband who masquerades as a physician, and the Reverend Arthur Dimmesdale, her lover, have a philosophical discussion about public confession. "Why should not the guilty ones sooner avail themselves of this unattainable solace?" Chillingworth asks his patient, who harbors a devastating secret. In keeping with Hawthorne's narrative, Darley depicted the doctor as a wizened old man with a hunchback—a physical manifestation of his bent for revenge—standing at his laboratory table and holding a weed that he found growing out of a sinner's grave. Seated at an open window, the young minister, with his brow furrowed in anguish, clutches his breast. This gesture symbolically links Dimmesdale to Hester, who wears a scarlet *A*, labeling her as an adulterer, on her chest. Darley further built up the narrative with rich descriptions of period costume and furnishings, including the latticed windows and straight-backed chair. Chillingworth's studio is cluttered with books and the paraphernalia used for distilling his medicinal concoctions. Darley's attention to detail is evident in the trunk at lower left. Its padlock suggests Dimmesdale's tightly guarded secret, which the doctor will figuratively unlock at the end of the chapter.

Largely self-taught, the Philadelphia-born Darley became the most prominent and prolific American illustrator of the middle decades of the nineteenth century. His designs appeared in popular magazines and books and were reproduced as independent prints. Influenced by the linear style of the European artists John Flaxman (1755–1826) and Moritz Retzsch (1779–1857), Darley developed his distinctive approach with an eye toward historical accuracy and narrative clarity, often working closely with authors. His lively renderings helped to popularize distinctive American types (such as the Pilgrim and the frontiersman) and literary classics, including the works of James Fenimore Cooper, Washington Irving, Charles Dickens, and Henry Wadsworth Longfellow, to whom Darley dedicated his *Scarlet Letter* illustrations.

1. Nathaniel Hawthorne, *The Scarlet Letter* (Boston: Houghton, Mifflin and Co., 1878), illustration between pages 162 and 163. Darley's twelve Hawthorne illustrations were also issued as a collection of plates, *Compositions in Outline from Hawthorne's Scarlet Letter by F. O. C. Darley* (Boston: Houghton, Osgood and Company, 1879).

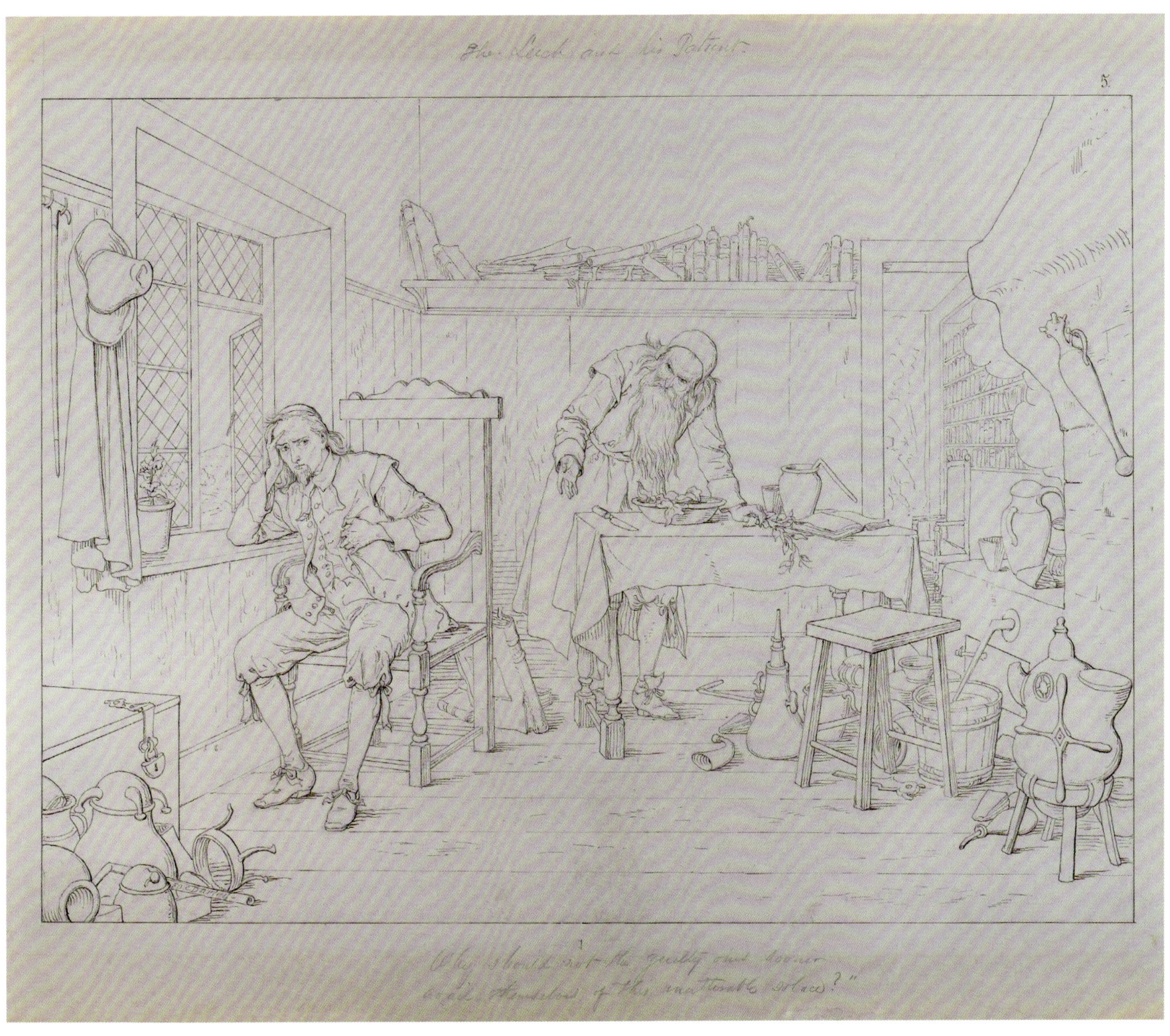

Elihu Vedder

American, 1836–1923

64 Study for "Prayer for Death in the Desert," circa 1867

Charcoal, white chalk, pastel, and black crayon on gray-green, moderately thick, slightly textured wove paper, 12⁵⁄₁₆ × 17⁷⁄₁₆ in. (31.3 × 44.3 cm)
Signed in graphite, lower right: "E. V."
Lent by Mr. and Mrs. Wilbur L. Ross, Jr., L81.62

Set in a barren, rocky landscape, this spare though powerful image takes as its theme the existential crisis of a man contemplating death to relieve his extreme suffering. Elihu Vedder depicted a hermit at the end of his quest for spiritual enlightenment, after first rejecting worldly comforts and concerns for a period of solitary wandering in the desert. The protagonist kneels on a rock with his head thrown back and his arms raised heavenward as he prays for divine intervention. His ragged robes and gaunt physique testify to the physical deprivation he has endured, while the tools discarded on the ground suggest his resignation to his fate. Vedder maintained the narrative tension of this scenario by leaving the ultimate outcome uncertain. Will the man's prayers be answered, the viewer wonders, and, if so, what form will his deliverance take?

Created as a preparatory study for a larger painting, this drawing demonstrates Vedder's technical virtuosity as a draftsman and his efficiency as a storyteller.[1] He rendered the figure with academic precision, modeling anatomical forms with firm outlines and tonal shadings. The hermit's suppliant pose creates a dramatic silhouette against the stark desert landscape, which is described with charcoal and pastel in subtle shades of pink and yellow.

Vedder spent much of his adult life in Europe. After preliminary training in various towns in New York State, he went abroad in 1855 to study in Paris and Florence. In Italy he joined a large community of artists and writers and was influenced by Early Renaissance art and by the Macchiaioli, contemporary plein air Realists with whom Vedder went on sketching trips around Italy. The rugged terrain in this drawing evokes the landscapes of Volterra and along the Tyrrhenian coast.

During the early part of his career, Vedder was preoccupied with themes of death and the meaning of life. In his 1910 memoir, he recalled that works such as his painting *Prayer for Death in the Desert* reflected "that rich, romantic sadness of youth. I had it very badly and enjoyed it immensely; otherwise, how account for my preparations for dying young, preparations for which event were amply provided for in numberless subjects I then conceived . . . the alchemist dying just as he made his grand discovery; the young hermit praying for death; the old man at the gate of a graveyard."[2] Vedder went on to earn international regard for his enigmatic Symbolist subjects and his classicizing treatment of the human figure (see also number 34).

1. The painting *Prayer for Death in the Desert*, circa 1867, is also in the Brooklyn Museum's collection (acc. no. 55.40). Although Vedder extended the landscape horizontally in the finished work, its main vignette follows this study very closely.

2. Elihu Vedder, *The Digressions of V.* (Boston: Houghton Mifflin Company, 1910), 145.

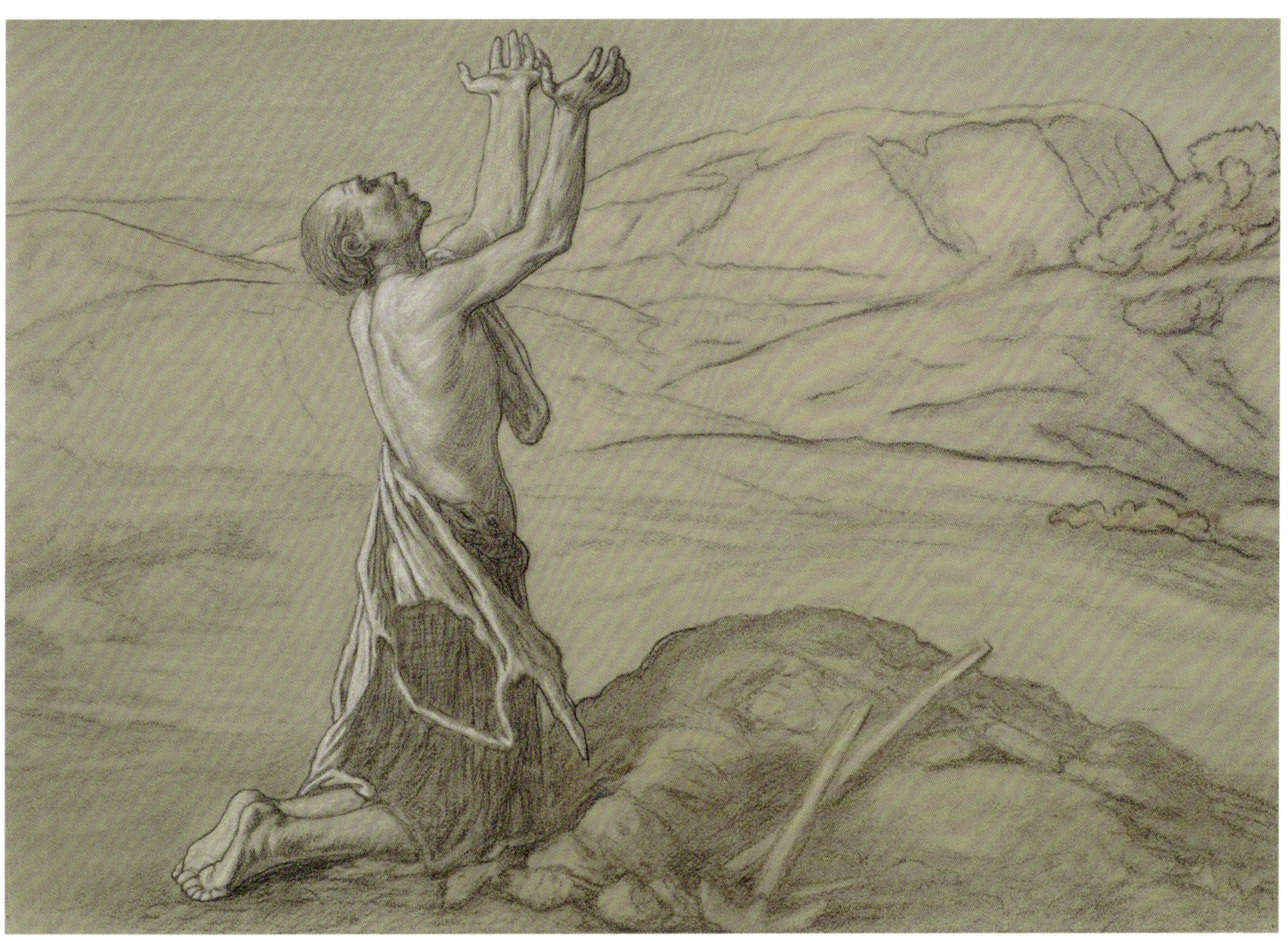

Winslow Homer

American, 1836–1910

65 The Swimming Hole, undated

Graphite on beige, moderately thick, moderately textured wove paper, 7⅝ × 9⅞ in. (19.4 × 25.1 cm)
Signed in graphite, lower right: "W. H."
Frederick Loeser Fund, 28.209

In this animated image, Winslow Homer depicted a group of young boys playing around a swimming hole. Several stand along the leafy banks, drying themselves off and cheering on their buddies in the water—all under the watchful gaze of a large dog seated in profile in the foreground. Two schematized heads and a hand popping out of the water suggest the forms of boys engaged in some sort of aquatic contest. The casual attitudes of the boys and the quick execution of the drawing convey the sense of an on-the-spot sketch. Less concerned with reportorial naturalism than with the overall impression of the genre scene, Homer rendered the image in an abbreviated fashion, using strong outlines and passages of rubbed shading. His line is economical yet expressive: a few scribbles suggest foliage or ripples on the water's surface, and the figures lack anatomical details. Notwithstanding this essentialized approach, the artist vividly captured the gleeful exuberance of youths enjoying a sun-drenched day.

Throughout his career as one of America's best-known Realist artists of the late nineteenth century, Homer drew avidly in many media and kept scores of drawings in his studio.[1] An apprenticeship in a Boston lithography shop from 1855 to 1857 led to his early work making illustrations for sheet-music covers and popular magazines such as *Harper's Weekly* and *Every Saturday*.

This experience honed his ability to tell stories with pictures that engaged the viewer and were immediately legible. By the time he gave up his successful work as an illustrator in 1875, he had also established his reputation as a painter in oils and was beginning to gain attention for his watercolors. His subject matter frequently focused on modern American leisure pursuits—hunting, hiking, and frolicking on the beach. Rural children in idyllic settings were among his most critically acclaimed and favorite themes (see also numbers 29, 30). Homer regularly spent his summers in the countryside or at the seashore, away from his New York studio, and most likely made *The Swimming Hole* during one such sojourn. The work probably dates from the late 1870s or later, when he was moving away from the literal realism of his illustration style to a more abstract and simplified approach to representation in his drawings.

1. In the months following Homer's death, mice in his studio destroyed an estimated three hundred drawings. David Tatham, *Winslow Homer Drawings, 1875–1885: Houghton Farm to Prout's Neck* (Syracuse, N.Y.: Joe and Emily Lowe Art Gallery, Syracuse University, 1979), unpag.

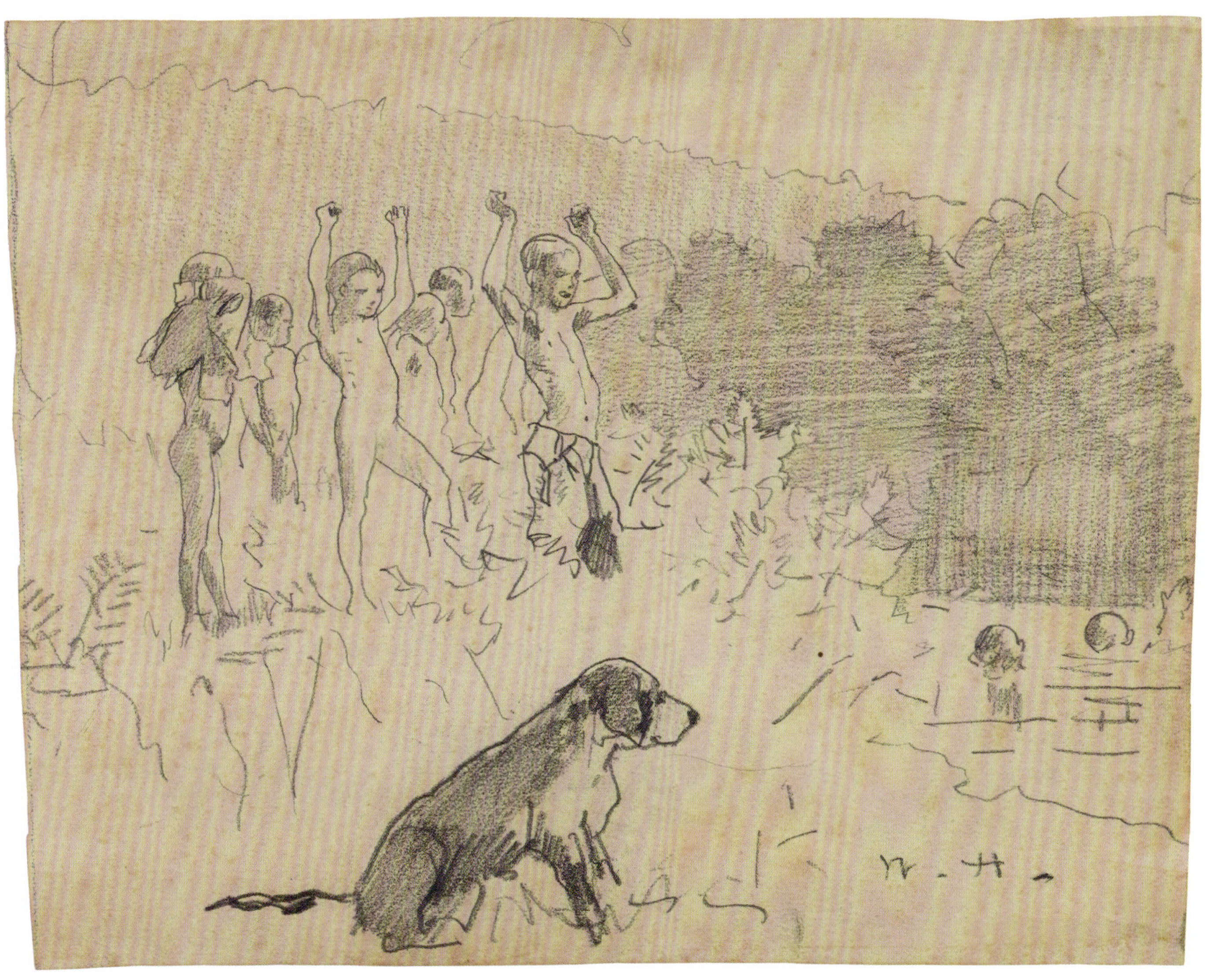

Thomas Eakins

American, 1844–1916

66 "Thar's Such a Thing as Calls in This World," illustration for "Mr. Neelus Peeler's Conditions," 1879

Black ink with opaque white highlights on cream, medium-weight, smooth wove paper, 10⁷⁄₁₆ × 12¼ in. (26.5 × 31.1 cm)
Brooklyn Museum Collection, 30.1452

This genre scene by the Philadelphia Realist painter Thomas Eakins was reproduced as an illustration for "Mr. Neelus Peeler's Conditions," a story about a family in rural Georgia by the local-color writer Richard M. Johnston that was published in the June 1879 issue of *Scribner's Monthly Magazine*.[1] Set in a sparsely furnished domestic interior, the image depicts the story's opening scene, in which the perennially lazy Neelus Peeler tells his industrious wife, Betsy, "Thar's such a thing as calls in this world." To justify his lack of employment, Peeler claims that he is awaiting his "calls," or his true vocation, which he later realizes as a traveling preacher specializing in maudlin tales of his own purported sufferings. Eakins effectively communicates the opposing characters of husband and wife through body language. Neelus is all talk, leaning over the table with a gesture of self-righteous earnestness, while Betsy, turned away from him and unmoved by his familiar excuses, concentrates on her sewing.

The artist's storytelling abilities are also evident in the figure of the Peelers' son on the floor. Although Elijah does not appear at this point in the narrative, his supine pose reflects his indolence (inherited from his father) and foretells a future incident of drunkenness.

Rendered in monochromatic washes of black ink with white highlights, this drawing demonstrates Eakins's exacting realism in the handling of human anatomy and spatial depth. He carefully modeled the figures through tonal variations to create an illusion of their volume: Elijah's dramatically foreshortened body is a virtuoso example of Eakins's skills. As was typical of his working method, Eakins made preparatory studies for this image, including a drawing with both a perspectival grid to plot the precise placement of the figures and sketches of some of the decorative objects in the margins (figure 18).[2] In contrast to the main vignette, Eakins described the background in summary fashion, although a portrait of George Washington is legible on the wall above the mantelpiece.

The son of a writing master, Eakins excelled in draftsmanship from a young age. He received a rigorous academic training, focused on drawing and the figure, first at Philadelphia's Pennsylvania Academy of the Fine Arts (where he later taught) and then during his advanced studies in Paris. Best known for unsparingly realistic portraits of his friends in Philadelphia's artistic and scientific communities as well as sporting scenes, Eakins occasionally painted literary or other historical subjects. Around the time of this illustration, he produced a series of works depicting a woman in colonial attire sewing or spinning (Betsy recalls this type), possibly to capitalize on the interest in America's past fostered by the centennial. His drawing for "Mr. Neelus Peeler's Conditions" was one of only a few commercial illustrations that Eakins made for popular magazines.[3]

Fig. 18. Thomas Eakins. *Perspective Study for Illustration for Magazine Story, "Mr. Neelus Peeler's Conditions,"* 1879. Ink and pencil on paper mounted on paper board with original wood engraving by Alice Barber, 14¹⁄₁₆ × 17 in. (35.6 × 43.2 cm). Hirshhorn Museum and Sculpture Garden, Smithsonian Institution, Gift of Joseph H. Hirshhorn, 1966, 66.1525. Photograph: Lee Stalsworth

1. Richard M. Johnston, "Mr. Neelus Peeler's Conditions," *Scribner's Monthly Magazine* 18, no. 2 (June 1879): 256–67. Eakins's illustration, the only one that accompanies this story, appears on page 256; it was engraved by Alice Barber (1858–1932), one of his students.

2. Eakins also made an oil sketch of Neelus Peeler's figure, now titled *The Timer* (New Britain Museum of American Art, New Britain, Connecticut, acc. no. 1950.05).

3. For Eakins's illustration work, see Ellwood C. Parry III and Maria Chamberlin-Hellman, "Thomas Eakins as an Illustrator, 1878–1881," *American Art Journal* 5 (May 1973): 20–45.

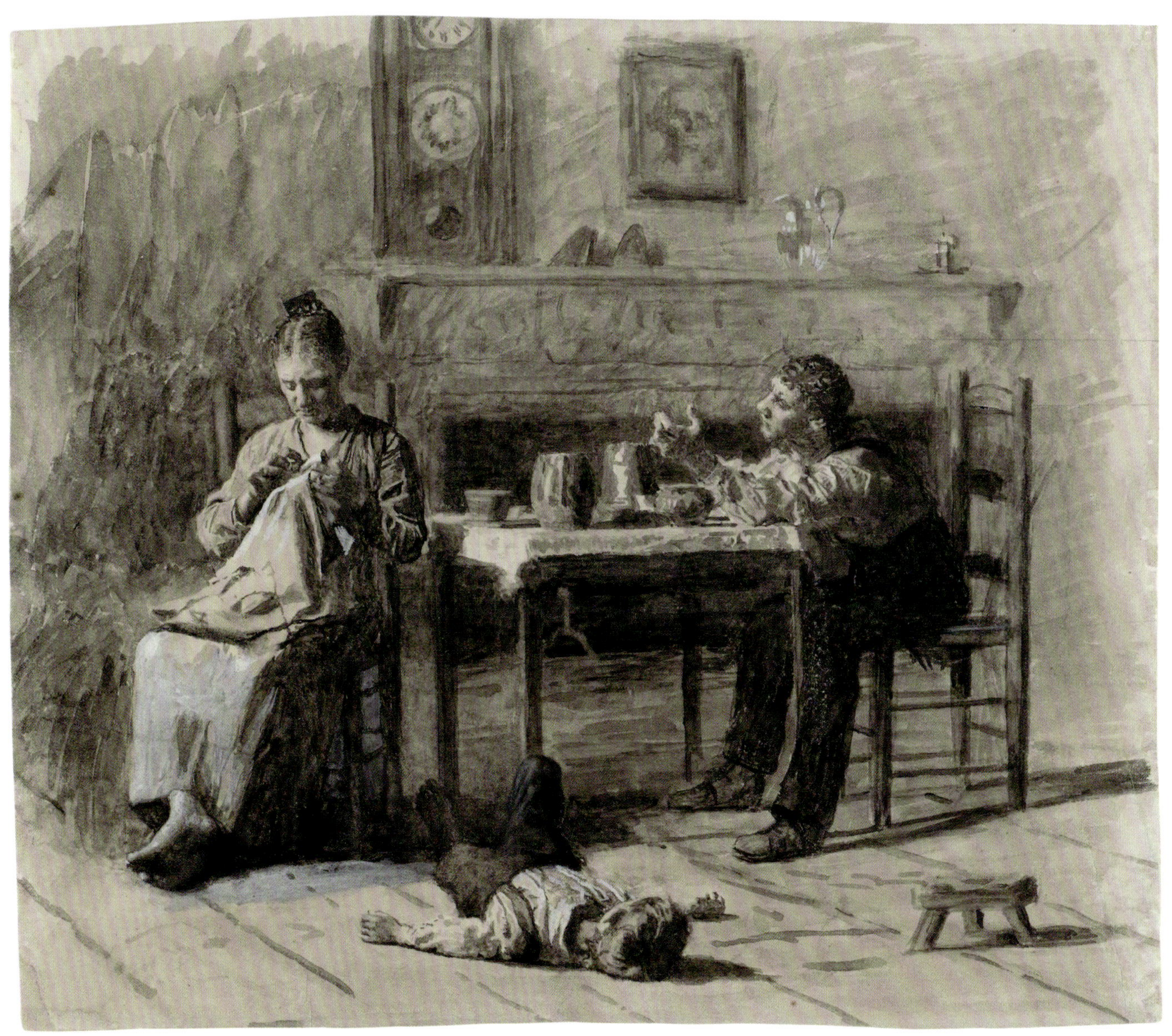

Winslow Homer

American, 1836–1910

67 Study for "The Unruly Calf," circa 1875

Graphite and white opaque watercolor on blue-gray, moderately thick, moderately textured wove paper, 4¹¹⁄₁₆ × 8½ in. (11.9 × 21.6 cm)
Signed in graphite, lower right: "W H"
Museum Collection Fund, 24.241

About 1875 Winslow Homer created a small series of works depicting a young African American boy weaning a calf by dragging it away from its mother. This drawing focuses solely on the central characters of this drama: the boy and the resisting animal. (In his most elaborate version of the subject, Homer included two white boys as onlookers and, in the background, a farmer restraining the mother cow.[1]) Engaged in a tug-of-war of wits and brawn, the boy braces his body in a wide-legged stance and pulls on a rope tied around the calf's neck, using a slim tree trunk as leverage for his grip. His determination seems matched by that of the calf, which leans in the opposite direction and arches its tail in indignation. A faint outline indicates that Homer experimented with the placement of the tail before he settled on this more animated pose. The artist rendered the scene with his typical realistic style and deft execution. His line is particularly expressive in the frayed threads of the boy's tattered clothing and the abstracted scribbles indicating the grassy meadow. He followed this preparatory study very closely in an oil painting, but he refined the composition by changing the trees in order to keep the emphasis on the figures (figure 19).

At the time he made *The Unruly Calf* and related works, Homer was best known for his images of the Civil War and of rural children. Both subjects afforded him the opportunity to portray blacks, as did his visits to Petersburg, Virginia, in 1875–76, when he sketched in African American communities. The young boy in this drawing appears in several other works of this period. These pictures were noted by critics at the time for their sympathetic and naturalistic treatment of blacks—qualities that distinguished Homer's imagery from the racist caricatures that proliferated in nineteenth-century visual culture. As one contemporary writer observed, "His negro studies, recently brought from Virginia, are in several respects—in their total freedom from conventionalism and mannerism, in their strong look of life, and in their sensitive feeling for character—the most successful things of the kind that this country has yet produced."[2] More recently, art historians have suggested that the subject of a black boy weaning a calf—while recording a typical farm activity—also has deeper significance as a metaphor of the struggles of African Americans for self-determination in the Reconstruction-era South.[3]

1. *Weaning the Calf*, 1875, oil on canvas (North Carolina Museum of Art, Raleigh). For reproductions of this and related pictures, see Nicolai Cikovsky, Jr., and Franklin Kelly, *Winslow Homer* (Washington, D.C.: National Gallery of Art, 1995), 116–17.
2. G. W. Sheldon, "American Painters—Winslow Homer and F. A. Bridgman," *Art Journal*, n.s., 4 (1878): 227.
3. See Peter H. Wood and Karen C. C. Dalton, *Winslow Homer's Images of Blacks: The Civil War and Reconstruction Years* (Austin: Menil Collection and University of Texas Press, 1988), 70–72, and Linda J. Docherty, "A Problem of Perspective: Winslow Homer, John H. Sherwood, and *Weaning the Calf*," *North Carolina Museum of Art Bulletin* 16 (1993): 32–48.

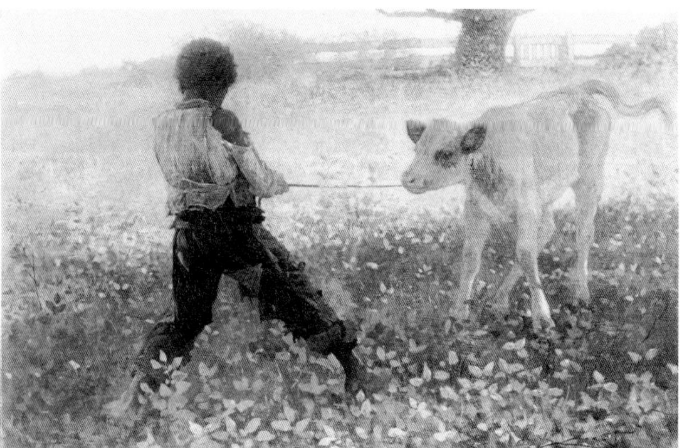

Fig. 19. Winslow Homer. *The Unruly Calf*, 1875. Oil on canvas, 24¼ × 38½ in. (61.6 × 97.8 cm). Private collection

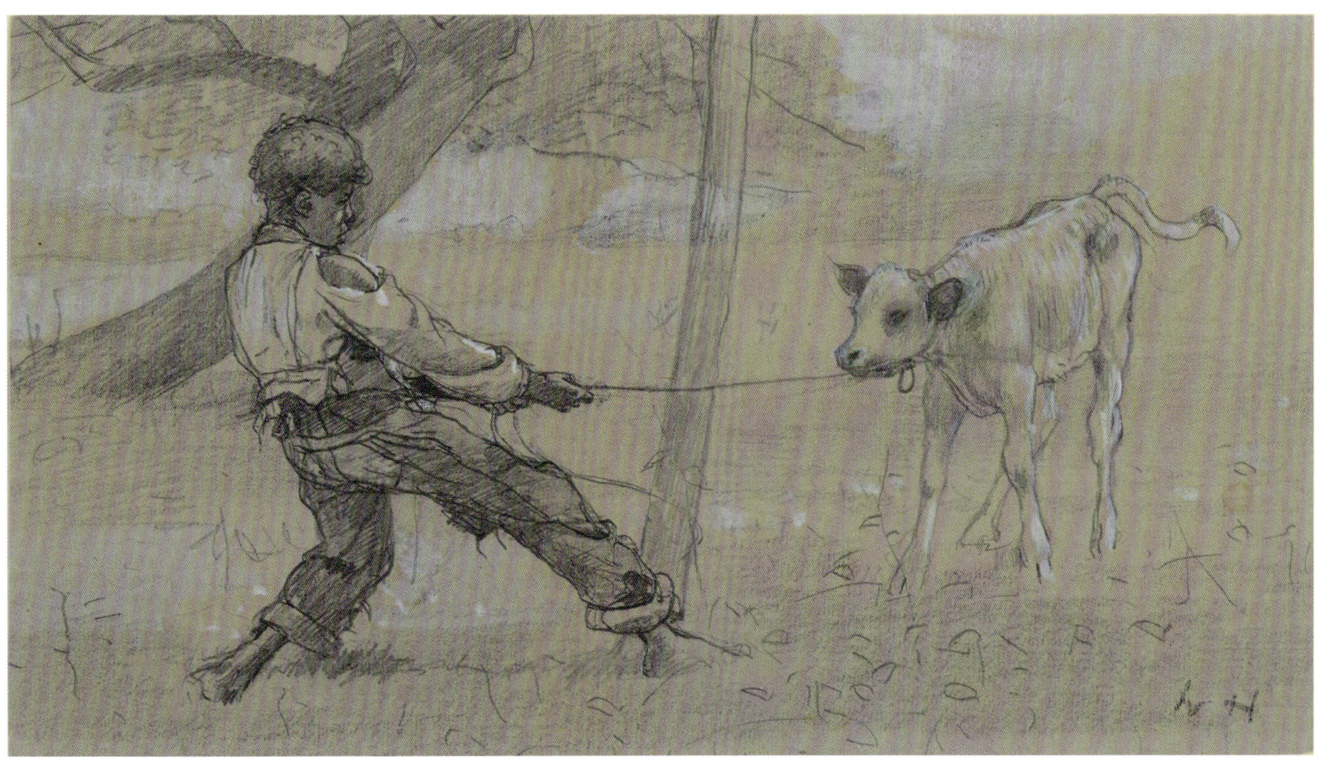

Edward Henry Potthast

American, 1857–1927

68 Illustration for "George Washington Jones: A Christmas Gift That Went A-Begging," 1903

Charcoal, watercolor, and white crayon on cream, medium-weight, slightly textured wove paper, 19¾ × 14¹³⁄₁₆ in. (50.2 × 37.6 cm)
Signed in charcoal, lower right, "E Potthast"
Peter F. Schofield Fund, 33.392

This work is the original drawing for one of four illustrations Edward Henry Potthast made for Ruth McEnery Stuart's *George Washington Jones: A Christmas Gift That Went A-Begging* (1903), a sentimental novel that follows the shifting fortunes of a young African American orphan in Reconstruction-era New Orleans.[1] George Washington Jones, the plucky protagonist, seeks to follow his family's tradition of working in a white household. His late grandfather was enslaved and given as a Christmas present to the master's daughter to be her personal servant. George's quest ends happily when, after several trials, he is hired by the same family that his grandfather served. In its suggestion that blacks were content to reproduce slavery-era social hierarchies and patterns of servitude, the tale functioned to assuage white audiences' anxieties about post–Civil War racial tensions.

Potthast's drawing depicts George getting dressed to present himself as a Christmas gift to potential employers. Wanting to make a good impression but having limited means, the boy inspects his tattered, secondhand outfit in the mirror and laments, "Wush't I was a little purtier."[2] Potthast captured both the humble circumstances and complex emotions of the protagonist with careful attention to telling details, such as the crumbling wall in the cramped garret, the cracked mirror, and the too-short jacket sleeve. George's erect posture and uptilted head convey determination and pride, but his reflected expression in the mirror is apprehensive. The strong contrast between the dark foreground, where the figure stands in shadow, and the well-lit background further enhances the narrative drama; these lighting effects could also foretell George's brighter future.

Using a combination of charcoal and watercolor, Potthast rendered his drawing in a monochromatic palette of blacks and grays with accents of white, for reproduction as a black-and-white illustration. Although best known as a painter of vividly colored Impressionist-inspired beach scenes, he began his career as a lithographer and illustrator in Cincinnati and continued to supplement his painting income with freelance illustration work. Potthast often created images for stories involving African Americans. His attention to detail and realistic style made this rendering particularly well suited for the novel *George Washington Jones*, an example of American local-color fiction, which was characterized by a focus on regional dialects and customs.

1. Ruth McEnery Stuart, *George Washington Jones: A Christmas Gift That Went A-Begging* (Philadelphia: Henry Altemus Company, 1903). This illustration appears facing page 28.

2. This scene is described on pages 26–29; the quote—from page 29—is also the caption for the illustration.

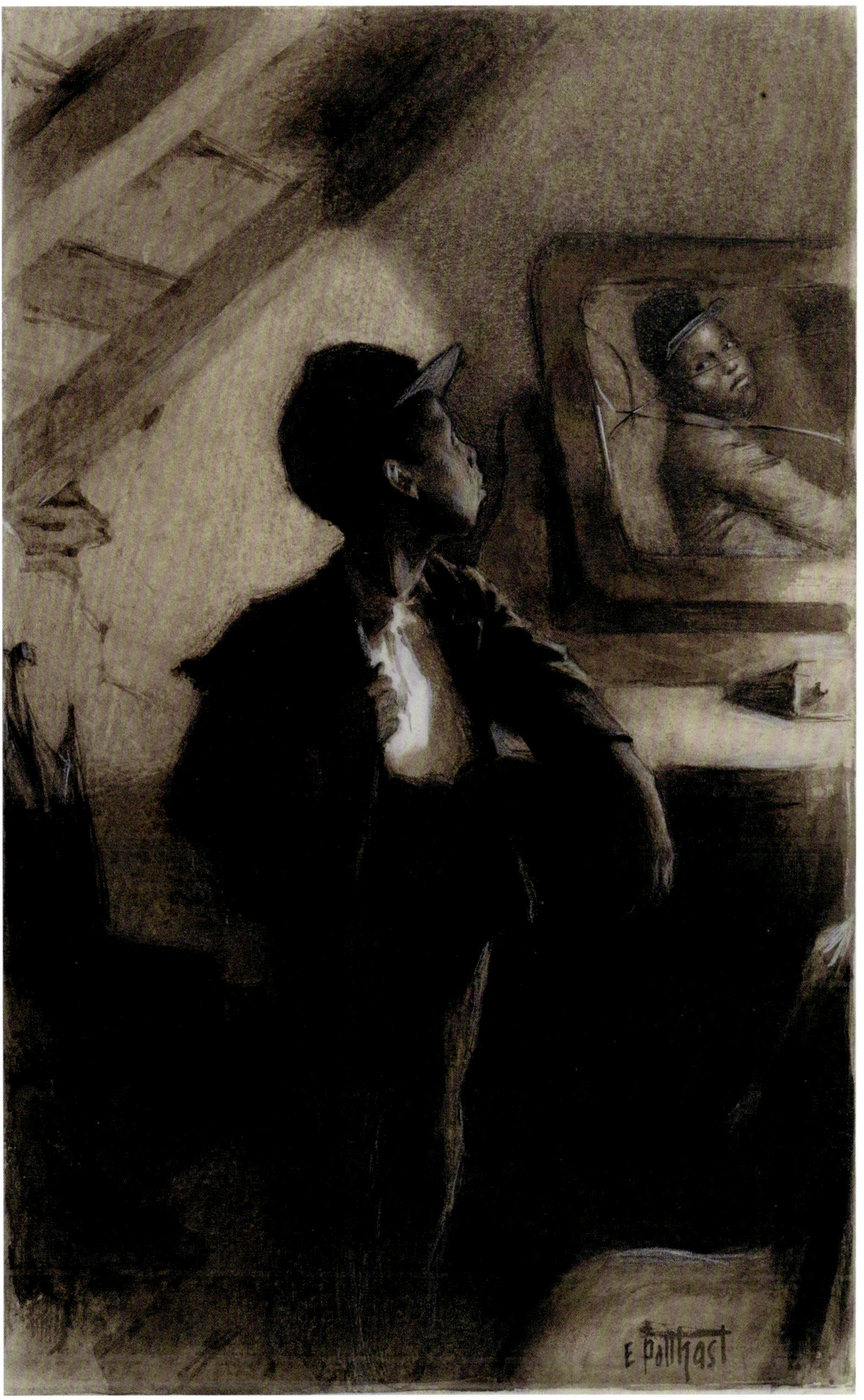

Everett Shinn

American, 1876–1953

69 Frédérique Follows Her Husband, illustration for *Frédérique*, 1906

Black crayon (probably Conté) on beige, medium-weight, slightly textured wove paper, 15⅝ × 21 in. (39.7 × 53.3 cm)
Signed in crayon, lower left: "E SHINN / 1906"
Dick S. Ramsay Fund, 42.101

Published in 1907, Charles Paul de Kock's two-volume novel *Frédérique* contained sixteen illustrations by Everett Shinn, including this highly finished drawing, *Frédérique Follows Her Husband*.[1] The novel's protagonist, Charles Rochebrune, narrates a tale about love and adultery in Parisian society. Rochebrune meets the amiable Frédérique Dauberny, who recounts the story of twice disguising herself in men's clothing to pursue her husband on his evening outings, eventually confirming her suspicions about his extramarital escapades. Shinn's rendering conflates these two incidents, combining the gentleman's outfit that Frédérique dons in the first pursuit with the shadowy side street she describes in the second account: "[H]e turned into a narrow, muddy street, the houses of which were of a very gloomy aspect. . . . I trembled as I thought that I was perhaps going to be forced to follow my husband into a house of ill-repute."[2]

Here, Shinn depicted a dark urban street with two cloaked figures, Frédérique at left and her husband, who turns away from the viewer as he rounds a corner, at right. The angled view of the composition and disappearing figure, as well as the contrast between Shinn's precise application of crayon in the figure at left and rapid strokes of the medium in the architecture and pavement, heightens the mystery of the scene on this gloomy street corner.

From 1893 to 1897, Shinn worked as an illustrator at the *Philadelphia Free Press*. There he mastered the quick sketches of urban subjects that were typical of the newspaper's illustration style; it was a manner that reappeared in his later independent work. After settling in New York in 1897, Shinn became involved with **Robert Henri**'s circle of urban Realists and focused more seriously on his own art, especially pastels (see number 104). Drawing on his early experience in illustration, he continued to depict city subjects, particularly the struggles of the urban working class.[3]—CG

1. Charles Paul de Kock, *Frédérique*, 2 vols. (Boston: F. J. Quinby, 1907). This illustration appears in volume 1, chapter 10, between pages 270 and 271, with the caption, "I must follow M. Dauberny to be better informed."
2. Ibid., 278.
3. Janay Wong, *Everett Shinn: The Spectacle of Life* (New York: Berry-Hill Galleries, 2000), 10, 47.

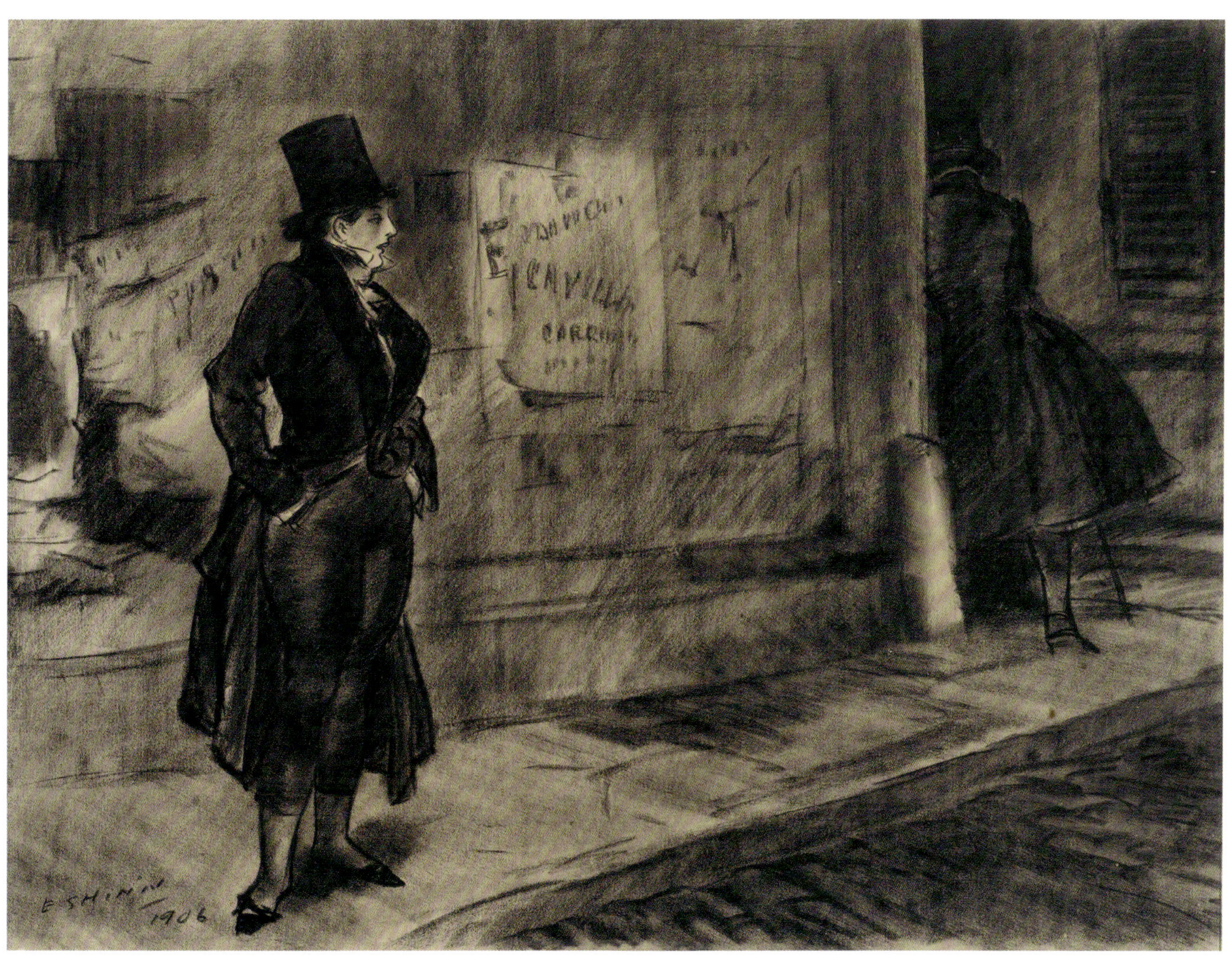

Jerome Myers

American, 1867–1940

70 Central Park Concert, undated

Black crayon (probably Conté) on cream, medium-weight, slightly textured wove paper with watermarks, 7½ × 9 in. (19.1 × 22.9 cm)
Signed in graphite, lower right: "JEROME / MYERS"
John B. Woodward Memorial Fund, 18.165.1

Like the progressive urban Realists of the Ashcan School with whom he was acquainted, Jerome Myers embraced the unvarnished aspects of modern city life as subject matter for his art. He was particularly drawn to society's less fortunate classes and became well known for his sympathetic portrayals of the poor immigrant populations—especially children—of New York's Lower East Side. Throughout his career, he wandered through the city with sketch pad in hand; the artist Guy Pène du Bois (1884–1958) described him as "a sort of day and night prowler, a phantom in the city streets."[1] In *Central Park Concert*, a typical example of Myers's on-the-spot records of the city's human spectacle, his primary interest was the audience rather than the

concert itself. With deft and energetic strokes of crayon, Myers portrayed a motley group listening to an outdoor musical performance. As the different levels of finish among the figures reveal, he worked by lightly sketching the forms and then reinforcing his initial conception with darker lines. This drawing combines his quick execution with careful observation. The artist individualized the physiognomy and dress of each person, including the bearded old man wearing a rumpled suit and clenching a pipe between his teeth who sits on the bench and the little girl with a cherubic face and bow in her hair who stands at the left. Although there is no ostensible narrative, Myers conveyed both diversity and unity within the urban community in this vignette, in which people of varying ages and stations share an appreciation for the music. Because the artist frequently depicted outdoor concert scenes (figure 20), it is difficult to date *Central Park Concert* more precisely than before its 1918 acquisition.

Born in Virginia, Myers settled in New York in 1886. While working various jobs, including as an illustrator for the *New-York Tribune*, he studied part-time at the Cooper Union and the Art Students League. His frustrations with the academic environment and a brief trip to Paris in 1896 confirmed his commitment to American urban subjects, which had begun appearing in his art during the late 1880s. Over the course of his career, Myers maintained a visible profile in the art scene through the regular exhibition of his paintings and works on paper. His drawings were particularly admired. One critic, writing on the occasion of the artist's memorial exhibition, stated that "as a draughtsman [Myers] leaves little to be desired. The drawings are extremely personal, entirely free from derivative or academic attributes and present themselves with the freshness of life itself. It seems to me that these qualities place him among the greatest draughtsmen of all time."[2]

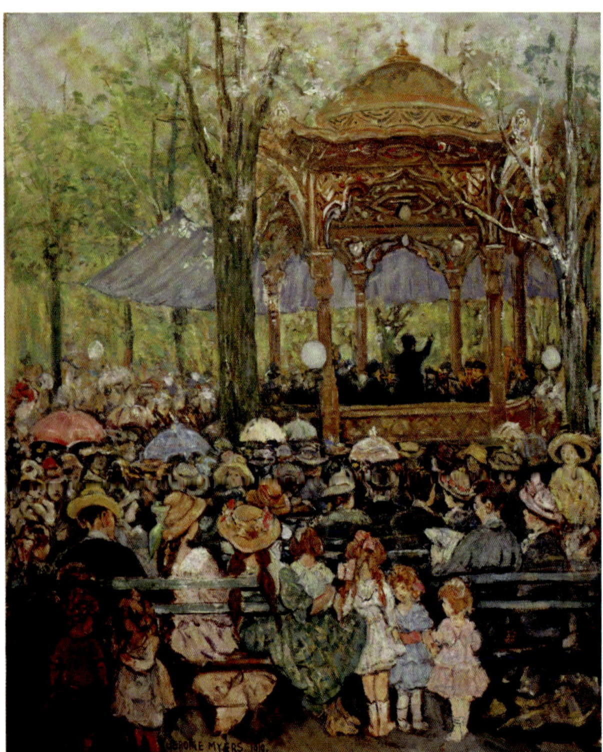

Fig. 20. Jerome Myers. *Concert in Central Park, New York*, 1919. Oil on canvas, 30 × 25 in. (76.2 × 63.5 cm). Norton Museum of Art, West Palm Beach, Florida, Gift of Elsie and Marvin Dekelboum, 2005.61

1. Guy Pène du Bois, "Artist in the Wilderness of New York," *New York Herald Tribune*, Mar. 31, 1940, sec. 9, p. 7, quoted in Grant Holcomb, "The Forgotten Legacy of Jerome Myers (1867–1940): Painter of New York's Lower East Side," *American Art Journal* 9 (May 1977): 81.

2. Harry Wickey, *Jerome Myers Memorial Exhibition* (New York: Whitney Museum of American Art, 1941), 5.

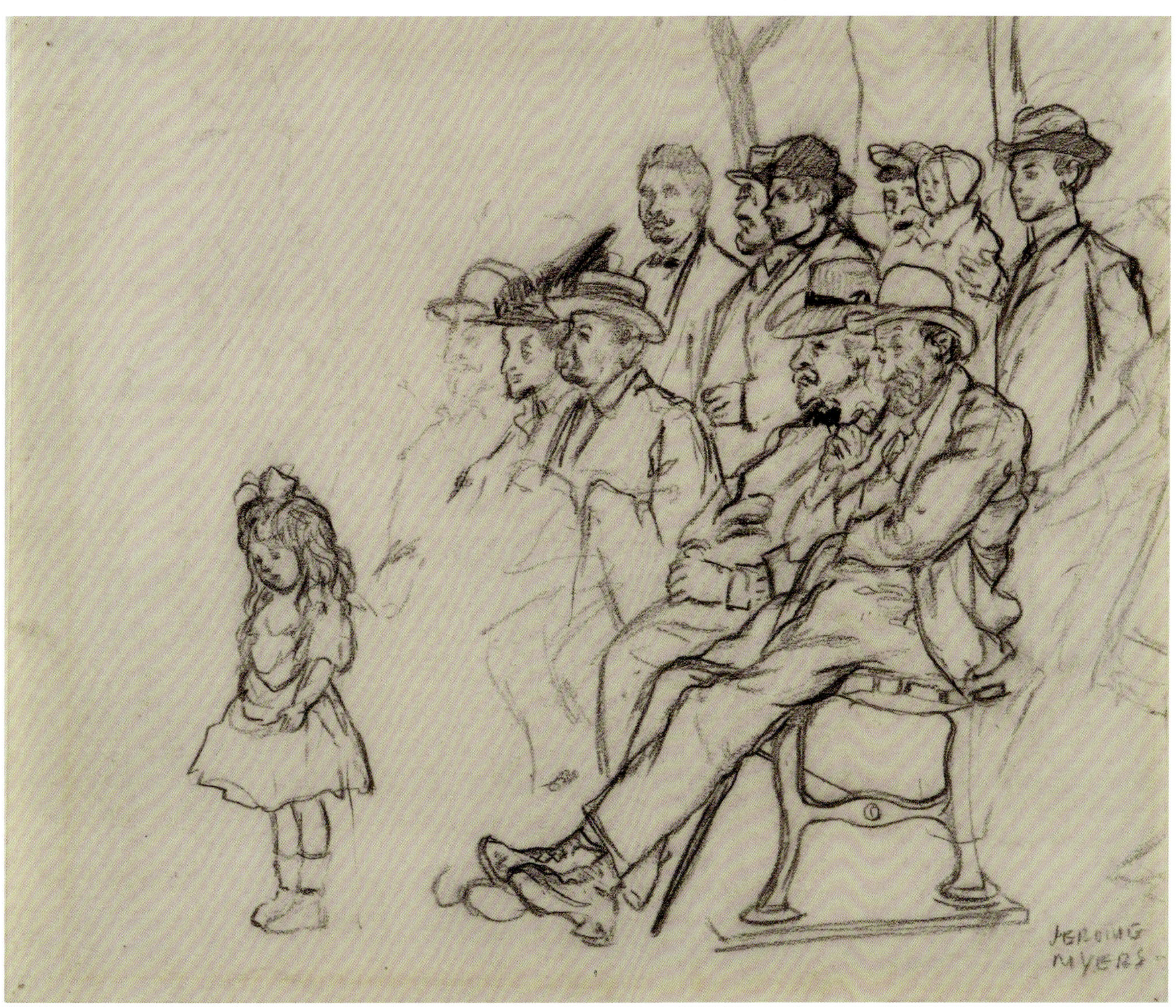

George Benjamin Luks

American, 1867–1933

71 **Pony Ride,** undated

Black Conté crayon on beige, moderately thick, smooth wove paper, 10⅛ × 7¾ in. (25.7 × 19.7 cm)
Dick S. Ramsay Fund, 58.43.5

George Benjamin Luks, a member of **Robert Henri**'s circle of urban Realists, found his inspiration in the lives of everyday New Yorkers. He wandered constantly throughout the city, filling sketchbooks with unembellished, spontaneous records of the people and places he encountered (see also number 39). This drawing, a typical example of his on-the-spot sketches, depicts a small concession stand giving pony rides to children in an urban park. Several of the diminutive animals await their turn under a striped canopy along with their handlers or parents of customers, while two ponies with riders and guides trot up and down a trail. Luks broadly described the scene with slashing strokes of Conté crayon, rendering forms as generalized shapes with minimal detailing. Based on the incline of the path, the setting could be Central Park or one of the other parks he frequented, including Prospect Park in Brooklyn and High Bridge Park in northern Manhattan, near his home-studio of the 1910s. In Progressive Era New York, parks were championed as a retreat from the noise, overcrowding, and hustle-bustle of the city, and urban inhabitants of diverse classes used these outdoor spaces for various recreational activities. For children, parks offered many entertainments, including playgrounds, carousels, puppet shows, and petting zoos, as well as pony rides.

Like many of the Ashcan School artists, Luks began his professional career as an illustrator for several newspapers in Philadelphia and then in New York, where he settled in 1896. As a result of his illustration work, he became adept at recording his observations quickly and accurately in both drawings and paintings. One critic described him as "a hand and an eye. His powers of observation are enormous. . . . He employs any method, the looser in the handling the better to secure his end—i.e., the rapid transference to canvas of reality."[1] Luks and his Realist peers revolutionized American art at the turn of the century by embracing subject matter that had traditionally been considered unsuitable for art—the everyday lives of the city's poor and immigrant classes, and the seedier parts of the urban scene (such as slum districts and dives). Luks represented these humble subjects in a frank, realistic style, unembellished by moralizing or didacticism, earning him both critical praise and condemnation.

1. James Huneker, "George Luks," *Sun* (New York), Mar. 21, 1907, 8.

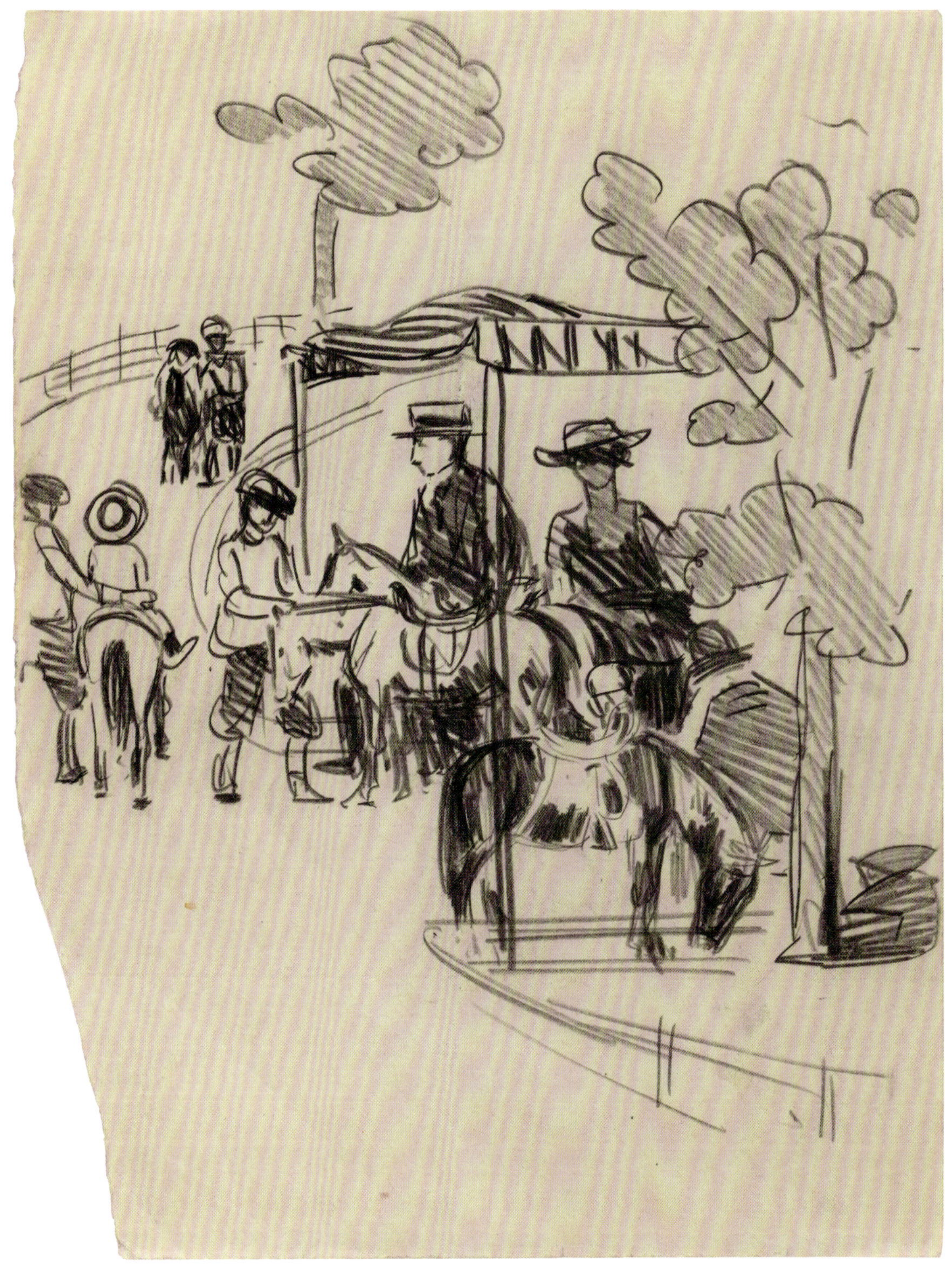

William Glackens

American, 1870–1938

72 Merry Christmas (Yuletide Revels), circa 1910

Graphite, Conté crayon, ink, and transparent and opaque watercolor on laminated board adhered to wood-pulp board, 24⅜ × 18½ in. (61.9 × 47 cm)
Signed in Conté crayon, lower right: "W. Glackens"
Gift of Ira Glackens, 63.58

A member of the Ashcan School of urban Realists who was also a renowned illustrator, William Glackens produced this delightfully humorous scene for reproduction in *Collier's Weekly*, one of the nation's most popular magazines at the turn of the century.[1] Set in a large room decorated for the holidays, *Merry Christmas (Yuletide Revels)* depicts a motley group of children playing with their new toys. Their antics are tumultuous, full of mischief, and often painful. Some of the richly detailed vignettes include a sobbing boy who has cut his finger with a knife (lower left), a budding "artist" with a watercolor set who paints the face of another child who is forcibly restrained by a buddy (lower right), and a boy dressed in an Indian costume who chases a girl clutching her doll (center). Other children bang drums, launch toy airplanes, scribble on the walls, and climb up the Christmas tree, which teeters precariously. A few adults in the margins of the composition attempt to instill discipline—dragging one boy up the stairs by his ear or spanking a child as he tries to slide down the banister—but their efforts are largely futile.

Conveying a chaotic atmosphere with easily legible imagery, *Merry Christmas (Yuletide Revels)* reveals Glackens at the height of his powers as a draftsman and storyteller. He rendered forms with vivid black outlines and hatched shading, then added washes of color—particularly accents of red—for visual interest. His figure style is slightly cartoonish but incorporates descriptive details of gesture, facial expression, and costume that endow each child with a distinct personality. Glackens also made subtle references to social tensions, as in the scene at the foot of the stairs in which a middle-class boy dressed foppishly as the literary character Little Lord Fauntleroy (with long blond curls, a large, frilly collar, pink sash, and black tights) is bullied by two young thugs, one of whom wears boxing gloves. With his keen eye for comic drama, the artist created an entertaining image as well as an ironic commentary on the innocence of children and the "joys" of the holiday season.

Glackens began his career as an artist-reporter in Philadelphia, where he befriended other newspaper illustrators, including John Sloan (1871–1951), **Everett Shinn**, and **George Benjamin Luks**, and their charismatic mentor **Robert Henri**. The members of this group eventually moved to New York, rebelled against artistic conventions with their grittily realistic urban subjects, and formed the Eight (subsequently dubbed the Ashcan School). Although Glackens considered himself primarily a painter, he continued to work prolifically and with great acclaim as an illustrator through the mid-1910s; he won a gold medal for illustration at the Pan-American Exposition in Buffalo, New York (1901). He also helped to organize progressive exhibitions, such as the Armory Show (1913), and he selected Impressionist and modernist art in Europe for the collector Albert Barnes, an old school friend.

1. *Collier's Weekly*, Dec. 10, 1910, 30 (full-page illustration).

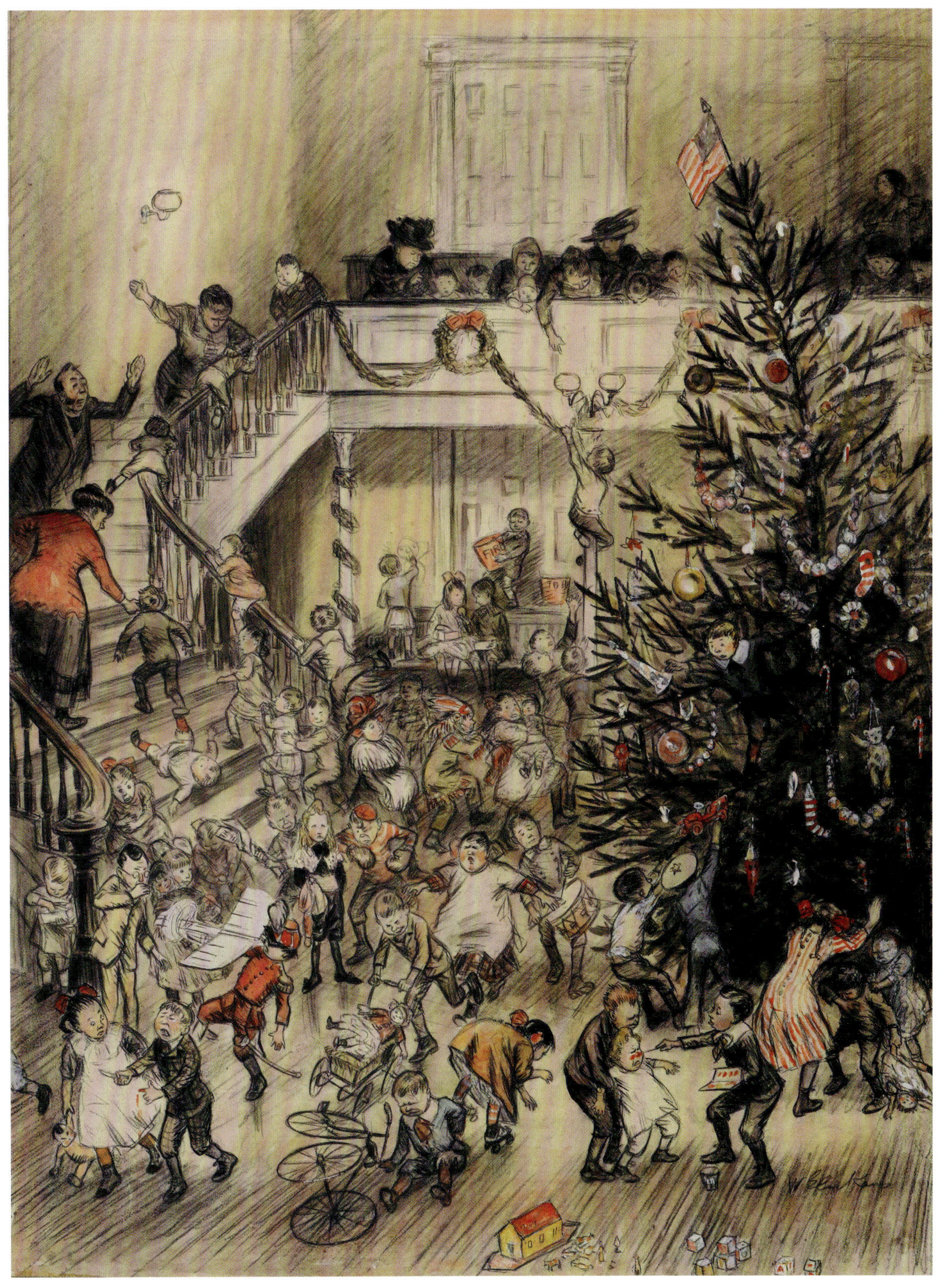

EXPLORING NATURE

The easy portability of drawing materials has historically made this art form well suited to documenting nature in its infinite variety through on-the-spot observation. Ranging from panoramic vistas to detailed, close-up studies of a particular species of flora or fauna, the drawings in this section exemplify various approaches to plein air sketching. The rise of the Hudson River School in the second quarter of the nineteenth century established landscape as a significant genre in American art. Although the artists of the group never formed an official organization, they shared a vision of nature that combined accurate transcription of natural forms with metaphoric and nationalistic symbolism. Asher B. Durand (1796–1886), one of the leaders of the school and a leading proponent of plein air sketching, advised young artists to forgo training with a teacher and, instead, to seek "sure and safe instruction" in "the STUDIO of Nature."[1] The English art critic John Ruskin (1819–1900), whose highly influential treatise

Modern Painters (1843–60) was widely read in the United States, also called for absolute fidelity to nature. The documentary impetus of landscape representation placed a premium on accuracy, and many artists spent the summer months working outdoors, recording their observations in drawings and oil studies that were subsequently used as source material for paintings made in the studio.

Later in the nineteenth century and into the twentieth, plein air sketching remained a vital practice. As artists became influenced by the French Barbizon School, Impressionism, and other modern movements, they increasingly turned to portraying the fleeting impressions of atmosphere and climate as well as their subjective and emotional responses to nature in their landscape drawings. Some sought respite in more pristine locales away from the hustle-bustle of urban life, and many used landscape subjects to experiment with new styles and aesthetic concerns.

1. Asher B. Durand, "Letters on Landscape Painting—Letter 1," *Crayon* 1 (Jan. 3, 1855): 2, reprinted in *Kindred Spirits: Asher B. Durand and the American Landscape*, ed. Linda S. Ferber (New York: Brooklyn Museum in association with D Giles, London, 2007), 233.

David Johnson

American, 1827–1908

73 Sketchbook, Conway, New Hampshire, July–October 1851

Graphite, chalk, and opaque watercolor on beige, medium-weight wove paper, 4⅞ × 6¾ × 5⁄16 in. (12.4 × 17.1 × 0.8 cm)
Signed and inscribed in ink, inside front cover: "David Johnson. / Cor[ner] of Pearl and Chatham / St. New York."
Gift of Blair Effron, 1997.157

One of the second generation of artists of the Hudson River School of landscape painters, David Johnson embraced plein air work as fundamental to his art. Rarely without a sketchbook in hand, he used drawing both as a method of understanding nature and as material for his paintings.[1] This example from the beginning of his career was done while he was on a sketching excursion in New Hampshire's White Mountains in 1851—the first of many trips Johnson would make to this region throughout his life. He traveled to New Hampshire and worked side by side with fellow artists Jasper Francis Cropsey (1823–1900), with whom he had taken formal lessons in the preceding year; John William Casilear (1811–1893); and Benjamin Champney (1817–1907). Johnson's drawings demonstrate his technical mastery as well as his commitment to close observation of nature. The sketch on page 7, for instance, depicts a splintered tree trunk along a streambed with meticulous attention paid to its rough textures and irregular forms. The close-up format and humble subject of this image recall the intimate forest interiors by Asher B. Durand (1796–1886), one of the founding fathers of the Hudson River School and a leading proponent of plein air study in the United States. Trees were Johnson's favorite subjects,[2] and page 14, executed in October in Bartlett, contains a striking image of a cluster of trees set against distant hills. He clearly delighted in the expressive arrangement of the branches of these pines, which dominate the composition in both scale and level of finish (the smaller trees or shrubs are rendered much more loosely with quick scribbles). Although most of the images in this sketchbook represent pure landscapes, Johnson occasionally included evidence of human presence, as in the scene of a farmstead with a cart and a sleeping dog in the yard on page 17.

A native New Yorker, Johnson had limited formal training, consisting of life-drawing classes at the National Academy of Design from 1845 to 1847 and the lessons with Cropsey in 1850. In 1849 Johnson exhibited his first landscape paintings and began his lifelong practice of nature study in the summer followed by studio work in the winter. He traveled throughout the Northeast; the Adirondack, Catskill, and White Mountains were among his favorite sketching haunts. His oeuvre was characterized by highly detailed and naturalistic landscapes until the 1880s, when he adopted a looser, more painterly approach to topography influenced by the French Barbizon School.

1. John I. H. Baur and Margaret C. Conrads, *Meditations on Nature: The Drawings of David Johnson* (Yonkers, N.Y.: Hudson River Museum of Westchester, 1987), 11.
2. Ibid.

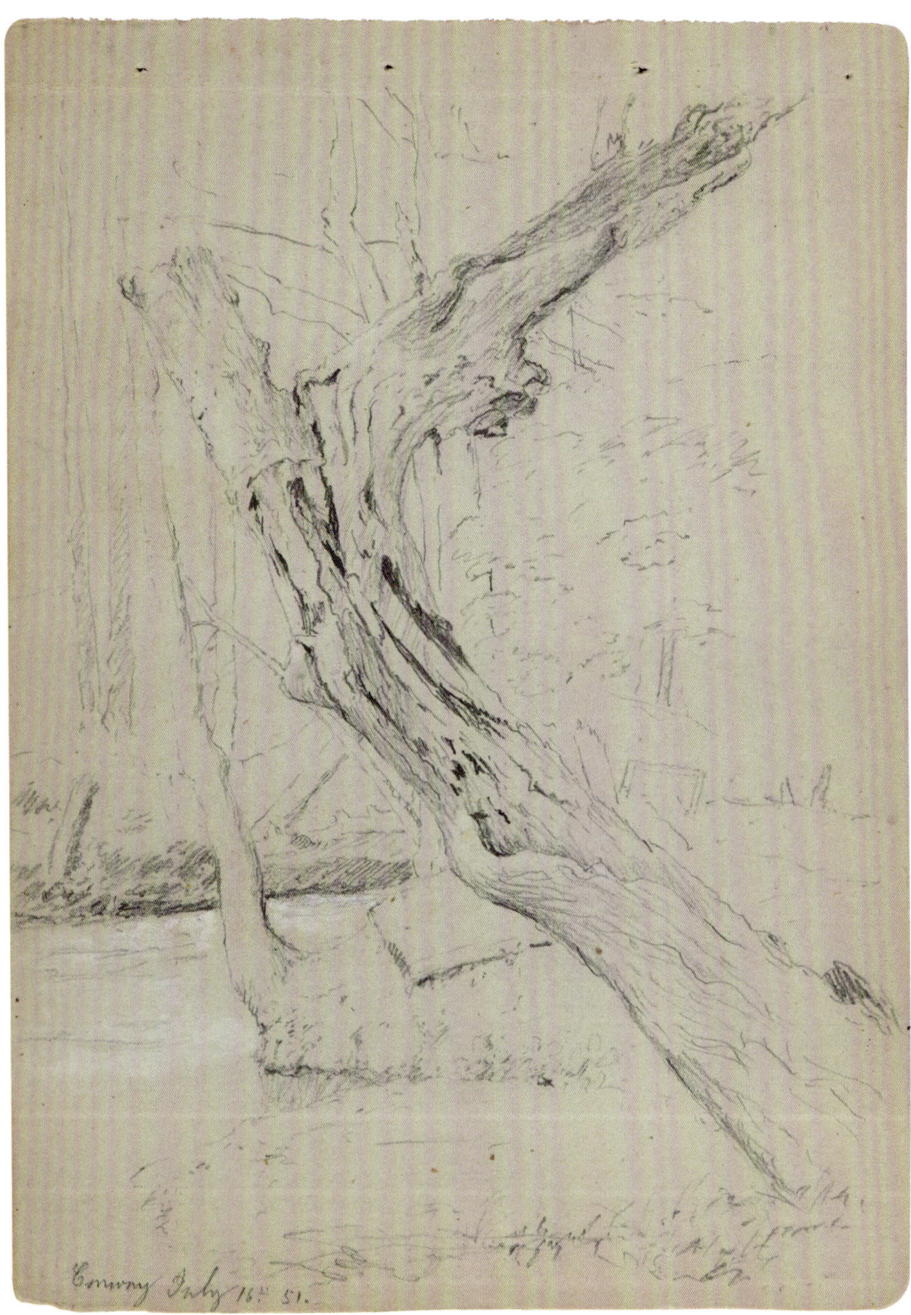

1997.157, page 7

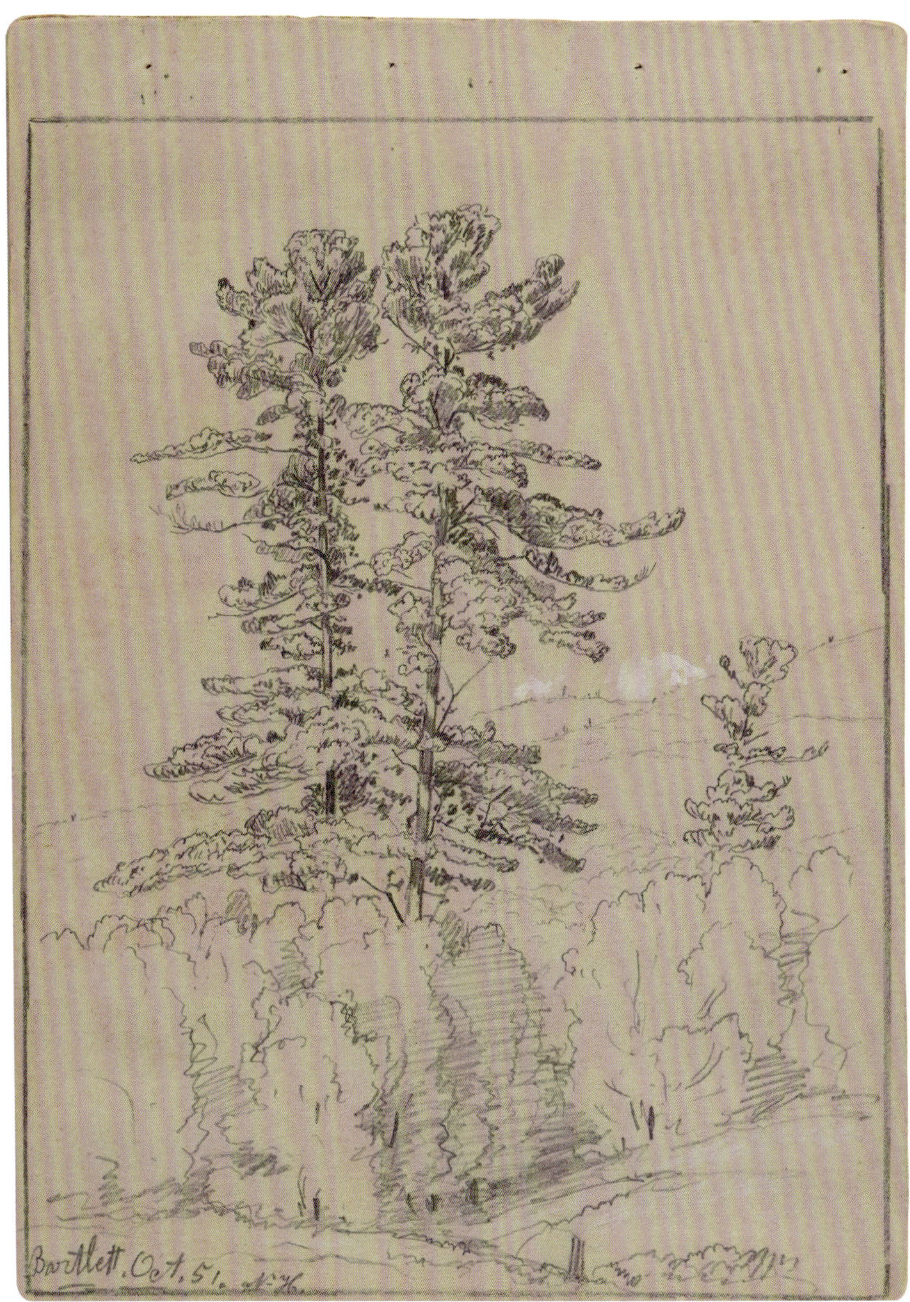

1997.157, page 14

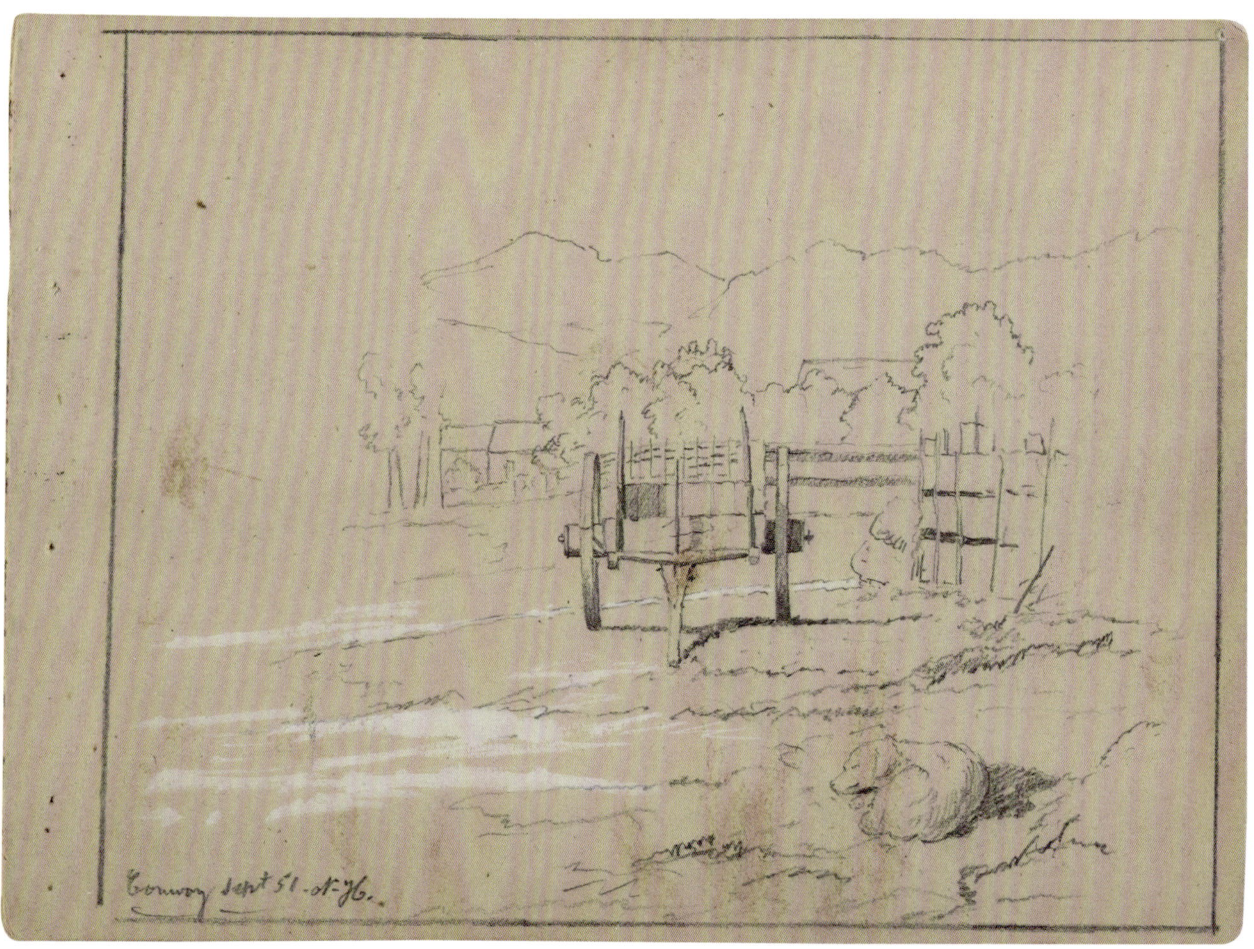

1997.157, page 17

George Henry Hall

American, 1825–1913

74 Sketchbook, various dates, 1852–93

Graphite and opaque watercolor on cream, blue, and beige, medium-weight, slightly textured wove papers, 11¹⁄₁₆ × 16¹³⁄₁₆ × ¹³⁄₁₆ in. (28.1 × 42.7 × 2.1 cm)
Gift of Jennie Brownscombe, 16.758.1

George Henry Hall's sketchbook documents a variety of subjects and locations in Italy and the United States, mostly from his early career in the 1850s. Hall began his studies abroad at the Düsseldorf Royal Academy in 1849, opened a studio in Paris by 1850, and later traveled extensively throughout Italy. Using this sketchbook to record sights from his Italian travels in the spring of 1852, Hall created polished drawings of stunning panoramas and natural landscape formations. Executed primarily in graphite and white watercolor, the sketches follow the picturesque landscape conventions established by the practitioners of the Hudson River School. In a sweeping view of the southern Italian city of Sorrento on page 31, Hall used white highlights to lead the viewer's eye away from the open expanse of the foreground to the architecture of Sorrento lining the coast. These highlights create the effect of sunlight hitting the buildings, setting the middle ground apart from the mountainous background. An intimate landscape of Lake Nemi, located about twenty miles south of Rome, on page 27 contains an even more distant view of a city, framed by the branches of a tree in the foreground. White wash illuminates the water, tree trunk, and architecture, capturing the brilliance of Italian light. In the view of Capri on page 33, craggy cliffs frame the dramatic rock formations that jut out of the calm water. The elongated strokes of graphite used to represent shadows on the smooth surface of the water are juxtaposed with sharp, rapidly executed hatch marks that

indicate the rough texture of the rocks. After returning to New York in the summer of 1852, Hall continued to fill this sketchbook with scenes from subsequent travels in upstate New York and New Hampshire.

To fund an extended period of study in Spain beginning in 1860, Hall held a sale of 143 works completed in the 1850s.[1] At least thirty of these paintings (now unlocated) depicted ruins, nature studies, or landscapes from Italy, Massachusetts, New York, and New Hampshire—subjects that may have been based on preparatory images from this sketchbook. Hall traveled to Spain twice during his career, in 1860–61 and again in 1866–67, in order to focus on figure paintings of peasants. These pictures, along with his Italian figural subjects, became some of his best-known works.[2] Because Hall was primarily a genre and still-life painter, this sketchbook provides a rare glimpse into the artist's experiments with landscape composition.—CG

1. The total proceeds of this sale, held at Henry H. Leeds & Co. in New York, exceeded $3,600. See *Catalogue of Pictures, Fruit & Flower Studies, and Sketches from Nature, Painted by Mr. Geo. H. Hall, now on exhibition at the Academy of Design, Tenth Street, near Broadway*, sale cat., Henry H. Leeds & Co., New York, Feb. 29, 1860.
2. See "Obituary: George Henry Hall," *American Art News* 11, no. 20 (Feb. 22, 1913): 3.

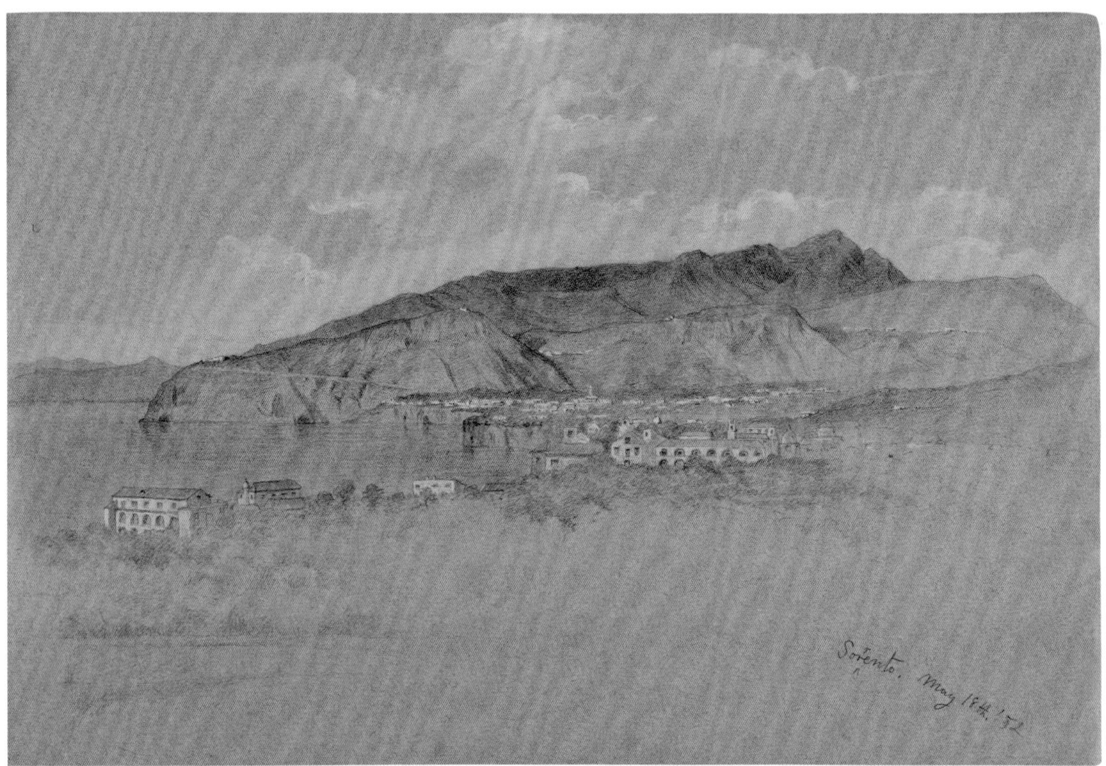

16.758.1, page 31

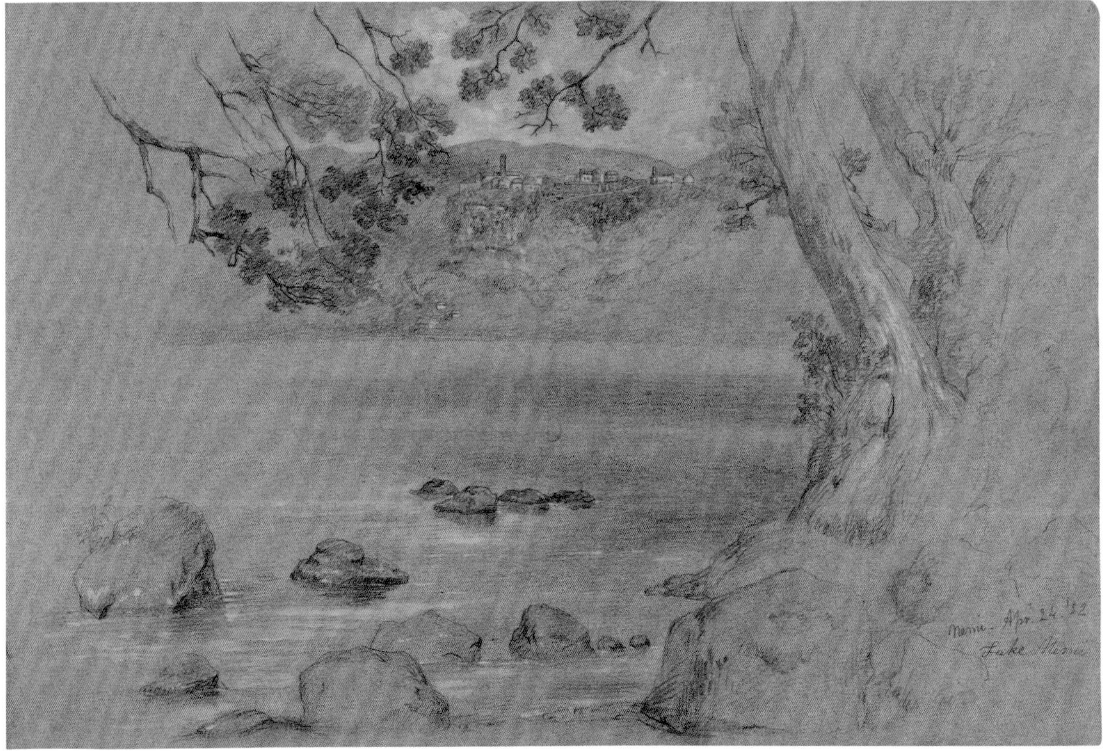

16.758.1, page 27

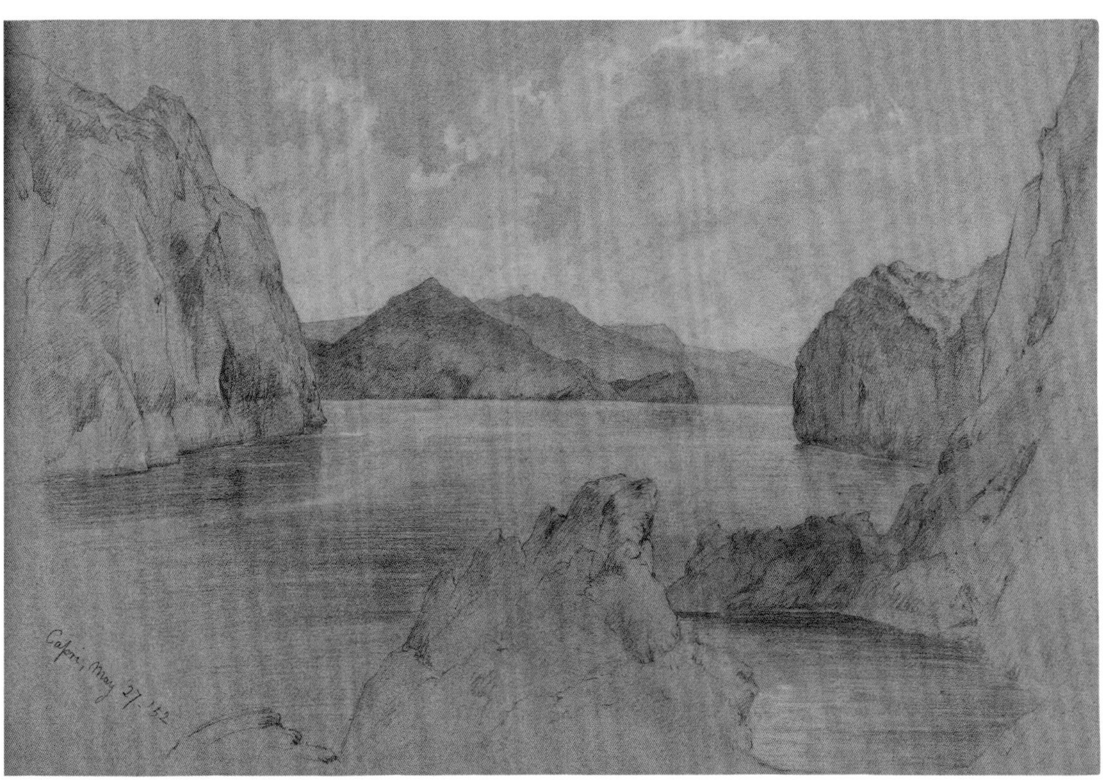

16.758.1, page 33

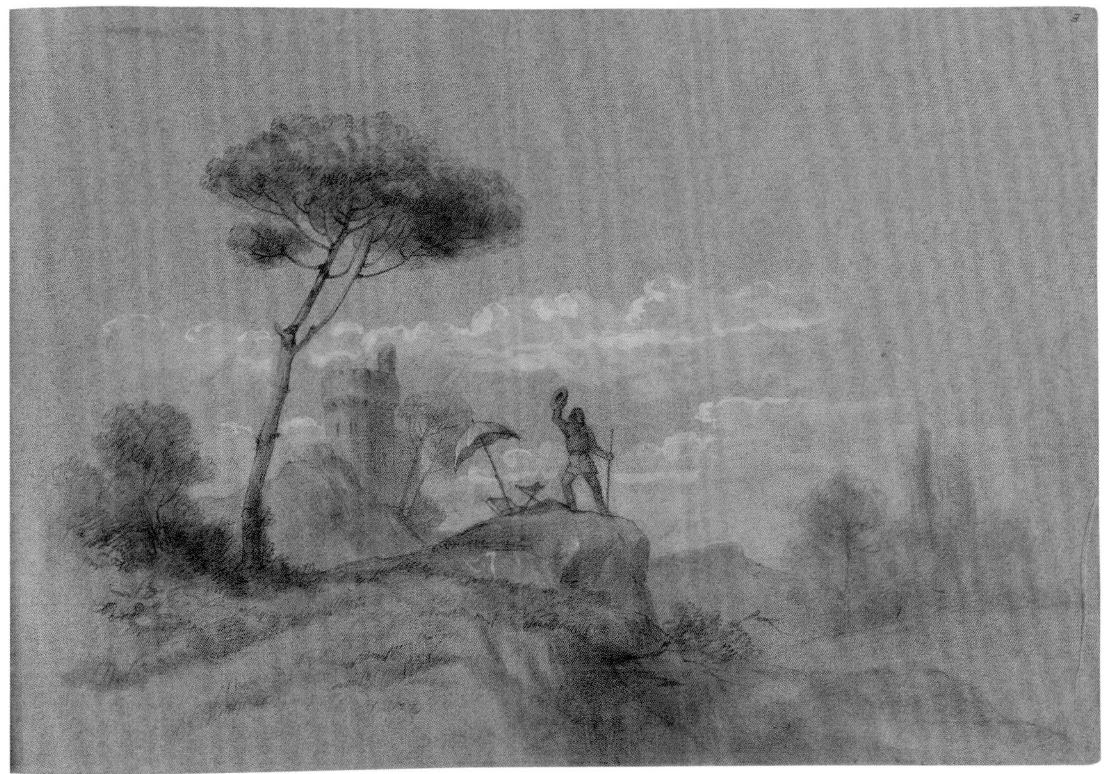

16.758.1, page 3

William Trost Richards

American, 1833–1905

75 Niagara Falls, 1856

Graphite on cream, medium-weight, smooth wove paper, 9¼ × 12⁹⁄₁₆ in. (23.5 × 31.9 cm)
Lent by Mr. and Mrs. David Price, TL70.281.104

On this sheet torn from a sketchbook (at an unknown time), William Trost Richards executed a rapid sketch of Niagara Falls, North America's most famous and recognizable natural wonder, seen from the American side in New York State. His vantage point situates the viewer on a ledge at the top of the falls. Richards heightened the visual sensation of awe and vertigo by leaving the area at the lower left of the composition largely blank: the viewer's eye moves quickly across these white passages to follow the path of the powerful river as it pours over the edge. The artist used shaded rubbings of graphite to depict the water and thin, jagged outlines to articulate the rocky topography, as well as the trees and clouds in the far distance. He again exploited the blank paper to describe the mist that obscures parts of the Horseshoe Falls in the middle distance.

Richards traveled to Niagara Falls in 1856 for his honeymoon, following his marriage to Anna Matlack. Since the beginning of the nineteenth century, this spectacular landmark had been drawing artists and other visitors who went to marvel at nature's sublime power. The area's tourism industry developed concurrently with the emergence of the Hudson River School. Symbiotic relationships between landscape tourism and landscape painting also arose around sites in other parts of the country (such as the Catskill Mountains in New York and the Natural Bridge in Virginia), fostering widespread interest in images of these distinctive American places.

As the Philadelphia-born Richards began his artistic career in the early 1850s, he modeled his work on that of the luminaries of the Hudson River School, including Thomas Cole (1801–1848), John Frederick Kensett (1816–1872), and Jasper Francis Cropsey (1823–1900). Such influences are evident in the panoramic sweep, topographic naturalism, and on-the-spot production of *Niagara Falls*. Over the course of his long and productive career, Richards's approach to landscape evolved to incorporate the meticulously detailed mode of representation advocated by John Ruskin (see numbers 77, 78) and the Barbizon-inspired interest in capturing atmospheric effects—especially in coastal scenes, for which he became best known. His commitment to sketching in nature remained constant, as evidenced by the great volume of drawings and oil studies that he produced.[1]

1. The Brooklyn Museum also owns twenty-seven sketchbooks by Richards, as well as numerous other drawings, watercolors, and oil paintings.

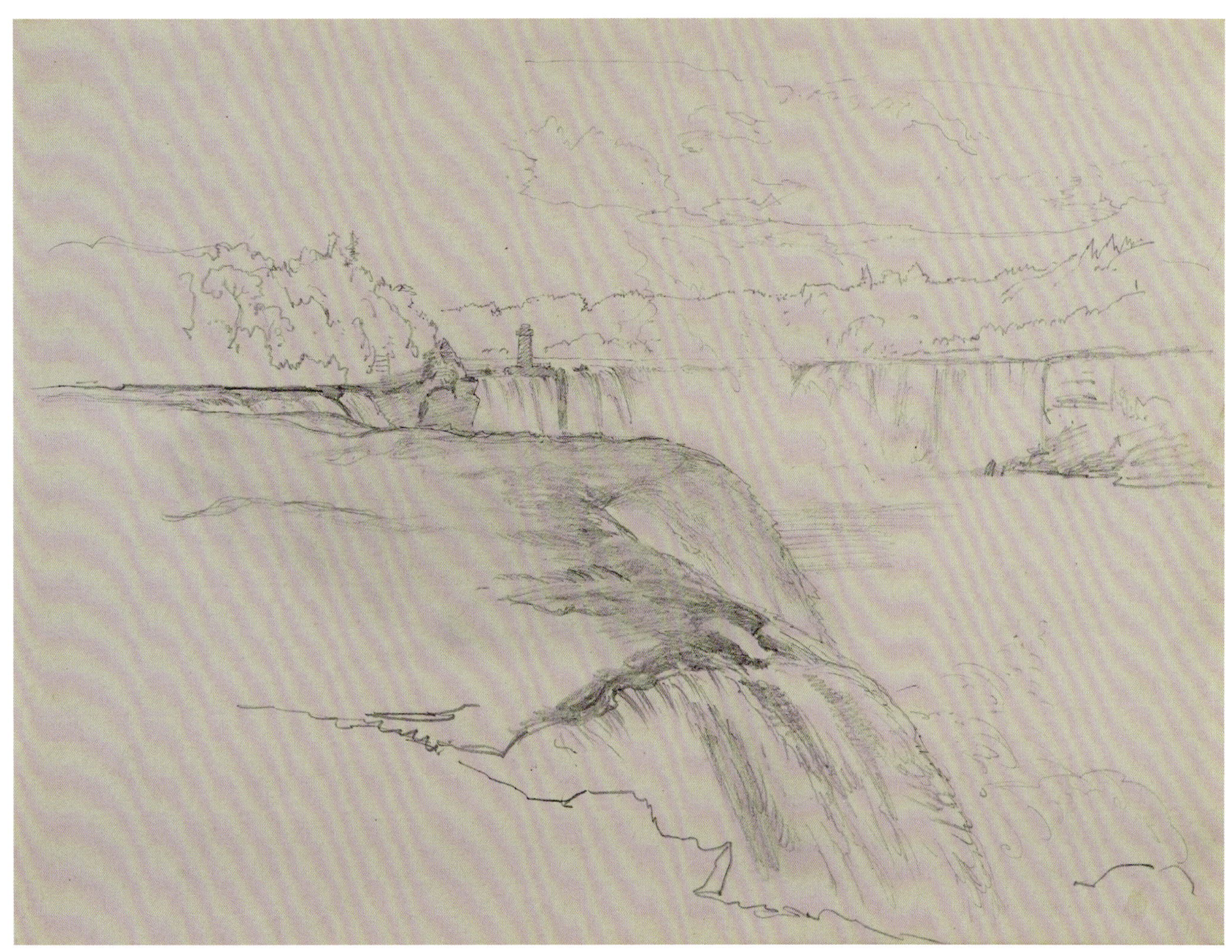

Albert Bierstadt

American, born Germany, 1830–1902

76 Study of a Ewe, circa 1855

Black crayon and red and white chalk on blue-green, medium-weight, slightly textured laid paper, 10⁹⁄₁₆ × 14¹⁄₁₆ in. (26.8 × 35.7 cm)
Purchased with funds given by Mr. and Mrs. Leonard L. Milberg, 1990.101.2

Albert Bierstadt's *Study of a Ewe* was most likely executed during a summer sketching tour of the German countryside while the artist was studying in Düsseldorf between 1853 and 1857. Using black crayon and highlights of white chalk, Bierstadt captured with great naturalism and precision the volume and texture of the ewe's full coat, while rendering the face and legs only in outline. The sheet also includes, at the upper right, a loosely sketched male face in profile, possibly representing one of Bierstadt's traveling companions. In Germany, Bierstadt mastered the typical Düsseldorf style, associated with highly detailed paintings using localized color and intense light and shade. In style, subject matter, and execution, *Study of a Ewe* is similar to the drawings of farm animals, peasants, and landscapes contained in Bierstadt's 1854 sketchbook from his time in Germany (Addison Gallery of American Art, Andover, Massachusetts).[1]

In 1857 Bierstadt returned to the United States and eventually established his career with monumental panoramic views of the Alps and the American West—subjects that combined spectacular scenery with meticulous natural details, demonstrating the artistic skill and techniques the artist had acquired during his four years abroad. In preparation for these complex compositions, Bierstadt traveled extensively, making drawings and oil sketches of flora and fauna, as well as geological studies. Many such sketches of bison, oxen, donkeys, and other animals document the artist's close observation of these creatures for his grand compositions. *Study of a Ewe*, like Bierstadt's later sketches of animals, was a live nature study, most likely intended for use in a finished painting.—CG

1. Harrison House, *Albert Bierstadt: Painter of the American West* (New York: Harry N. Abrams, 1988), 34.

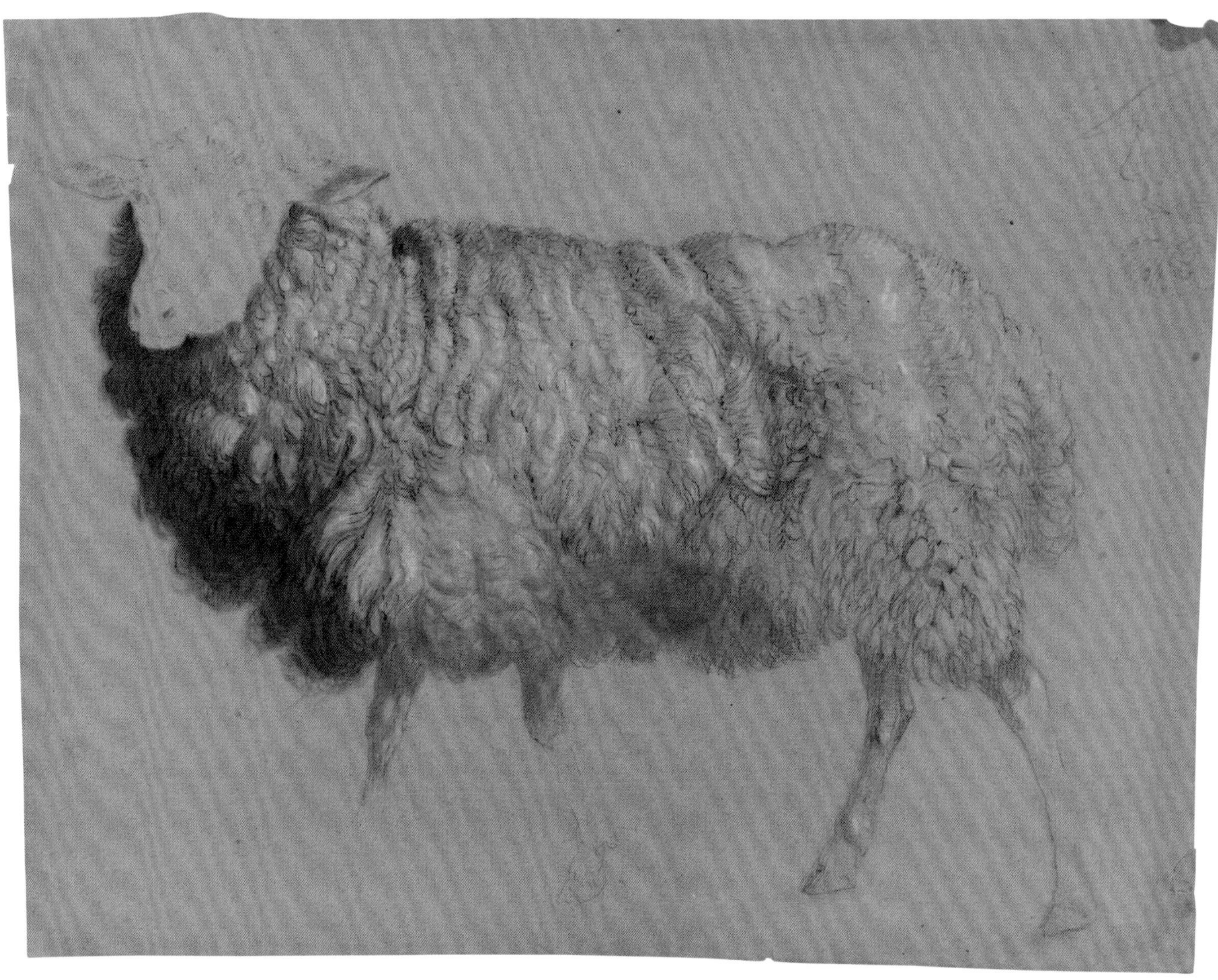

William Trost Richards

American, 1833–1905

77 Plant Study, August 1860

Graphite on beige, moderately thick, slightly textured wove paper, 5⅝ × 8¹⁄₁₆ in. (14.3 × 20.5 cm)
Inscribed in graphite, left center: "Aug 1ˢᵗ 1860."; bottom center: "Aug 4ᵗʰ 1860"; upper right: "white flower / green center"
Gift of Edith Ballinger Price, 72.32.12

78 Flower Study, July 9–14, 1860

Opaque watercolor and graphite on brown, moderately thick, slightly textured wove paper, 8⅛ × 5⅝ in. (20.6 × 14.3 cm)
Inscribed in graphite, left center: "July 9ᵗʰ 1860"; near stalks of wild grass: "little less / than size / nature" and "July 14ᵗʰ";
lower right: "about size of / nature"
Gift of Edith Ballinger Price, 72.32.9

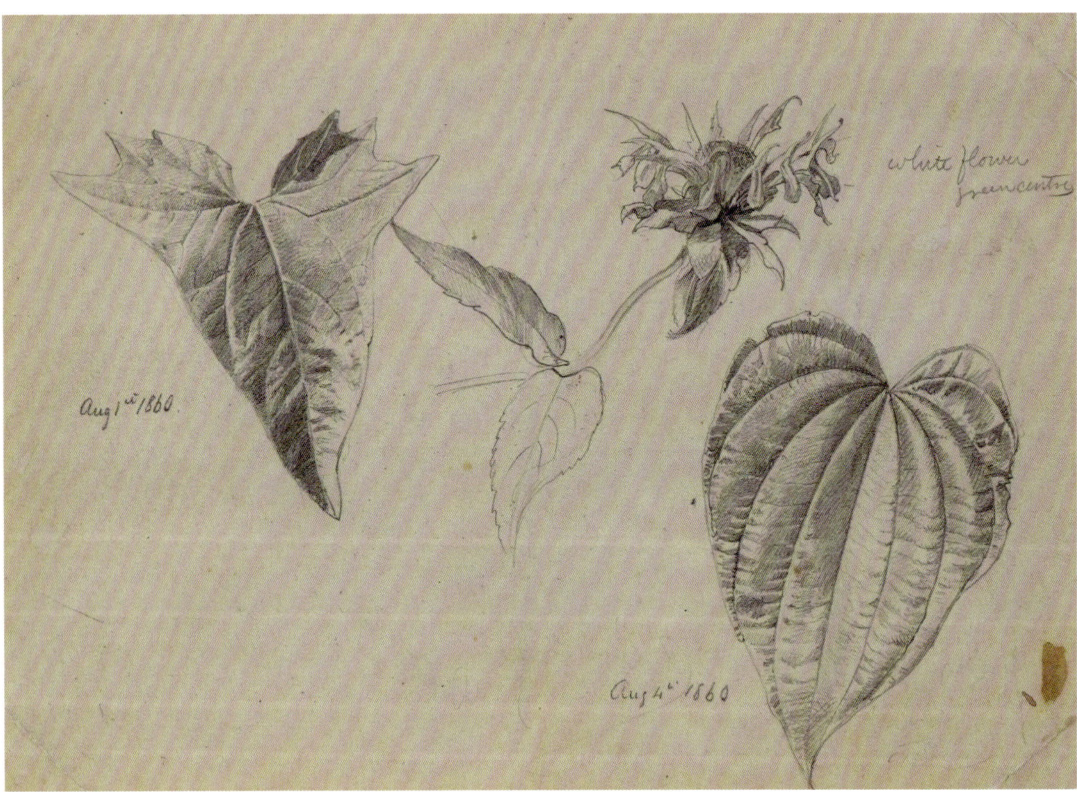

In the late 1850s, William Trost Richards ardently embraced John Ruskin's philosophy of "truth to nature," based on careful study of botanical forms. The English critic articulated these ideas in *Modern Painters*, a highly influential five-volume work published between 1843 and 1860. Excerpts also appeared in the *Crayon*, America's leading arts and culture journal of the period, and Ruskin's work became a sensation in the United States.[1] His ideas were sympathetically received by the English Pre-Raphaelite Brotherhood (founded in 1848) and by its American counterpart, the Association for the Advancement of Truth in Art (also known as the American Pre-Raphaelites), a short-lived group founded in 1863 of which Richards was a member.

In their precise accuracy and close-up format, these two carefully detailed nature studies exemplify Richards's new

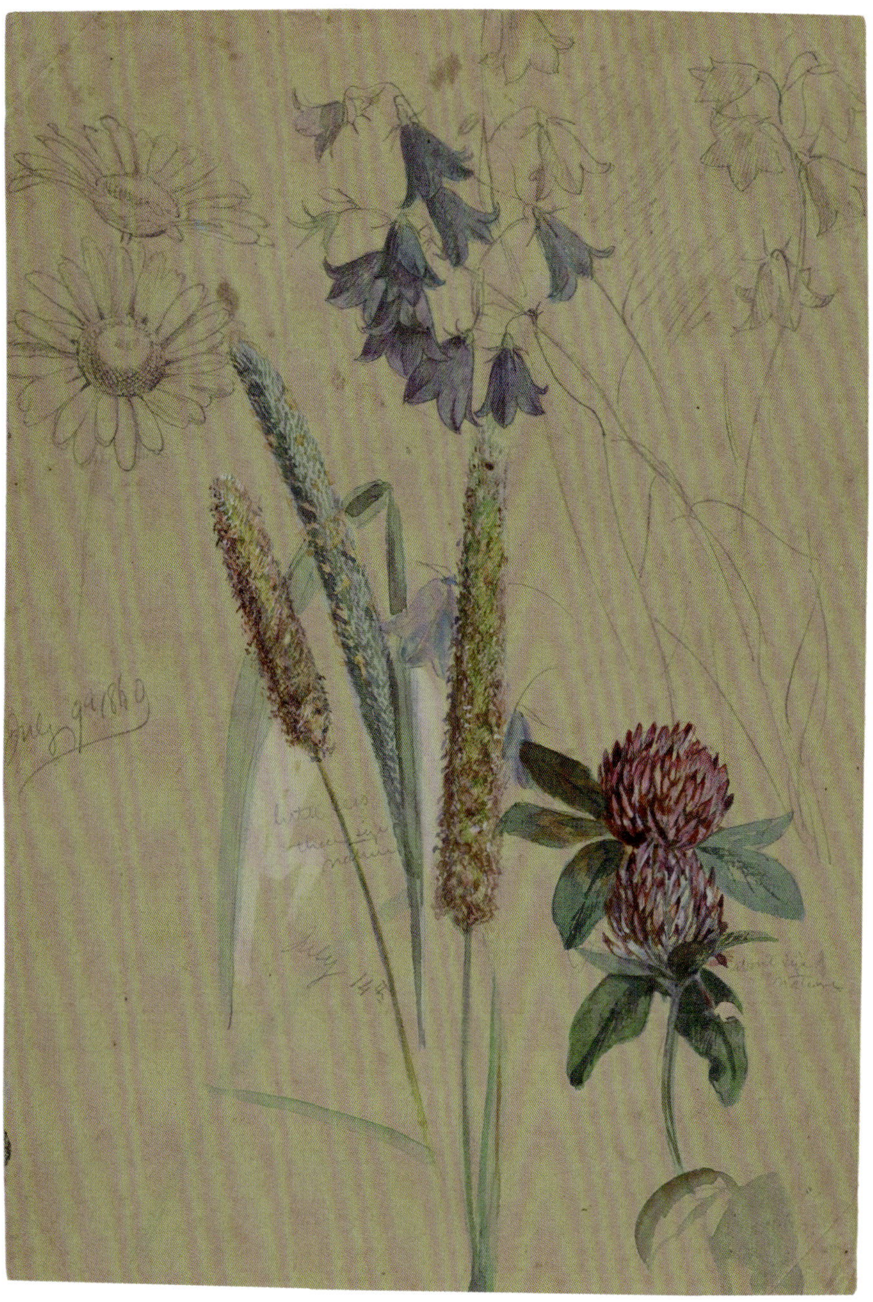

Ruskinian approach. He meticulously delineated the forms of various plants with fine graphite lines, adding hatch marks for shading. His great technical skill is particularly evident in *Plant Study*, executed entirely in graphite, in which his refined tonal modulation of the medium captures every vein of each leaf and its crinkly surface. *Flower Study* displays the same degree of botanical exactitude but adds the further dimension of color,

achieved through watercolor washes added in some of the field flowers. Inscriptions on both drawings record the day a particular specimen was drawn (each sheet contains studies from different days) and other visual notes, such as "white flower green center" or "about size of nature." The artist's concern for realism jibes with the Ruskinian notion that God is manifest in the tiniest details of the natural world.

Born in Philadelphia, Richards was forced to drop out of high school to support his family; he worked as a commercial draftsman designing ornamental metalwork. He also took informal lessons with Paul Weber (1823–1916), a German-born landscape and portrait painter. Richards began exhibiting Hudson River School–inspired landscapes in the early 1850s and, with the help of local patrons, made the first of many trips abroad in 1855–56. His travels to Paris, Florence, and Düsseldorf allowed him to complete his artistic training. Back in the Philadelphia area, he began working in the transcriptive and highly detailed manner seen in these two drawings. The mixed critical response to his Pre-Raphaelite landscapes led to another stylistic shift in the late 1860s, when he concerned himself with capturing the shifting atmospheric and meteorological conditions along the coast. Throughout his career, he was a prolific draftsman devoted to plein air work.

1. For a succinct discussion of Ruskin's influence in America, see Linda S. Ferber and William H. Gerdts, *The* *New Path: Ruskin and the American Pre-Raphaelites* (New York: Brooklyn Museum, 1985), 14–16.

— • ● • —

William Trost Richards

American, 1833–1905

79 Forest Scene with Rocky Brook, circa 1864–67

Charcoal on cream, moderately thick, slightly textured wove paper mounted to paper, 22¹³⁄₁₆ × 17¹³⁄₁₆ in. (57.9 × 45.2 cm)
Gift of Edith Ballinger Price, 72.32.2

Between 1864 and 1867, during his involvement with the short-lived American Pre-Raphaelite group known as the Association for the Advancement of Truth in Art, William Trost Richards produced large, highly finished drawings of woodland interiors such as this one. The scale and allover treatment of the picture surface constituted a departure from his typical graphic oeuvre, which consists of small sketches of panoramic landscapes and detailed nature studies, as seen in numbers 75, 77, and 78. In *Forest Scene with Rocky Brook*, he described the rugged topography and dense foliage of the woods in his typical naturalistic style. He applied the charcoal in both hard-edged lines and smudged passages, masterfully varying the tone to represent the forms and textures of the landscape motifs convincingly. White areas of blank paper break up the shadowy darkness of the forest interior by creating the effect of dappled sunlight poking through the canopy of leaves.

Although Richards had been an avid and talented draftsman from the outset of his career, drawing assumed special impor-tance for the American Pre-Raphaelites in their quest to make faithful depictions of nature. The group's manifesto, published in the inaugural issue of its organ, the *New Path*, declared that it was the artist's "duty to strive for the greatest attainable power of drawing."[1] Densely worked scenes of forest interiors had begun appearing in Richards's oils and watercolors about 1860. Although such pictures garnered praise for their accuracy and painstaking craftsmanship, they were also criticized for being unrelentingly literal. In reviewing a painting titled *Wood Scene*, one critic observed: "[Richards] forgot that seeing nature as a botanist is not seeing nature as a poet. . . . Of spiritual or poetic insight we see no sign. . . . For the rare and remarkable work which Mr. Richards has given us we are grateful, but must conclude that he is not destined to give us great creative art."[2] Such criticism led the artist to turn his energies primarily to marine subjects, particularly coastal scenes, after 1867.

1. "Association for the Advancement of Truth in Art," *New Path* 1, no. 1 (May 1863): 11.
2. "Art: Three Pictures by W. T. Richards," *Round Table* 1, no. 10 (Feb. 20, 1864): 153, quoted in Linda S. Ferber and William H. Gerdts, *The New Path: Ruskin and the American Pre-Raphaelites* (New York: Brooklyn Museum, 1985), 224. The painting described may be *Woodland Interior*, 1861 (private collection).

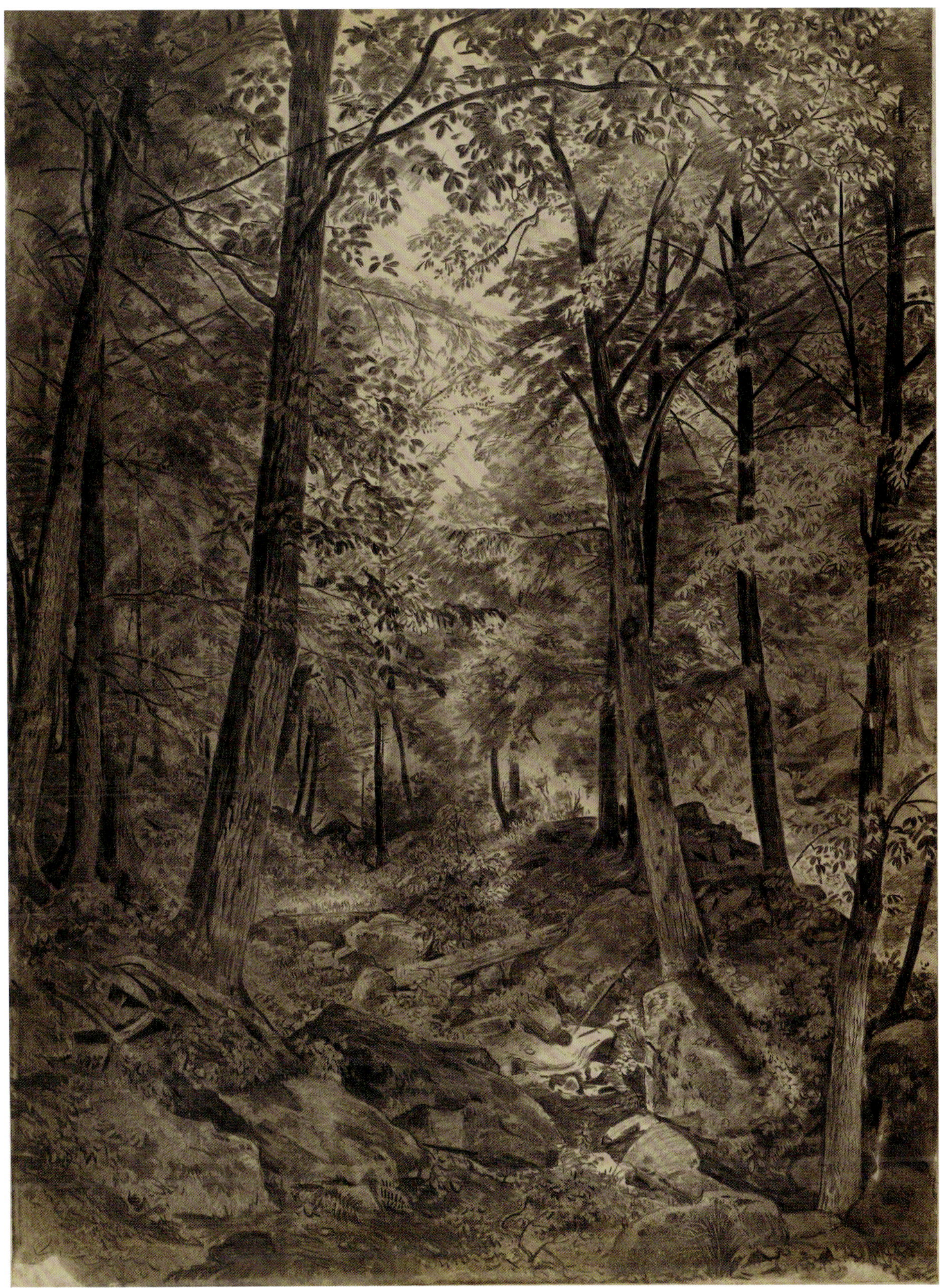

Robert Brandegee

American, 1849–1922

80 Anemones (Grasses and Flowers), April 15, 1867

Graphite on cream, moderately thick, smooth wove paper mounted to paper, 4¼ × 6⅝ in. (10.8 × 16.8 cm)
Signed in graphite, lower left: "RB"
Signed and inscribed, in graphite, on mount: "(Robert Brandegee) April 15th. 1867"
Charles Stewart Smith Memorial Fund, 82.134.1

With its high level of detail, this stunning graphite drawing is typical of Robert Brandegee's work from the early phase of his career. A member of the American Pre-Raphaelite group that followed the writings of the English critic John Ruskin, Brandegee embraced the group's philosophy of transcribing exacting observations of nature. From about 1867 to 1872, he focused on minutely observed, close-up views of nature, particularly flowers and birds, studies that also demonstrated his dual interests in art and science. In *Anemones*, he rendered the softness and lightness of the delicate flowers by alternating blank paper with heavily shaded areas to create contrast between the white anemones and the tangled brush. The firm lines in the grass and fine touches of graphite within the flowers display the confidence and precision of the artist's pencil in rendering the intertwined vegetation and each filament and anther, which together make up the stamen, of the flowers. This drawing expresses not only Brandegee's interest in botany but also his familiarity with the landscape and his attraction to the anemone, of which he wrote: "But loveliest of all was the anemone, the Thalictrum Anenenordes. . . . My delight in these flowers never changes even after many years."[1]

Brandegee completed his early artistic training with Thomas C. Farrer (1840–1891) and either John William Hill (1812–1879) or his son John Henry Hill (1839–1922), all three of whom were members of the Association for the Advancement of Truth in Art, the official name of the American Pre-Raphaelite movement. The group published the *New Path* magazine and championed the topographic recording of nature in landscape and still-life paintings so that viewers from the fields of both science and art could enjoy meticulous depictions of the natural world. By 1872 Brandegee relocated to Paris, where he lived and received academic training for almost a decade. When he returned to New York in about 1881, he opened a studio, where he completed landscapes and portraits and focused on his teaching at Miss Porter's School in Farmington, Connecticut. He later turned to writing and publishing his own books, as well as the *Farmington Magazine*, until his death in 1922.—CG

1. Robert B. Brandegee, manuscript autobiography, Collection of Robert L. Brandegee, Salisbury, Conn., quoted in Linda S. Ferber and William H. Gerdts, *The New Path: Ruskin and the American Pre-Raphaelites* (New York: Brooklyn Museum, 1985), 236.

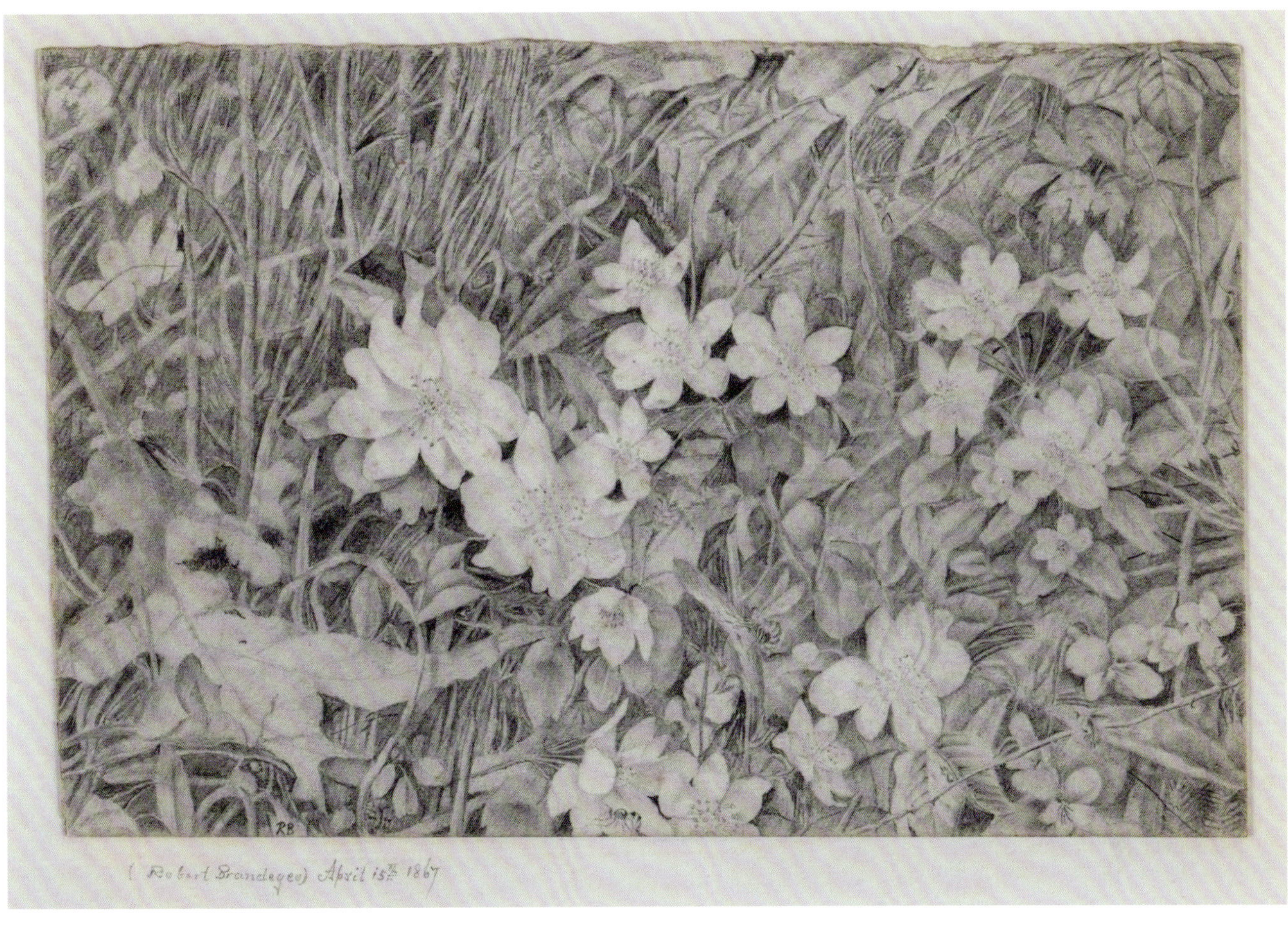

(Robert Brandegee) April 15th 1867

Aaron Draper Shattuck

American, 1832–1928

81 **Plants by a Stream,** undated

Graphite on off-white, moderately thick, smooth wove paper, sheet 3⅜ × 7¾ in. (8.6 × 19.7 cm)
Gift of Mr. and Mrs. Eugene Emigh, 77.106. © Estate of Aaron Draper Shattuck

The landscape painter Aaron Draper Shattuck most likely created this detailed study of flowers, grasses, tree trunks, and a stream organized within an arched frame during a summer sketching excursion. Typical of his plein air nature studies, the composition emphasizes the delicate flowers in the foreground, making them appear disproportionately large compared to the tree trunk at right.[1] Shattuck rendered the petals, leaves, and stems by alternating blank paper with refined and precise shading. This tight handling is juxtaposed with his vigorous yet controlled application of graphite strokes in the shadowy and at times indistinct background. The unusual arched frame, a picturesque motif that appears occasionally in Shattuck's work, is reminiscent of a stained-glass window, possibly alluding to the artist's reverence for nature. The critic Henry T. Tuckerman noticed the emotional character of Shattuck's meticulously realistic images, describing them as "elaborately true in details, and yet imbued with feeling."[2]

Beginning in 1851, Shattuck studied with the portraitist Alexander Ransom (active circa 1840–65) in Boston and in New York, where he also was enrolled at the National Academy of Design by 1852. Despite his training with Ransom, Shattuck developed an early interest in landscape painting and took annual sketching trips in the summers beginning in 1854, traveling primarily to New Hampshire as well as to the Catskills, the Adirondacks, Maine, Vermont, and Virginia. His early landscapes were well received by critics, who praised their fidelity to nature.[3]

Shattuck was best known for his small nature paintings, although he also produced larger landscapes and animal scenes. His detailed plein air studies such as *Plants by a Stream* merged traditional Hudson River School techniques with the theories of the English critic John Ruskin, whose writings, championed by the Hudson River School painter Asher B. Durand (1796–1886) and the Pre-Raphaelite movement, advocated faithful, topographic representations of nature. In 1870 Shattuck moved to a twenty-eight-acre farm in Danbury, Connecticut, where he focused on pastoral landscapes in a manner that resembled the developing American Barbizon style. Failing eyesight cut his art career short in 1888, after which he worked as an inventor and violin maker.—CG

1. Kevin J. Avery, *American Drawings and Watercolors in the Metropolitan Museum of Art*, vol. 1, *A Catalogue of Works by Artists Born before 1835* (New York: Metropolitan Museum of Art, 2002), 257.

2. Henry T. Tuckerman, *Book of the Artists: American Artist Life* (New York: G. P. Putnam and Son, 1867), 560.

3. See, for example, the review in "Domestic Art Gossip," *Crayon* 2, no. 21 (Nov. 21, 1855): 330.

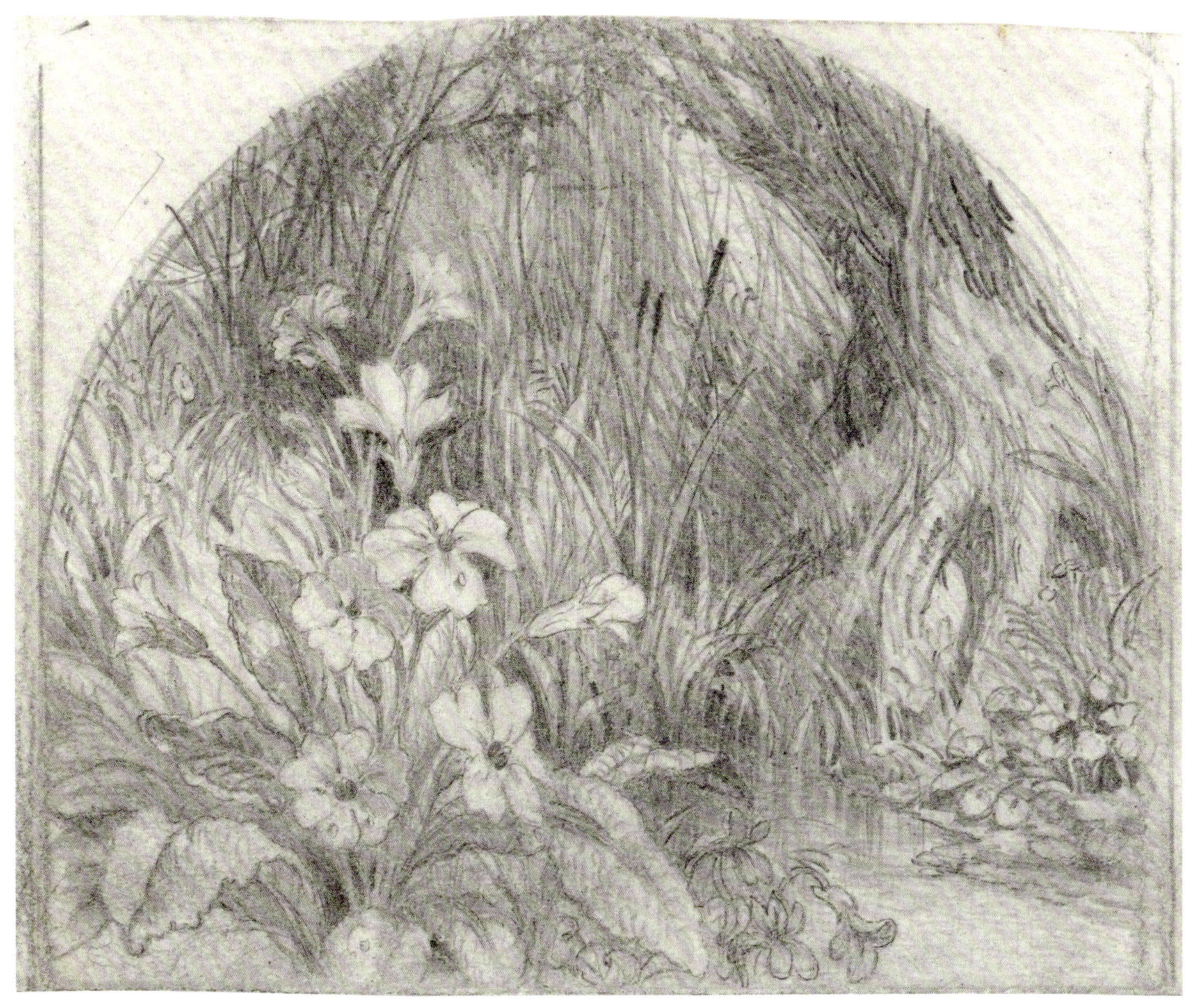

Sanford Robinson Gifford

American, 1823–1880

82 Italian Sketchbook, 1867–68

Graphite on tan, medium-weight, slightly textured wove paper, 5 × 9 × ⁷⁄₁₆ in. (12.7 × 22.9 × 1.1 cm)
Signed and inscribed in graphite, inside front cover: "S R Gifford / Studio Building 51 West 10th. St / New York" and "Maggiore / Como / Sicily / Rome / Genoa / 1868"
Gift of Jennie Brownscombe, 17.141

A leading figure of the Hudson River School of landscape painting, Sanford Robinson Gifford was a devoted practitioner of plein air sketching, which provided raw material for paintings executed later in his studio. He used this sketchbook on his travels in Europe and the Middle East during his second European sojourn, which included a three-month stay in Rome. Composed of seventy-six pages, sixty-five of which contain drawings of locations visited by the artist, the book documents his trips around Italy between July and October 1868, beginning with his passage through the Alps from Switzerland to northern Italy.

Many of these sketches are based on Gifford's travels around the lakes in Lombardy. After recording mountain views in the Alps such as the Matterhorn, Gifford traveled to Lake Orta, where he sketched the Basilica of Saint Julius on the Isola San Giulio (page 29). Following a short stay in Milan, Gifford proceeded to Stresa, on Lake Maggiore, where he sketched Monte Ferro rising above Laveno, located across the lake (pages 32–33). Gifford's sketch documents the massive shape and volume of Monte Ferro, emphasizing its sharp peaks, and captures the grandness of the mountain form rising above the calm lake; when he returned to the United States, he completed a finished painting of the subject (figure 21). The details of daily life in the lake region are depicted on page 32, where Gifford quickly sketched boats and the lake-side town of Laveno. This compositional format—a two-page panoramic view—appears throughout the sketchbook and is often accompanied by these small, sometimes framed sketches of figures, buildings, or possible composition designs. Gifford later based other paintings on these sketches, including scenes of the Matterhorn and Tivoli.[1]

From Stresa, Gifford crossed to Lake Maggiore's eastern shore and found himself at the church of Santa Caterina del Sasso (page 35), "a church hung on a shelf of rock on the face of a cliff—a very picturesque spot."[2] He then journeyed both west and south, to Genoa, Rome, and Sicily, stopping in Tivoli outside Rome, where he sketched the Arch of Nero (pages 70–71).—CG

1. The Matterhorn painting is lost but is known from an etching. See Ila Weiss, "Sanford R. Gifford in Europe: A Sketchbook of 1868," *American Art Journal* 9, no. 2 (Nov. 1977): 85. *Tivoli*, 1869, oil on canvas, is now in the collection of the Metropolitan Museum of Art, New York (acc. no. 12.205.1).
2. Sanford Robinson Gifford Papers, Aug. 11, 1868, Archives of American Art, Smithsonian Institution.

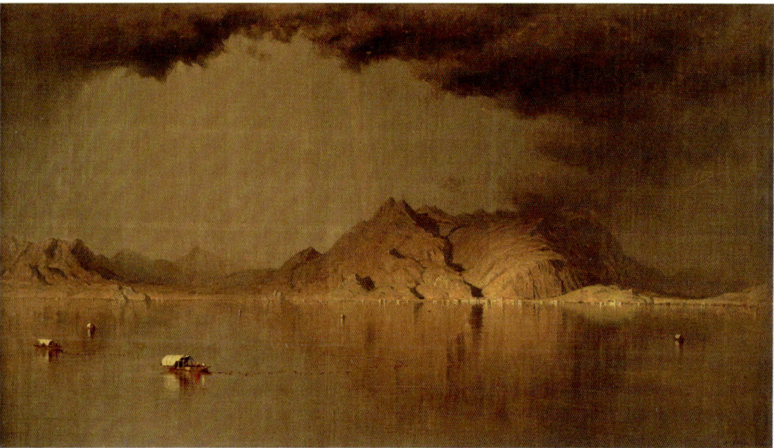

Fig. 21. Sanford Robinson Gifford. *Monte Ferro from Lago Maggiore*, 1871. Oil on canvas, 22½ × 40¼ in. (57.2 × 102.2 cm). Picker Art Gallery, Colgate University, Hamilton, New York, Gift of James Colby Colgate

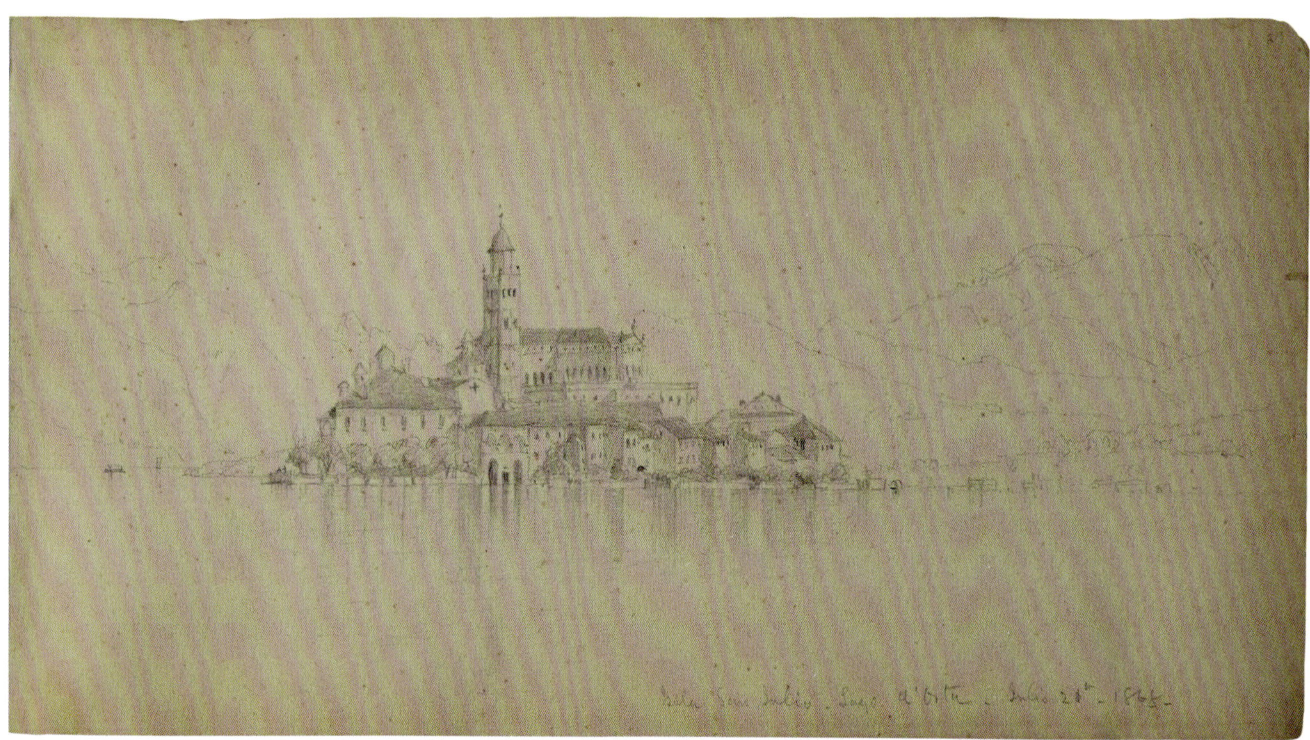

17.141, page 29

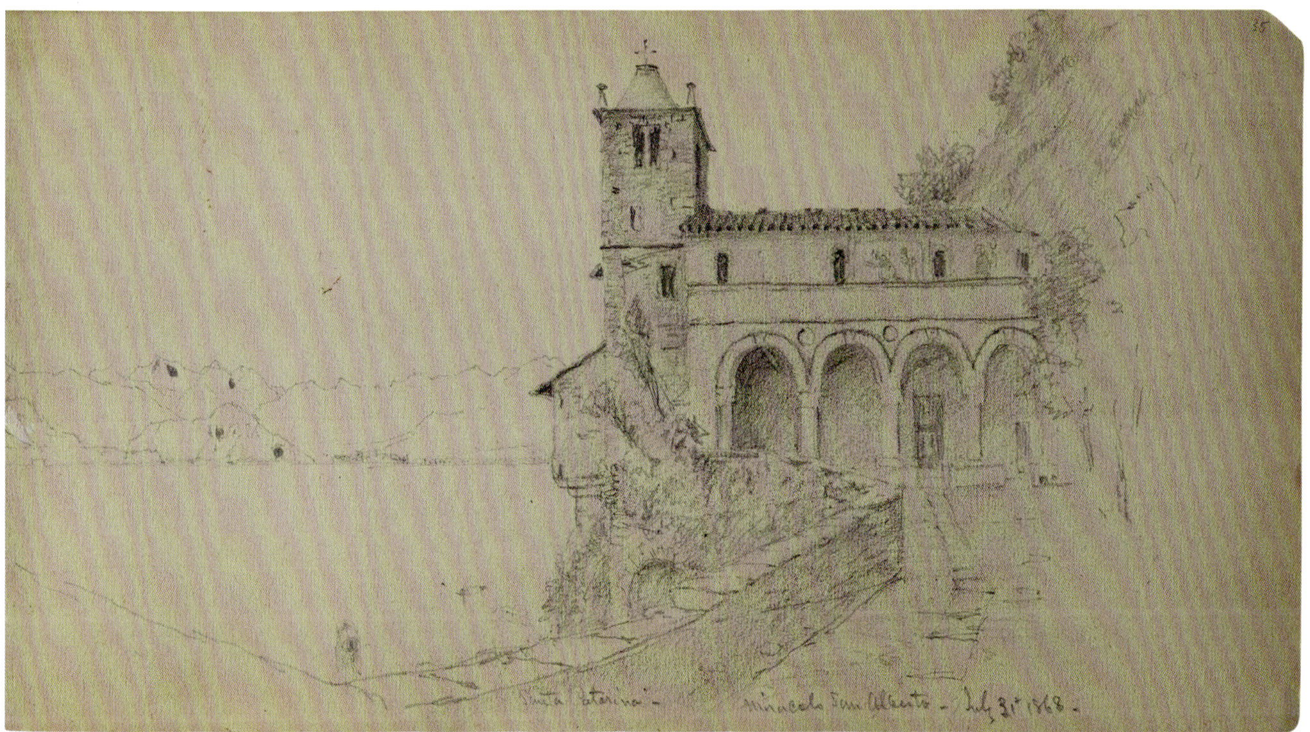

17.141, page 35

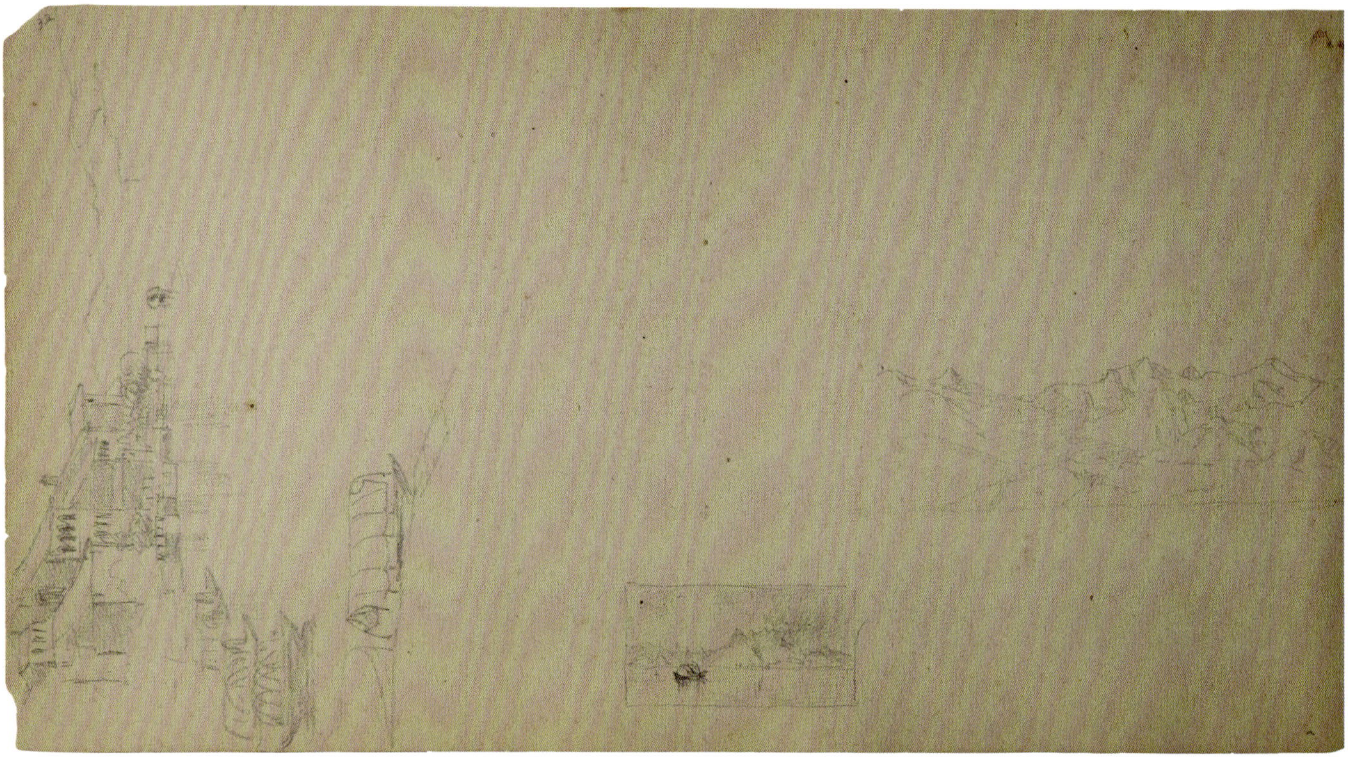

17.141, page 32 and (opposite) page 33

17.141, page 70 and (opposite) page 71

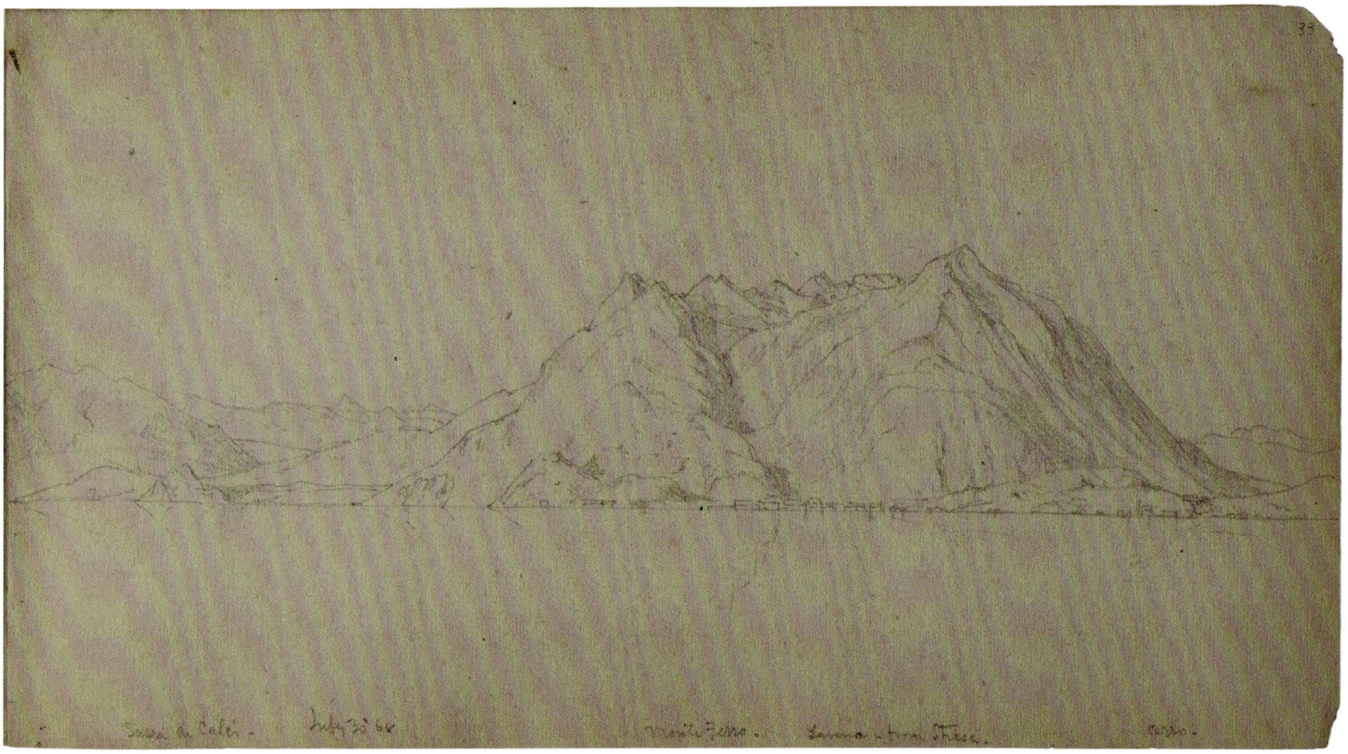

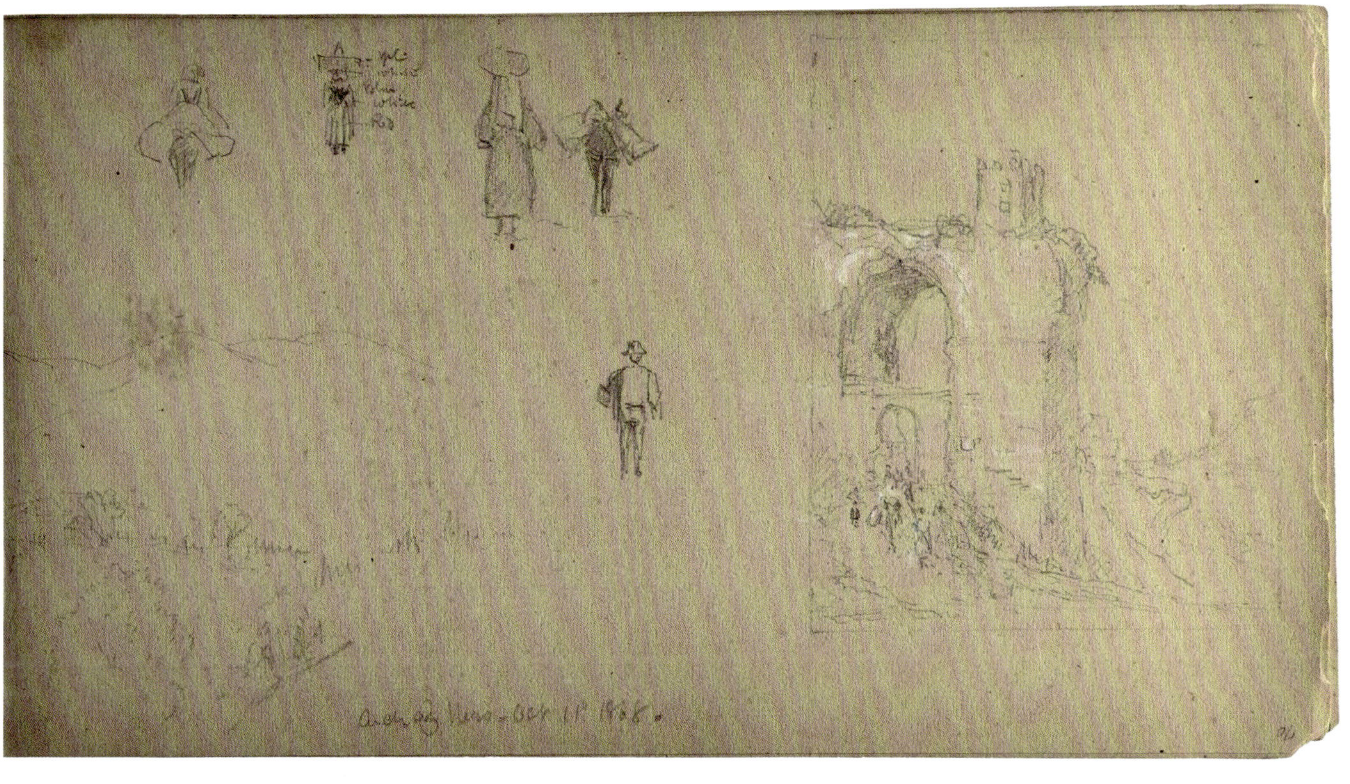

Ralph Albert Blakelock

American, 1847–1919

83 Pitch Pine, Point Arena, California, circa 1869–72

Ink and graphite on cream, moderately thick, moderately textured wove paper, $10^{15}/_{16} \times 8^{1}/_{2}$ in. (27.8 × 21.6 cm)
Signed in ink over graphite, lower right: "Pitch Pine / Pines / Pt. Arena Cal / Blakelock"
Gift of Mr. and Mrs. E. LeGrand Beers in memory of Edwin Beers, 27.17

84 Russian Gulch, California, circa 1869–72

Ink on off-white, medium-weight, smooth wove paper, $6^{11}/_{16} \times 5^{3}/_{8}$ in. (17 × 13.7 cm)
Signed in ink over graphite, lower right: "R.A. Blakelock / Russian Gulch Cal."
Gift of Mr. and Mrs. E. LeGrand Beers in memory of Edwin Beers, 27.12

In 1869, early in his career, Ralph Albert Blakelock set off for the Pacific coast to seek inspiration in the relatively pristine landscapes of the American West. En route to California, he traveled through various states and territories, often alone and on horseback, and also spent time among Native American tribes. His return took him through Mexico, Panama, and Jamaica before he arrived home in New York City in 1872.[1] During these travels, Blakelock produced more than a hundred on-the-spot drawings, including the two landscapes shown here of Russian Gulch and Point Arena, sites along the coast north of San Francisco. As is typical of this body of work, he executed each image in pencil and then traced over his graphite line in ink, possibly at a later date. *Russian Gulch* depicts a panoramic vista of the craggy peaks of this dramatic landscape, while *Pitch Pine* focuses on a more intimate, close-up view of trees. In both sketches, Blakelock described the forms in an economical outline, with only minimal shading in occasional passages of parallel hatch marks. The vigorous quality of his draftsmanship, however, endows these spare pictures with energy. Rarely continuous and flowing, the lines are jagged or broken into short dashes, or they twist and loop in animated fashion; such effects are particularly evident in *Pitch Pine*. Although these western drawings are not closely linked to any of Blakelock's later paintings, they foretell the expressive and idiosyncratic nature of his mature art.

Largely self-taught as an artist, the New York–born Blakelock dropped out of medical school to pursue a painting career and, in 1867, made his debut at the National Academy of Design with a landscape painting. His early pictures, based on sketching trips in the Northeast, reflect the influence of the Hudson River School. After returning from his travels out west, Blakelock abandoned the detailed naturalism of this style and began painting western landscapes in a broadly brushed and evocative manner inspired by his own Romantic sensibilities and by the French Barbizon aesthetic. Deeply subjective, his dark, moody, and heavily impastoed mature works often depict moonlit forest scenes containing Native American vignettes. He struggled with both financial and mental problems and was institutionalized from 1899 until his death. Although critical recognition came late in his life, Blakelock is considered, along with Albert Pinkham Ryder (1847–1917), one of the most original and visionary American artists around the turn of the twentieth century.

1. The exact itinerary and dates of Blakelock's western travels are unclear, but it seems likely that he made two separate trips during a three-year period (one from 1869 to 1871 and another in 1872).

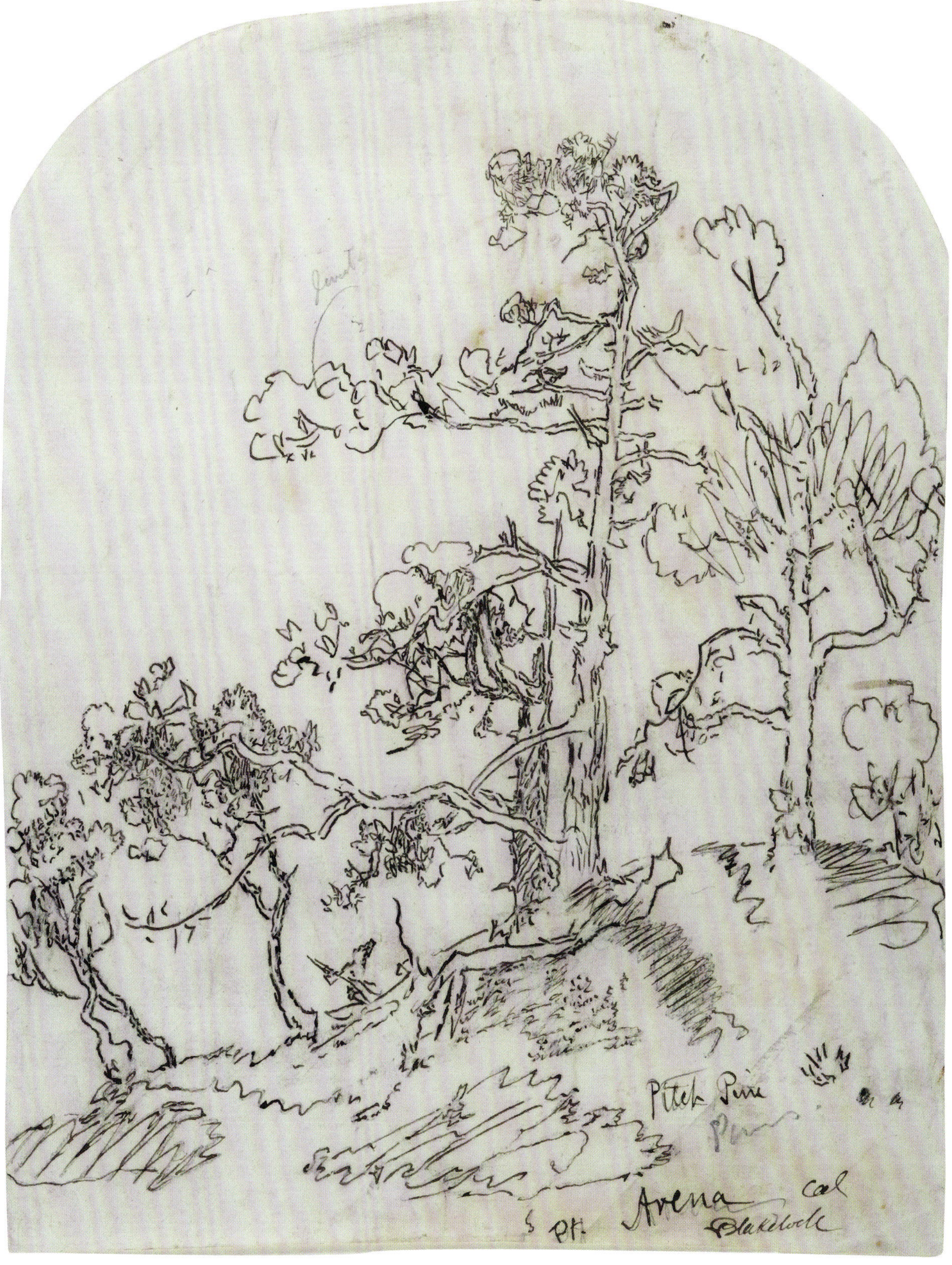

83

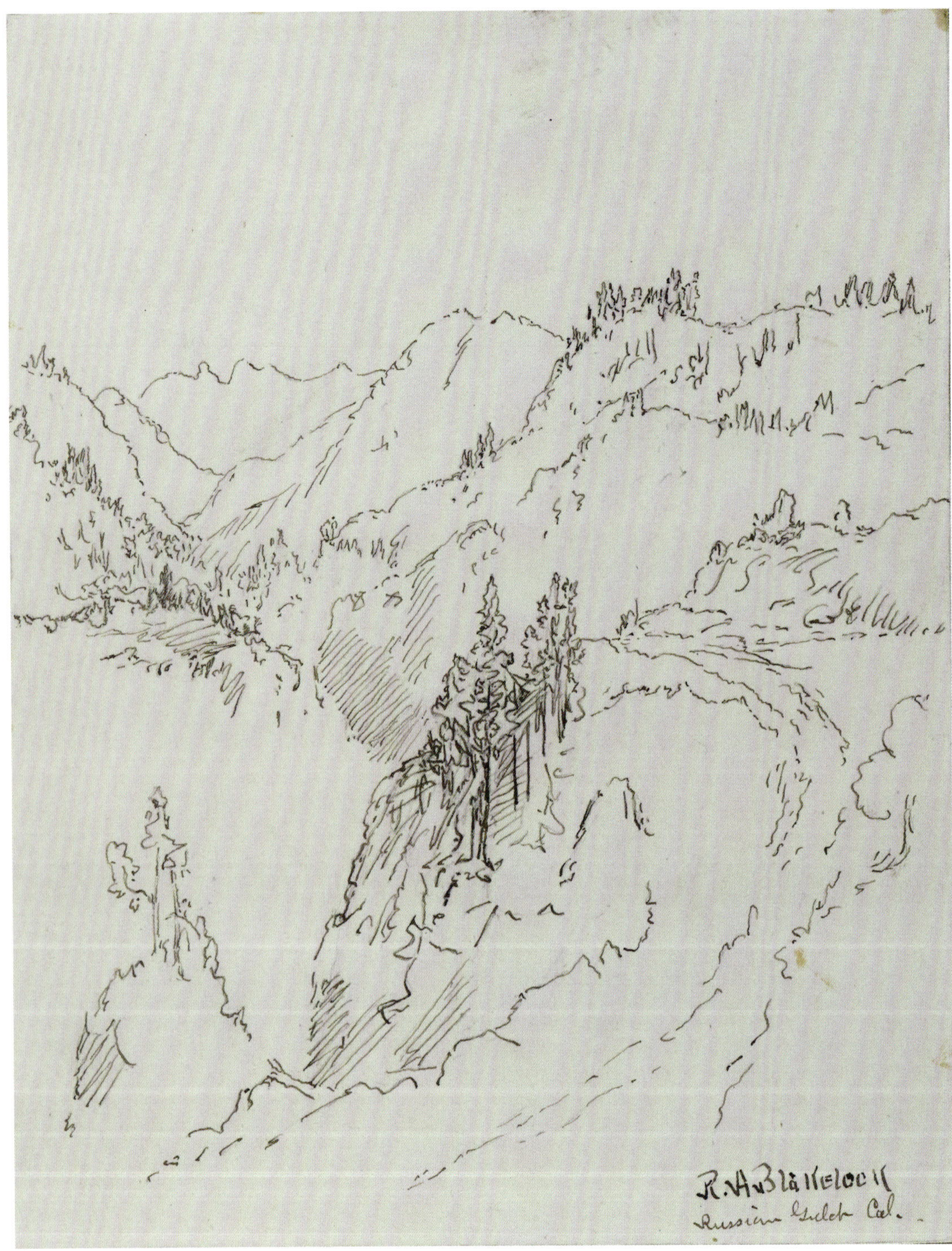

84

Esther Frances (Francesca) Alexander

American, 1837–1917

85 S. Zita, 1874–82

Brown ink on cream, moderately thick, slightly textured wove paper, 14¹⁵⁄₁₆ × 10¹⁵⁄₁₆ in. (37.9 × 27.8 cm)
Dick S. Ramsay Fund, 83.33.1

Between 1868 and 1882, Esther Frances (also called "Francesca") Alexander created 122 ink drawings—including *S. Zita*—that were reproduced in *Roadside Songs of Tuscany* (1884–85), a compilation of Italian folk ballads. This exquisite sheet consists of a minutely detailed image of a buttercup plant nestled between two rectangular registers containing the lyrics of a song about the thirteenth-century saint Zita in both Italian and English. Most likely working from direct observation,[1] Alexander accurately described the forms and textures of each botanical part with thin, precise pen strokes applied in a stippled pattern (figure 22). She lavished equal care on the text, using faint pencil guidelines for the rows of verse and emphasizing some letters with bold outlines while embellishing others with ornamental serifs. Although the floral decoration is not explicitly related to the song, the plant seems to interact with the verse in that a few bladelike leaves cross over the border of the text register.

Born in Boston, Alexander settled permanently in Florence, Italy, in 1853. Under the protective watch of her mother and father, the portraitist Francis Alexander (1800–1880), she pursued the art of drawing and her fascination with the folk music of the local peasantry, many of whom she befriended. These interests converged in *Roadside Songs of Tuscany*, a compilation of the words and melodies of traditional Italian songs illustrated with her drawings, including portraits, floral motifs, and genre scenes. Her cosmopolitan family's home was frequented by many artists and cultural luminaries, including the watercolorist Henry Roderick Newman (1843–1917), the poet John Greenleaf Whittier, and the doctor-writer Oliver Wendell Holmes. When John Ruskin visited in 1882 at Newman's suggestion, the famous English art critic was so impressed with Alexander's work that he purchased the original manuscript for *Roadside Songs*. The meticulous realism of her drawings and her unaffected piety (she regularly ministered to the poor) embodied Ruskin's own aesthetic tenet that propounded faithful transcriptions of nature in order to reveal God's presence. (Earlier in his career, Ruskin had championed the Pre-Raphaelites for similar reasons.) After returning to England in 1883, he promoted Alexander through his lectures and helped with the publication of *Roadside Songs*. Of these drawings he wrote: "In absolute skill of drawing, and perception of all that is loveliest in human

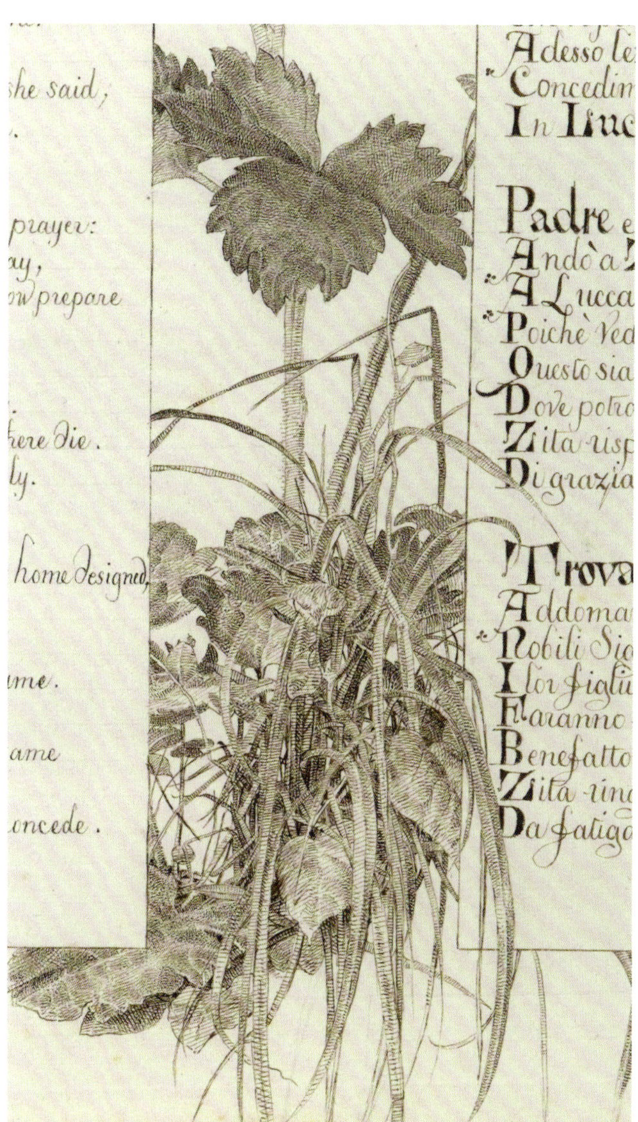

Fig. 22. Detail of number 85

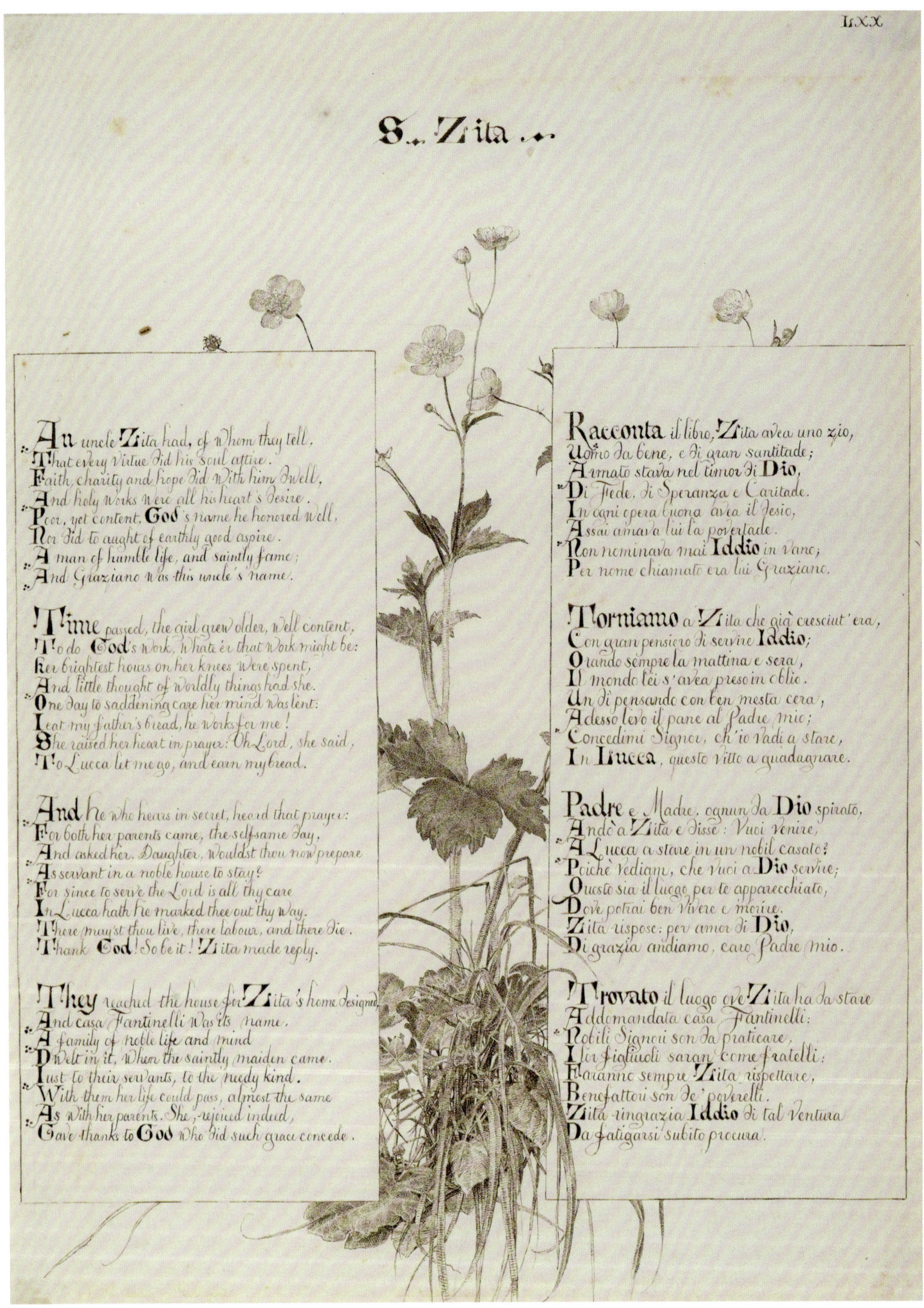
LXX

S. Zita

An uncle Zita had, of whom they tell,
That every virtue did his soul attire.
Faith, charity and hope did with him dwell,
And holy works were all his heart's desire.
Poor, yet content, God's name he honored well,
Nor did to aught of earthly good aspire.
A man of humble life, and saintly fame;
And Graziano was this uncle's name.

Time passed, the girl grew older, well content,
To do God's work, whate'er that work might be:
Her brightest hours on her knees were spent,
And little thought of worldly things had she.
One day to saddening care her mind was lent:
I eat my father's bread, he works for me!
She raised her heart in prayer: Oh Lord, she said,
To Lucca let me go, and earn my bread.

And he who hears in secret, heard that prayer:
For both her parents came, the selfsame day,
And asked her, Daughter, wouldst thou now prepare
As servant in a noble house to stay?
For since to serve the Lord is all thy care
In Lucca hath he marked thee out thy way.
There may'st thou live, there labour, and there die.
Thank God! So be it! Zita made reply.

They reached the house for Zita's home designed,
And casa Fantinelli was its name.
A family of noble life and mind
Dwelt in it, when the saintly maiden came.
Just to their servants, to the needy kind.
With them her life could pass, almost the same
As with her parents. She, rejoiced indeed,
Gave thanks to God who did such grace concede.

Racconta il libro, Zita avea uno zio,
Uomo da bene, e di gran santitade;
Armato stava nel timor di Dio,
Di Fede, di Speranza e Caritade.
In ogni opera buona avea il desio,
Assai amava lui la povertade.
Non nominava mai Iddio in vano;
Per nome chiamato era lui Graziano.

Torniamo a Zita che già cresciut'era,
Con gran pensiero di servire Iddio;
Orando sempre la mattina e sera,
Il mondo lei s'avea preso in oblio.
Un dì pensando con ben mesta cera,
Adesso lievo il pane al Padre mio;
Concedimi Signor, ch'io vadi a stare,
In Lucca, questo vitto a guadagnare.

Padre e Madre, ognun da Dio spirato,
Andò a Zita e disse: Vuoi venire,
A Lucca a stare in un nobil casato?
Poiché vediam, che vuoi a Dio servire;
Questo sia il luogo per te apparecchiato,
Dove potrai ben vivere e morire.
Zita rispose: per amor di Dio,
Di grazia andiamo, caro Padre mio.

Trovato il luogo ove Zita ha da stare
Addomandata casa Fantinelli:
Nobili Signori son da praticare,
I lor figliuoli saran come fratelli:
Faranno sempre Zita rispettare,
Benefattori son de' poverelli.
Zita ringrazia Iddio di tal ventura
Da faticarsi subito procura.

creatures—and in the flowers that live for them—I think these works are in their kind unrivalled, and that they do indeed represent certain elements of feeling and power peculiar to this age."[2] Ruskin's advocacy brought Alexander international fame, and the two became close friends. Failing eyesight in the mid-1880s truncated her artistic activities, but she continued her lifelong devotion to the local peasantry through charitable work.

1. A visitor to the artist's studio noted, "[T]he chief decoration of the room was the flowers—huge Tuscan jars of blue and yellow ware filled with anemones, tulips, violets, and a spray of almond blossom"; quoted in *Francesca Alexander (1837–1917): Drawings for "Roadside Songs of Tuscany"* (Woodside, Calif.: Sven H. A. Bruntjen Fine Arts, 1981), 3.

2. Ruskin praised Alexander's works in a letter to her mother (Oct. 7, 1882), which appeared in M. H. Spielmann, "Francesca Alexander and 'The Roadside Songs of Tuscany,'" *Magazine of Art* 18 (1895): 297–98.

Homer Dodge Martin

American, 1836–1897

86 Newport, 1881

Black and white Conté crayon on green-gray, moderately thick, slightly textured wove paper, 6¼ × 10⅝ in. (15.9 × 27 cm)
Inscribed in graphite, lower left: "Newport"
Gift of Mrs. William A. Putnam, 36.487

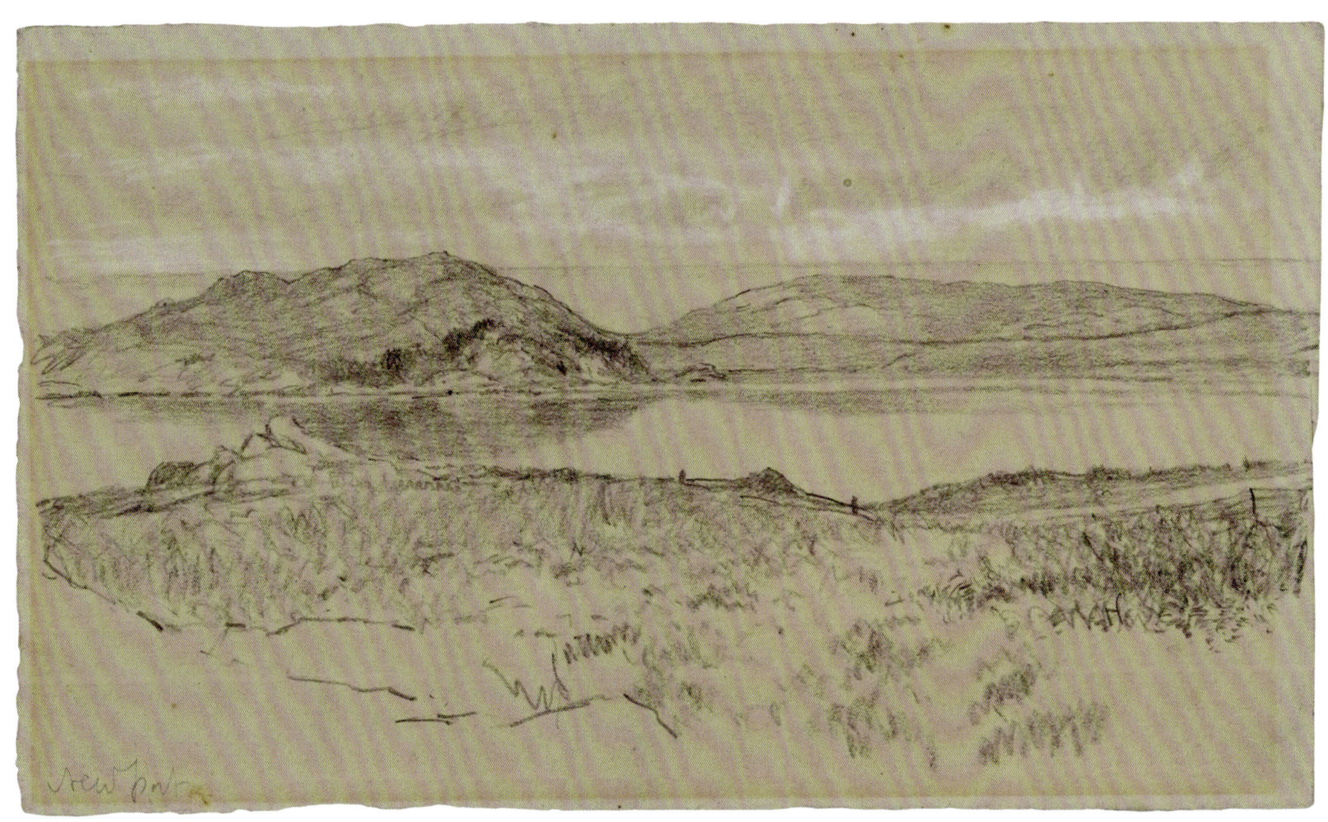

The self-taught Hudson River School artist Homer Dodge Martin produced this sketch during a visit to Newport, on the Isle of Wight off the southern coast of England, in 1881.[1] Executed in Martin's typical compositional and technical style, *Newport* captures an expansive landscape of rolling hills and glistening water stretching into the distance. After precisely outlining the contours of the topographic features, the artist described the grassy areas using looser strokes and scribbles of Conté crayon. This freer handling of the medium allowed him to capture quickly the precise geologic forms and visual effect of the panoramic sweep. Martin's use of white crayon in the sky illustrates the hazy atmosphere of the locale. Elizabeth Gilbert Martin described the sense of isolation in many of her husband's landscapes, noting "an austerity, a remoteness, a certain savagery in even the sunniest and most peaceful of them."[2] Nevertheless, glimpses of human intervention in the landscape, such as the fence and dirt road in the foreground here, occasionally appear in Martin's images. Such structures allude to the presence of humans while simultaneously underscoring their absence from the scene, emphasizing the mood of solitude.

Although as a young artist Martin associated with the Hudson River School painters William Hart (1823–1894) and James M. Hart (1828–1901), after his first visit to Europe in 1876, his style began to reflect the growing popularity of Barbizon landscapes. As exemplified by *Newport*, these Barbizon-inspired plein air drawings and oil studies convey the artist's emotional response to the landscape, departing from the traditional Hudson River School approach of documenting the minute details of nature. After leaving England with his wife in October 1882, Martin settled for four years in Normandy, France, where his work evolved further under the influence of Impressionism. Back in New York in 1886, Martin suffered from alcoholism, problems with his eyesight, and diminishing public interest in his work, conditions that led to sporadic production and poor sales. He eventually joined his wife and son in Saint Paul, Minnesota, where he lived until his death in 1897.—CG

1. Elizabeth Gilbert Martin, *Homer Martin: A Reminiscence* (New York: William Macbeth, 1904), 22. According to Martin's wife, the artist visited Newport on his second trip abroad in 1881.
2. Ibid., ix.

Joseph Frank Currier

American, 1843–1909

87 Study of Trees, circa 1880

Charcoal on cream, medium-weight, slightly textured laid paper,
4⁷⁄₁₆ × 6⁷⁄₈ in. (11.3 × 17.5 cm)
Gift of Mrs. John White Alexander, 31.202.1

88 Study of Trees, circa 1880

Charcoal on cream, medium-weight, slightly textured laid paper,
4³⁄₁₆ × 7⅜ in. (10.6 × 18.7 cm)
Gift of Mrs. John White Alexander, 31.202.2

89 Study of Trees, circa 1880

Charcoal on cream, medium-weight, slightly textured laid paper,
4⅝ × 6⁵⁄₁₆ in. (11.7 × 16 cm)
Gift of Mrs. John White Alexander, 31.202.3

90 Study of Trees, circa 1880

Charcoal on cream, medium-weight, slightly textured laid paper,
3⅞ × 7⁷⁄₁₆ in. (9.8 × 18.9 cm)
Gift of Mrs. John White Alexander, 31.202.4

The landscape and figure painter Joseph Frank Currier's deep love of nature made him a committed pleinairist. As his daughter recalled, "I cannot remember ever seeing him paint in his studio."[1] Using various media, including oil, watercolor, pastel, and—as in this group of tree studies—charcoal, he sketched outdoors in all kinds of weather and at all times of day, seeking to document the changing conditions of light and atmosphere, as well as the shifting moods of the landscape. An expatriate artist who lived in Germany from 1870 to 1899, Currier did most of his outdoor work in the picturesque countryside around Munich. These small, vigorously executed sketches were most likely made in Schleissheim, six miles north of the city. Currier began visiting this Bavarian village regularly in the late 1870s and settled there in 1882.[2]

In each drawing, trees dominate the composition with their outstretched branches and billowing canopies. Occasionally, a glimpse of a farmhouse or town buildings can be found in the background, as in numbers 87 and 88. Currier first established each scene in broad tonal masses made with rubbings and smudges of charcoal and then articulated the contours of trunks, branches, and other forms with dark lines applied with the tip of the stick. Staccato strokes serve as a kind of visual shorthand for leaves and blades of grass. The resulting effect conveys an overall impression of the landscape rather than botanically specific details. Notwithstanding this generalized treatment, expressive lines individualize each tree. Furthermore, the energetic execution of the crackling lines endows the natural world with a sense of dynamism, as if the trees are possessed of an inner life force. An early biographer of the artist aptly described Currier's charcoal studies as "almost titanic in their force and freedom."[3]

Born in Boston, Currier was one of the most progressive of the colony of young American artists—including **William Merritt Chase**, Frank Duveneck (1848–1919), and **John Henry Twachtman**—who gathered in Munich in the 1870s and embraced a vigorous manner of Realism. Currier's landscape pictures, which seemed like "glimpses from the window of an express train," created a sensation when they were first exhibited in New York in 1878.[4] He continued working *en plein air* in his expressive style until the early 1890s, when a stroke drastically reduced his output.

1. Quoted in Nelson C. White, *The Life and Art of J. Frank Currier* (Cambridge, Mass.: privately printed at the Riverside Press, 1936), 33.
2. When the Brooklyn Museum acquired these drawings, the donor provided the date of 1870. Currier was doing plein air work in the environs of Paris in the summer of 1870, but, to judge from their appearance and medium, these sketches likely date from his later period in Schleissheim. See also ibid., 67–68.
3. Quoted in ibid., 67.
4. "The Younger Painters of America," *Scribner's Monthly* 20, no. 1 (May 1880): 13.

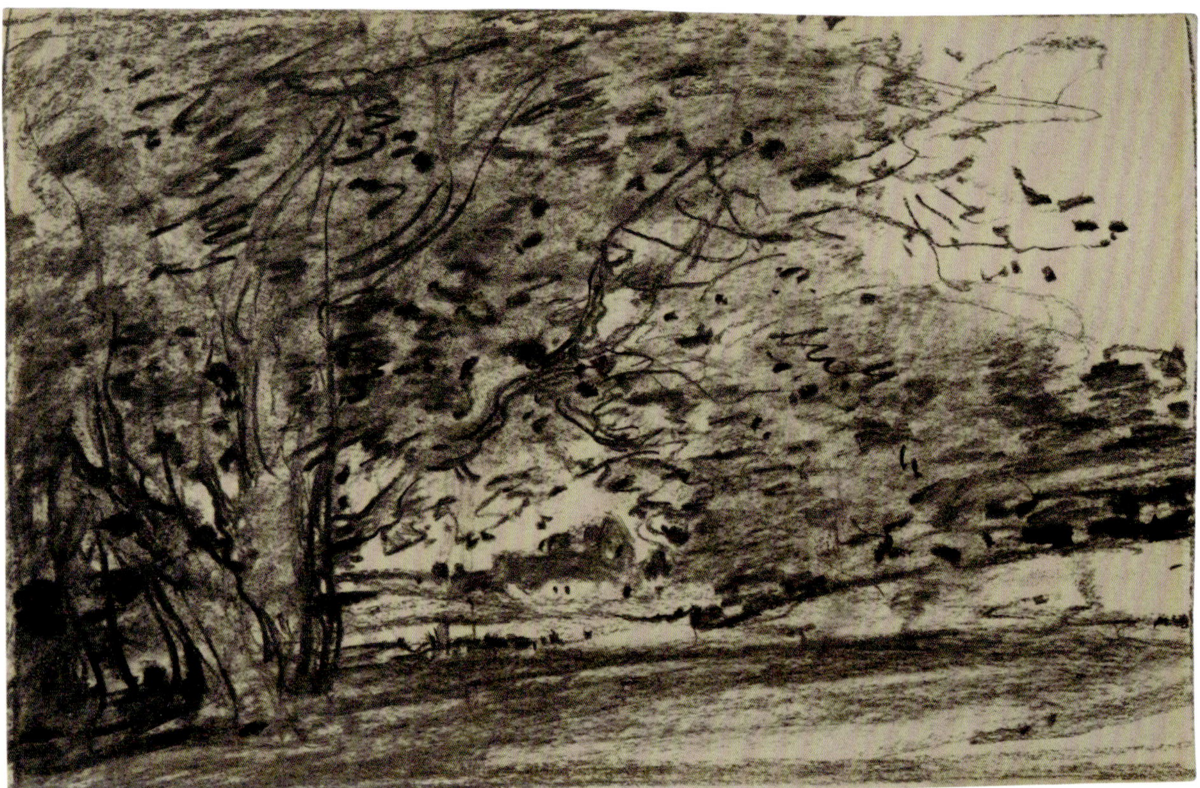

87

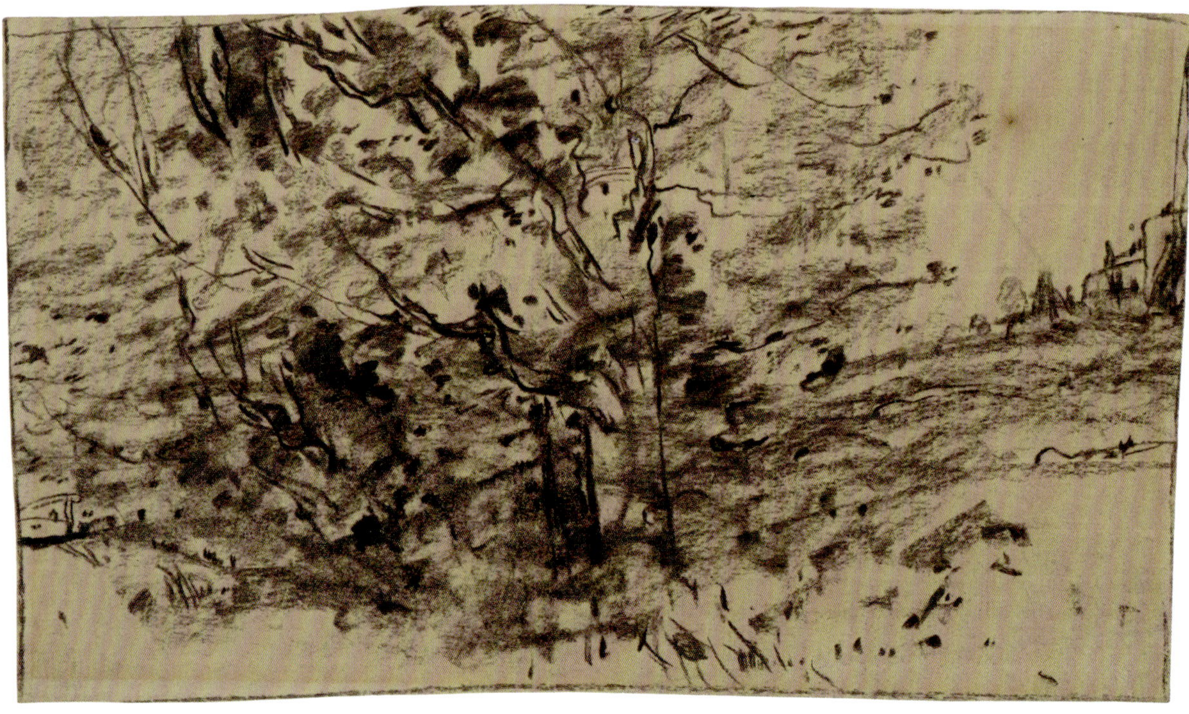

88

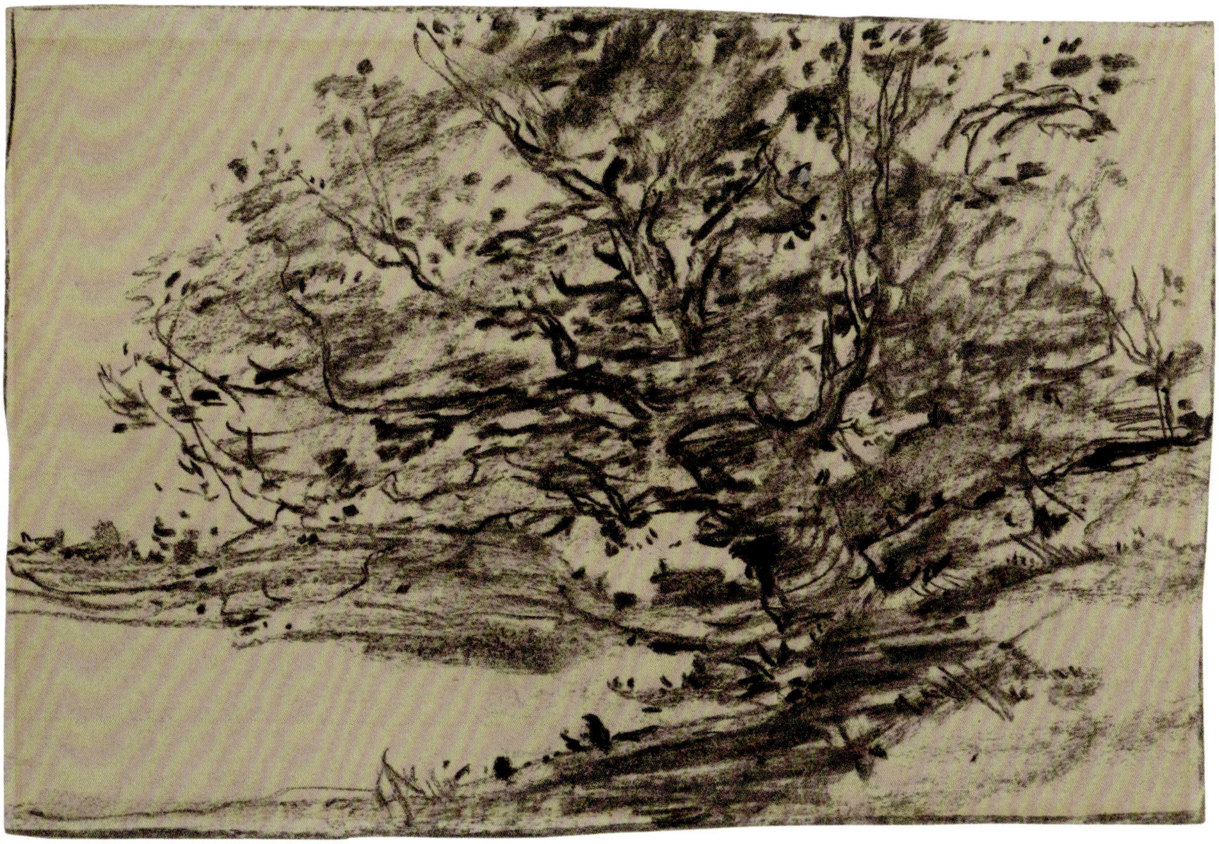

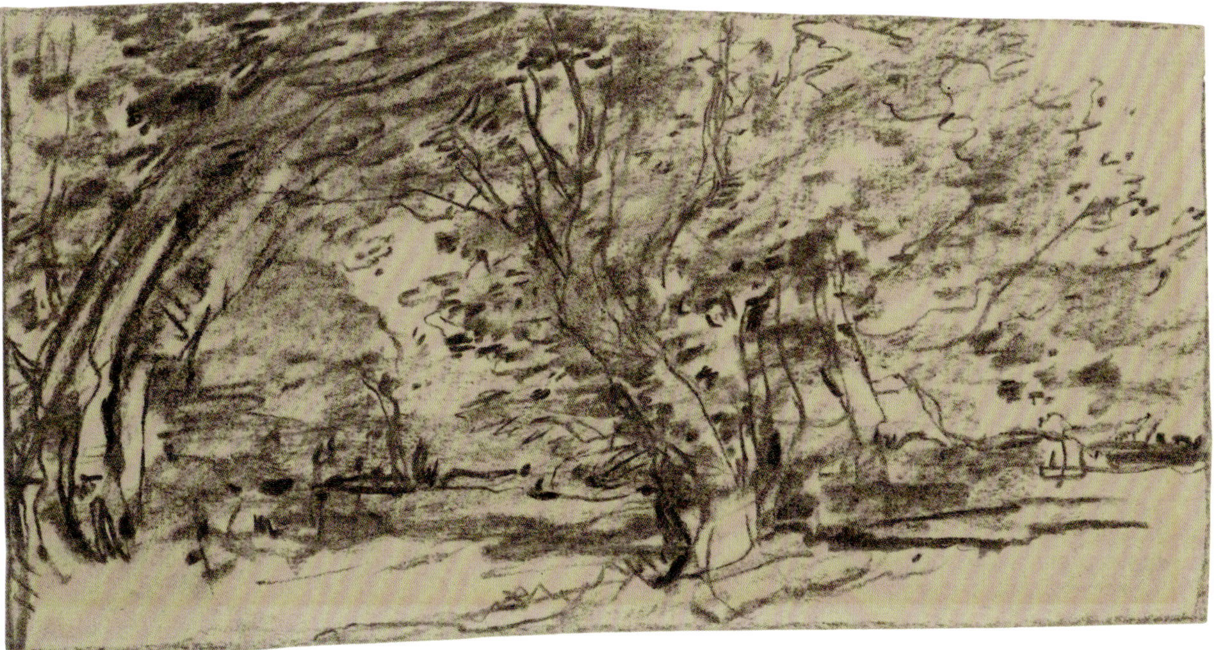

89

90

John Henry Twachtman

American, 1853–1902

91 Three Trees, circa 1888–95

Pastel on gray-brown, moderately thick, moderately textured wove paper with black, blue, and red threads, 14 × 18 in. (35.6 × 45.7 cm)
Signed in pastel, lower left: "J.H. Twachtman"
Museum Surplus Fund, 25.416

Recognized as one of the most innovative American Impressionists, John Henry Twachtman began working in pastel in the mid-1880s, at a time when this medium was enjoying a revival among artists (see number 35). He participated in the activities of the Society of Painters in Pastel, an organization founded in 1882 by his friends **Robert Frederick Blum**, **William Merritt Chase**, and others. Made during a period when Twachtman was particularly active in pastel, *Three Trees* typifies his subject matter and handling of the medium. This work, which depicts a sunny hillside punctuated with a stand of trees and rocks in the foreground and farm buildings on the horizon, was most likely inspired by the artist's own seventeen-acre property outside Greenwich, Connecticut. Seeking spiritual renewal in nature, he moved to this rural setting in 1889, and it became the dominant subject of both his paintings and pastels.[1] Concerned more with recording his subjective impression than with descriptive accuracy, Twachtman rendered the natural forms loosely, using lightly applied layers of pastel in soft green, gray, and blue hues. His sensitive understanding of the medium is also evident in the way that he fully integrated the brownish color and rough texture of the paper into the design. The overall effect is of a landscape dematerialized into an aesthetic arrangement of airy touches of color on the picture surface.

Although Twachtman's career was short (he died at age forty-nine), his work encompassed many of the progressive developments in American art in the late nineteenth century, including the broadly brushed style of Munich Realism and the Aestheticism and japonisme inspired by James McNeill Whistler (1834–1903), as well as Impressionism. Born in Cincinnati, Twachtman studied in Munich, joining the lively colony of artists in that city (see also numbers 47 and 87–90), and then in Paris. Throughout his career, he traveled frequently with fellow artists to sketch *en plein air* in picturesque locales in the United States and Europe. He maintained strong ties with the New York art world through exhibitions, teaching, and involvement in artists' organizations. With other American Impressionists, Twachtman established the summer artists' colony in Cos Cob, Connecticut, and the Ten American Painters group. In an appreciation published the year following the artist's death, one critic had the following praise for Twachtman's work: "His color sense was rare and delicate, his harmonic instinct invariable, and his note strongly individual."[2]

1. Alternatively, *Three Trees* might represent the country home of his fellow Impressionist J. Alden Weir (1852–1919) in nearby Branchville, where Twachtman was a regular visitor.

2. Katherine Metcalf Roof, "The Work of John H. Twachtman," *Brush and Pencil* 12, no. 4 (July 1903): 243.

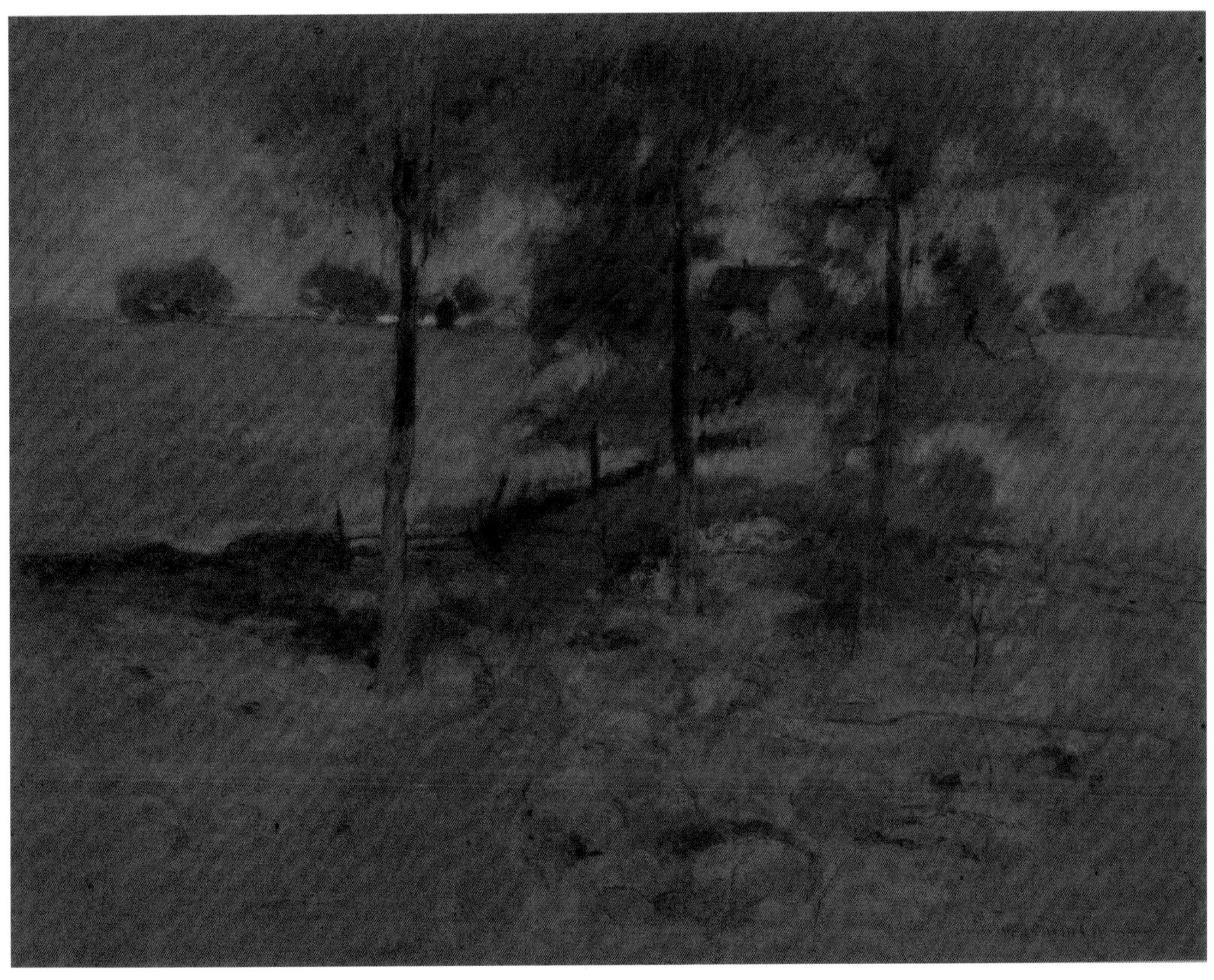

William Merritt Chase

American, 1849–1916

92 Shinnecock Hills, circa 1895

Pastel on commercially preprimed canvas, with hand-applied gray ground, 20 × 24 in. (50.8 × 61 cm)
Signed lower left, in pastel: "Wm M. Chase"
Gift of William A. Putnam, 19.96

This pastel is one of the many works William Merritt Chase made between 1891 and 1902, while he was running the Shinnecock Summer School of Art, the first school in the United States devoted to plein air practice. Located on Shinnecock Bay at the eastern end of Long Island, this school was founded at the urging of Mrs. William Hoyt, an amateur painter and summer resident of the area, and supported by other wealthy patrons. The Art Village, as the campus was called locally, consisted of cottages for housing about fifty students and a larger residence for Chase, the school's director. During his tenure at Shinnecock, Chase spent the summers instructing the many students who came to work with the famous artist and teacher, as well as making his own pictures of the surrounding landscape and his family's activities.

Shinnecock Hills depicts a broad expanse of the characteristic terrain—sandy dunes covered in grasses and bayberry bushes—on a sunny day. A rugged path in the center recedes into the distance, drawing the viewer into this bright and pleasing composition. Chase applied the pastel in soft, feathery strokes of pure color, some of which he smudged and blended with either a finger, cloth, or stumping tool.[1] The gritty texture of the support, which provides tooth for holding the particles of pigment, adds to the powdery, loose quality of this picture. As was typical of his practice, Chase undoubtedly executed *Shinnecock Hills* quickly, to capture the fleeting effects of nature. He told his students, "I believe in single-sitting impressions. If you will acquire the ability and facility to do rapidly the thing that might otherwise cause you great trouble and time, you will place yourself in a position to record a great many things that do not last long. Nature rarely repeats itself."[2]

This work exemplifies the high-keyed colors and Impressionist style that Chase adopted in the 1880s, after turning away from the darker palette of his Munich training (see number 47). During his student years, he established the practice of plein air sketching that he continued for the remainder of his career. One of the most celebrated painters of his generation, Chase also gained recognition as a master of pastel. He was a founding member of the Society of Painters in Pastel, an organization established in 1882 that helped to spur renewed appreciation for the medium in the late nineteenth century (see number 35).

1. Chase used pastel in a manner similar to his handling of oil paint. See Marjorie Shelley, "Assimilating Modernism: The Pastel Technique of William Merritt Chase," in Ronald G. Pisano, *The Complete Catalogue of Known and Documented Work by William Merritt Chase (1849–1916)*, vol. 1, *The Paintings in Pastel, Monotypes, Painted Tiles and Ceramic Plates, Watercolors, and Prints* (New Haven, Conn.: Yale University Press, 2006), 97–111.

2. William M. Chase, "Address of Mr. William M. Chase before the Buffalo Fine Arts Academy, January 28, 1890," *Studio* 5, no. 13 (Mar. 1, 1890): 124, quoted in Ronald G. Pisano, *Summer Afternoons: Landscape Paintings of William Merritt Chase* (Boston: Little, Brown and Company, 1993), 13.

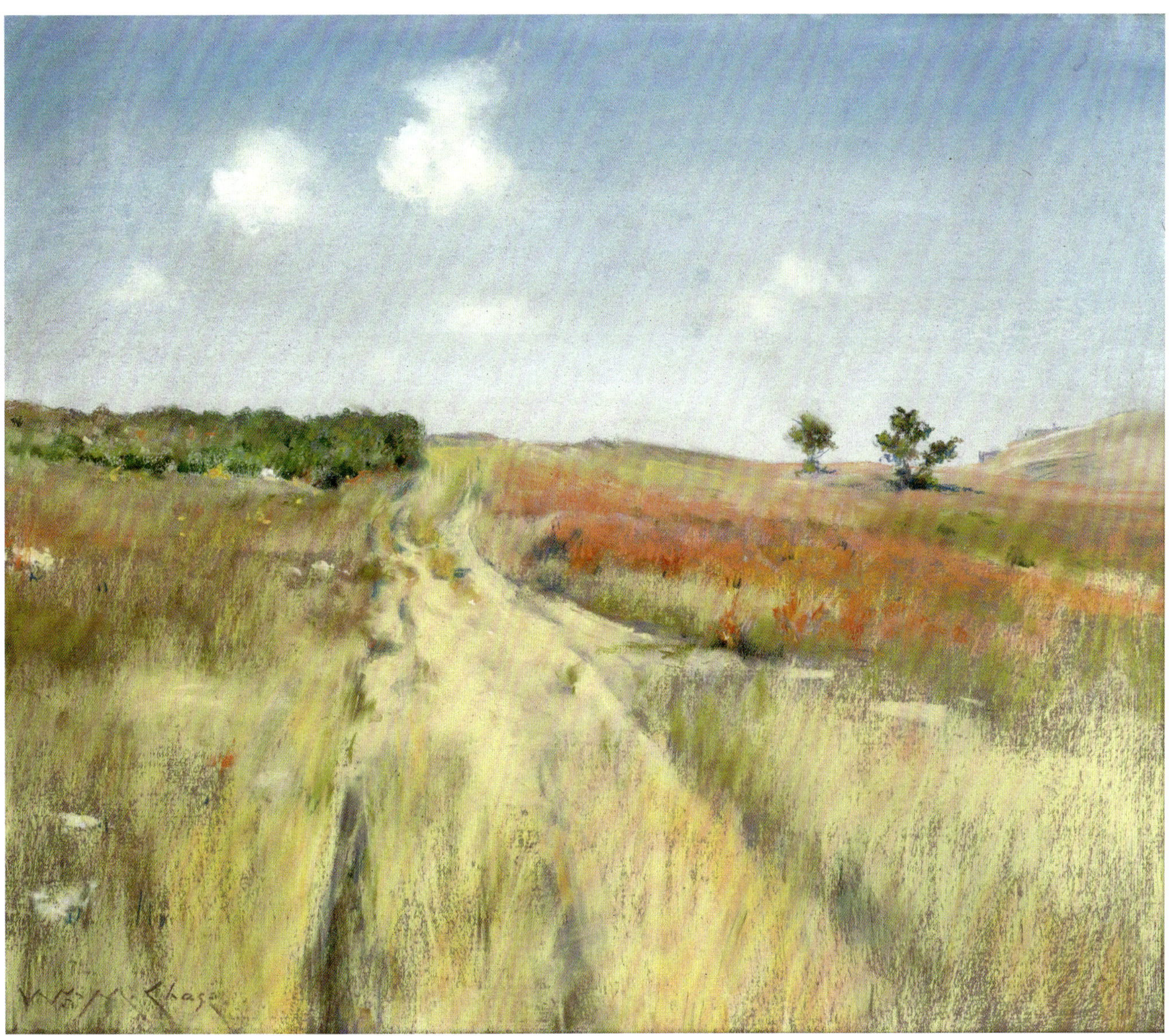

Charles Caryl Coleman

American, 1840–1928

93 A Shower of Ashes upon Ottaviano, April 14, 1906

Pastel on gray-blue laid paper, mounted to board, 10⁹⁄₁₆ × 8⁷⁄₁₆ in. (26.8 × 21.4 cm)
Signed in blue pastel, lower left: "CCC [in monogram] / 10 A.M. / April 14 – 1906"
John B. Woodward Memorial Fund, 20.656

A Shower of Ashes upon Ottaviano is one of a series of drawings, watercolors, and oils that Charles Caryl Coleman made to document the eruption of Mount Vesuvius that lasted many months and culminated in April 1906, gripping the world's attention.[1] An expatriate artist, he had a direct view of this landmark from his home and studio on the island of Capri. In this delicate pastel, the peak of Mount Vesuvius and a towering plume of smoke rise from an expanse of water—the Bay of Naples—in the lower half of the composition. Coleman's documentary impulse was more focused on atmospheric effects than on topographic detail. As the precise reference to time in the inscription suggests, he wanted to capture the meteorological and atmospheric conditions of a specific moment in which the heavy, ash-filled air cloaked the Italian landscape in a smoky haze. Coleman summarily described this vista with short, controlled strokes in the mountain and clouds and broad, sweeping lines in the sea. The pastel's powdery texture, combined with the restricted palette of white with a few shades of blue (turquoise and cobalt) against a gray-blue paper, further enhances the overall vaporous impression. As one critic remarked, "The group of pastels, drawings and tempera [watercolor] which Mr. Coleman aptly designates as 'Songs of Vesuvius' . . . are in the truest sense lyrics of art, delicate fleeting notes of exquisite color in which the majesty of an awful natural phenomenon is interpreted with great seriousness, yet made to serve as a basis for a sensuous effect, extraordinarily light, subtle and tender."[2]

A native of Buffalo, New York, Coleman spent the majority of his career abroad, living in Italy from 1866 on. With his good friend **Elihu Vedder**, whom he met during their student days in Paris, he was part of a lively expatriate community first in Rome and then on Capri, where he settled in 1886. Coleman maintained ties with the United States through frequent travel and exhibition of his works. He became known primarily for his oil paintings of picturesque Italian landscapes, figure subjects, and architectural scenes.

1. This event received almost daily coverage in the *New York Times* during the month of April; on April 10, 1906, for example, one front-page article detailed the volcanic activities (including lava flows, ash accumulation, and seismic rumblings), evacuation plans, and destruction of life and property, while a second feature on page 2 recounted the famous ancient eruption of Vesuvius in 79 C.E., which buried the towns of Pompeii and Herculaneum.
2. "Exhibition of Works by Charles Caryl Coleman at the Albright Art Gallery," *Academy Notes* 11 (Jan.–Oct. 1916): 57.

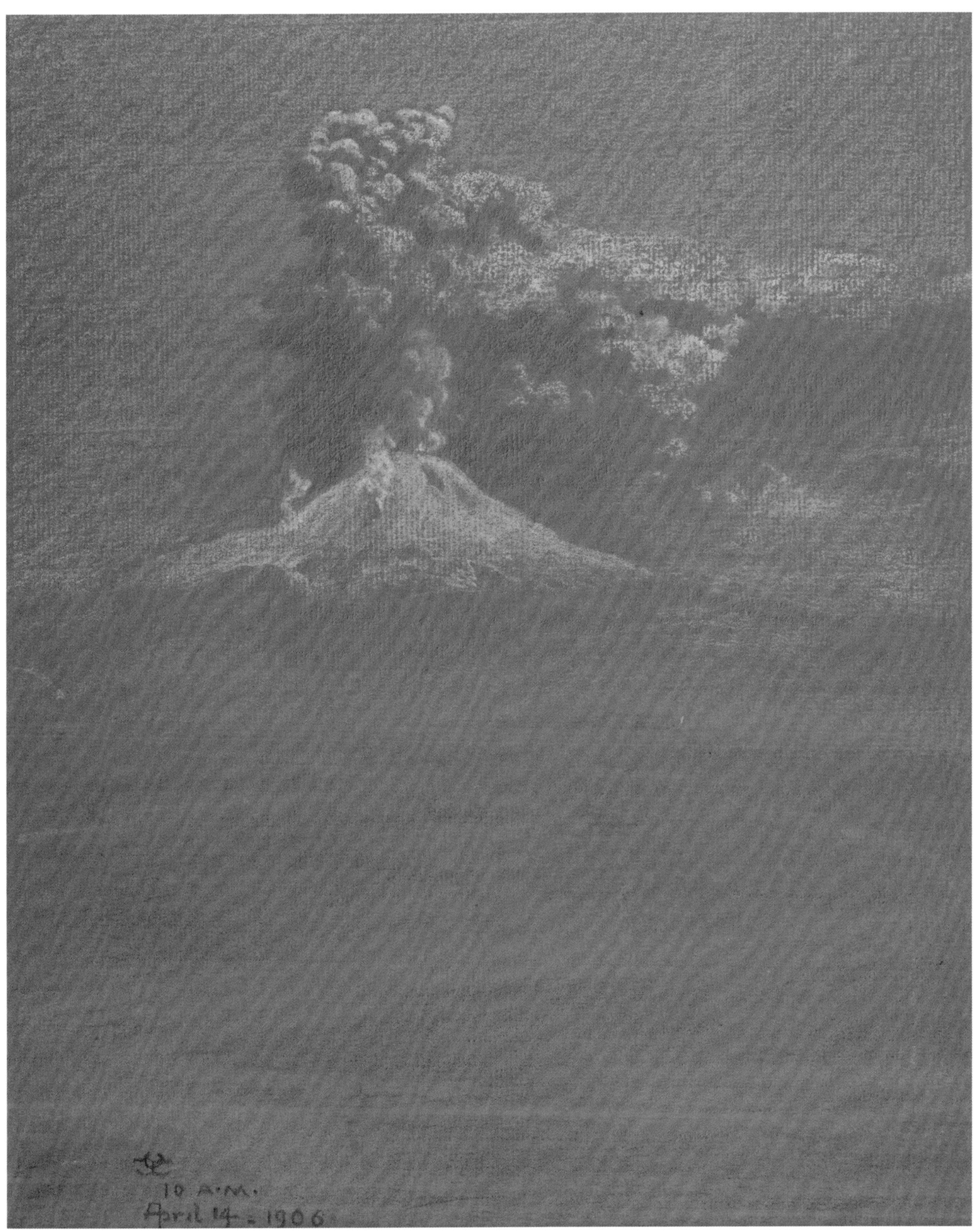

10 A.M.
April 14 - 1906

Oscar F. Bluemner

American, born Prussia, 1867–1938

94 The Harbor at Sea Cliff, Long Island, 1911

Crayon on cream, medium-weight, slightly textured wove paper, 7³⁄₁₆ × 11¼ in. (18.3 × 28.6 cm)
Inscribed in black crayon, lower right: "Sea Cliff [?]413 / E. 5 P L. 5. —11"
Signed in black crayon, lower right: "O F B" [in monogram]
Gift of Stuart Feld, 79.297.1

The Harbor at Sea Cliff, Long Island exemplifies the depictions of local landscapes and experiments with color that defined Oscar F. Bluemner's oeuvre. Using a palette of crisp greens and blues with touches of vibrant red and yellow, the artist evoked the freshness and vitality of the Long Island seaside and the joy he experienced in this escape from his life in New York City. Modest buildings, docks, and small boats are rendered in the middle ground, set against dense trees and sloping hills that dwarf the development of the harbor. Bluemner expressed these forms almost abstractly, using pure, unmodulated colors that are juxtaposed to create depth. At the lower right, loose strokes and scribbles of yellow, red, and green crayon describe the texture of the land as it changes from gnarled grass and earth to soft, pristine sand. In the first decade of the 1900s, Bluemner generally executed his most brilliantly colored landscapes in crayon or colored pencil, but by the 1910s, he began to brighten his palette and expand his media to include oil paint. This drawing is on the cusp of the artist's transition from crayon and pencil drawings to oil paintings of similar subjects.

After a brief career in architecture, Bluemner began painting professionally about 1900, primarily using vibrant color to express emotion. Stating the importance of color in his art, he wrote, "I work—the usual way from Form to Color, reversed—from Color to Form; from inward experiences to their outer realization, through creative imagination."[1] In *The Harbor at Sea Cliff, Long Island*, Bluemner used pure blue to stand for the serenity he felt while gazing on the harbor scene and green to symbolize repose; he rendered built structures mostly in bright red, to represent the vitality of human activity within the peaceful landscape.[2] Throughout his oeuvre, Bluemner conveyed strong emotions or moods through color, believing this technique to be an "Emotional language."[3] To viewers of his expressive pictures, the artist advised, "Look at my work in a way as you listen to music—look at the space filled with colors and try to feel; do not insist on 'understanding' what seems strange. When you 'FEEL' colors, you will understand the 'WHY' of their forms. It is so simple."[4]—CG

1. Oscar Bluemner, *Oscar Florianus Bluemner* (Minneapolis: University Gallery, University of Minnesota, 1939), unpag. This retrospective exhibition catalogue with an introduction by Bluemner was published posthumously.
2. For Bluemner's list of colors and their emotional significance, see Oscar Bluemner, painting diary, Apr. 21, 1918, Oscar Bluemner Papers, Archives of American Art, Smithsonian Institution.
3. Bluemner, *Oscar Florianus Bluemner*, unpag.
4. Ibid.

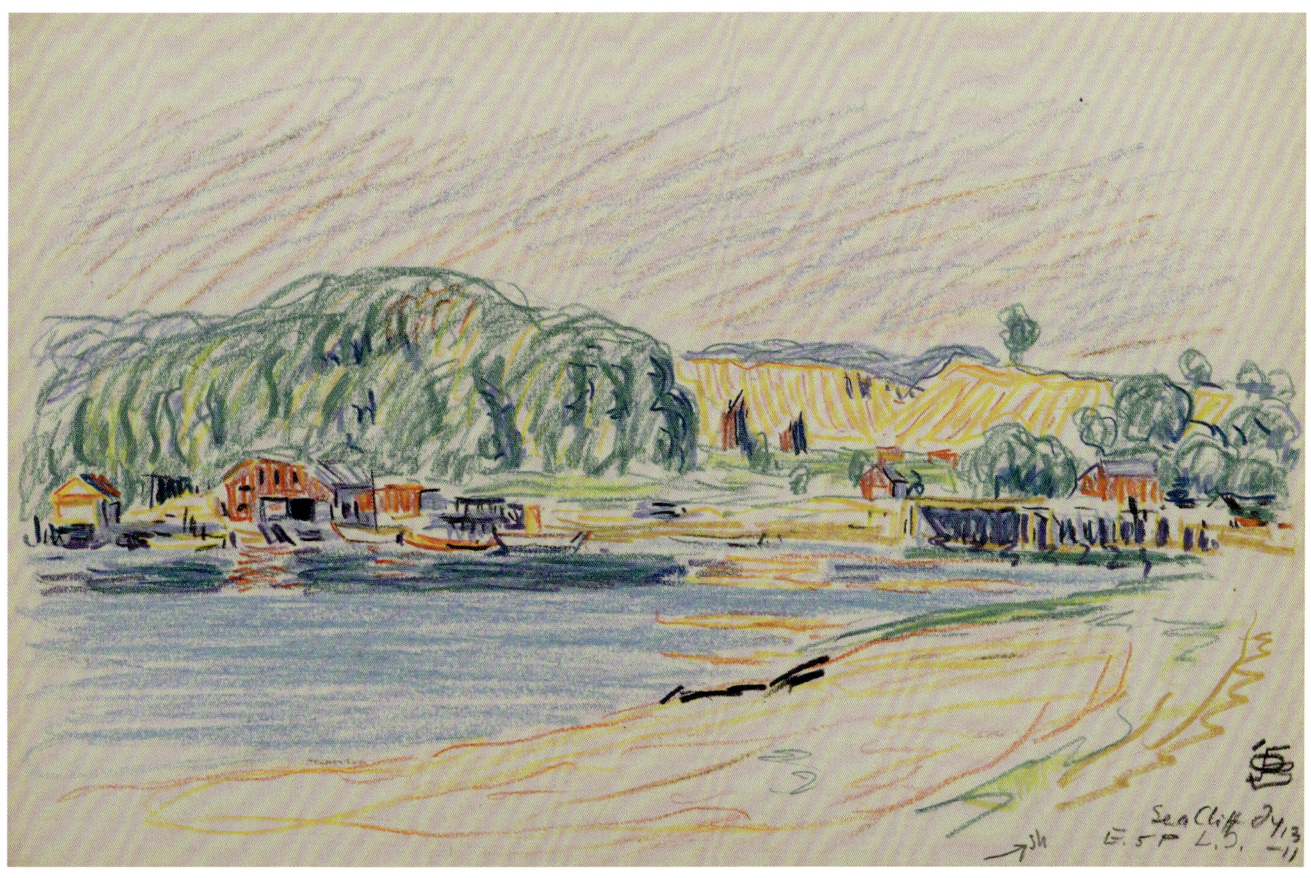

Marsden Hartley

American, 1877–1943

95 **New Mexico,** circa 1918–19

Pastel on beige laid paper mounted to wood-pulp board, 16⁵⁄₁₆ × 26⁷⁄₁₆ in. (41.5 × 67.2 cm)
Anonymous gift, 39.274

Throughout a career marked by constant wandering and stylistic experimentation, the modernist artist Marsden Hartley regularly sought spiritual rejuvenation and transcendence in nature. After World War I, he set his sights on leaving New York for New Mexico, avowing: "I want to get down out of here and really get on my way to the southwest for in that lies the only salvation that is in evidence for me. . . . I want an open space for my eyes to regain their vision, and my mind to feel itself free again."[1] The Southwest appealed to Hartley because it was both distinctly American and—with its strong Native American and Hispanic cultures—different from the "deadly" East Coast.[2]

In 1918 he traveled to Taos, where he met his friend Mabel Dodge, a wealthy patron of the arts who had settled there the preceding year and whose home would become the center of a lively community of artists, writers, and intellectuals in the 1920s. Hartley also spent time in Santa Fe and California before returning to New York in 1919. During his southwestern sojourn, he created a series of pastels, including this one, based on direct observation of the surrounding landscape. The medium allowed him to record his subjective responses quickly, in a departure from his usual practice of oil painting.[3] *New Mexico* depicts the rugged topography of the high desert landscape (possibly Arroyo Hondo, where he often sketched) under a brilliant blue sky. Hartley outlined the generalized masses of the mesas and winding gulch and then built up their forms with patches of variegated shades of yellow, peach, and pink applied in parallel, feathery strokes of pastel. There are also touches of green in the scrubby bushes and dark browns in the shadows. Ironically, despite Hartley's desire to find a fresh artistic vision out west, his application of color and slightly abstracted approach to representation in this drawing recall his debt to the French Post-Impressionist Paul Cézanne (1839–1906; see number 97).

Throughout Hartley's career, a change in location typically instigated a change in his art, and he moved on to different artistic concerns after he left the Southwest. New Mexican imagery continued to appear in his art until 1924, however, often in works he called "recollections."

1. Marsden Hartley to Alfred Stieglitz, May 24, 1918, quoted in Heather Hole, *Marsden Hartley and the West: The Search for an American Modernism* (New Haven, Conn.: Yale University Press in association with Georgia O'Keeffe Museum, 2007), 24.
2. Ibid.
3. Ibid., 8, 28–29.

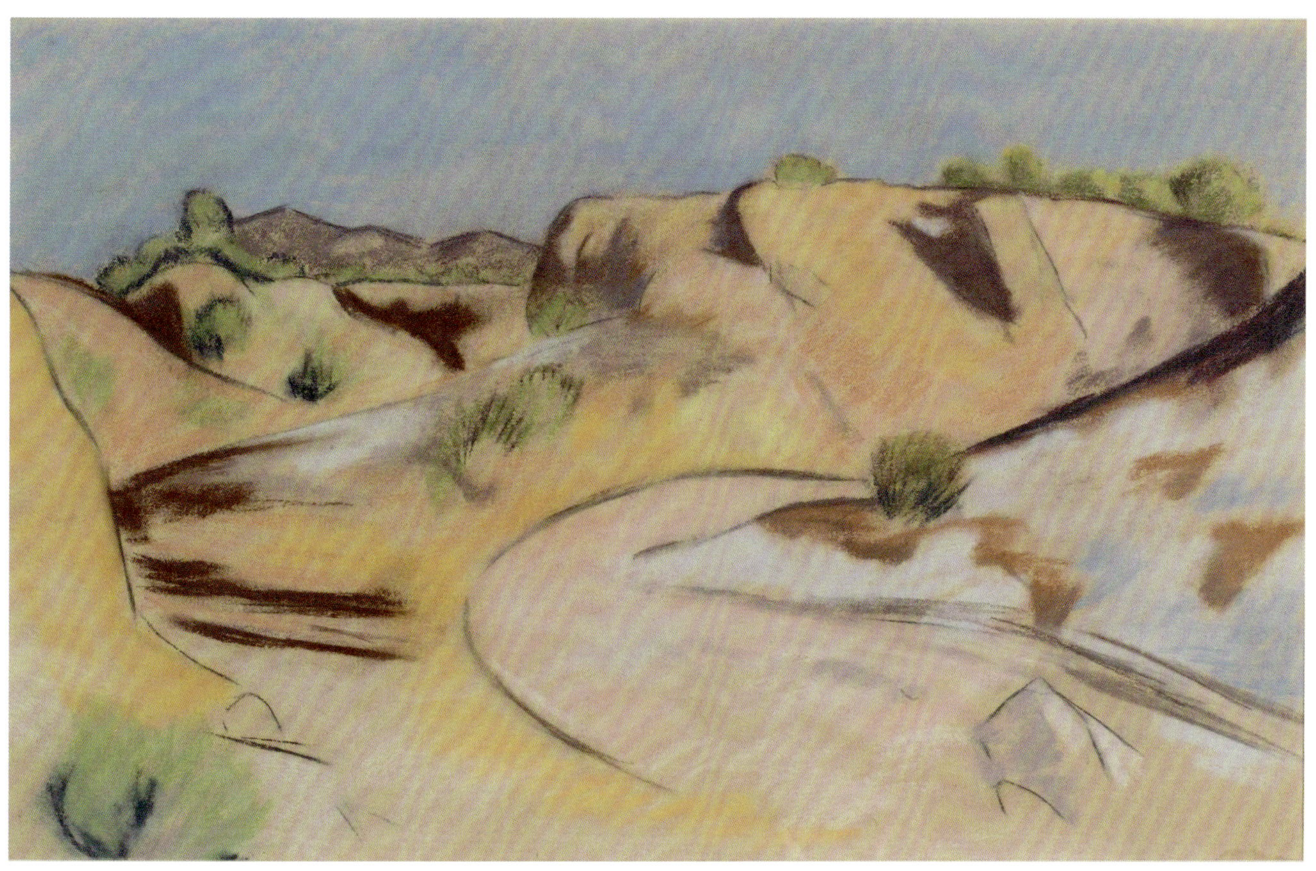

William Zorach

American, born Lithuania, 1887–1966

96 Three Figures under a Tree, 1917

Graphite on beige, medium-weight, slightly textured wove paper, 11⅟₁₆ × 8½ in. (28.1 × 21.6 cm)
Signed in graphite, lower right: "William Zorach / 1917"
Gift of William Bloom, 84.46.8

When they married in 1912, the American modernists William and **Marguerite Zorach** resolved to "spend their summers in nature" as a respite from the daily grind of life in New York City.[1] The destinations for their summer retreats included Robinhood, Maine (where they bought a cottage in 1923), Provincetown, Massachusetts, and—in 1917, the year this work was created—Plainfield, New Hampshire. In this graphite drawing, Zorach depicted a large tree in a hilly landscape with three nude, probably male figures relaxing under its lush canopy. He abstracted the forms into schematized shapes, first drawing simple outlines and then adding parallel hatchings throughout to indicate shading or to enhance his outlines. This combination of descriptive and decorative tonal patterning is evident in the tree. Loosely scribbled hatch marks in varying densities suggest the clusters of leaves, while tighter, more controlled passages of hatching trace the silhouette of the tree's trunk and branches. Zorach treated both figures and botanical motifs in the same manner, pointing to a harmonious relationship between humankind and the natural world that reflects his own idyllic experience of nature. As he recalled in his autobiography of one summer in the countryside, "There were no problems . . . no gloomy forebodings, no literary solving of the world's ills, only a joyous awareness of the world about us. Flowers bloomed, wildlife carried on, clouds floated, trees designed themselves in the landscapes. Nude figures lay around pools, played with children, made love, dreamed."[2]

The theme of the nude figure or bather in the landscape had a long tradition in Western art and, at the turn of the twentieth century, was subjected to modernist reevaluation and revision by such artists as Paul Cézanne (1839–1906), Pablo Picasso (1881–1973), and Henri Matisse (1869–1954). Zorach encountered their works on a formative trip he took to Paris in 1910–11. When he returned to the United States, he embarked on a decade of modernist experimentation, combining in his paintings Cubist abstraction with Fauvist coloring. He also made drawings, watercolors, prints, and sculpture. In the early 1920s, Zorach abandoned painting to devote his creative energies primarily to sculpting in a direct-carving technique. Nonetheless, drawing continued to play a vital role in his art (see numbers 15, 43, and 55).

1. Quoted in Efram L. Burk, "The Prints of William Zorach," *Print Quarterly* 19, no. 4 (2002): 10.
2. William Zorach, *Art Is My Life: The Autobiography of William Zorach* (Cleveland: World Publishing Company, 1967), 36–37.

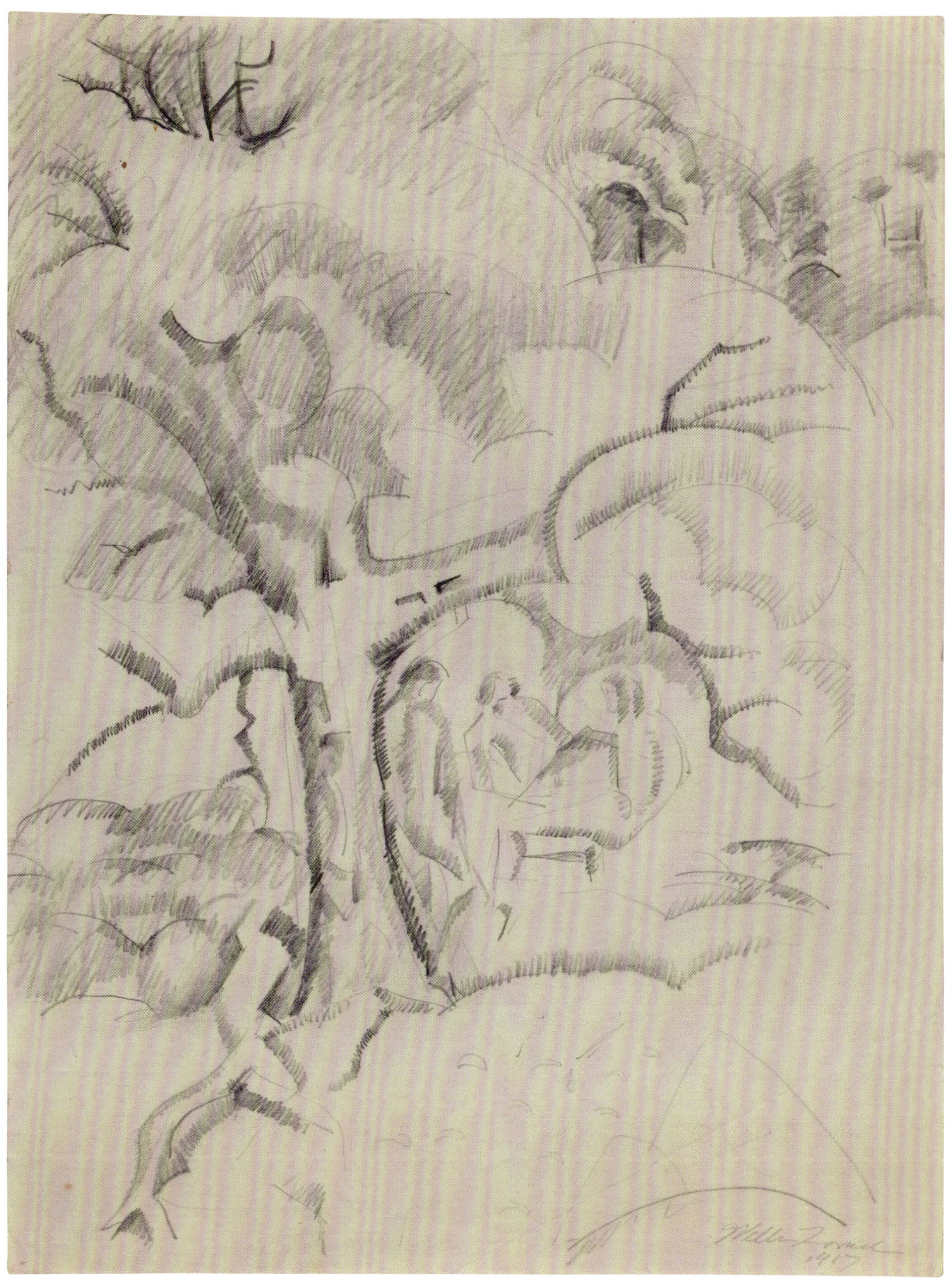

Marsden Hartley

American, 1877–1943

97 Mont Sainte-Victoire, 1926–27

Graphite on cream, thick, rough-textured wove paper, 22⅝ × 31³⁄₁₆ in. (57.5 × 79.2 cm)
Dick S. Ramsay Fund, 61.4.1. © Estate of Marsden Hartley, Yale University Committee on Intellectual Property

In describing Paul Cézanne's (1839–1906) formative impact on modern art in both Europe and the United States, Marsden Hartley called him "the prophet of the new time."[1] Hartley's deep appreciation for Cézanne's art found its most direct expression in 1926–27, when the American lived in Aix-en-Provence, in the South of France, working in the very places and manner of the French master.[2] This large, spare drawing is one of several that Hartley made of Mont Sainte-Victoire, a subject that became synonymous with Cézanne's art (figure 23). Hartley's rendition of this landmark captures the mountain's distinctive profile and stark monumentality. Using delicate strokes of graphite, he outlined the forms of the peak, darkening a line to create tonal variations, and added shaded rubbings to describe the mountain's sculpturesque contours. With Mont Sainte-Victoire as his focal point, Hartley treated the foreground of his image—the expansive landscape of the Arc River valley—more schematically. It is composed of large areas of blank paper punctuated by a few simplified buildings, depicted with a planar faceting that recalls Cézanne's handling of such motifs, and truncated tree trunks at the right. Although Hartley was working in front of the natural motif, he envisioned this landscape through the lens of another's art.

Born in Maine, Hartley received his early training in academic and Realist styles in Cleveland and New York. In 1909 he met the photographer and gallery owner Alfred Stieglitz (1864–1946), a passionate champion of modernism in the United States, and became part of his inner circle of progressive artists. Hartley first encountered the art of Cézanne at Stieglitz's gallery 291 the following year. With Stieglitz's financial support, he made several formative trips to Europe between 1912 and 1915, spending time in Paris and Berlin, where he familiarized himself with the latest developments in modern art and met many vanguard artists. Assimilating these various influences, he forged his unique style of modernism, which combined Cubist pictorial structure, Expressionist color and bold brushwork, and personal symbolism. Hartley's restless spirit, combined with financial and emotional difficulties, led to a peripatetic existence. He traveled constantly throughout his career, often seeking creative renewal in new places (see number 95). He spent his late career in his native state, making powerfully original images of New England landscapes, still lifes, and figures.

1. Marsden Hartley, *Adventures in the Arts: Informal Chapters on Painters, Vaudeville and Poets* (New York: Boni and Liveright, 1921), 36.
2. For a succinct discussion of Cézanne's influence on Hartley, see Gail Stavitsky and Katherine Rothkopf, *Cézanne and American Modernism* (New Haven, Conn.: Yale University Press, 2009), 214–16.

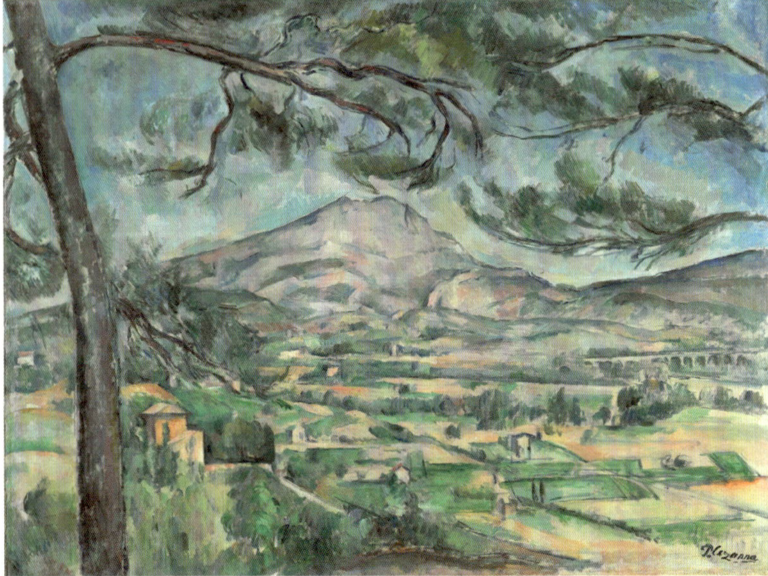

Fig. 23. Paul Cézanne (French, 1839–1906). *Montagne Sainte-Victoire with Large Pine*, circa 1887. Oil on canvas, 26¼ × 36⁵⁄₁₆ in. (66.8 × 92.3 cm). Courtauld Gallery, London, The Samuel Courtauld Trust, P.1934.SC.55

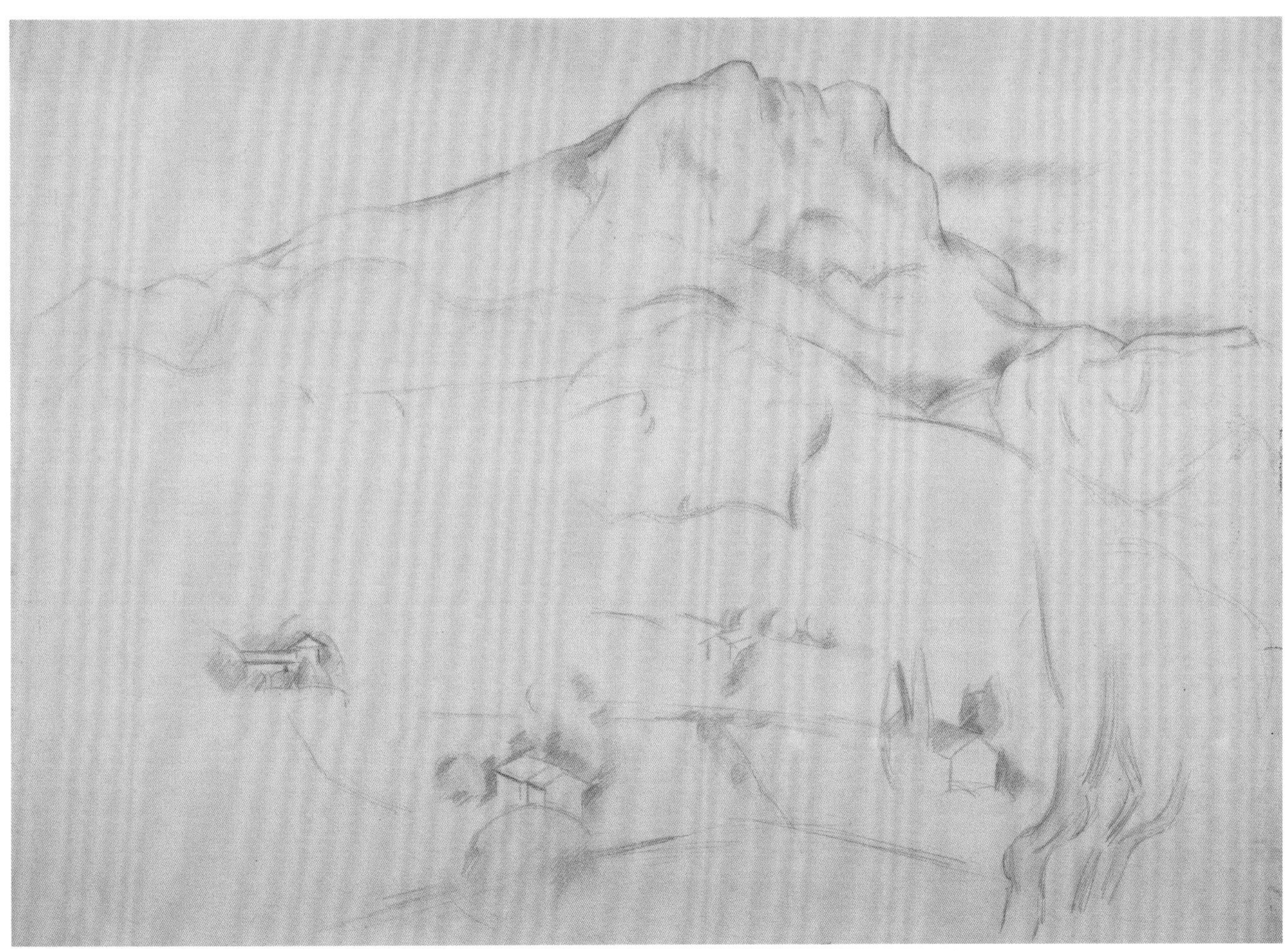

Georgia O'Keeffe

American, 1887–1986

98 Red Hills with the Pedernal, 1936

Pastel on paper mounted to wood-pulp board, 21½ × 27¼ in. (54.6 × 69.2 cm)
Bequest of Georgia O'Keeffe, 87.136.4

Like **Marsden Hartley**, Georgia O'Keeffe was one of the modernists in the Stieglitz circle who found renewal and inspiration in the natural beauty of New Mexico (see number 95). Her engagement with the Southwest was much more sustained than Hartley's, however. After falling in love with the region during her first visit in 1929, she spent summers there annually until 1946, when she moved to New Mexico permanently. The sights she encountered in the landscape—including dramatic geologic formations, desert vegetation, adobe structures, and desiccated animal bones—provided a constant source of artistic inspiration throughout her long career. One such landmark was the Pedernal, a mesa in the Jemez Mountains that O'Keeffe could see from Ghost Ranch, her home and studio northwest of Santa Fe. This motif appeared regularly in her paintings and works on paper. In an interview late in life, she joked: "It's my private mountain. It belongs to me. God told me if I painted it enough, I could have it."[1]

In *Red Hills with the Pedernal*, the mesa juts into the sky above a row of terracotta-colored hills with accents of green shrubbery. The Pedernal's light blue color suggests both its distance and the atmospheric conditions of a particular day. O'Keeffe rendered this landscape in her typical mode of reductive realism, simplifying forms into their essential shapes. It appears that she made a preparatory underdrawing to establish this composition: a few faint, cream-colored lines are visible in the small area of uncovered, tan-colored paper at the center right. She then worked up her image with thick strokes of opaque pastel, blending and smoothing them with a finger or brush. Her technique allowed her to achieve subtle modulations of hues and values, effects also evident in her oil paintings.[2]

Widely considered the most famous and original American artist of the twentieth century, O'Keeffe is best known for her paintings of magnified botanical forms and New Mexico landscapes. Her first critical recognition, however, came from a series of abstract charcoal drawings that brought her to the attention of Alfred Stieglitz in 1916. He encouraged her to move from Texas to New York in 1918 and became her most ardent promoter, as well as (in 1924) her husband. During the 1910s and 1920s, O'Keeffe also produced critically acclaimed watercolors. From the 1930s on, she devoted her energies primarily to painting rather than works on paper, although she occasionally dabbled in pastel to remarkable effect, as in *Red Hills with the Pedernal*.

1. Amei Wallach, "Georgia O'Keeffe," *Newsday*, Oct. 30, 1977, quoted in Laurie Lisle, *Portrait of an Artist: A Biography of Georgia O'Keeffe* (Albuquerque: University of New Mexico, 1986), 237.

2. For a thorough discussion of O'Keeffe's use of pastel, see Ruth E. Fine and Barbara Buhler Lynes, *O'Keeffe on Paper* (Washington, D.C.: National Gallery of Art, 2000), 69–77.

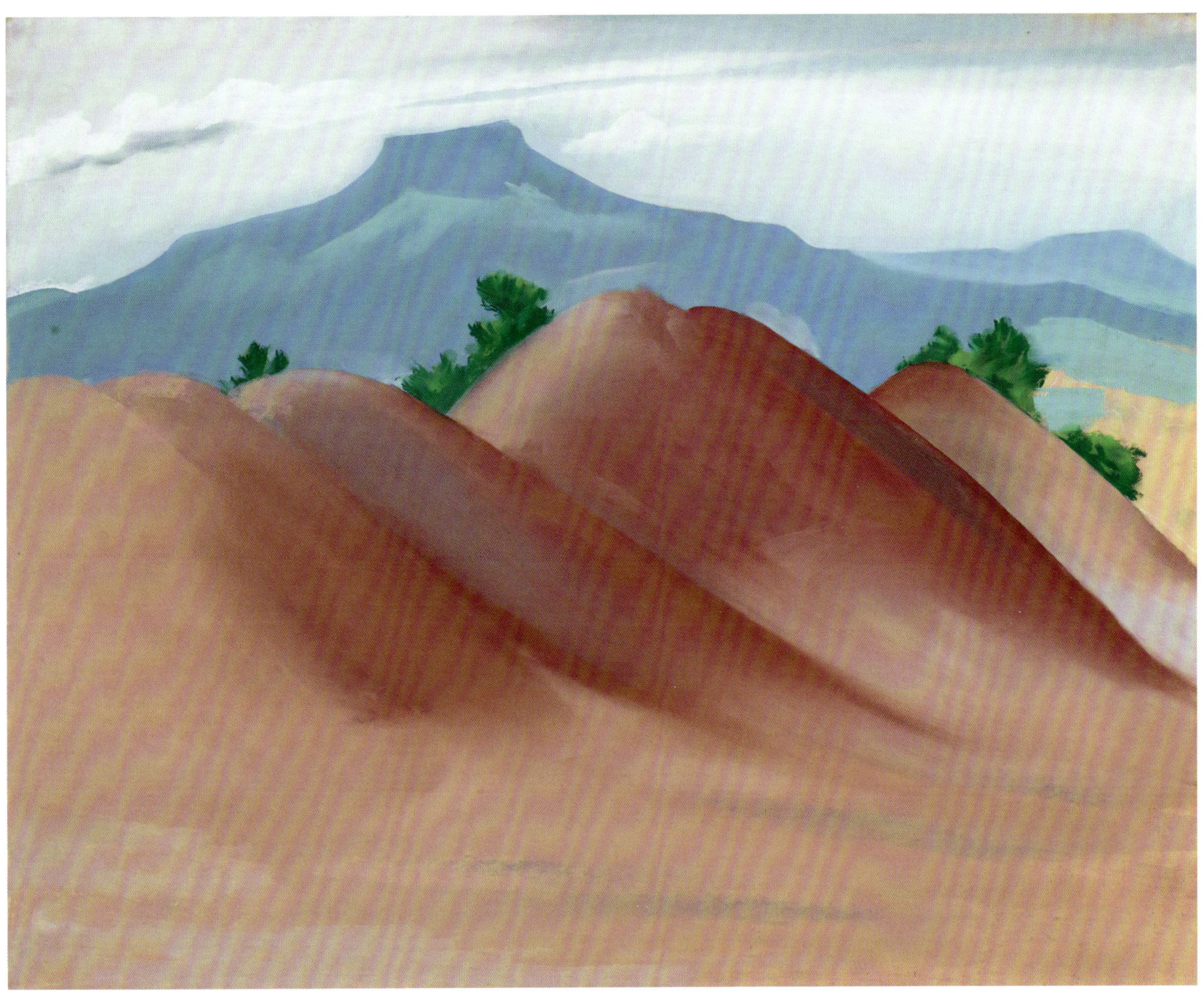

OBSERVING THE BUILT ENVIRONMENT

For artists, the impulse to document the world around them with sketches made on the spot extended both to the wonders of nature and to the constructions of humankind. As they traveled around their neighborhoods and around the globe with sketchbook in hand, artists created images of the structures they encountered. Depictions of buildings and urban environments—the focus of this section—present some distinct artistic concerns. The drawings of architectural edifices and cityscapes included here address the structural, spatial, and aesthetic properties of built things, as well as the formal and symbolic relations between organic and synthetic forms.

Throughout the eighteenth and nineteenth centuries, renderings of archaeological sites and historical architecture documented these structures and invited philosophical musings about the passage of time and humankind's transformation of the natural world. As the United States developed into a more urbanized and industrialized society during the nineteenth and twentieth centuries, artists found aesthetic inspiration in the new vertical thrust of skyscrapers and the gridded geometries of cities and mechanical forms. The dramatically altered landscape of the modern metropolis prompted artists to seek new ways of representing the visual and physical experience of the urban environment by investigating modern and abstract styles.

Alexander Robertson

American, born Scotland, 1772–1841

99 From the Mill, September 11, 1796

Black ink on off-white, moderately thick, moderately textured laid paper, 8¾ × 11½ in. (22.2 × 29.2 cm)
Inscribed in ink, lower right: "11. Sept. 1796"
Purchased with funds given by Mr. and Mrs. Leonard L. Milberg, 1990.216.2

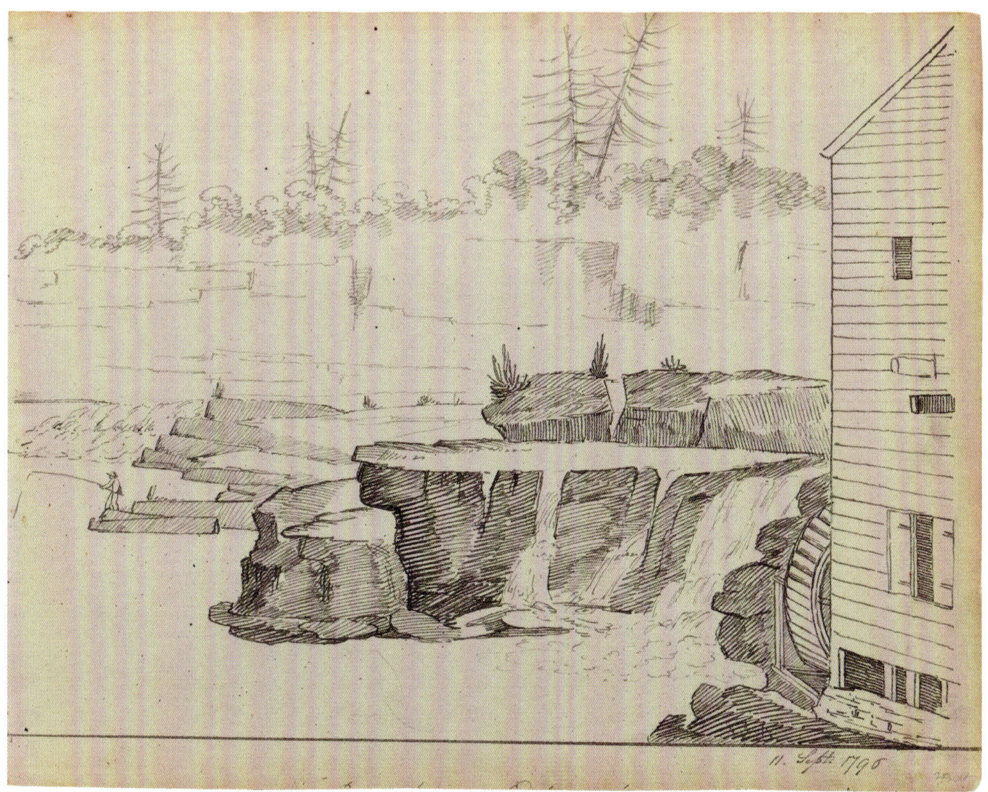

This pen-and-ink drawing was originally a page in a sketchbook that Alexander Robertson used in New York City and on travels in the Hudson River valley between 1796 and 1798.[1] Although made on-site, *From the Mill* exemplifies the artist's generalized approach to nature and stylized drawing technique. In keeping with British conventions of the picturesque landscape, Robertson framed the scene with a strong vertical element (the building) and created a gradual progression from foreground to background. Strong contrasts—such as the natural contours of trees, waterfalls, and rocks against the more rigid geometries of the mill—were also characteristic of the picturesque. In a kind of graphic shorthand, the artist quickly rendered leafy trees with looping strokes of his pen, indicated volume and shading with parallel diagonal lines, and implied spatial distance by using lighter outlines for background motifs. While the presence of the mill suggests the beginning of industrial development, the drawing presents a harmonious vision of man in nature, with its tiny figure of a fisherman tucked among the rocks at the left.

In both aesthetic approach and graphic style, the artist followed the practice of his older brother, Archibald Robertson (1765–1835), who came to New York from Scotland in 1791 and established the Columbian Academy of Painting, which offered drawing classes to both men and women, professionals and amateurs. The elder Robinson was the author of *Elements of the Graphic Arts* (1802), the first drawing manual published in the United States, whose chapter on landscape outlines the shorthand drawing technique and compositional formulas followed in *From the Mill*. Alexander Robertson, who studied at

King's College in Aberdeen, Scotland, and at the Royal Academy of Arts in London, joined his brother in New York in 1792 to teach at the highly successful Columbian Academy and formed his own school, the Academy of Painting and Drawing, ten years later. He was also active in the Academy of the Fine Arts, an early artists' organization and forerunner of the National Academy of Design. Both Robertsons played a formative role in promoting drawing (and watercolor painting) at a time when there were few art schools in the United States. In addition to

their teaching, their art helped foster a taste for topographic views of the American landscape. This burgeoning appreciation set the stage for the rise of the Hudson River School in the second quarter of the nineteenth century.

1. The sketchbook is in the collection of the Albany Institute of History and Art, Albany, New York. See also *American Drawings, Pastels and* *Watercolors, Part One: Works of the Eighteenth and Early Nineteenth Centuries* (New York: Kennedy Galleries, 1967), 18–24.

James L. Dick

American, 1834–1868

100 **Farmhouse in Brooklyn,** November 1863

Graphite on cream, medium-weight, smooth wove paper, 6⅞ × 9 in. (17.5 × 22.9 cm)
Inscribed in graphite, lower left: "Nov/63"
Gift of Dr. Clark Marlor, 1993.38.4

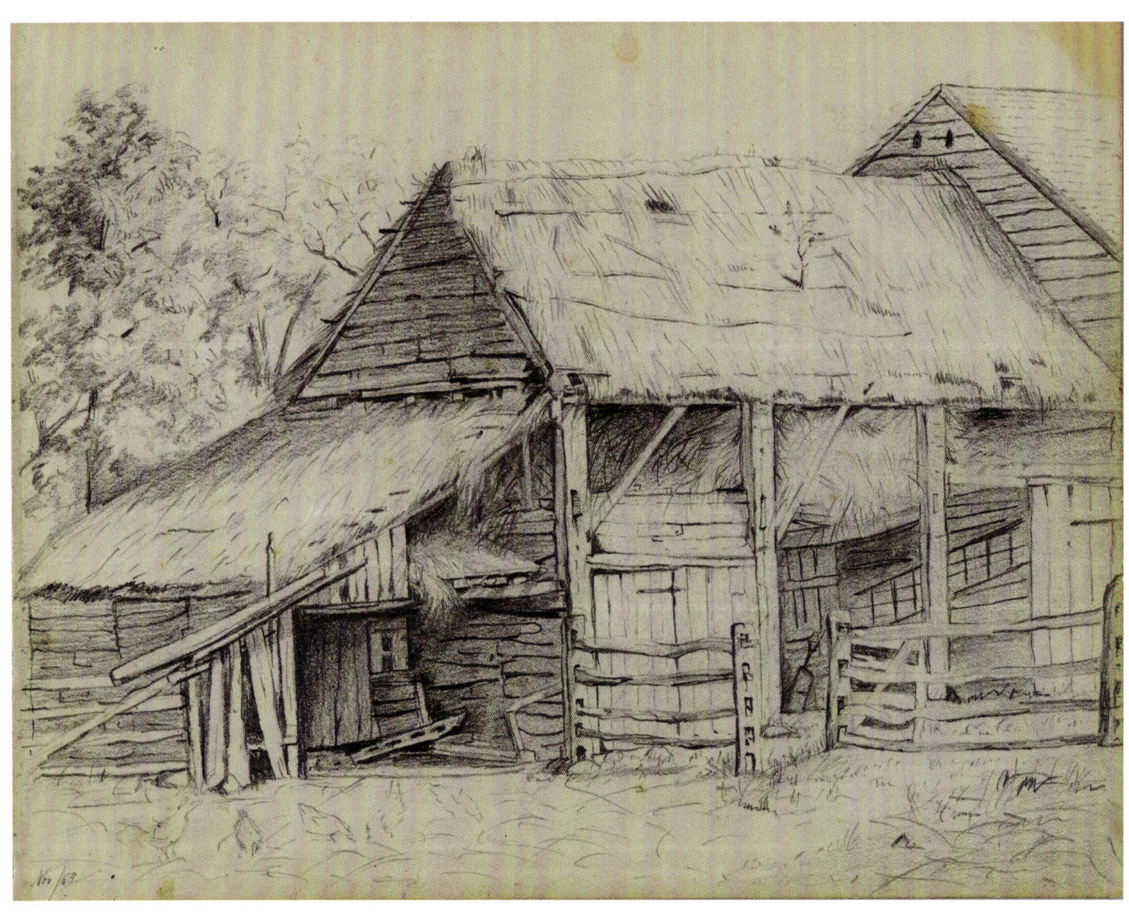

Originally a page from a sketchbook, this drawing by the Brooklyn artist James L. Dick depicts a thatched-roof barn, showing signs of disrepair, attached to a wooden farmhouse (visible at the far right). Dick's inviting composition—with fence gate left slightly ajar and the faint outlines of chickens in the foreground—creates a nostalgic view of a typical seventeenth-century Dutch farm structure in rural Brooklyn. At the same time, this intimate scene meditates on a transitional moment in Brooklyn history as burgeoning industrialization and urbanization led to the disappearance of such traditional structures and the agrarian way of life.

The 1850s and 1860s, when Dick was active as an artist, witnessed a great influx of Irish and German immigrants to Brooklyn. Originally a wealthy residential neighborhood, Brooklyn Heights, where Dick lived most of his life, became the city's financial center. Despite Brooklyn's rapid industrial and economic development and booming population growth in the mid-nineteenth century, areas outside the city center, including Flatbush, Flatlands, New Utrecht, and Gravesend, remained rural and less populated.

One of the founders of the Brooklyn Academy of Design and Brooklyn Art School (later the Brooklyn Art Association), Dick exhibited portraits and genre paintings of rural subjects at the National Academy of Design.[1] In 1861, two years before he completed this drawing, he exhibited at the National Academy a painting (now unlocated) of another Brooklyn scene titled *Old Mill—Red Hook Point*.—CG

1. The Brooklyn Museum's collection also contains a cache of other drawings and sketchbooks by Dick depicting farm structures, tools, and animals.

Francis William Edmonds

American, 1806–1863

101 British Isles Sketchbook, 1841

Graphite on cream, moderately thick, slightly textured wove paper, 4¾ × 6⁵⁄₁₆ × ¼ in. (12.1 × 16 × 0.6 cm)
Purchase gift of Mr. and Mrs. Leonard L. Milberg, 1999.6.2

On June 18, 1841, after traveling through continental Europe, Francis William Edmonds set out from London for northern England and Scotland. This fourteen-page sketchbook constitutes a visual record of his itinerary during that three-week journey through the British Isles. Completed on June 30, one of the most striking sketches in this book is that of Jedburgh Abbey in Scotland (page 6). The early twelfth-century abbey, shown rising above modest residences, exemplifies the transition from Romanesque to Gothic architecture over the course of the building's construction. With fine attention to detail, Edmonds precisely rendered the large, solid Romanesque bell tower at the right and the more delicate Gothic colonnade and rose window at the left. While in Britain, he made numerous sketches of important monuments during stops in Birmingham, Warwick, Kenilworth, Liverpool, Glasgow, Edinburgh, Abbotsford, and other major cities and tourist sites.[1] The view of Stratford-upon-Avon, made from the riverbank (page 13), also includes vignettes of human industry. A loosely sketched man operates a mill in the foreground, while a horse-drawn carriage crosses a bridge and the steeple of a church pokes up among trees in the distance.

Much of Edmonds's time abroad between 1840 and 1841 was spent studying both Old Masters and contemporary artists in London, Paris, and throughout Italy. His own genre pictures were compared with the works of the Scottish painter David Wilkie (1785–1841) for their "attention to design, composition, and light and shade."[2] Edmonds's interest in and admiration for Wilkie were renewed after studying the older artist's work, which combined the Italian Old Master tradition with Dutch and Flemish genre painting.[3] The land- and townscapes in Edmonds's sketchbooks were unusual subject matter for this figure painter; the drawings served as travel diaries and exercises rather than as preparatory sketches for later paintings.

Edmonds studied at the National Academy of Design, where he was elected an academician in 1840. Active as a professional artist, he also worked in the banking industry to support his family. When he experienced a nervous breakdown after the economic Panic of 1837 and the death of his wife, Edmonds was prescribed rest in a Mediterranean climate. He took this opportunity to pursue artistic study abroad, making a grand tour of Italy, England, Scotland, and France (Paris). Parts of his itinerary are documented in this and a second sketchbook in the Brooklyn Museum's collection.[4] —CG

1. The itinerary of Edmonds's travels, as documented in his travel diary, has been thoroughly summarized in Maybelle Mann, "Francis William Edmonds: Mammon and Art" (PhD diss., New York University, 1972), 52–57.
2. "Editor's Table: The Fine Arts," *Knickerbocker* 16 (July 1840): 83, quoted in H. Nichols B. Clark, *Francis W. Edmonds: American Master in the Dutch Tradition* (Washington, D.C.: Smithsonian Institution Press, 1988), 57.
3. Clark, *Francis W. Edmonds*, 58.
4. *European Sketchbook* (acc. no. 1999.6.1) includes images from the Italian portion of his journey.

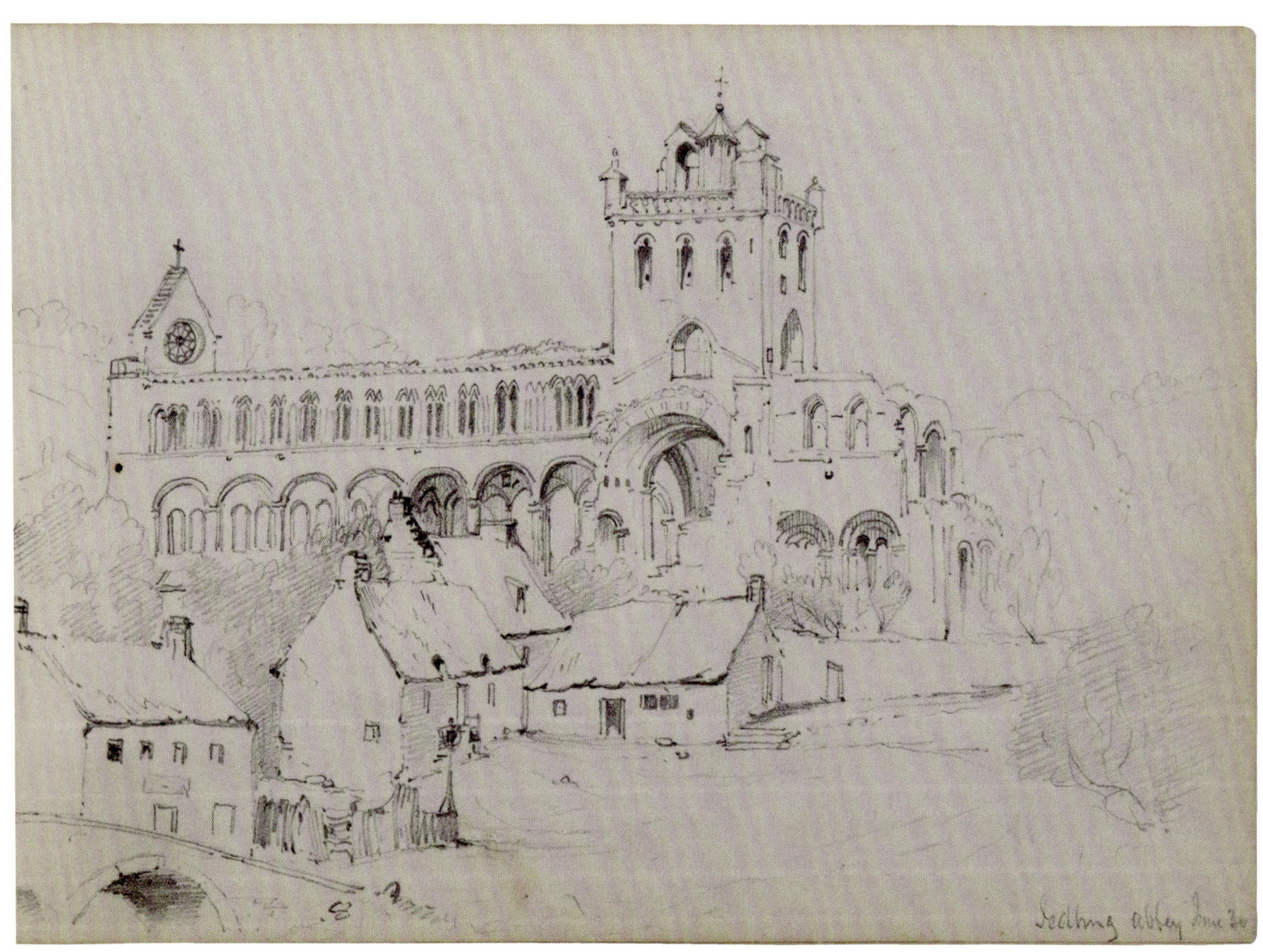

1999.6.2, page 6

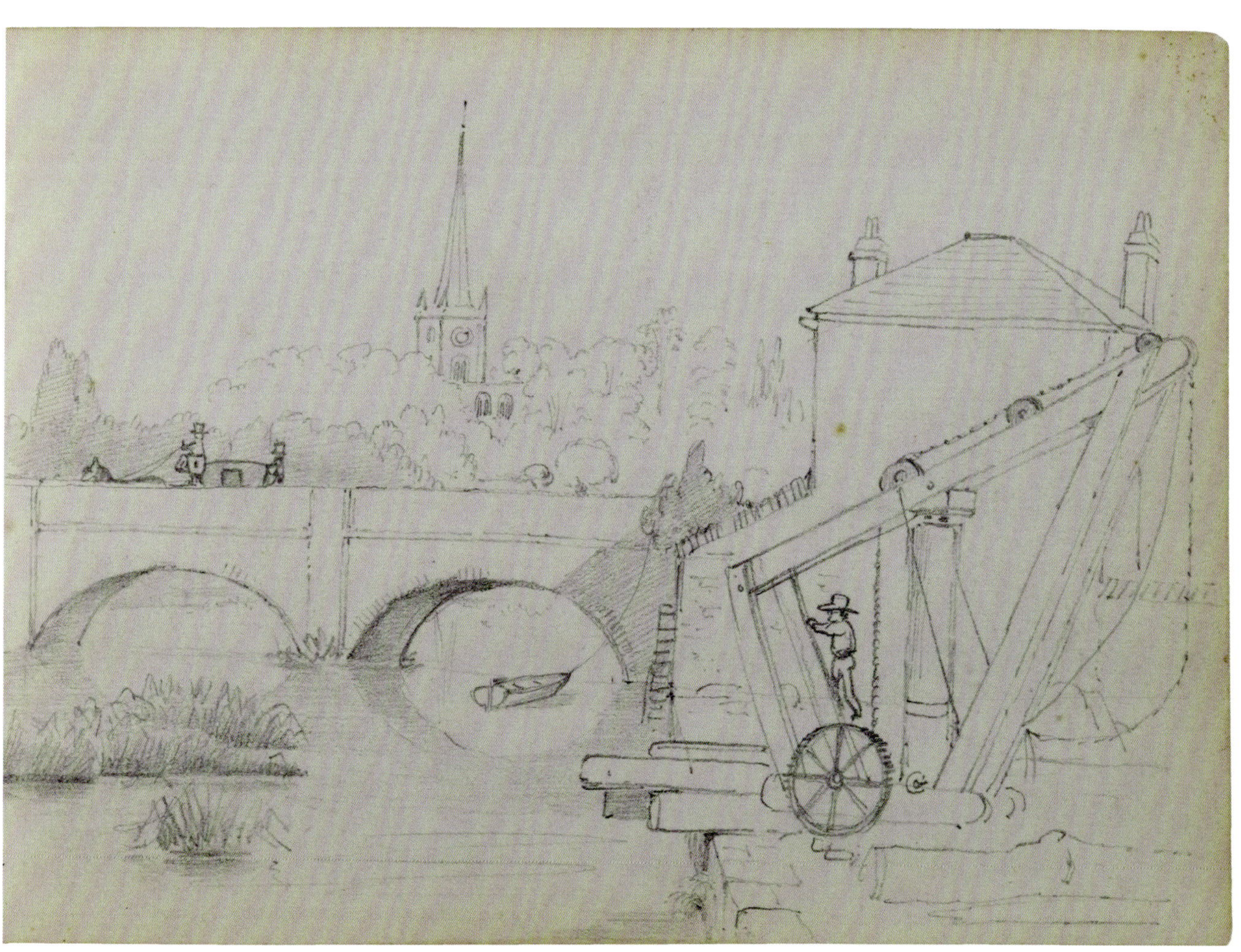

1999.6.2, page 13

Edwin Howland Blashfield

American, 1848–1936

102 Early Christian (Coptic) Monastery at Esna, March 1, 1887

Graphite on cream, medium-weight, smooth wove paper, 8¼ × 10¾ in. (21 × 27.3 cm)
Signed in graphite, lower right: "BY. / E. H. BLASHFIELD '87"
Gift of John H. Field, 48.217.1

103 Temple of Khonsu at Karnak, 1887

Graphite on cream, medium-weight, slightly textured wove paper, 10⅝ × 13¾ in. (27 × 34.9 cm)
Signed in graphite, lower right: "BY / E. H. BLASHFIELD '87"
Gift of John H. Field, 48.217.8

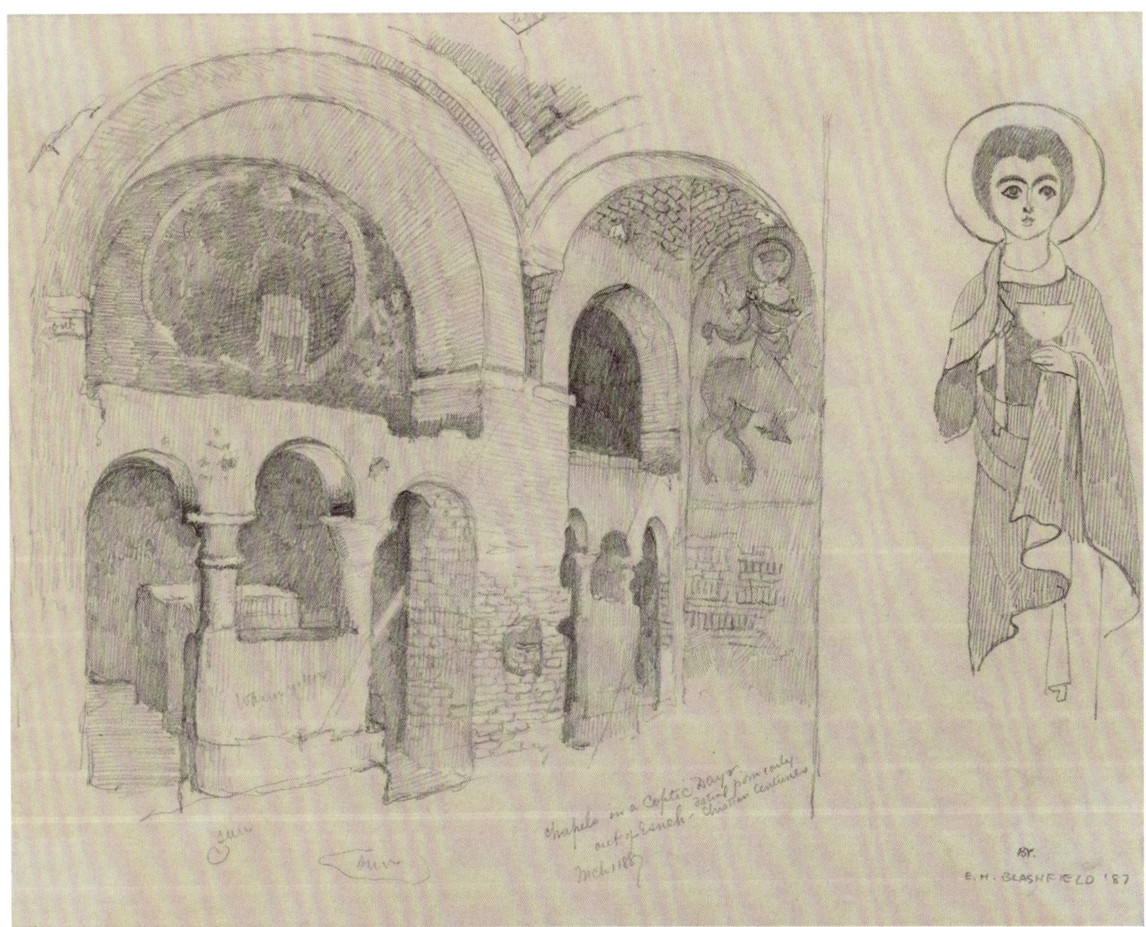

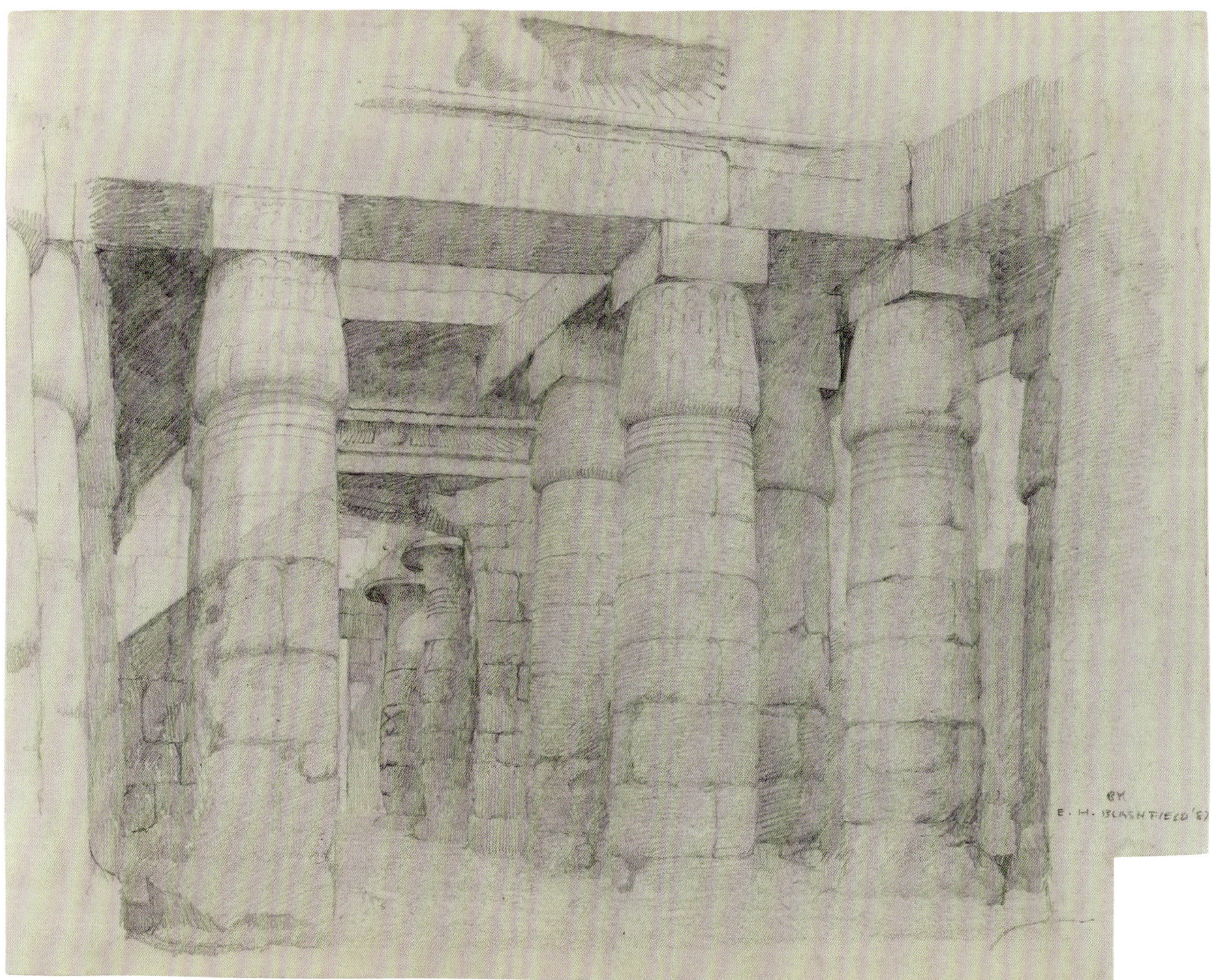

These two graphite drawings are part of a series of sketches Edward Howland Blashfield made in the winter of 1886–87 while sailing up the Nile River with Charles Edwin Wilbour, a noted American Egyptologist and the artist's father-in-law. Best known as a leading muralist in the American Renaissance style, Blashfield also published, with his wife, Evangeline Wilbour Blashfield, a series of articles about their travels in *Scribner's Magazine* illustrated with his images. The colorfully descriptive stories about the people and places they encountered appealed to the popular taste for exotic or orientalist subjects among audiences in Gilded Age America.[1]

Referring to John Murray's *Handbook for Travelers in Lower and Upper Egypt* (1880),[2] the party stopped in the city of Edfu, where Blashfield visited the eleventh-to-twelfth-century Coptic monastery Deir el-Shuhada on the road to Esna. His resulting drawing (number 102) depicts the interior of the transept of the northernmost structure in the Deir el-Shuhada complex (figure 24). The left portion of the sheet contains a precise architectural rendering of the structure, juxtaposing the grand arches of the transept with the exposed brick, which had crumbled in places over time. Blashfield lightly applied evenly spaced lines to create texture on the walls and used dense hatching to suggest shade and depth in the side aisles. The artist's notations regarding color and sunlight effects are found at lower left. The image of Saint Claudius on horseback on the south wall of the transept is roughly sketched in comparison to the architecture. At the far right, a detailed depiction of Saint Stephen demonstrates Blashfield's close study of this mural, which is actually located within the archway next to the image of Saint Claudius.[3]

After leaving Edfu, Blashfield and his companions stopped in Luxor to visit the Karnak temple complex, which developed over several building campaigns from the fifteenth to the fourth

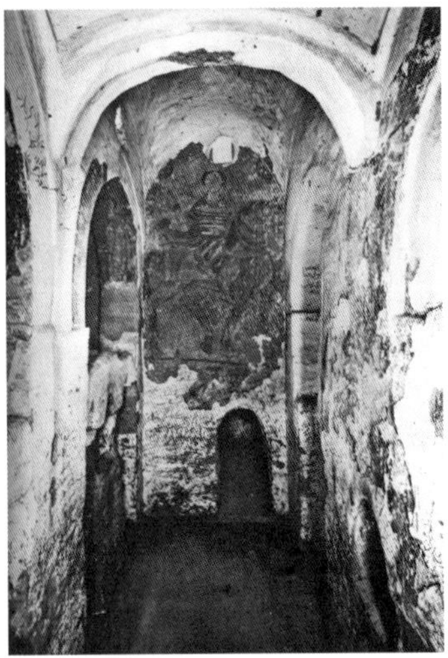

Fig. 24. South wall of the transept of Deir El-Shuhada, Esna, Egypt. © IFAO. Reproduced from Jules Leroy, *Les Peintures des couvents du désert d'Esna* (Cairo: Institut Français d'Archéologie Orientale, 1975), page 39

century B.C.E. The temple of Khonsu, which Blashfield recorded in the other drawing shown here, was built beginning in the twelfth century B.C.E. during the reign of Ramesses III. This sketch depicts the temple's famous peristyle court, renowned for its gridded arrangement of twenty-eight colossal columns

decorated with hieroglyphs. Combining geometric precision with deep recession, this drawing conveys the artist's astonishment at the height and width of the columns and the impressive architectural design. During a later visit to this location in the winter of 1889–90, Blashfield expressed his feeling of wonder while navigating the shadowy spaces amid this dense forest of monumental columns: "100 men might stand on the top of a Karnak capital. Confusion mystery vertigo occur in this deception of the Karnak col[umns]."[4]—CG

1. Edward Howland Blashfield and Evangeline Wilbour Blashfield, "Afloat on the Nile," *Scribner's Magazine* 10, no. 6 (Dec. 1891): 663–81; and Edward Howland Blashfield and Evangeline Wilbour Blashfield, "A Day with the Donkey-Boys," *Scribner's Magazine* 11, no. 1 (Jan. 1892): 32–50.
2. John Murray, *A Handbook for Travelers in Lower and Upper Egypt* (London: John Murray, 1880). Charles Wilbour recorded in his travel journal, "The rest are going to a convent you will find mentioned in Murray and I shall go to the temple [of Edfu]"; Charles Wilbour, entry, Mar. 1, 1887, quoted in *Travels in Egypt (December 1880 to May 1891): Letters of Charles Edwin Wilbour*, ed. Jean Capart (New York: Brooklyn Museum, 1936), 424–25.
3. For additional information about these murals, see Jules Leroy, *Les Peintures des couvents du désert d'Esna* (Cairo: Institut Français d'Archéologie Orientale, 1975), 12. It is an important testament to the documentary value of Blashfield's sketches that the Museum's drawing helped Egyptologists in 1967 learn of the existence of these early mural paintings, which had been covered with whitewash.
4. Edwin Howland Blashfield, "Egypt Notes," winter 1889–90, Edwin Howland Blashfield Travel Diaries, Brooklyn Special Collections, Brooklyn Museum.

Everett Shinn

American, 1876–1953

104 Fifth Avenue, 1910

Pastel on beige, moderately thick, moderately textured laid paper, 12⅜ × 15¼ in. (31.4 × 38.7 cm)
Signed in pastel, lower left: "E SHINN / 1910"
Gift of Samuel A. Lewisohn, 43.227

Using a muted palette of black, gray, and white against a tan-colored paper, Everett Shinn captured the misty atmosphere of a rainy day along New York's Fifth Avenue. Seen from behind, a man and woman, both dressed in black, draw the viewer's eye into the scene as they scurry down the sidewalk huddled under their shared umbrella. This figural group stands out as a stark silhouette against the sketchy forms of the surrounding setting—a row of buildings that recedes into the distance at the right and a broad street dotted with horse-drawn carriages and other pedestrians at

the left. The skyscraper in the left background, with its distinctive triangular profile, is recognizable as the Flatiron Building, located at the intersection of Fifth Avenue and Twenty-third Street. At the turn of the century, this newly developed area—which included Madison Square Park—was considered one of the city's most elegant districts. Commentators likened it to London's Trafalgar Square and Paris's place de la Concorde in beauty and grandeur.[1] Shinn lived a few blocks away and frequently portrayed the urban spectacle around the park under different weather conditions.

Here his primary concern was to record an overall impression rather than transcribe specific details of place. Indeed, the buildings and other forms—rendered with broad strokes of thinly layered pastel—appear dematerialized in the hazy effects of inclement weather.

Born in New Jersey, Shinn became a talented draftsman and spent his early career as an illustrator. He was one of the Philadelphia newspapermen in the orbit of **Robert Henri**—the group that would form the core of the Eight, or Ashcan School, of urban Realists. Shinn received his art training through classes at the Pennsylvania Academy of the Fine Arts and his participation in the Charcoal Club, a group of artists who met

regularly to sketch from live models and to receive critiques from Henri and John Sloan (1871–1951). After moving to New York in 1897, Shinn devoted himself more seriously to art, although he continued to do illustration work (see number 69). His pastels, which focused on urban and theatrical subjects and displayed the influence of the French Impressionist Edgar Degas (1834–1917), were widely acclaimed. As one critic noted, "Shinn is a master of pastel; he knows thoroughly both the possibilities and the limitations of his medium. . . . [I]f technically his pastels are great achievements, pictorially they are also so."[2]

1. See Janay Wong, *Everett Shinn: The Spectacle of Life* (New York: Berry-Hill Galleries, 2000), 23–24.

2. A[lbert]. E. Gallatin, "Studio Talk," *International Studio* 30 (Nov. 1906): 86.

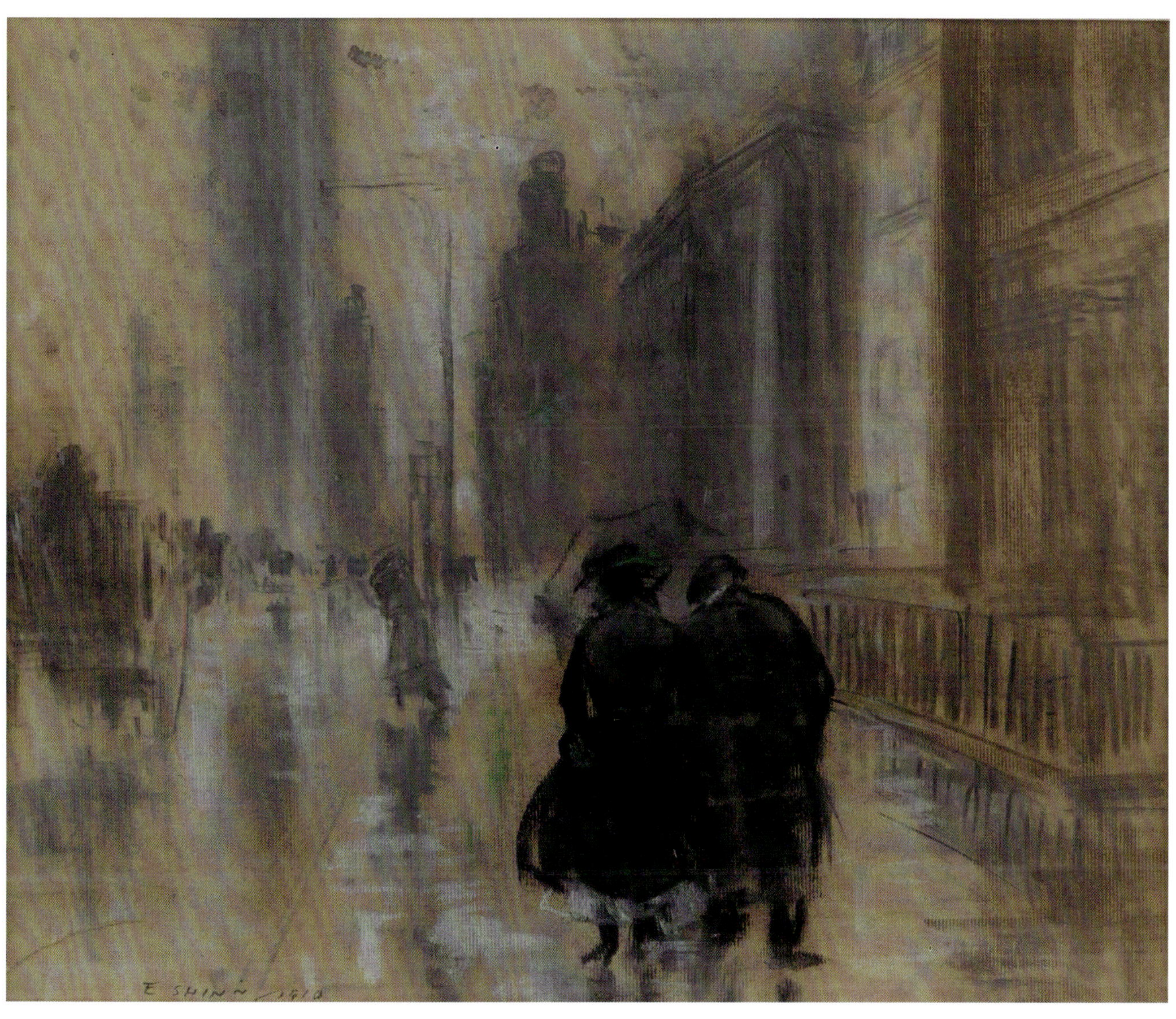

Abraham Walkowitz

American, born Siberia, 1878–1965

105 Improvisations of New York, 1914

Ink on cream, thin, smooth wove paper mounted to paper, 10½ × 7¼ in. (26.7 × 18.4 cm)
Signed in ink, lower left, on mount: "A. WALKOWITZ 1914"
Bequest of Mrs. Carl L. Selden, 1996.157.31

Improvisations of New York was made during a time when Abraham Walkowitz was experimenting with the styles of Fauvism, Cubism, and Futurism in an attempt to capture the vitality of urban life. In comparison with his earlier, more representational views of the city, *Improvisations* evokes skyscrapers abstractly through its vertical composition and the energetic upward thrust of its angled and squiggled lines. Dots suggest the hundreds of windows rising above a crowded street, represented by increasingly dense strokes of ink concentrated across the bottom of the composition. The spontaneous, frenetic rhythm of lines conjures up crowds and skyscrapers, while the dynamism of the ink application dematerializes the architecture into abstract notations and suggests the fast-paced excitement of New York life. This sense of speed and motion is also a nod to Futurism.

Walkowitz recorded his urban impressions in an extensive series of *Improvisations* made over the course of several decades. As he did for his Isadora Duncan drawings (see numbers 20–22), he compiled many of his city views into a publication. The book, *Improvisations of New York: A Symphony in Lines* (1948),[1] constitutes a composite view of the city that expresses its pulsing energy.

After studying at the National Academy of Design in New York, Walkowitz went to Paris to continue his training at the Académie Julian. While in France, he witnessed some of the latest developments in modern art and met a number of avant-garde artists, including **Marsden Hartley**. In 1912 Hartley introduced Walkowitz to the photographer and gallery owner Alfred Stieglitz (1864–1946), who advocated a greater understanding of European avant-garde art and its translation into a uniquely American modernism. After making Fauvist-inspired images of nude female bathers in bright colors, Walkowitz began experimenting with the expressive possibilities of simple black line, which led to later work in pure abstraction, including his *Improvisations*.—CG

1. Abraham Walkowitz, *Improvisations of New York: A Symphony in Lines* (Girard, Kans.: Haldeman-Julius Publications, 1948). The Brooklyn Museum's drawing is not reproduced in this publication.

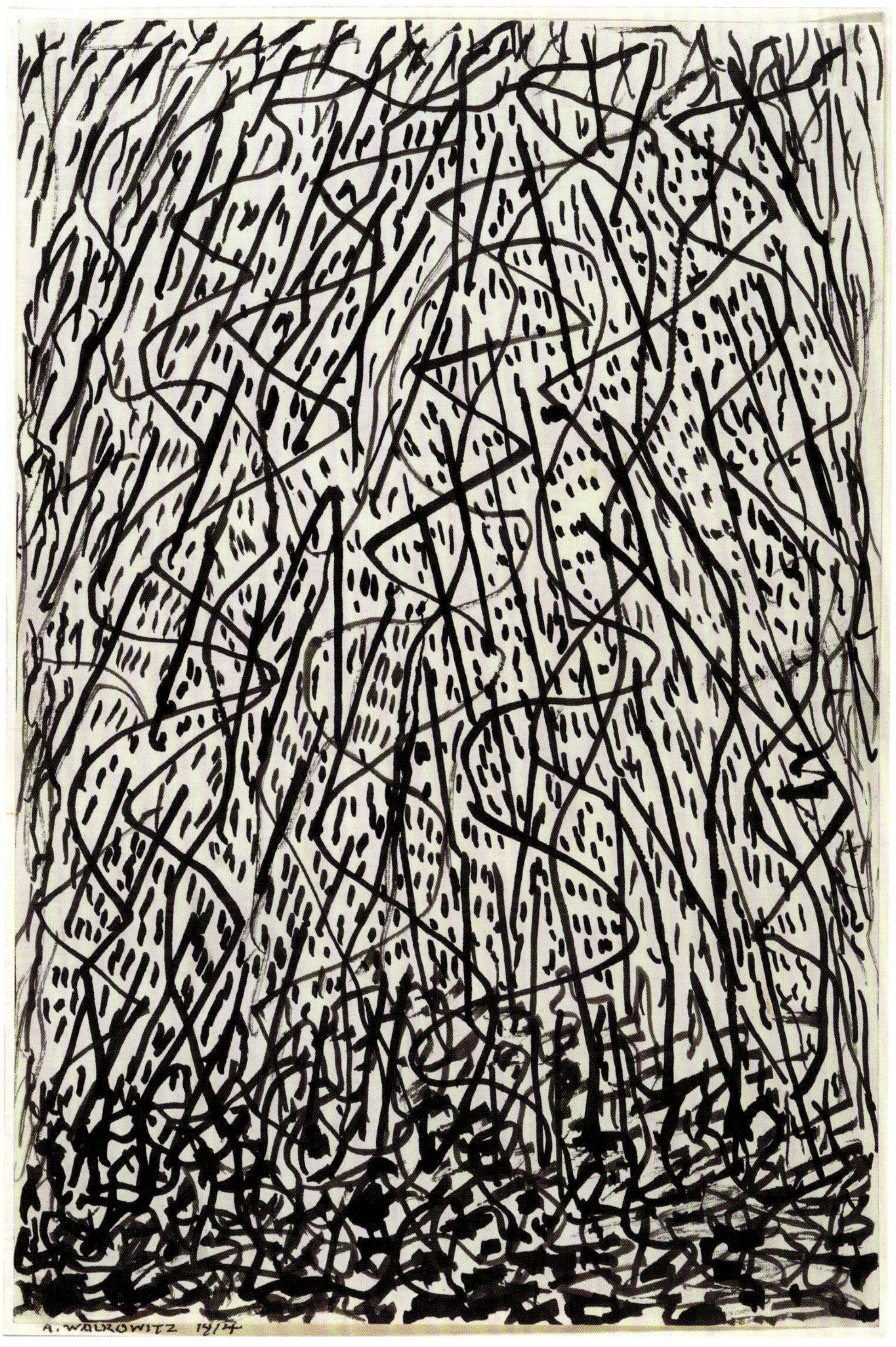

Stuart Davis

American, 1892–1964

106 Serviceable Boxes among the Rocks, 1917

Graphite on cream, moderately thick, moderately textured wove paper, 14¹⁵⁄₁₆ × 19 in. (37.9 × 48.3 cm)
Signed in graphite, lower right: "Stuart Davis 1917"
Purchased with funds given by Mr. and Mrs. Leonard L. Milberg, 1992.224

This sketch of the fishing town of Gloucester, Massachusetts, demonstrates both the artist's facility with the pencil and his preoccupation with geometric forms. With strokes that are quick yet assured, Stuart Davis described the densely clustered houses in hilly topography as well as key architectural details, such as chimneys, dormer windows, and fences. (The clock tower of the town hall is visible in the background at right.) Davis contrasted the rigid linearity of these buildings with the undulating branches of trees and the roughly circular shapes of rocks and shrubbery in the center of the composition. The origin and significance of the drawing's title—*Serviceable Boxes among the Rocks*—are unknown, but it may refer to the boxlike structure, stacked appearance, and functional simplicity of these residences.[1]

Drawing always played a pivotal role in Davis's art, from his earliest illustrations for newspapers and magazines to his mature modernist paintings.[2] He used drawing to record his subjective impressions of a motif and to work out his complex, often esoteric theories about art, explaining in 1948, "Drawing is a method for giving permanent Form to experience with subject matter. The drawing is the Form of the experience, not of the subject."[3] Even as his pictures became increasingly abstract over the course of his career, Davis continued to take his inspiration from the world around him.

The son of artists (his mother was a sculptor and his father an illustrator and art director for the *Philadelphia Press*), Davis studied art in New York for three years with **Robert Henri**, the leader of the Ashcan School of urban Realists. Like many artists in Henri's circle, Davis embraced modern American life as subject matter—in particular, its urban and industrial landscapes and its fleeting sensory experiences of billboards and jazz music—and he regularly took to the streets with sketchbook in hand. From 1915 to 1934, he spent summers in Gloucester, and he incorporated its "topographical severity and the architectural beauties of the Gloucester schooner" in his art.[4] Davis produced *Serviceable Boxes among the Rocks* during a transitional period. Whereas this drawing reflects the realistic, reportorial style of his early work, its planar geometries hint at his later Cubist-inspired landscapes with dramatically simplified, hard-edged forms.

1. This title is inscribed in an unknown hand (not Davis's) on the verso; the first word has been erroneously transcribed as "Servicala" and "Servicale" in past exhibitions. See Ani Boyajian and Mark Rutkoski, eds., *Stuart Davis: A Catalogue Raisonné*, 3 vols. (New Haven, Conn.: Yale University Art Gallery in association with Yale University Press, 2007), 2:52, cat. no. 114.
2. Of the more than 1,700 works recorded in the Stuart Davis catalogue raisonné, over 700 are individual drawings; furthermore, his voluminous notebooks include many sketches and diagrams. For these statistics, see Mary Birmingham, *Dynamic Impulse: The Drawings of Stuart Davis* (New York: Hollis Taggart Galleries, 2007), 10.
3. Stuart Davis Papers, reel 8, Sept. 27, 1948, Fogg Museum, Harvard Art Museums, quoted in Karen Wilkin and Lewis Kachur, *The Drawings of Stuart Davis* (New York: American Federation for the Arts in association with Harry N. Abrams, 1992), 24.
4. Stuart Davis, *Stuart Davis*, American Artists Group Monograph, no. 6 (New York: American Artists Group, 1945), 14.

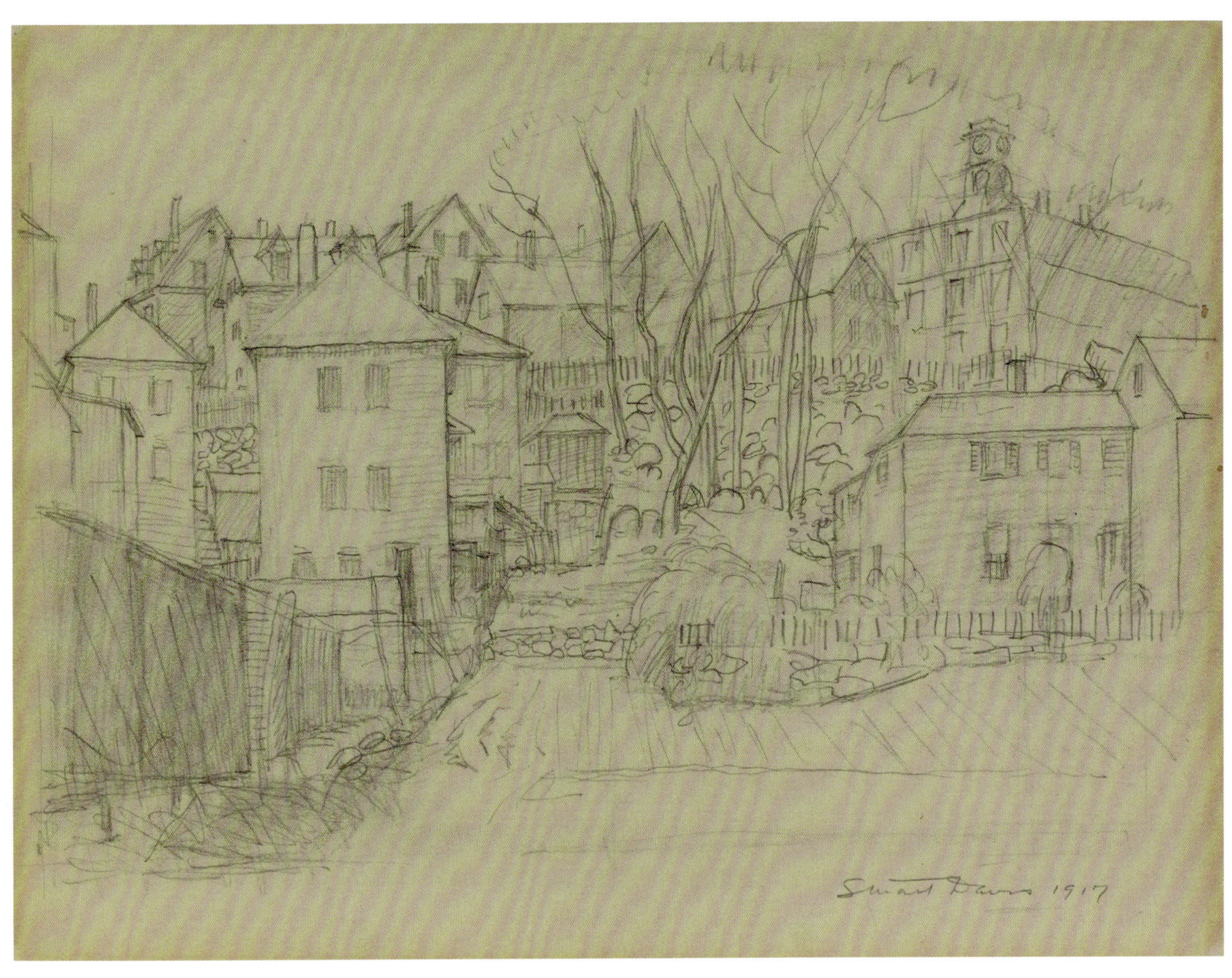

George Copeland Ault

American, 1891–1948

107 Shipboard, 1924

Graphite on cream, medium-weight, slightly textured wove paper, 9 × 6 in. (22.9 × 15.2 cm)
Signed in graphite, upper left: "G.C. Ault '24."
Gift of Manhattan Art Investments, LP, 2007.46

Depicting a cluster of smokestacks, ducts, and pipes on an ocean liner, this drawing features the kinds of mechanical and industrial imagery embraced by Precisionist artists as icons of modern America. By cropping the view of the ship's machinery, George Copeland Ault focused attention on the aesthetic potential of his subject—the play of rounded and linear shapes and dark and light tones—rather than its practical function. He articulated these geometric forms with thin outlines and delicately nuanced modeling, achieved by rubbing the side of his pencil along the textured surface of the paper, that provides the illusion of volume and spatial depth. Some motifs are difficult to read: for instance, the rectangular form and bent tube that appear to emerge from the central smokestack could be either parts of the ventilation system or an abstracted depiction of billowing smoke. The drawing's geometrized composition, absence of people, and overall mood of distilled stasis are all characteristic of Precisionism.

Ault completed this work on a 1924 visit to Paris during a transitional period of his career. Beginning in the 1920s he abandoned his early Impressionist manner and began painting urban and industrial subjects with hard-edged, simplified geometries and flat paint application. His interest in modern architecture and Machine Age forms was inspired in part by his move to New York City and a short stint working in his father's printing-ink factory in New Jersey.[1] In Paris, Ault was exposed to Surrealism and the work of the Italian painter Giorgio de Chirico (1888–1978), whose influence is evident in the sense of disquiet that often infuses Ault's pictures. During the 1920s, Ault exhibited regularly in progressive galleries in New York and enjoyed critical success. Chronic personal struggles—including poor health, family deaths, and depression—increasingly interfered with his art, and in 1937 he settled in Woodstock, New York, hoping to find respite and renewed inspiration in the rural landscape. One critic described the unique quality of Ault's oeuvre: "In his pictures, which are flawlessly designed, precision, austerity, and careful definition merge with a poetic sense, mystery and awe. Definite realism is welded with certain and strong abstraction. Quietude and gentle melancholy are combined with tension, a 'pull' akin to gravity."[2]

1. Susan Lubowsky, *George Ault* (New York: Whitney Museum of American Art, 1988), 14–15.
2. John Ruggles, *George Ault Memorial Exhibition* (Woodstock, N.Y.: Woodstock Art Gallery, 1949), unpag.

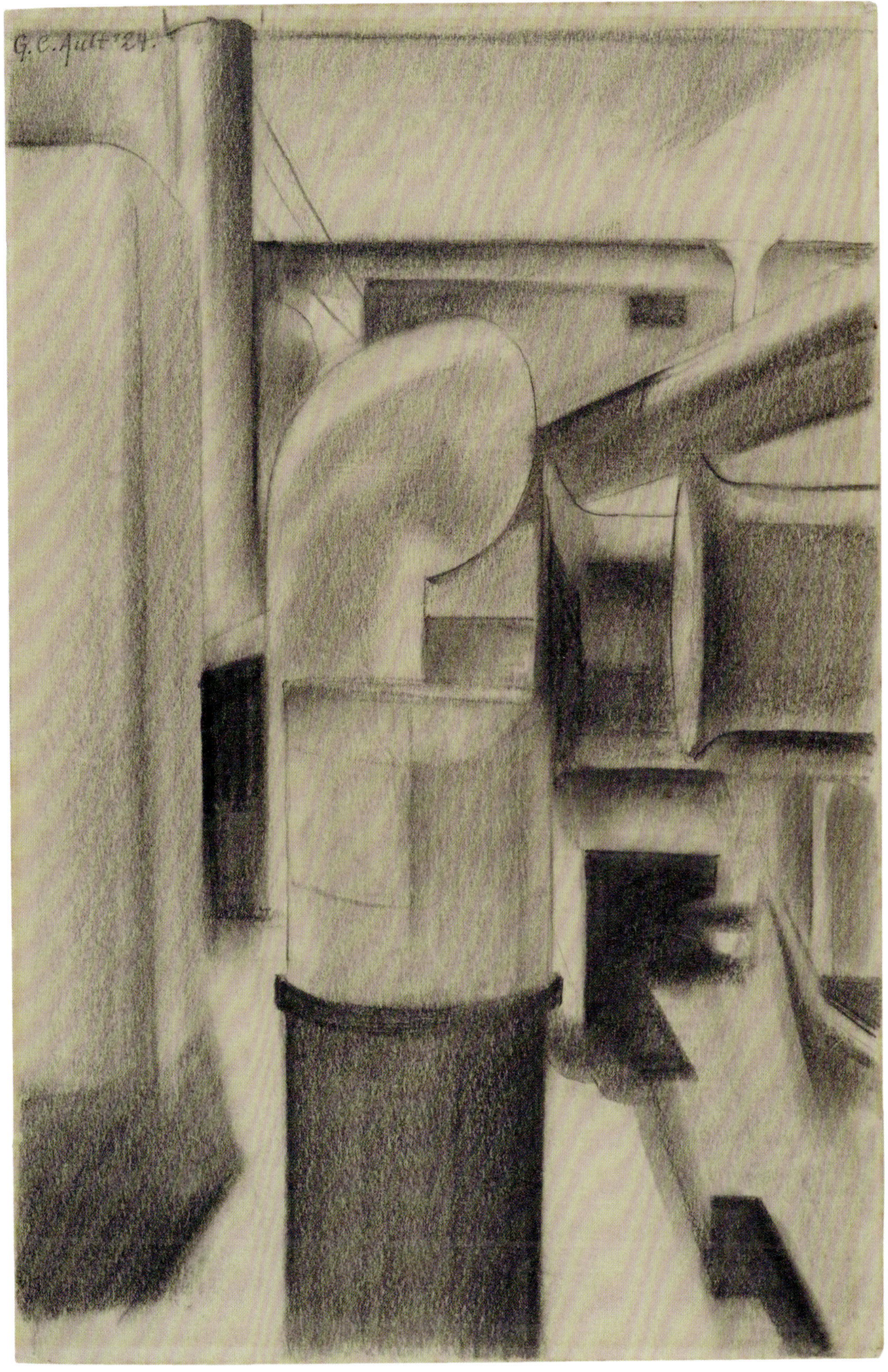
G. C. Ault '24.

Blanche Lazzell

American, 1879–1956

108–12 Five Sketches for "Abstract Composition," 1924

Graphite on cream, thin, smooth paper, each 10⅝ × 8¼ in. (27 × 21 cm)
Gift of Dr. Abram Kanof and Theodore Keel, by exchange, Charles Stewart Smith Memorial Fund, and the Dick S. Ramsay Fund, 2006.43.2, .5, .7, .8, .12. © Estate of Blanche Lazzell

113 Abstract Composition, 1924

Opaque watercolor and graphite on cream, thin, smooth wove paper mounted to board, 10¾ × 8¼ in. (27.3 × 21 cm)
Signed in graphite, lower right: "Blanche Lazzell, 1924"
Inscribed in graphite, on verso, by Albert Gleizes: "Je voudrais dans cette composition moins d'éparpillement / Les [mesures?] sont trop uniformes—L'action doit être / écrite plus fortement." (I would like less scattering in this composition / The [proportions?] are too uniform—The action must be inscribed more forcefully.)
Gift of Dr. Abram Kanof and Theodore Keel, by exchange, Charles Stewart Smith Memorial Fund, and the Dick S. Ramsay Fund, 2006.43.1. © Estate of Blanche Lazzell

Always eager to expand her knowledge and practice, the American modernist Blanche Lazzell traveled to Paris at age forty-five to study with the French Cubists Albert Gleizes (1881–1953), Fernand Léger (1881–1955), and André Lhote (1885–1962). Gleizes, with whom she took private lessons from February to August 1924, had the greatest impact on her. These six objects—part of a series of fourteen related works in the Brooklyn Museum's collection (one watercolor and thirteen studies in graphite)—were made as an exercise for Gleizes. They provide a rare and fascinating glimpse into Lazzell's process of transforming a townscape into an abstract composition.[1]

An early drawing in this group (number 108) is the most representational among them: Lazzell articulated the buildings, staircases, and trees around a plaza as simplified, geometric forms. While working through the subsequent sketches and culminating in the final watercolor (number 113), she broke down the initial composition into ever more reductive, abstract shapes that she then rearranged and filled with different patterns and tones. This kind of experimentation allowed Lazzell to explore the expressive possibilities of abstraction in keeping with Gleizes's tutelage. He theorized that the juxtaposition of flat forms—through their relation to each other and the picture's support—provided a nonrepresentational way to signify spatial depth.[2] Because Lazzell was partially deaf, Gleizes frequently wrote out his critiques, as can be seen on the reverse of this watercolor.[3]

Born on a farm near Maidsville, West Virginia, Lazzell made the unconventional decision early in her life not to marry so that she could devote herself to a professional career. In 1918, after studying at West Virginia University, at the Art Students League in New York, and at several ateliers on her first trip to Paris (1912–14), she settled in Provincetown, Massachusetts, and became a leading figure of its thriving artists' colony. Lazzell also maintained contact with avant-garde circles in the New York art world, such as the Société Anonyme.[4] She worked in various media—including oil, woodblock prints, and textile design—depicting still lifes and landscapes in a Cubist-inspired style of flattened, decorative shapes. Her works from the mid-1920s, produced under Gleizes's influence, were among her most daring creations and made her a pioneer of abstraction in American art.

1. The following year, Lazzell created an oil painting after this series, *Painting III* (West Virginia and Regional History Collection, Morgantown, acc. no. 1995.007.004).
2. For a discussion of Lazzell's studies with Gleizes and his theories, see Peter Brooke, "Studying with Albert Gleizes in 1924," in *Blanche Lazzell: The Life and Work of an American Modernist*, ed. Robert Bridges, Kristina Olson, and Janet Snyder (Morgantown: West Virginia University Press, 2004), 207–27.
3. The author thanks Jane Boyd and Hélène Valance for suggesting that the inscrutable word in Gleizes's inscription may be *mesures*.
4. Founded in 1920 by the artist-collector Katherine Dreier (1877–1952), the Société Anonyme was devoted to promoting vanguard art; other members included Marcel Duchamp (1887–1968) and Man Ray (1890–1976).

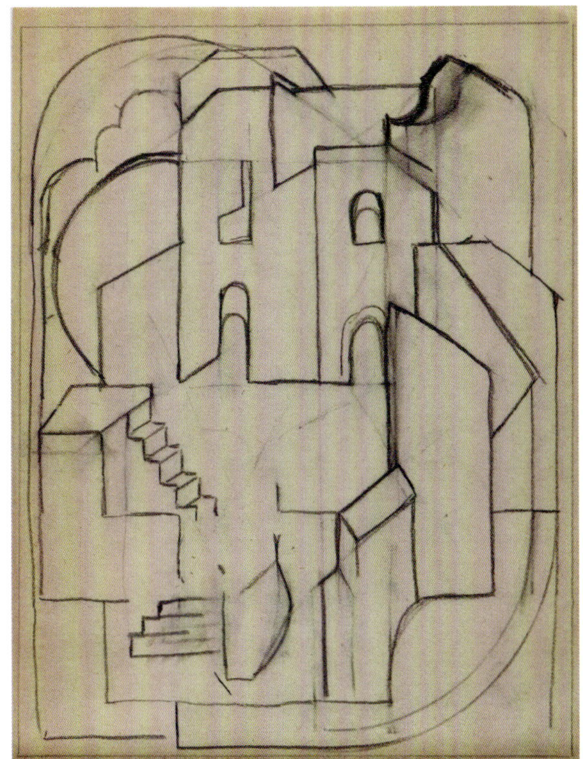

108

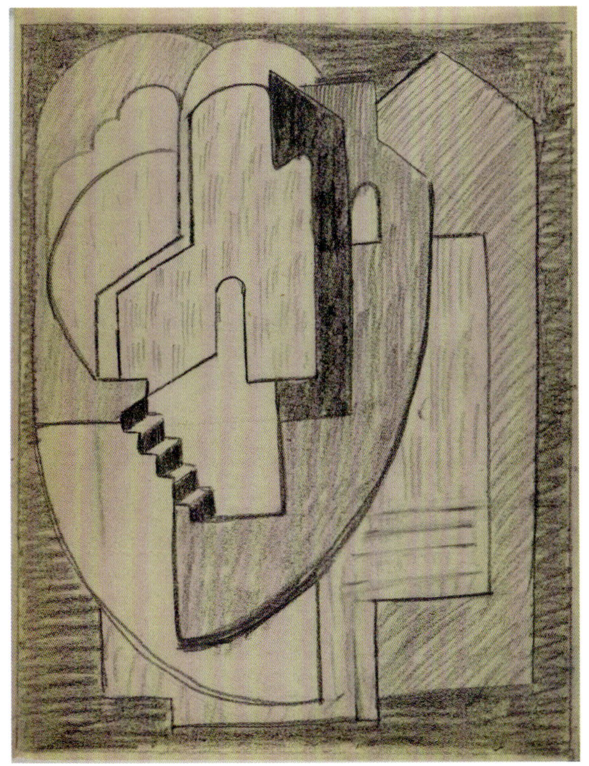

109

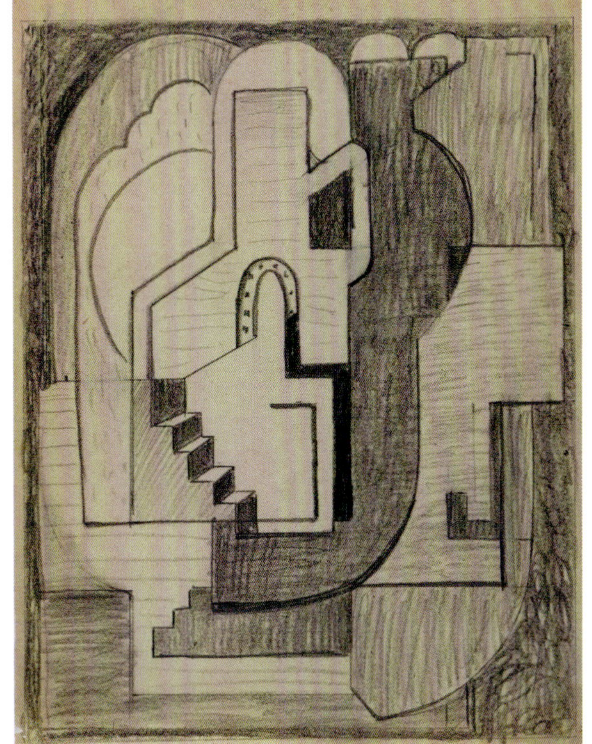

110

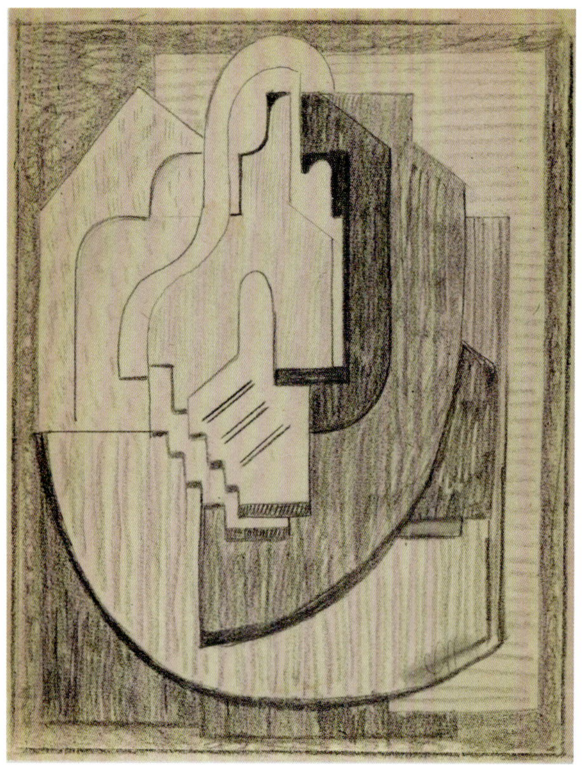

111

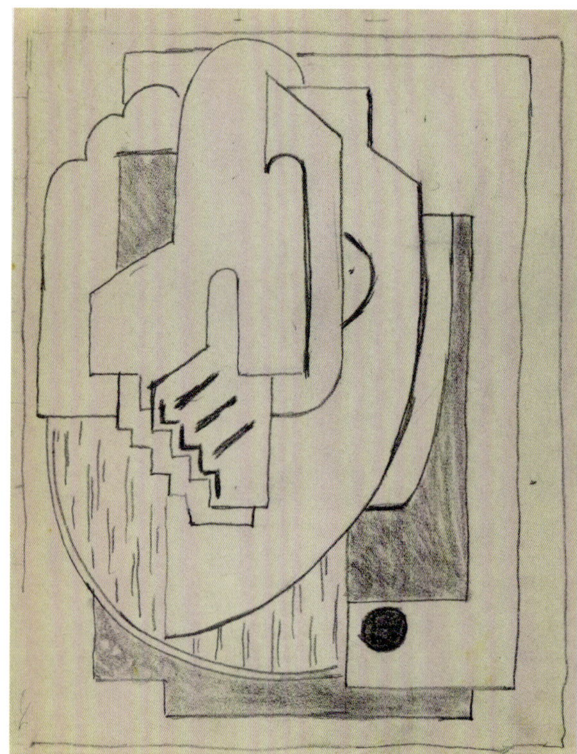

112

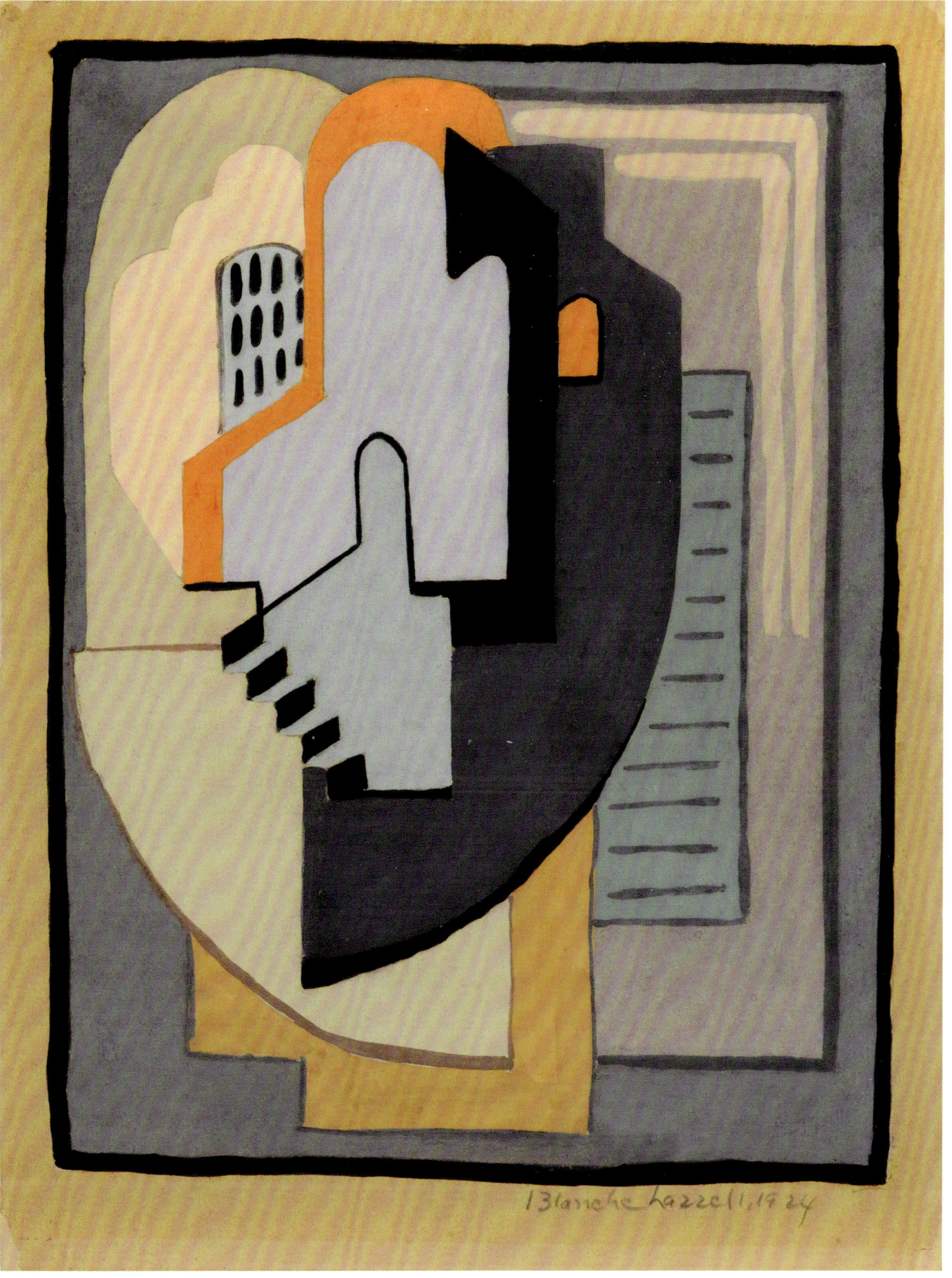

113

Reginald Marsh

American, 1898–1954

114 Wall Street, March 18, 1931

Brown ink with graphite underdrawing on cream, medium-weight, slightly textured wove paper, 9 × 6⁷⁄₁₆ in. (22.9 × 16.4 cm)
Signed and inscribed in graphite, lower center: "Reginald Marsh March 18 1931 / (F. M. M.)"
Designated Purchase Fund, 77.232.3. © 2012 Estate of Reginald Marsh / Art Students League, New York / Artists Rights Society (ARS), New York

Wall Street, by the illustrator, painter, and printmaker Reginald Marsh, depicts a narrow vista of the lower Manhattan skyline with its densely packed cluster of buildings soaring above the busy harbor, seen from the southeast.[1] Marsh's technique here is particularly well suited to the rigid geometries of his subject matter. After outlining the architectural forms faintly in graphite, he used a thin pen to apply brown ink in a series of lively parallel lines in horizontal, vertical, or diagonal strokes—altering their thickness and density and using cross-hatching to create tonal variations. The curling plumes of smoke rising from tugboats in the foreground provide relief from the urban grid. Marsh's linear approach also relates to the etching process, and this drawing served as the model for one of his prints (figure 25).

Early work as an illustrator for New York newspapers and magazines made Marsh an astute observer of urban life, and he regularly prowled the city's streets and waterways, filling sketchbooks with the characters and scenes he witnessed, rendering them in an energetic Realist style. He was particularly fascinated by the city's social diversity and seamier side, frequently taking as his subjects the denizens of the Bowery district, burlesque theatricals, and Coney Island bathers. The architectural and industrial infrastructure also captured his enthusiasm. "I felt fortunate indeed to be a citizen of New York, the greatest and most magnificent of all cities," he stated in 1926. "New York City was in a period of rapid growth, its sky-scrapers were thrilling by growing higher and higher. There was a wonderful waterfront with tugs and ships of all kinds and steam locomotives on the Jersey shore. In and around were dumps, docks and slums all wonderful to paint and in the city, subways, people and burlesque shows."[2] Many of the structures he depicted in *Wall Street* in 1931 had been erected over the preceding five years, including the City Bank–Farmers Trust Company Building (20 Exchange Place) and the Bank of Manhattan Trust Building (40 Wall Street), the two tallest office towers at left and right, respectively.

1. Marsh possibly made this sketch from the Brooklyn residence of the modernist sculptor Robert Laurent (1890–1970) at 104–110 Columbia Heights, a locus for artists and writers. Laurent had inherited the house from his mentor Hamilton Easter Field, an important supporter of modern art. Marsh also regularly traveled around New York Harbor by boat.
2. Marsh was describing his emotions after returning from a trip to Europe; quoted in Lloyd Goodrich, *Reginald Marsh* (New York: Harry N. Abrams, 1972), 34.

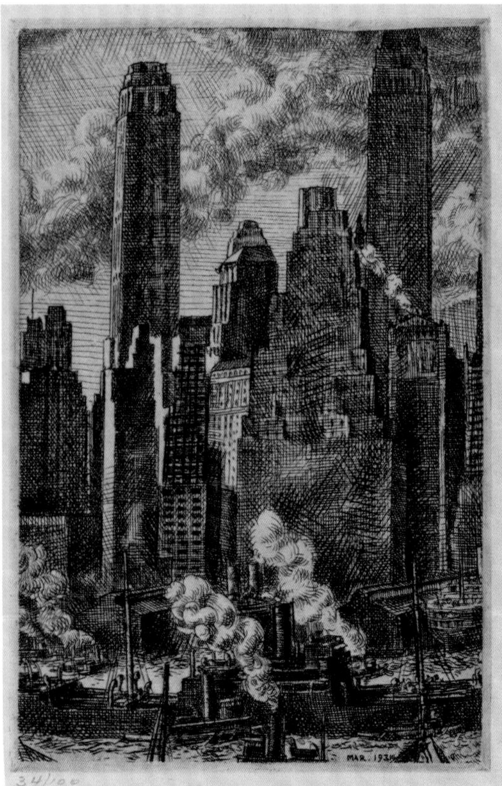

Fig. 25. Reginald Marsh. *Wall Street*, 1931. Etching with black ink on off-white, heavyweight, slightly textured wove paper, 15⁹⁄₁₆ × 13 in. (39.5 × 33 cm). Brooklyn Museum, Gift of Associated American Artists, 77.223

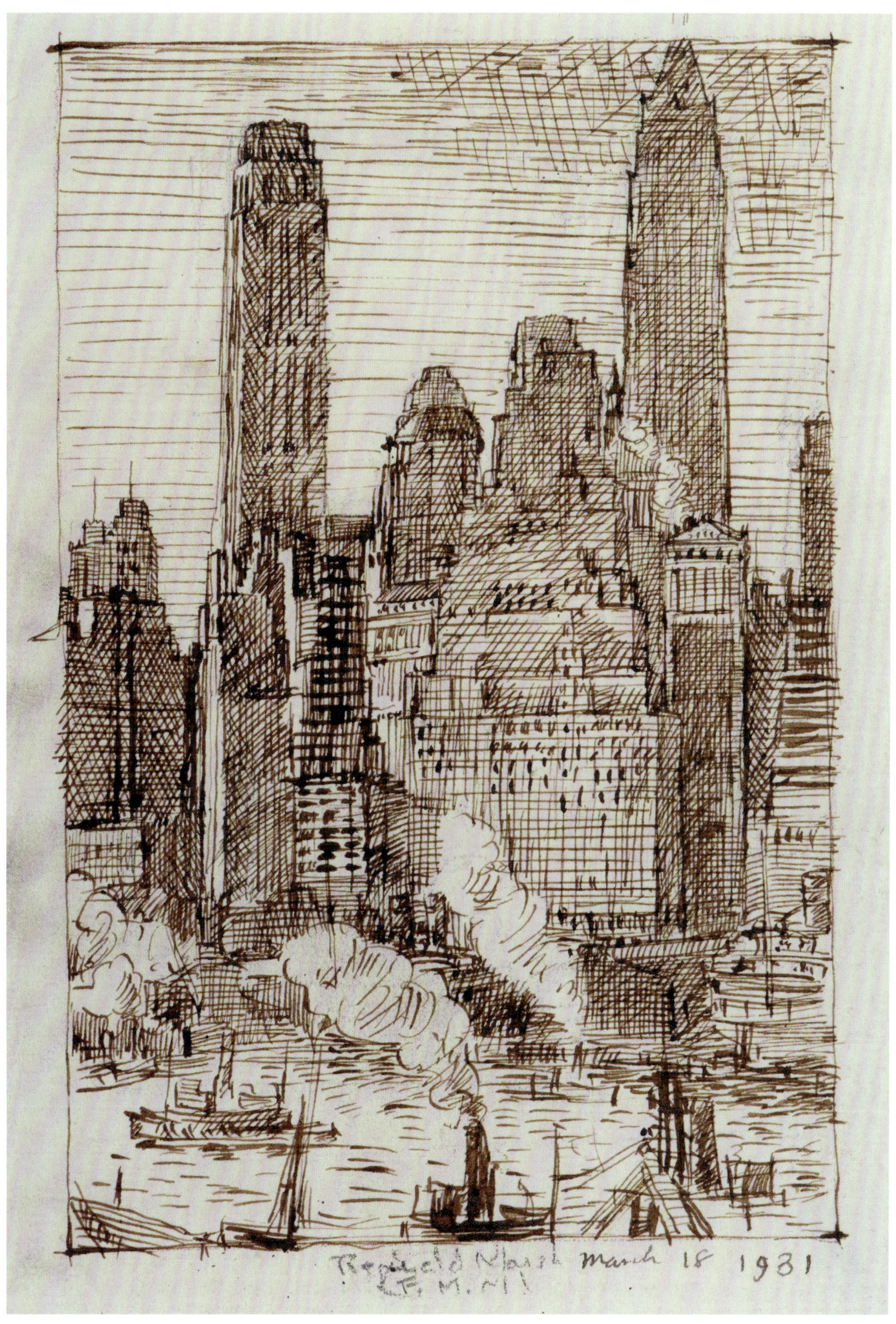

THE CONSERVATOR'S EYE: EXAMINING A COLLECTION

CAITLIN JENKINS

Conservation is a critical component and the key to understanding the material nature and technique of a work of art, thus ensuring its long-term preservation. This exhibition and catalogue, *Fine Lines: American Drawings from the Brooklyn Museum*, provides a unique opportunity for an in-depth study of the working methods of many of the American artists represented in the Museum's drawings collection. The materials available to American artists from the late eighteenth to the mid-twentieth century[1]—years that witnessed sweeping industrial and technological changes—have been the subject of much scholarship. With the aid of this research and in close collaboration with the curator, conservators at the Brooklyn Museum were able to study the works in this catalogue extensively for the first time, achieving a better appreciation of this collection of American drawings.

In preparation for the publication and exhibition of drawings selected for *Fine Lines*, each work was examined in the conservation lab and detailed technical analysis of its composition and condition observed and recorded. Conservators looked for instability of media and signs of degradation or damage, noted changes in the work's appearance from the time the artist created it, and evaluated the housing and mounting materials that have an impact on the long-term preservation of the artwork. Conservators paid close attention to the paper supports and to colored media, such as **watercolor** and colored pencil,[2] which can fade or become discolored as a result of exposure to light. Other media, such as **charcoal** and **pastel**, were checked for friability, or loose, crumbling pieces. Conservators tested certain inks that were thought to be **iron gall ink**, an acidic medium that can degrade the paper support in the areas where it is applied. White pigments such as lead white and zinc white were distinguished and identified. Lead white has been in use since antiquity (and can sometimes blacken over time owing to pollutants in the atmosphere), whereas zinc white was available only after 1834. Thus, one could examine drawings within this collection and establish that these white pigments were used within the appropriate time period. Tears, losses, and other types of damage to the paper support were noted, along with poor-quality mounting materials and evidence of past nonarchival storage. All of these can accelerate the degradation of paper, which is prone to becoming brittle and discolored when in contact with acidic materials.

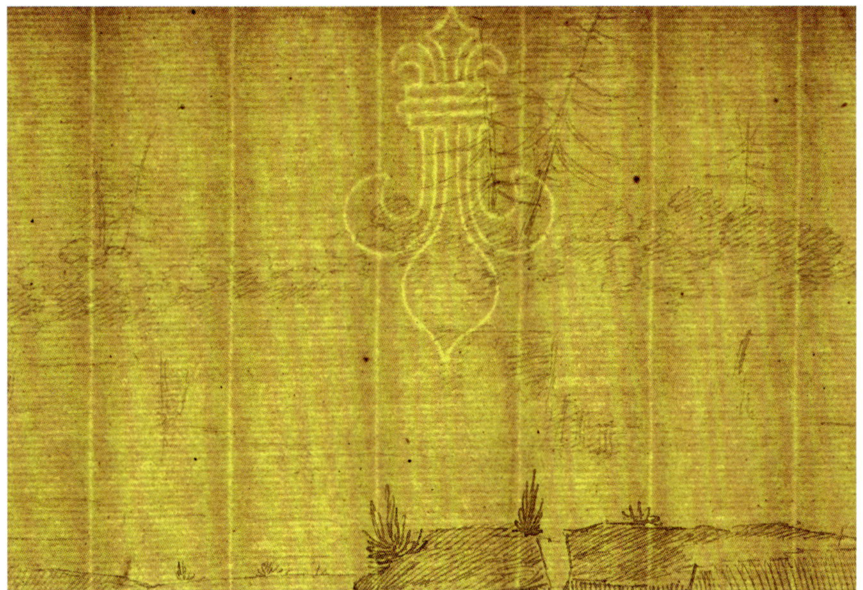

Fig. 26. Detail, Alexander Robertson, *From the Mill* (number 99), as seen under transmitted illumination, which emphasizes the laid and chain lines that characterize laid paper

The main emphasis of the conservation staff's review was the study and identification of types of supports, media, and artists' technique. Various illumination techniques, the use of a microscope, and close inspection with the naked eye revealed how and why a particular artist may have selected a paper, drawn a line, or applied a brushstroke in various media.

The Support: Paper

In analyzing a drawing, one of the first characteristics that a conservator notes is the paper support. Initial examination of the works in this volume was carried out with the unaided eye, using various kinds of illumination, including natural daylight as well as artificial illumination from lamps. Under these lighting conditions, the conservators made observations about support color, surface texture, and other characteristics. **High magnification** with a stereo-microscope and special lighting techniques known as **raking, specular**, and **transmitted illumination** were utilized to obtain a different perspective not only on the support but also on the media. Fiber analysis is another means of identifying components making up the paper support. Under high magnification, a minute fiber is removed from an inconspicuous place in the drawing. Several such

samples were taken from Benjamin West's *Know Thy Self*, 1768 (see number 61), a work that entered the collection with an insecure attribution. Viewed through a polarizing light microscope, the fibers were identified as a mixture of flax, wool, and a small amount of cotton, a composition that is consistent with papers from the mid-eighteenth century. This, and the unusual chain line pattern of the paper, which matched exactly those found in known and dated drawings by West, helped to confirm both the attribution and the date of the drawing.

Another significant attribute of paper is how it is made, whether laid or wove, hand- or machine-made. Of the 114 drawings featured in this catalogue, 26 are on **laid paper**, while the rest are on **wove paper**. Until the mid-eighteenth century, laid paper was the only type made in the West. Laid paper is characterized by the pattern of fiber distribution imparted by the wire mould on which the sheet was formed, as seen in Alexander Robertson's *From the Mill*, 1796 (see number 99), one of the earliest examples in this volume, or in Thomas Sully's *Figure Studies*, circa 1830s (see number 26). This pattern consists of closely spaced lines—horizontal (laid) and vertical (chain)—which are most easily observed in transmitted light (figures 26, 27). Even when more choices of paper became

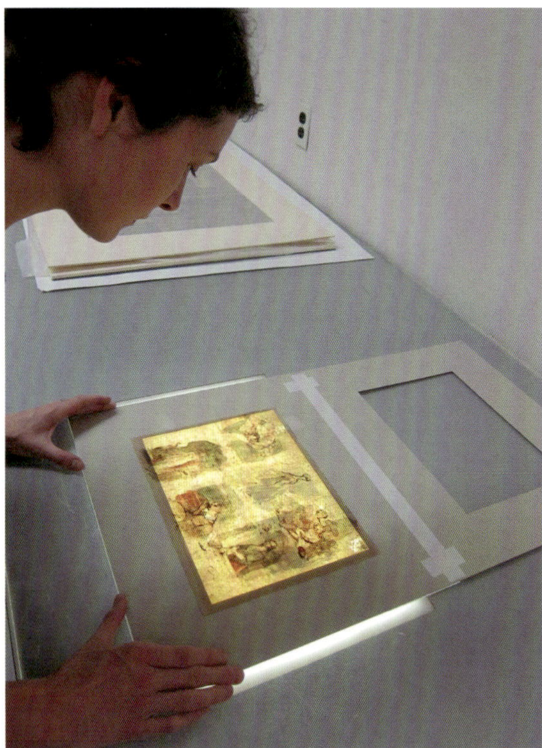

Fig. 27. Examination in the conservation lab of Thomas Sully, *Figure Studies* (number 26, recto), using transmitted light from a light box to make the laid and chain lines more visible

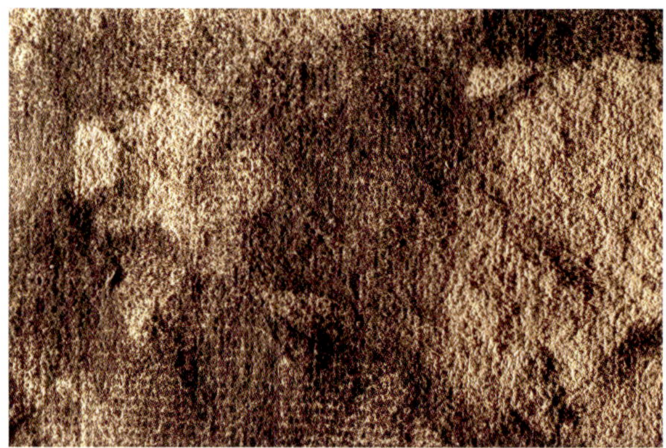

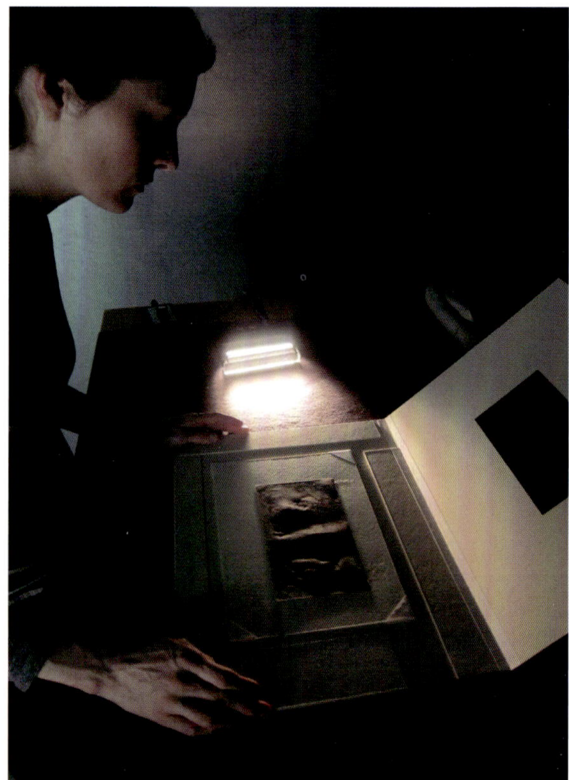

Top: Fig. 28. Detail, Charles Sprague Pearce, *Study for "The Beheading of Saint John the Baptist"* (number 49), as seen under raking illumination, which highlights the surface texture of the laid paper and the media

Above: Fig. 29. Examination in the conservation lab of Winslow Homer, *Study for "The Unruly Calf"* (number 67), using raking illumination, provided by light from a light line, to help illuminate surface features on a textured wove paper

available over time, many artists deliberately selected laid paper because they desired the aesthetic effect or the appearance of this texture. In Charles Sprague Pearce's *Study for "The Beheading of Saint John the Baptist,"* circa 1881 (see number 49), for example, raking illumination highlighted how the powdery charcoal medium adheres to the high points or "peaks" of the textured surface but not to the low points or "valleys" (figure 28). A similar effect can be seen in Winslow Homer's *Study for "The Unruly Calf,"* circa 1875 (figure 29; see number 67).

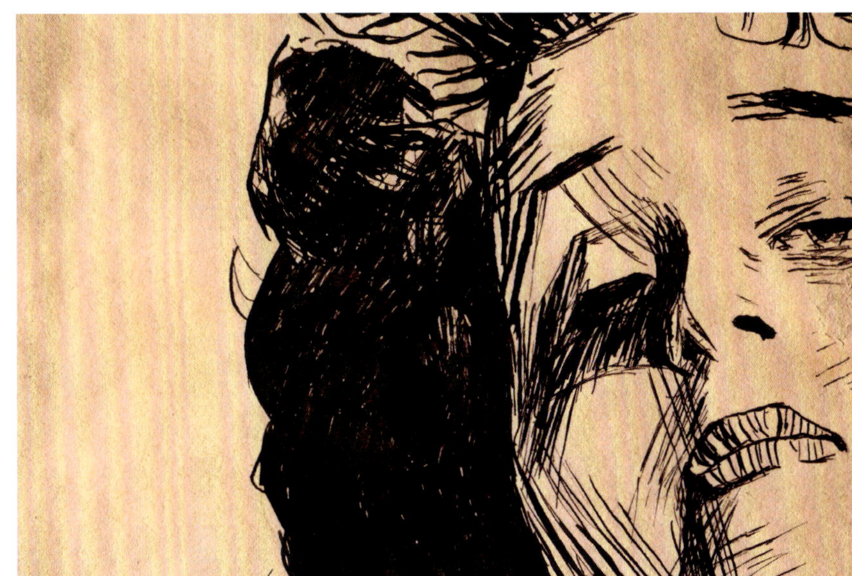

Fig. 30. Detail, Charles Dana Gibson, *Young Woman Struck with Cupid's Arrows* (number 53), as seen under raking illumination, which reveals the smooth surface texture of the wove paper

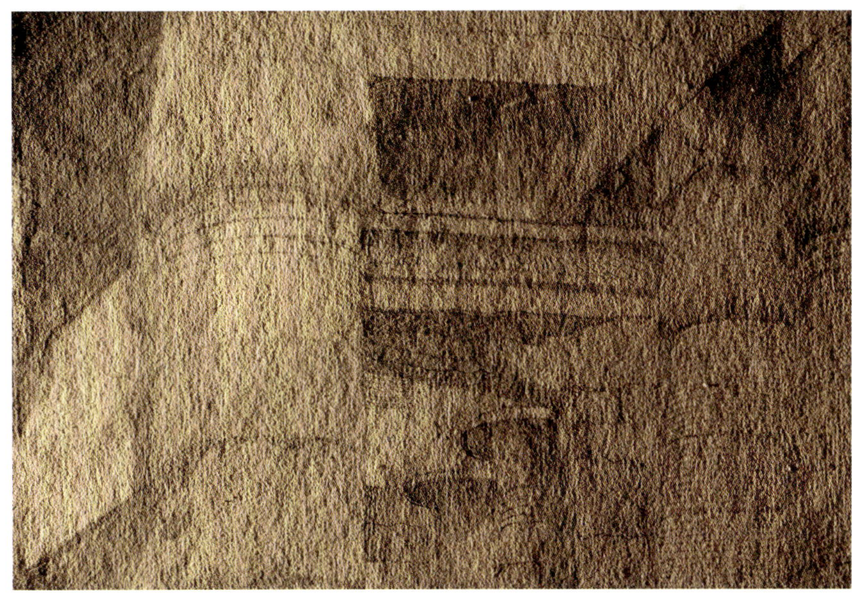

Fig. 31. Detail, Edwin Howland Blashfield, *Temple of Khonsu at Karnak* (number 103), as seen under raking illumination. This wove paper has a slightly rougher texture than the wove paper in figure 30.

Wove paper, first introduced in the 1750s, was not readily available to artists until the end of the eighteenth century. This paper can be identified by its lack of laid and chain lines, because the sheets are formed on a fine-mesh wire screen. Many artists, including Charles Dana Gibson and Edwin Howland Blashfield, preferred to avoid the gridlike pattern of laid paper and therefore sought out wove papers, which were also offered in a range of surface textures, from smooth to rough. Viewed under raking illumination, Gibson's *Young Woman Struck with Cupid's Arrows*, circa 1900 (see number 53), and Blashfield's *Temple of Khonsu at Karnak*, 1887 (see number 103), show different surface textures (figures 30, 31). The paper that Gibson chose for his ink drawing is slightly smooth, allowing for an even, uninterrupted application of ink, whereas Blashfield's has a slightly rough surface, which imparts a texture to the graphite.

By the early nineteenth century, a papermaking machine had been patented and put into use, first in Europe and then

Above: Fig. 32. Photomacrograph, reverse of Everett Shinn, *Frédérique Follows Her Husband* (number 69). This brown paper is made from short-fibered wood pulp.

Below: Fig. 33. Photomacrograph, Albert Sterner, *Nude* (number 9), showing its long-fibered paper, in contrast to the short-fibered wood-pulp paper seen in figure 32

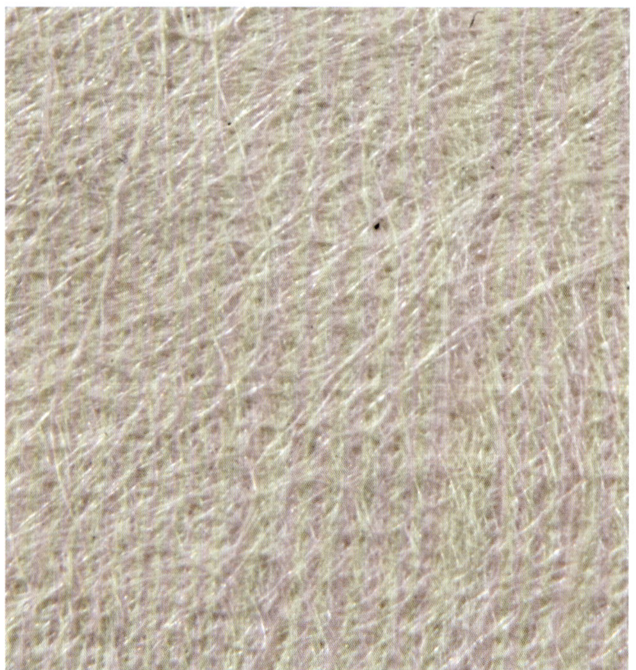

(in 1827) in the United States.[3] This technological development meant that both laid and wove papers could be manufactured with greater speed and in greater quantity and were available to artists in a wide range of textures. Early machine-made papers were generally made of the same high-quality materials as handmade papers until about the middle of the nineteenth century; at that time the supply of cotton and linen rags could not keep up with the increased demand for paper, leading to the use of wood pulp (figure 32) and short-fibered cotton.

In general, papers made with long fibers are more durable than those made with short fibers, because they create a stronger interlocking network and a sturdier sheet, as seen in the paper that Albert Sterner selected for his *Nude* of 1916 (figure 33; see number 9). Wood-pulp paper is not only made of short fibers but is also more acidic than cotton paper and thus more prone to becoming brittle and discolored. The switch to wood pulp and short-fibered cotton, as well as the introduction of chemical bleaching and acidic internal sizings, resulted in a decline in the durability and permanence of many machine-made papers. As the price of high-quality papers rose, the use of lower-grade papers increased among professional and amateur artists. Some continued to seek out well-crafted papers: Eastman Johnson may have chosen the high-quality paper of *Three Dutch Figures*, circa 1852, for its individually colored cotton fibers and subtly fibrous surface texture, just as Homer did for his *Study for "The Unruly Calf,"* best seen using high magnification (figures 34, 35; see numbers 27, 67). Many artists, however, opted for lower-grade papers, which can be identified by increased degradation, such as yellowing and brittleness, that naturally occurs over time (figure 36).

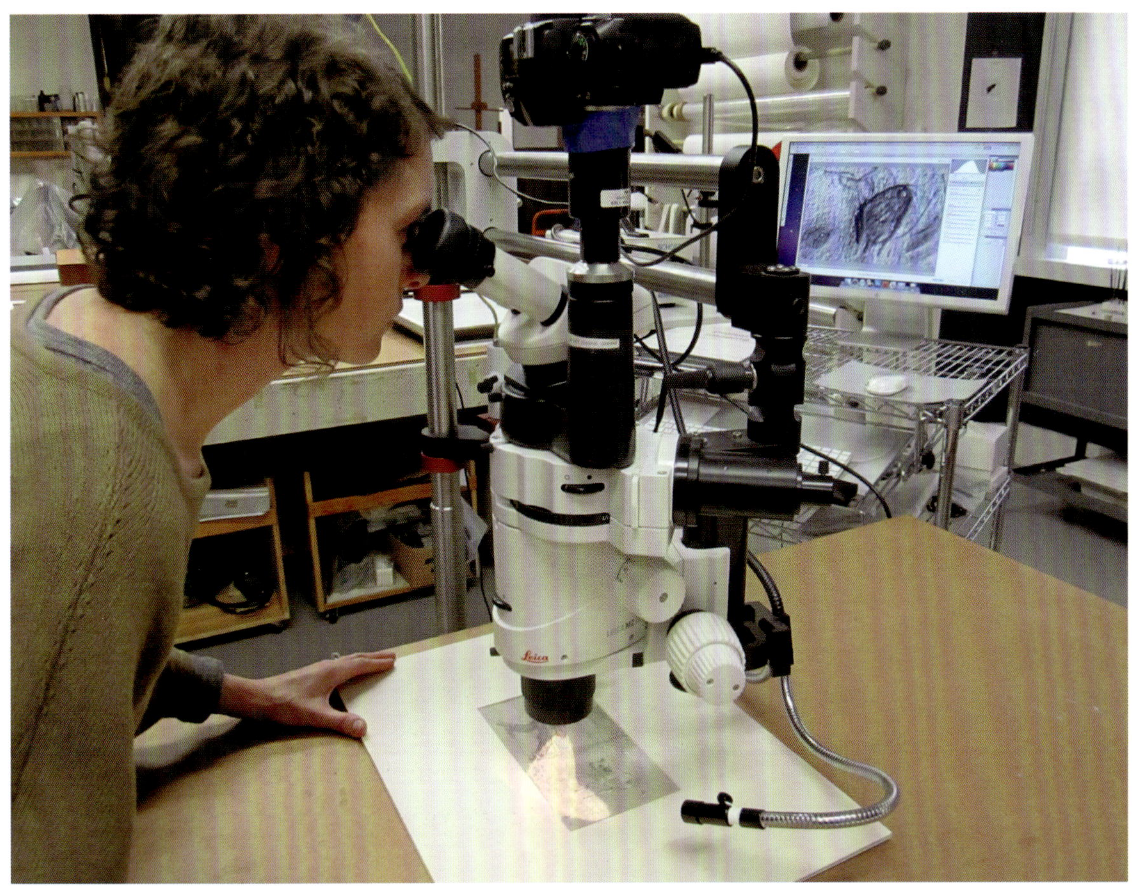

Above: Fig. 34. Examination in the conservation lab of Winslow Homer, *Study for "The Unruly Calf"* (number 67), using a high-powered microscope to achieve high magnification to better view the surface texture of the paper as well as Homer's application of graphite

Right: Fig. 35. Detail, Eastman Johnson, *Three Dutch Figures* (number 27), showing the individual cotton fibers and the surface texture of the paper

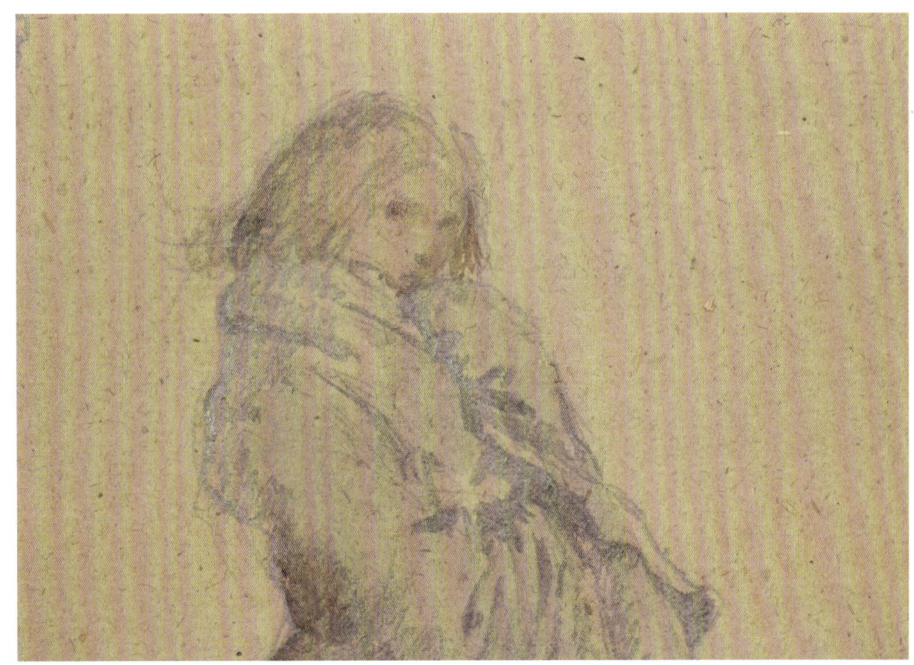

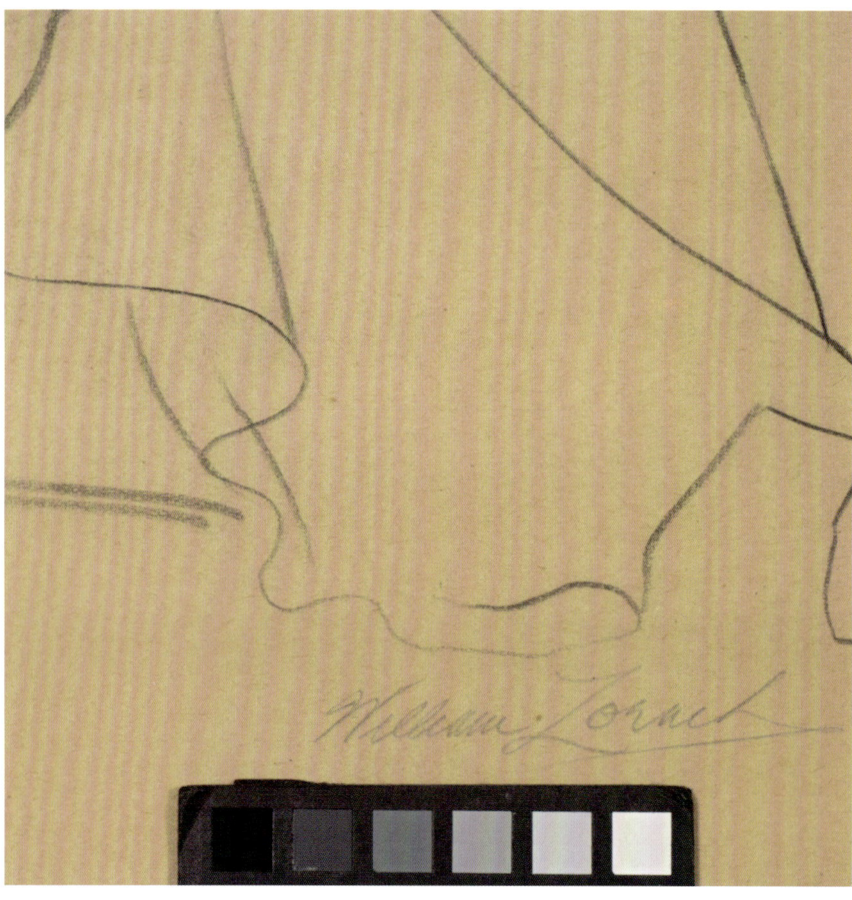

Fig. 36. Detail, William Zorach, *Seated Nude* (number 15). Zorach used a short-fibered wood-pulp paper; overexposure to light on this already somewhat unstable paper caused an overall darkening to the sheet.

As papermaking itself became increasingly mechanized, so too did the ways in which dyes and pigments were added, expanding the variety of colored papers available to artists. Many chose colored paper for the effect it would have on the tonality of a composition. In *Three Trees*, circa 1888–95 (number 91), for example, John Henry Twachtman let the rich gray-brown color of the paper become one of the hues in his landscape scene, visible in parts of the sky and foreground earth. Such papers were used infrequently by American artists before the nineteenth century. An early exception was John Singleton Copley, who often made preparatory drawings on blue paper, as in *Studies for "Saul Reproved by Samuel for Not Obeying the Commandments of the Lord,"* 1797–98 (see number 25). Blue was the most common paper color, other than the typical shades of cream and ivory, and before the nineteenth century, blue paper was formed by adding colored

rags to the pulp. Under high magnification, the individual tinted fibers of a colored paper are distinguishable.

Although a wide variety of papers was available in the United States and Europe, many Western artists often chose Asian papers, particularly Japanese ones, for their drawings. These papers are notable for their unique tonal qualities, translucency, absence of sizing, and variety of surface textures, ranging from extremely smooth to more rough and fibrous. High magnification shows the difference between the two Japanese papers chosen by Arthur Bowen Davies and Albert Sterner, respectively, for their drawings of nudes (figures 37, 38; see numbers 8, 9). Davies selected a thin, fibrous paper for his pastel, most likely because he liked the way the texture of the sheet affected the powdery medium. Sterner chose a thicker Japanese paper with a slightly rougher surface for his chalk drawing.

Fig. 37. Detail, Arthur Bowen Davies, *Nude* (number 8). Davies preferred the way the texture of this fibrous sheet affected the powdery pastel.

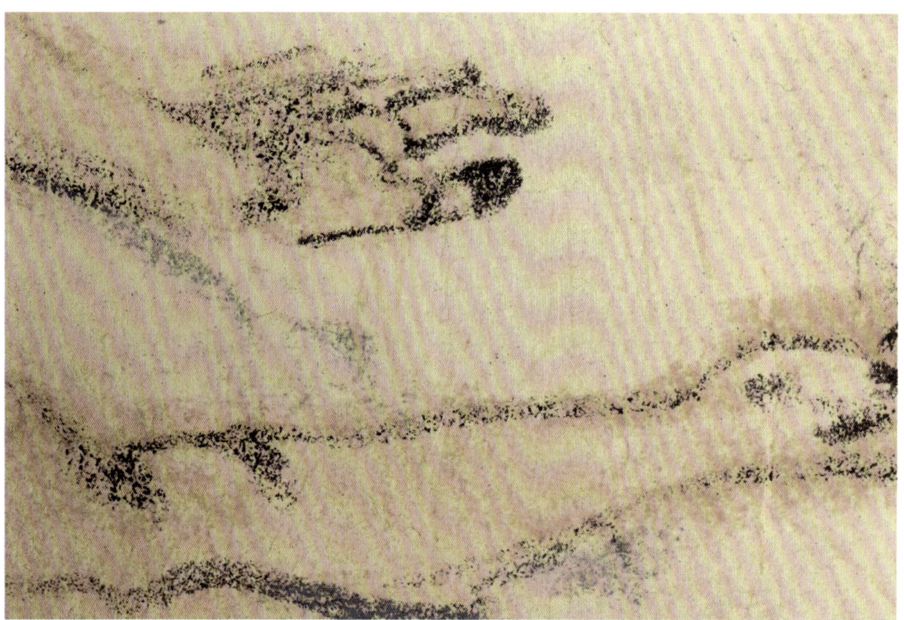

Fig. 38. Detail, Albert Sterner, *Nude* (number 9). For this chalk drawing, Sterner selected a Japanese paper that is thicker and has a slightly rougher surface than the paper in figure 37.

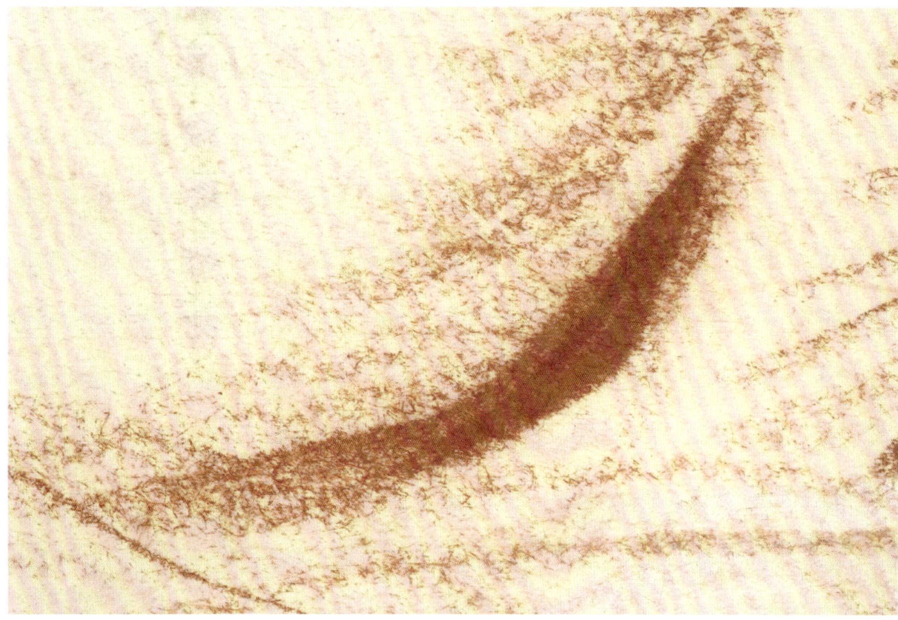

Media

Not only the range of papers but also the types of available graphic media had an impact on the output of American artists and the appearance of their drawings. By 1750 many art suppliers imported and stocked ready-made drawing materials from Britain, such as brushes, chalks, crayons, pencils, and inks and other pigments. Such materials continued to be imported throughout much of the nineteenth century, but eventually, they were also produced domestically. Beginning in the late eighteenth century, American artists had a wider array of materials available to them. This greater diversity poses a challenge to the conservator seeking to identify each material accurately. For example, black **chalk** and charcoal look similar to the naked eye, both appearing as a dark, powdery substance. Viewed under high magnification, however, charcoal has a characteristic appearance, as will be described below.

Many of the techniques used to examine the paper support—including high magnification and the various visible illumination techniques described above—are also employed to study the media. In addition, illumination in the invisible range such as **infrared reflectography** and **ultraviolet-induced visible fluorescence** proved important in identifying materials such as carbon-based ink and zinc white pigment.

Some types of media appear to be very similar but, when examined closely, have some very distinct qualities. The precise identification of the medium has an important impact on decisions concerning handling, mounting, and whether the work of art is stable enough for travel. For example, Joseph Frank Currier used charcoal in his studies of trees of circa 1880 (see numbers 87–90). Charcoal is very loosely bound and powdery and is often so fragile that it easily rubs off. Furthermore, the loose charcoal particles are sensitive to static electricity. To prevent damage to the drawing and losses of charcoal, the works are framed under antistatic glazing, which does not attract the loose particles. Charcoal was traditionally made by heating wood in an airtight container until it was reduced to charred carbon. When viewed under the microscope, individual charcoal particles appear dark, separated from one another, and are narrow and splintery. Many artists embraced charcoal for its softness and its ability to create seamless tonal gradations, as seen in Currier's landscape studies and also in Minerva Chapman's *Woman in Profile*, undated (see number 51). Another drawing medium that appears, with the unaided eye, similar to charcoal is black chalk, but under magnification black chalk lacks the splintery appearance of charcoal and is often less distinct and slightly more compact. Before 1800 natural black chalk, molded directly from carbonaceous shale, was one of the most common types of drawing media. Copley's *Studies for "Saul Reproved by Samuel for Not Obeying the Commandments of the Lord"* is executed in black chalk and heightened with white chalk.

By the end of the eighteenth century, natural black chalk was largely replaced by synthetic black chalks[4] and other types of fabricated media, such as **graphite**, **Conté crayon**, wax **crayon**, and compressed charcoal, that were becoming more popular and more widely available. Graphite was one of the most prevalent types of drawing media after 1800, and indeed, of the 114 works in this volume, 36 were executed solely in graphite, and another 24 were done in graphite in combination with another medium. Under magnification, graphite differs in appearance from charcoal in that the former's particles are quite shiny and more unified. Graphite

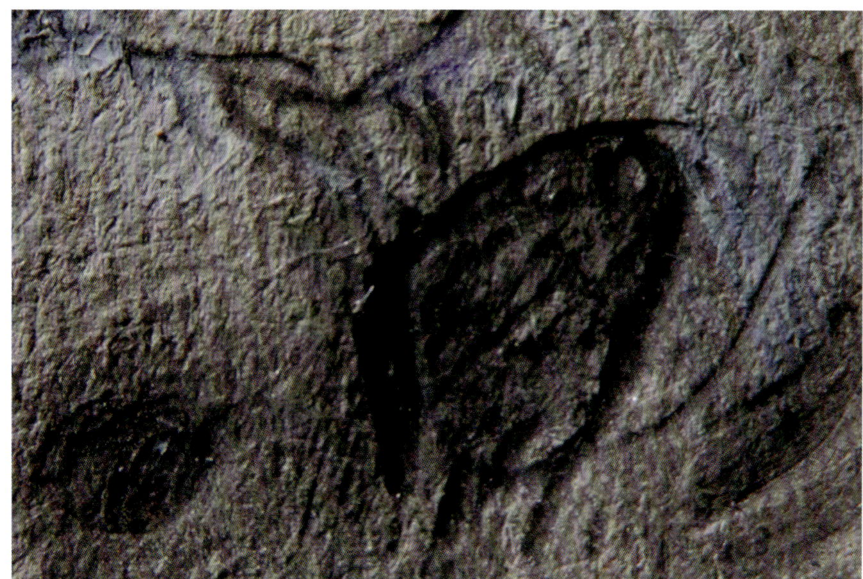

Fig. 39. Detail, Winslow Homer, *Study for "The Unruly Calf"* (number 67), as seen under raking illumination, which emphasizes the heavily incised lines

Fig. 40. Detail, Blanche Lazzell, *Sketch for "Abstract Composition"* (number 112), as seen under specular illumination, which shows the sheen of the heavily applied graphite

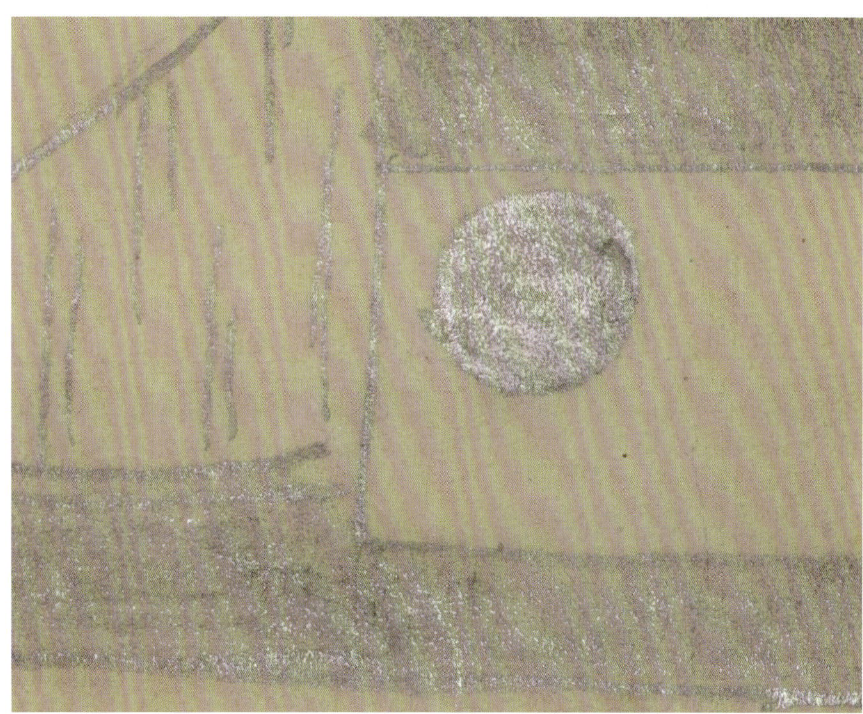

can be worked to produce many different effects. Winslow Homer used graphite to create dark marks and deeply impressed lines in the paper in such works as *Study for "The Unruly Calf"* (figure 39; see number 67), whereas Blanche Lazzell applied the graphite heavily to impart the medium's characteristic sheen in *Sketch for "Abstract Composition,"* 1924 (figure 40; see number 112). Conté crayon, a mixture of refined graphite and clay, patented by Nicolas-Jacques Conté in France in 1795, was favored by artists for its rich tone, cohesive texture, and more intense black than could be achieved with graphite, as seen in George Benjamin Luks's *Pony Ride*, undated (see number 71).

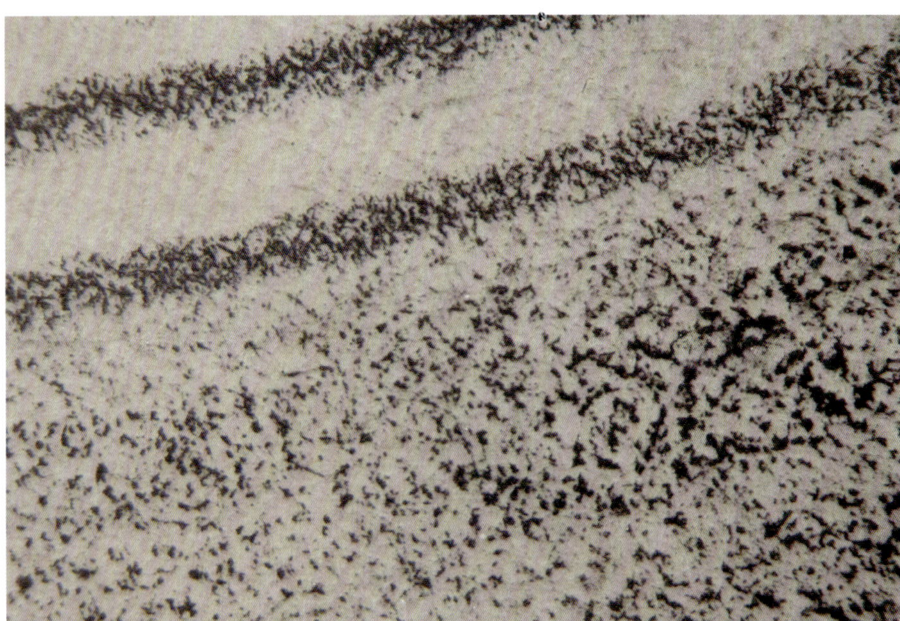

Fig. 41. Photomacrograph, Blanche Lazzell, *Sketch for "Abstract Composition"* (number 112), showing particles of graphite

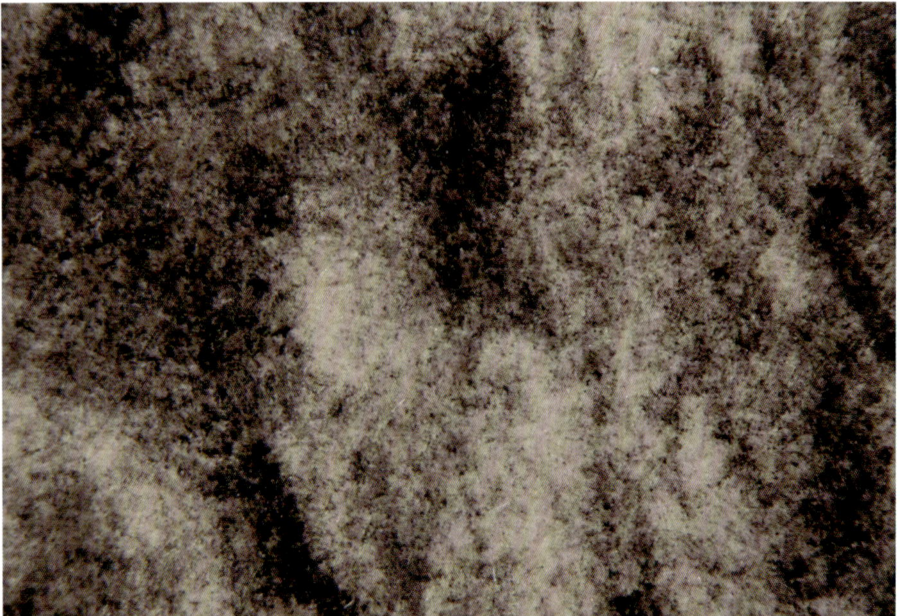

Fig. 42. Photomacrograph, Joseph Frank Currier, *Study of Trees* (number 87), showing particles of charcoal

Under high magnification, the differences between graphite, charcoal, black chalk, and Conté crayon are discernible. Graphite has a shiny appearance (figure 41). The particles of charcoal are lightweight, distinct, darker, narrow, and splintery (figure 42). Black chalk appears powdery, and black Conté crayon is rich in tone, and more compact (figures 43, 44).

To add color to a drawing, many artists use pastels, made by blending dry colored pigments with white pigments (such as clay or chalk), adding a minimal amount of liquid binder (such as gum tragacanth or gum arabic), and forming the mixture into sticks. When applied to the surface of a paper, the pastel medium produces a soft, powdery effect. The mid-nineteenth century saw a revival of interest in this medium,

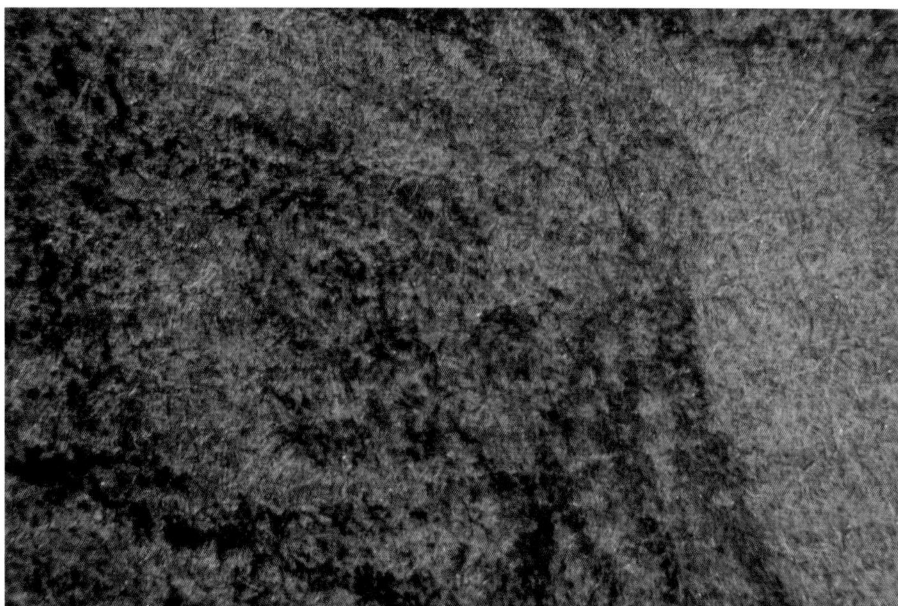

Fig. 43. Photomacrograph, John Singleton Copley, *Studies for "Saul Reproved by Samuel for Not Obeying the Commandments of the Lord"* (number 25, recto), showing particles of black chalk

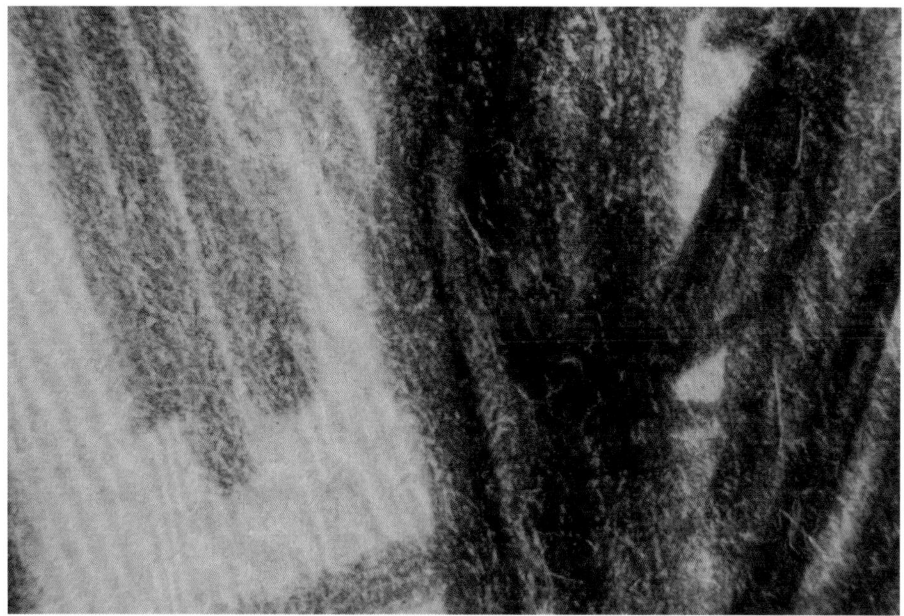

Fig. 44. Photomacrograph, George Benjamin Luks, *Pony Ride* (number 71), showing particles of Conté crayon

although pastels had been available for decades. Many American artists, such as Robert Blum (see number 35), were attracted to pastels for their vibrant colors and ease of use.

Approximately twenty-four works in this publication were executed in ink, almost always some type of black or brown ink. One exception is the blue-gray ink Max Weber used in *Standing Figure*, 1911 (figure 45; see number 11). In the

eighteenth century, ink was widely available as a writing material and thus was also employed by artists. Historically, the most common types of ink were **carbon black ink** and several types of brown ink, of which **bister**, **sepia**, and iron gall were the most prevalent. Iron gall ink, made from the nut galls of oak trees, vitriol (iron sulfate), gum, and water, is the easiest of the brown inks to distinguish because of its very dark, burnt

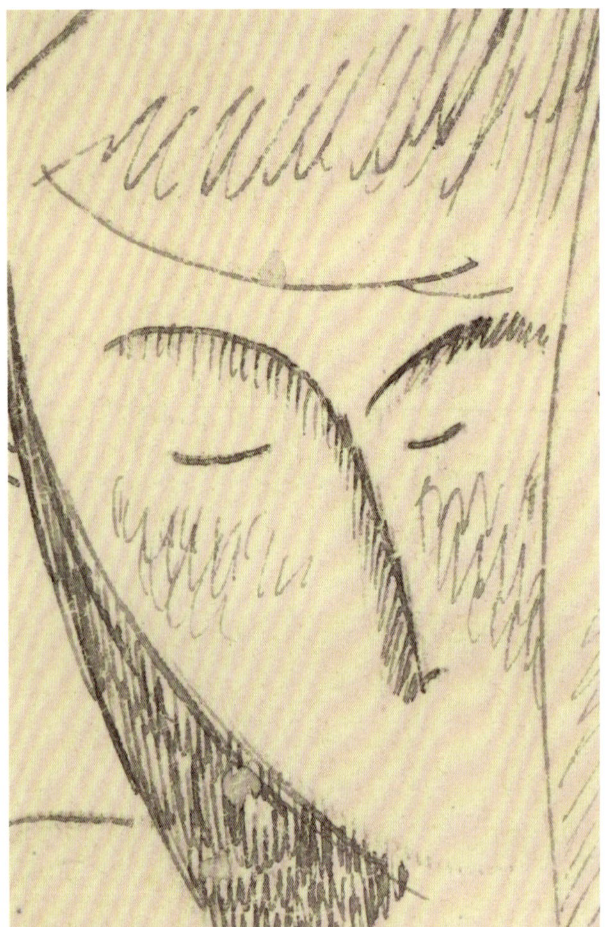

Fig. 45. Detail, Max Weber, *Standing Figure* (number 11), showing Weber's use of blue-gray ink

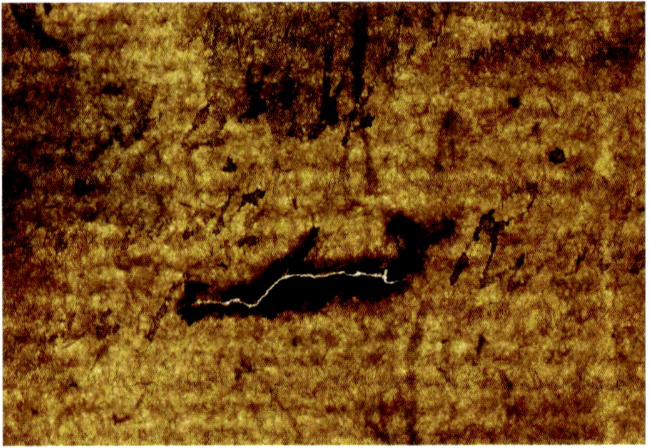

Fig. 46. Detail, Thomas Sully, *Figure Studies* (number 26, recto), as seen under transmitted illumination, which emphasizes the degradation of the paper in areas where iron gall ink was applied

appearance and also because its inherent acidic nature causes it to degrade and "eat through" the paper. These distinctive characteristics of iron gall are easy to identify with the naked eye and are accentuated with the use of transmitted illumination, as can be seen in Thomas Sully's figure drawings (figure 46; see number 26).

Carbon black ink, which has a rich, velvety appearance, is sometimes difficult to distinguish because it was often mixed with other inks that were not carbon based. Infrared reflectography is a technique that conservators often use to help in the identification of carbon-based materials: because carbon absorbs the infrared radiation, it appears dark, while non-absorbing materials seem to disappear. As a result, carbon-based materials stand out and can easily be identified. West's *Know Thy Self* was viewed with an infrared camera to examine the various inks in the composition. The iron gall ink, which does not contain carbon, became transparent, and the carbon-based inks appeared dark (figures 47, 48).

Many of the drawings featured in this catalogue incorporate watercolor as a secondary medium. By the nineteenth century, as watercolor became more commercially available and easier to use, it was widely embraced by American artists, both amateur and professional. Watercolor was favored for its transparency and the way that light goes through its washes and is reflected from the paper. Colors might be applied in transparent layers like the washes in Sully's figure studies (figure 49) or in several layers to the point of opacity, as in William Glackens's *Merry Christmas (Yuletide Revels)*, circa 1910 (figure 50; see number 72). Watercolor was used to accentuate simple line drawings, as in Winslow Homer's *Girl Seated on a Rail Fence*, circa 1878 (figure 51; see number 29), and to add

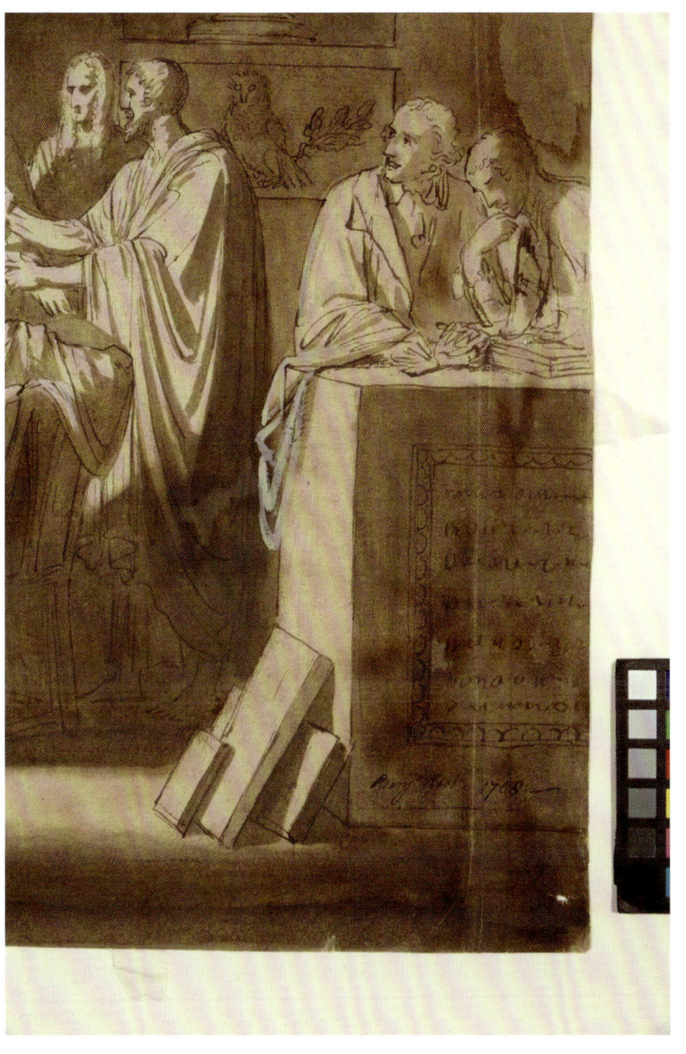

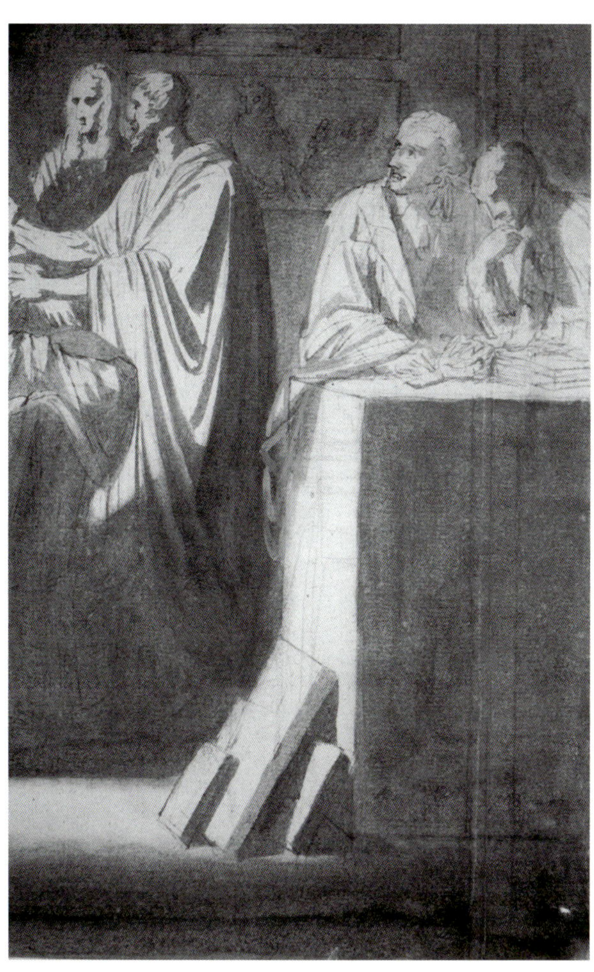

Above: Fig. 47. Detail, Benjamin West, *Know Thy Self* (number 61), as seen under normal illumination

Above right: Fig. 48. Detail, Benjamin West, *Know Thy Self* (number 61), as seen with the infrared camera. The inscription on the podium (right side of image), which can be seen under normal illumination (see figure 47), is not visible here because it was written in iron gall ink, but the carbon-based inks remain visible.

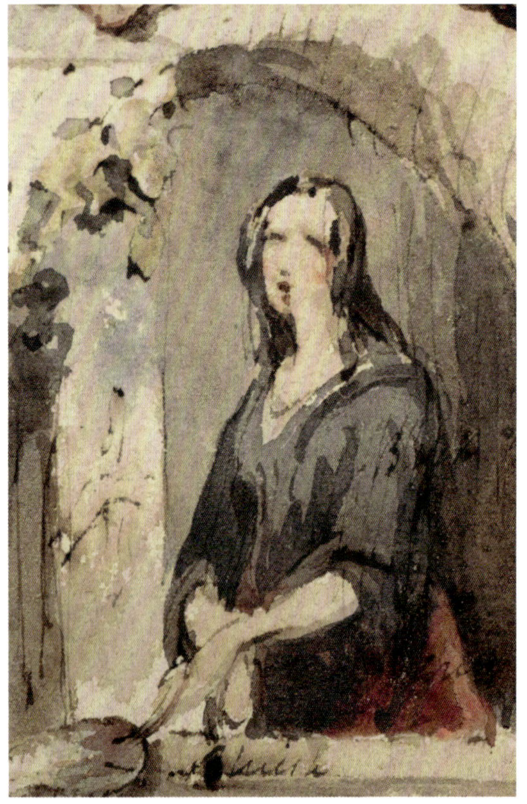

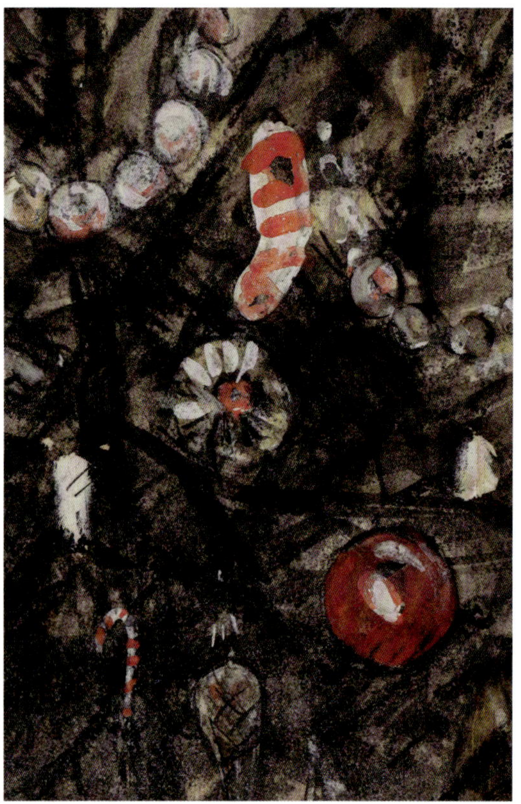

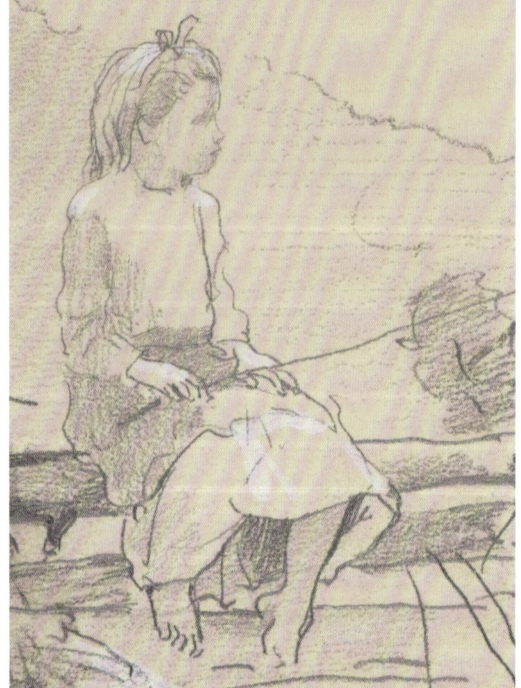

Above left: Fig. 49. Detail, Thomas Sully, *Figure Studies* (number 26, recto), showing the layering of various watercolor pigments

Above: Fig. 50. Detail, William Glackens, *Merry Christmas (Yuletide Revels)* (number 72), showing the application of opaque watercolor

Left: Fig. 51. Detail, Winslow Homer, *Girl Seated on a Rail Fence* (number 29), showing washes of white opaque watercolor

highlights, such as the touches of white in Edward Henry Potthast's *Illustration for "George Washington Jones: A Christmas Gift That Went A-Begging,"* 1903 (figure 52; see number 68). The latter work's opaque white highlights were examined in the conservation lab using ultraviolet-induced visible fluorescence to determine the components of the pigment (figure 53). Certain pigments have a characteristic fluorescence when viewed with ultraviolet radiation. Zinc white

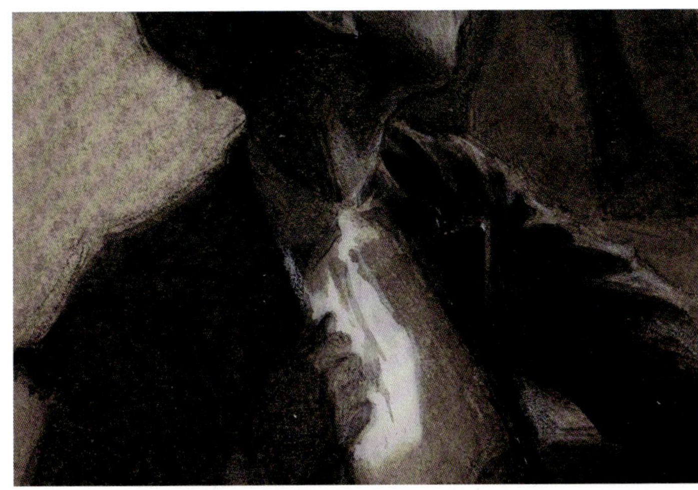

Left: Fig. 52. Detail, Edward Henry Potthast, *Illustration for "George Washington Jones: A Christmas Gift That Went A-Begging"* (number 68), showing white highlights

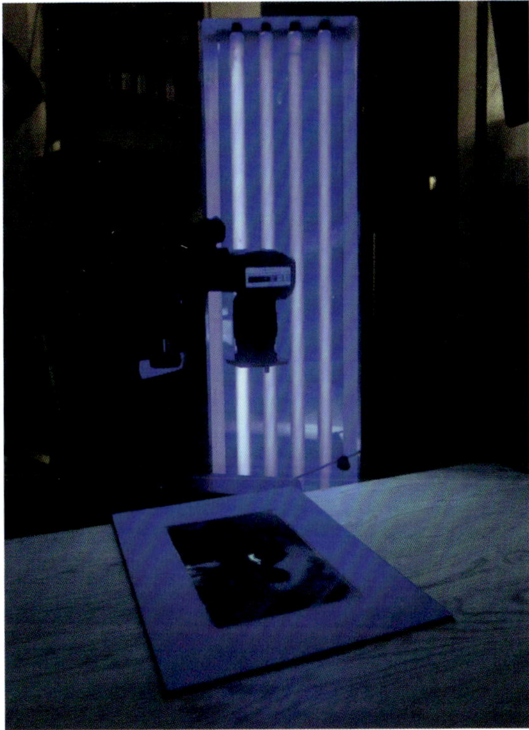

was identified as the pigment used for Potthast's highlights because of its characteristic yellow-green fluorescence (figure 54). The same examination technique was used to identify the white highlights in West's *Know Thy Self* as an oil-based medium, subsequently confirmed as lead white (figure 55). Because zinc white pigment was available only after 1834, it makes sense that it would be present in Potthast's work from 1903, but not in West's from 1768.

Above left: Fig. 53. Examination in the conservation lab of Edward Henry Potthast, *Illustration for "George Washington Jones"* (number 68), using ultraviolet-induced visible fluorescence

Above: Fig. 54. Detail, Edward Henry Potthast, *Illustration for "George Washington Jones"* (number 68), showing the white highlights fluorescing a yellow-green color under ultraviolet-induced visible fluorescence

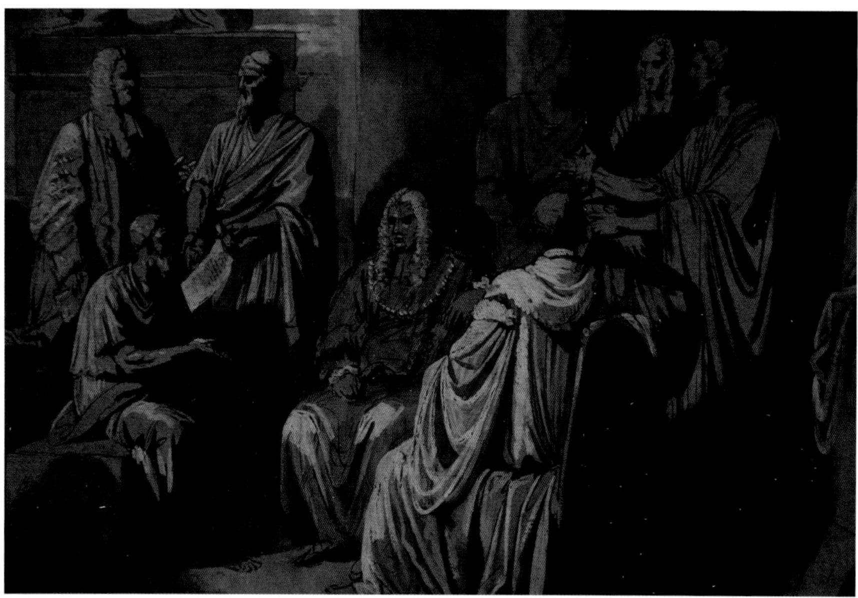

Fig. 55. Detail, Benjamin West, *Know Thy Self* (number 61), showing the oil component of the white highlights fluorescing under ultraviolet-induced visible fluorescence

Our close examination of this group of significant drawings provided a great deal of information about the materials available to American artists from the late eighteenth through the mid-twentieth century. The study also revealed many of the artists' working methods, which were sometimes apparent on close examination or after observation under a microscope, but in other cases were discovered only with the aid of various scientific techniques. Using the results gathered from these techniques, conservators were able to piece together a fuller comprehension of each artist's choices of media and methods, and to learn what the artist intended to convey in a given work, whether it observed the traditional boundaries of the materials or pushed far outside these conventions. In many cases, the information gathered through the conservator's examination of a drawing as a physical object, in conjunction with the curator's knowledge of its art-historical significance, led to a better understanding of the work of art as a whole.

To keep these fragile works available for viewing and study, it is also the conservator's role to ensure that they remain as close to their original condition as possible. This ongoing process of balancing their preservation with the need to make them accessible to the public will be critically important to future generations.

The author is grateful to the Andrew W. Mellon Foundation for the opportunity to undertake this research as a Mellon Fellow and would also like to thank the following people for their assistance with this chapter: Ken Moser, Antoinette Owen, Rachel Danzing, Carolyn Tomkiewicz, Pavlos Kapetanakis, Beatriz Centeno, Judith C. Walsh, and Marian Dirda.

1. Two particularly helpful sources are Cathleen A. Baker, *From the Hand to the Machine: Nineteenth-Century American Paper and Mediums; Technologies, Materials and Conservation* (Ann Arbor, Mich.: Legacy Press, 2010), and Marjorie Shelley, "The Craft of American Drawing: Early Eighteenth to Late Nineteenth Century," in Kevin J. Avery, *American Drawings and Watercolors in the Metropolitan Museum of Art*, vol. 1, *A Catalogue of Works by Artists Born before 1835* (New York: Metropolitan Museum of Art, 2002), 28–78.

2. Terms highlighted in boldface are defined in the Glossary of Drawing Materials and Conservation Techniques.

3. Baker, *From the Hand to the Machine*, 55.

4. Timothy David Mayhew, Margo Ellis, and Supapan Seraphin, "Natural Black Chalk in Traditional Old Master Drawings," *Journal of the American Institute for Conservation* 49, no. 2 (Fall/Winter 2010): 83–95.

GLOSSARY OF DRAWING MATERIALS AND CONSERVATION TECHNIQUES

CAITLIN JENKINS

bister. A brown ink made by extracting soluble tars from wood soot, dissolving the dark brown, greasy soot in water, filtering the resulting solution to remove the insoluble sediment, and boiling or evaporating part of the water in the solution to intensify the color.

carbon black ink. An ink made from carbon particles in the soot of burning oils, resins, or resinous woods, or the charcoal of many kinds of wood. These black particles are ground to a powder and combined with a binding medium.

chalk. A medium composed of natural earths. Black chalk is obtained from carbonaceous shale; red chalk from iron oxide in red ocher or in a variety of hematite; and white chalk from a variety of calcium carbonate or talc. For drawing purposes, lumps of these materials are reduced in size and inserted into holders. Chalks can be cut directly from stone, or they can be crushed, washed, and re-formed by compression, usually with the addition of a binder. Black chalk produces a black or grayish stroke, which is sometimes less intense in value than that of charcoal. White chalk is often employed to add highlights in drawings done in other media. Fabricated chalks include color pigments mixed with white pigments and combined with various binders such as gum arabic, sugar, or gum tragacanth.

charcoal. A medium made by heating wood in an airtight container until it is reduced to carbon. Frequently cut into pieces and used in holders, charcoal can be applied dry or after being soaked in linseed or olive oil to achieve a more intense and stable line.

Conté crayon. A **crayon**, made from a mixture of refined graphite and clay, that was invented in 1795 by Nicolas-Jacques Conté.

crayon. A medium in stick form made by mixing pigments with an oily, waxy, or greasy binder or with a combination of water-soluble and fatty binders.

graphite. A medium made by converting a crystalline, shiny, dark gray form of carbon to a powder, which is then mixed with various ingredients such as clay, wax, rosin, or gums.

high magnification. See **photomacrograph.**

infrared reflectography. An examination technique achieved with an imaging device, the infrared video camera, that is sensitive to waves on the electromagnetic spectrum just beyond the region of visible light. With this device, infrared waves make certain types of media more visible so that otherwise obscured features, such as inscriptions or underdrawings, can be discerned. Infrared luminescence can also be used to identify certain materials based on whether they appear opaque or transparent, as well as to provide information about the condition of a work, to show watermarks, and to emphasize the structure of a drawing's support.

iron gall ink. An ink obtained from a suspension of iron salts in gallic acid, taken from the nut galls of oak trees. The ink appears almost black when first applied but turns brown with time. It is acidic and corrosive in nature and causes degradation of the paper and ink where applied.

laid paper. Paper characterized by the surface pattern formed by the papermaking mould's closely spaced horizontal (laid) wires and more widely spaced vertical (chain) wires. Laid paper sheets are formed by depositing wet pulp onto this mould.

normal illumination. Lighting an object to create standard viewing conditions, with relatively flat and even lighting and minimal surface glare.

pastel. A medium in stick form made by blending dry powdered pigments with white pigments (such as clay or chalk) and adding a liquid binder such as gum tragacanth or gum arabic.

photomacrograph. A photograph taken at high magnification with a camera and lens with the aid of a microscope. High magnification reveals details about the condition of a drawing and sometimes about the composition of its media and support.

raking illumination. Lighting achieved by positioning a single light source at a low angle relative to the surface of the artwork. This reveals surface topography and texture in the paper such as laid lines, indentations, and media application.

sepia. An ink made from pigment, ranging from black to yellow-brown, extracted from the ink bladder of the cuttlefish. The sacs are dried in the sun, ground up, and mixed with boiling water; the liquor is then decanted several times and allowed to dry. The resultant sediment is ground fine and combined with gum arabic.

specular illumination. Lighting achieved by positioning a light source so that the viewer sees the reflection off the surface of the artwork in order to determine variations in surface sheen, the presence of a coating, or the general surface topography. Specular illumination is particularly useful with reflective surfaces.

transmitted illumination. Lighting an object from the side opposite the side being viewed. This type of illumination is used to show variations in the density and thickness of a sheet of paper, as well as paper structure, watermarks, tears, losses, and abrasions.

ultraviolet-induced visible fluorescence. An examination technique in which the art object is exposed to ultraviolet radiation, which is present on the electromagnetic spectrum just beyond visible light and makes visible many art materials, including certain adhesives, binders, and some pigments and dyes.

watercolor. A medium made of ground pigment commonly bound with gum arabic and diluted with water.

watermark. An image on a sheet of paper that is created by raised wires sewn or welded onto the papermaking mould. It generally identifies the manufacturer.

wove paper. Paper formed on a mould with a wove cover, composed of wires woven into a fine mesh.

SELECTED BIBLIOGRAPHY

Adams, Henry. *American Drawings and Watercolors from the Kansas City Region*. Kansas City, Mo.: Nelson-Atkins Museum of Art, 1992.

Ambers, Janet, Catherine Higgitt, and David Saunders, eds. *Italian Renaissance Drawings: Technical Examination and Analysis*. London: Archetype Publications, 2010.

Avery, Kevin J. *American Drawings and Watercolors in the Metropolitan Museum of Art*. Vol. 1, *A Catalogue of Works by Artists Born before 1835*. New York: Metropolitan Museum of Art, 2002.

Baker, Cathleen A. *From the Hand to the Machine: Nineteenth-Century American Paper and Mediums; Technologies, Materials and Conservation*. Ann Arbor, Mich.: Legacy Press, 2010.

Bermingham, Peter. *American Art in the Barbizon Mood*. Washington, D.C.: Smithsonian Institution Press for the National Collection of Fine Arts, 1975.

Bloch, E. Maurice. *Faces and Figures in American Drawings.* San Marino, Calif.: Huntington Library and Art Gallery, 1989.

Boime, Albert. *Strictly Academic: Life Drawing in the Nineteenth Century*. Binghamton, N.Y.: University Art Gallery, State University of New York, 1974.

Bolger, Doreen. "The Education of the American Artist." In *In This Academy: The Pennsylvania Academy of the Fine Arts, 1805–1976: A Special Bicentennial Exhibition*, 51–74. Philadelphia: Pennsylvania Academy of the Fine Arts, 1976.

Bolger, Doreen, et al. *American Pastels in the Metropolitan Museum of Art*. New York: Metropolitan Museum of Art, 1989.

Brooklyn Museum. *A Century of American Illustration*. New York: Brooklyn Museum, 1972.

The Brooklyn Museum: American Watercolors, Pastels, Collages: A Complete Illustrated Listing of Works in the Museum's Collection. New York: Brooklyn Museum, 1984.

Butler, Charles T., ed. *Lines of Discovery: 225 Years of American Drawings, the Columbus Museum*. Columbus, Ga.: Columbus Museum in association with D Giles, London, 2006.

Carlo, James, et al. *Old Master Prints and Drawings: A Guide to Preservation and Conservation*. Translated and edited by Marjorie B. Cohn. Amsterdam: Amsterdam University Press, 1997.

Corn, Wanda M. *The Great American Thing: Modern Art and National Identity, 1915–1935*. Berkeley: University of California Press, 1999.

Cummings, Paul. *Twentieth-Century Drawings from the Whitney Museum of American Art*. New York: Whitney Museum of American Art in association with W. W. Norton & Co., 1987.

Davidson, Marshall B. *The Drawing of America: Eyewitness to History*. New York: Harry N. Abrams, 1983.

Deák, Gloria Gilda. *Picturing America, 1497–1899: Prints, Maps, and Drawings Bearing on the New World Discoveries and on the Development of the Territory That Is Now the United States*. 2 vols. Princeton, N.J.: Princeton University Press, 1988.

Ferber, Linda S., and William H. Gerdts. *The New Path: Ruskin and the American Pre-Raphaelites*. New York: Brooklyn Museum, 1985.

Gerdts, William. *The Great American Nude: A History in Art*. New York: Praeger, 1974.

Goldman, Paul. *Looking at Prints, Drawings and Watercolours: A Guide to Technical Terms*. London: British Museum, 1988.

Grace, Trudie. *Paper Trail: Prints, Drawings, and Watercolors in the National Academy of Design*. New York: National Academy of Design, 2000.

Greenough, Sarah. *Modern Art and America: Alfred Stieglitz and His New York Galleries*. Washington, D.C.: National Gallery of Art, 2001.

Harvey, Eleanor Jones. *The Painted Sketch: American Impressions from Nature, 1830–1880*. Dallas: Dallas Museum of Art, 1998.

Haskell, Barbara. *The American Century: Art and Culture, 1900–1950*. New York: Whitney Museum of American Art in association with W. W. Norton, 1999.

Kornhauser, Elizabeth Mankin, ed. *American Moderns on Paper: Masterworks from the Wadsworth Atheneum Museum of Art*. New Haven, Conn.: Yale University Press in association with the Wadsworth Atheneum Museum of Art, 2010.

Lambert, Susan. *Reading Drawings: An Introduction to Looking at Drawings*. New York: Pantheon Books, 1984.

M. & M. Karolik Collection of American Water Colors and Drawings, 1800–1875. 2 vols. Boston: Museum of Fine Arts, 1962.

MacAdam, Barbara J. *Marks of Distinction: Two Hundred Years of American Drawings and Watercolors from the Hood Museum of Art*. Hanover, N.H.: Hood Museum of Art, Dartmouth College, 2005.

Mayhew, Timothy David, Margo Ellis, and Supapan Seraphin. "Natural Black Chalk in Traditional Old Master Drawings." *Journal of the American Institute for Conservation* 49, no. 2 (Fall/Winter 2010): 83–95.

Miller, Angela L., et al. *American Encounters: Art, History, and Cultural Identity*. Upper Saddle River, N.J.: Pearson Education, 2008.

Miller, Jo. *Drawings of the Hudson River School, 1825–1875*. New York: Brooklyn Museum, 1969.

Murray, Mary E., and Paul D. Schweizer. *Life Lines: American Master Drawings, 1788–1962, from the Munson-Williams-Proctor Institute*. Utica, N.Y.: Munson-Williams-Proctor Institute, 1994.

Olson, Roberta J. M. *Drawn by New York: Six Centuries of Watercolors and Drawings at the New-York Historical Society*. New York: New-York Historical Society, 2008.

On Paper: Masterworks from the Addison Collection. Andover, Mass.: Addison Gallery of American Art, 2004.

Pilgrim, Dianne H. "The Revival of Pastels in Nineteenth-Century America: The Society of Painters in Pastel." *American Art Journal* 10, no. 2 (Nov. 1978): 43–62.

Pohl, Frances K. *Framing America: A Social History of American Art*. 2nd ed. London: Thames and Hudson, 2007.

Rawson, Philip. *Drawing*. The Appreciation of the Arts 3. London: Oxford University Press, 1969.

Reaves, Wendy Wick. *Eye Contact: Modern American Portrait Drawings from the National Portrait Gallery*. Washington, D.C.: National Portrait Gallery, 2002.

Reed, Walt. *The Illustrator in America, 1860–2000*. 3rd ed. New York: Society of Illustrators, 2001.

Rosand, David. *Drawing Acts: Studies in Graphic Expression and Representation*. Cambridge: Cambridge University Press, 2002.

Ross, Barbara T. *American Drawings in the Art Museum, Princeton University: 130 Selected Examples*. Princeton, N.J.: Princeton University Press, 1976.

Shelley, Marjorie. "The Craft of American Drawing: Early Eighteenth to Late Nineteenth Century." In Kevin J. Avery, *American Drawings and Watercolors in the Metropolitan Museum of Art*. Vol. 1, *A Catalogue of Works by Artists Born before 1835*, 28–78. New York: Metropolitan Museum of Art, 2002.

Stebbins, Theodore E., Jr. *American Master Drawings and Watercolors: A History of Works on Paper from Colonial Times to the Present*. New York: Harper and Row, 1976.

Turner, Silvie. *The Book of Fine Paper*. London: Thames and Hudson, 1998.

Watrous, James. *The Craft of Old Master Drawings*. Madison: University of Wisconsin Press, 1957.

Weinberg, H. Barbara. *The Lure of Paris: Nineteenth-Century American Painters and Their French Teachers*. New York: Abbeville Press Publishers, 1991.

Weinberg, H. Barbara, and Carrie Rebora Barratt, eds. *American Stories: Paintings of Everyday Life, 1765–1915*. New York: Metropolitan Museum of Art, 2009.

Wilmerding, John. *American Art in the Princeton University Art Museum*. Vol. 1, *Drawings and Watercolors*. Princeton, N.J.: Princeton University Art Museum, 2004.

Wilton, Andrew, and Tim Barringer. *American Sublime: Landscape Painting in the United States, 1820–1880*. London: Tate Publishing, 2002.

Zurier, Rebecca, Robert W. Snyder, and Virginia M. Mecklenburg. *Metropolitan Lives: The Ashcan Artists and Their New York*. Washington, D.C.: National Museum of American Art, 1995.